Selling Britten

Selling Britten

Music and the Market Place

Paul Kildea

OXFORD
UNIVERSITY PRESS

OXFORD
UNIVERSITY PRESS

Great Clarendon Street, Oxford OX2 6DP

Oxford University Press is a department of the University of Oxford.
It furthers the University's objective of excellence in research, scholarship,
and education by publishing worldwide in

Oxford New York

Auckland Cape Town Dar es Salaam Hong Kong Karachi Kuala Lumpur
Madrid Melbourne Mexico City Nairobi New Delhi Shanghai Taipei Toronto

With offices in

Argentina Austria Brazil Chile Czech Republic France Greece
Guatemala Hungary Italy Japan South Korea Poland Portugal
Singapore Switzerland Thailand Turkey Ukraine Vietnam

Oxford is a registered trade mark of Oxford University Press
in the UK and in certain other countries

Published in the United States
by Oxford University Press Inc., New York

First published 2002

British Library Cataloguing in Publication Data

Data available

Library of Congress Cataloging in Publication Data

Kildea, Paul Francis.
Selling Britten: music and the marketplace/Paul Francis Kildea.
p.cm
Includes bibliographical references (p.) and index.
1. Britten, Benjamin, 1913-1976. 2. Mass media and music - Great Britain - 20th century.
3. Music trade - Great Britain - History - 20th century. 4. Music - Social aspects -
Great Britain - History - 20th century. 5. Opera - Great Britain - 20th century. I. Title
ML410.B853 K55 2003 780′.92 - dc21 2001058836

ISBN 0-19-816715-6 (hardback)

10 9 8 7 6 5 4 3

Typeset by Hope Services (Abingdon) Ltd.
Printed in Great Britain
on acid-free paper by
Biddles Ltd., King's Lynn, Norfolk

For Cyril

It takes many brains and many hands to carry music to the masses. Music must be composed, or adapted; someone has to choose the works which are to be performed, recorded on disc and tape or synchronized with films. Somebody has to engage the performers, for the big symphony orchestras and opera-houses, from the famous stars down to the cabaret and night-club singers. Somebody has to build transmitters and turntables, pay fees and salaries, print and sell tickets, put advertisements in papers and paste posters on hoardings. Somebody even has to print music, collect royalties, performing and mechanical fees and account for them—there is no end to what has to be done if music is to be available like drinking-water in a large city, and its material usefulness ensured.

(Ernst Roth, *The Business of Music*)

ACKNOWLEDGEMENTS

Grateful acknowledgement is made to Andrew Pinnock (Arts Council of Great Britain) who was very generous with his time and in providing access to the Aladdin's cave that is the Council's records. I am similarly indebted to Neil Sommerville and Jacqueline Kavanagh at the BBC's Written Archive Centre, Rosie Runciman (Glyndebourne), and Francesca Franchi (Royal Opera House).

I am grateful to Oxford University for supporting my candidature and thus allowing me to research and write what was the basis of this book, and to John Wagstaff and staff at the Library who were always helpful. I enjoyed the many conversations I had with Michael Burden, Suzanne Aspden, Keith Radford, Graeme Honner, Jack Turner, Glen Power, Andrew Comben, and Jonathan Wright.

I am also indebted to Peter L'Estrange, Chairman of the Archbishop Mannix Travelling Scholarship, and Warren Bebbington, Chairman of the Welsford Smithers Scholarship, for their financial support; funds from the Australian Music Foundation in London (Chairman Peter Andry) and an Overseas Research Students Award were also gratefully received.

I am greatly indebted to the late Nancy Evans and Eric Crozier for their generous hospitality and criticisms of my work on the English Opera Group.

I thank Malcolm Gillies for his friendship and all his stimulating comments and instruction over the past ten years. David Pear, Stuart Greenbaum, and Linda Kouvaras have also been great friends and colleagues. David and Merryn Oldham, Sue Hackett, and Olivia Gesini have long supported me in my work, and for that I am extremely thankful. I am similarly indebted to my wonderful parents Paul and Verlie.

Philip Reed and Paul Banks were generous with their expertise in my many visits to The Britten–Pears Library in Aldeburgh, as were Pamela Wheeler, Helen Risdon, Anne Surfling, and Keiron Cooke. More recently, Judith LeGrove read the entire book, making many helpful suggestions and an index, for which I am extremely thankful. Gratitude must also be expressed to Nigel Luckhurst for the photographic reproductions.

I am also grateful for the interest, knowledge, and support of Donald Mitchell, with whom I have enjoyed many stimulating and constructive conversations over a number of years; his comments on this book were gratefully received. I am similarly indebted to Roger Parker, Arnold Whittall, and Stephen Banfield.

I would like to thank Helen Moody, who read the book and had many, many helpful comments. The same can be said of Jenny Doctor, whose own remarkable work on the BBC I devoured. Bruce Phillips's early support of the project was an invaluable encouragement. The expertise of OUP's production, design, and music books staff has also been greatly appreciated: Mary Worthington, Dorothy McLean, Janet Moth, Helen Peres da Costa, and Michael Wood.

I also value my time with Brian Trowell whose wide knowledge of the period covered in this book was tapped, and whose comments on language and music have been most constructive.

For permission to reproduce copyright material I am grateful to the following organizations and individuals: Aldeburgh Productions; Richard Arnell; BBC Written Archives Centre; Philip Brett; The Decca Record Company Ltd.; EMI; Mark Deller; Christopher Donlevy; The Ronald Duncan Literary Foundation; Glyndebourne Festival Opera; Alfred A. Kalmus Ltd. and Universal Edition (London) Ltd.; the Yehudi Menuhin Estate; Metropolitan Opera Archives; Oxford University Press; Royal Opera House Covent Garden; Lady Susana Walton.

The excerpt from Michael Tippett's letter to Eric Walter White is quoted by permission of the Executors of the Estate of Sir Michael Tippett. The excerpt from Rutland Boughton's letter is reproduced by permission of the Rutland Boughton Music Trust; for further information on Boughton in this context see Michael Hurd, *Rutland Boughton and the Glastonbury Festivals* (OUP, 1993), 194–6. Excerpts from the Arts Council of Great Britain's files are reproduced by permission of the Arts Council of England. Extracts from letters of Eric Crozier are reproduced by kind permission of the Eric Crozier Estate. Extracts from Boosey & Hawkes correspondence are reproduced by kind permission of Boosey & Hawkes Music Publishers Ltd. The quotations from English Opera Group/English Music Theatre Company correspondence and other documents are © copyright the Trustees of the Britten–Pears Foundation and may not be further reproduced without the written permission of the Trustees. The quotations from the letters, diaries, and other writings of Benjamin Britten are © copyright the Trustees of the Britten–Pears Foundation and may not be further reproduced without the written permission of the Trustees. The quotations from the letters of Peter Pears are © copyright the Executors of the late Sir Peter Pears and may not be further reproduced without written permission.

While every reasonable attempt has been made to identify and contact copyright holders of material printed here, the author shall be pleased to hear from any individual he has been unable to trace.

Finally, I would like to thank Cyril and Felicity Ehrlich for their conversation, friendship, and hospitality. From my first meeting with Cyril to the final stages of this book, he has been the most remarkable and stimulating figure. His own work on the social and economic history of music has been a great example to me, as it is to anyone who works in this field.

PAUL KILDEA

January 2001

CONTENTS

LIST OF PLATES

(between pages 114–115)

1. Britten conducts the London Symphony Orchestra during the recording of *Peter Grimes* for BBC TV at Snape Maltings Concert Hall, February 1969. (photograph: BBC)
2. Britten (centre) in discussion with a Decca engineer during the recording of *Saint Nicolas*, Aldeburgh Parish Church, 1955. Imogen Holst (left) awaits a decision while Peter Pears (right) consults his score. (photograph: Kurt Hutton)
3. Britten conducting the English Chamber Orchestra and the contralto Helen Watts during the recording of Bach's *Christmas Oratorio* for BBC TV at Long Melford Church, 1967.
4. Britten in discussion with the conductor Ernest Ansermet during rehearsals for the first production of *The Rape of Lucretia* at Glyndebourne, 1946.
5. The English Opera Group arrives in Holland to give performances of *Albert Herring* and Britten's arrangement of *The Beggar's Opera* at the 1948 Holland Festival. Pears and Britten stand on the steps; other prominent members of the EOG are also visible, including Tyrone Guthrie (producer), Joan Cross and Jennifer Vyvyan (sopranos), Nancy Evans (contralto) and Eric Crozier (producer and librettist).
6. The catalogue of Britten's published works issued by Boosey & Hawkes in 1939.
7. Publicity for the 1951 'Britten Season' at the Lyric Theatre Hammersmith—an alternative 'Festival of Britten' in which the English Opera Group performed three of the composer's operas, a work by Monteverdi, and also gave the first performances of Britten's new realization of Purcell's *Dido and Aeneas*.

All photographs are reproduced by courtesy of the Britten–Pears Library, Aldeburgh (no. 6 also by courtesy of Boosey & Hawkes).

LIST OF TABLES

ABBREVIATIONS

ACGB	Arts Council of Great Britain (now Arts Council of England)
BBCBH	British Broadcasting Corporation Broadcasting House
BBCWAC	British Broadcasting Corporation Written Archives Centre
BL	British Library
BPL	The Britten-Pears Library
Britten's diary	Benjamin Britten's diary, BPL
Carpenter	Humphrey Carpenter, *Benjamin Britten: A Biography* (London: Faber & Faber, 1992)
CEMA	Council for the Encouragement of Music and the Arts
DMPR	Donald Mitchell and Philip Reed (eds.), *Letters from a Life: The Selected Letters and Diaries of Benjamin Britten 1913–1976*, vols. i and ii (London: Faber & Faber, 1991)
EOG	English Opera Group
GFO	Glyndebourne Festival Opera
OUP	Oxford University Press
PMA	*Proceedings of the Musical Association*
PRS	Performing Right Society
ROH	Royal Opera House, Covent Garden

Introduction

> Underneath the ceaseless speechifying about new starts, the dominant dream is of a Venetian twilight: a golden-grey steady state where staid arts and moderate politics join to preserve the tenor of things English. The true impulse is not really to 'catch up' with the greater, evolving world outside, but to hold one's own somehow, anyhow, and defend the tribe's customs and weathered monuments.[1]

> The story is about a recording engineer who is a frustrated composer. A woman comes to make a recording (with her manager), he falls in love with her and is inspired to write a masterpiece. There are several complications but the story does not have a happy ending—composer does not get woman.[2]

Before the 1950s or so classical or art musicians in Britain were notorious Luddites. Each technical advance or innovation was quickly derided, each threat to the status quo vilified. Part of this was snobbery: many musicians' vision of English culture was incompatible with growing industrialization. A pasture was the minimum constituent of a pastoral symphony—and not one cluttered with tractors. Larks did ascend, but certainly not in inner cities. Music critics were complicit in the promotion of this vision: in 1945 H. C. Colles wrote that 'English musicians must be glad to see their art enshrined in company with "Shakespeare", "The English Public School", "Cricket", and other matters which are part and parcel of our national inheritance'—a list that doesn't mention by name, but surely invokes in spirit, spinsters cycling to church, warm English ale, and the Henley Regatta.[3] The same critic noted in *The Times* that Vaughan Williams's 'Pastoral' Symphony 'speaks like that wide Down country in which, because there is no incident, every blade of grass and tuft of moss is an

[1] Tom Nairn, 'The Politics of the New Venice', *New Society*, 42 (17 Nov. 1977), 352, quoted in Martin Wiener, *English Culture and the Decline of the Industrial Spirit 1850–1980* (1981), 161.

[2] Synopsis of one-act opera by Richard Arnell, sent to the EOG for consideration, 9 Nov. 1954. BPL, EOG File 110.

[3] Robert Stradling and Meirion Hughes, *The English Musical Renaissance 1860–1940* (1993), 142.

incident'—different from, but at least not incompatible with, Philip Heseltine's mischievous suggestion that the piece depicted 'a cow looking over a gate', and miles away from the darker programme to this symphony—of post-war desolation and destruction—identified by critics today.[4] Music was an important element of England's 'Venetian Twilight'; the antics of Stockhausen had no part to play in the support of tribal customs and weathered monuments.

There was also an intellectual reaction against mass culture and its agents. John Carey suggests that 'the principle around which modernist literature and culture fashioned themselves was the exclusion of the masses, the defeat of their power, the removal of their literacy, the denial of their humanity',[5] and calls on Ezra Pound in his support:

> The artist has no longer any belief or suspicion that the mass, the half-educated simpering general . . . can in any way share his delights . . . The aristocracy of the arts is ready again for its service. Modern Civilization has bred a race with brains like those of rabbits, and we who are the heirs of the witch-doctor and the voodoo, we artists who have been so long the despised are about to take over control.[6]

Pound was writing in 1914—eight years or so before the establishment of the BBC and the introduction of electric recording, but his message is clear: the artist would triumph over the masses and their culture. *Real* culture was the providence of the intellectual elite. It is a great irony that, once formed, the BBC (an organ for the masses) spent much of its time promoting elitist music.

Yet the reactionary approach to new technology in musical circles was not purely the upshot of snobbery. To many, technology posed a real or perceived threat to their livelihood. Thomas Beecham spoke of a musical Armageddon, with audiences depending 'for every kind of music on the radio and musical reproduction by mechanical devices'.[7] The critic Leonid Sabaneev concurred: for 'every living musician we have several hundreds of thousands of mechanical reproducers, which have become the plague of the musical market, especially since their quality has improved and made artistically acceptable', and he predicted that fewer than 10 per cent of cinema musicians would find employment in the age of the 'talkies'.[8] Meanwhile, the Musical Association debated the question of 'Broadcasting and the Future of Music'. Throughout this, many musicians consoled themselves with the knowledge that quartets were still being written for four players and trios for three—but for how much longer? *The Listener* in 1933 published a photograph of the first electrical orchestra, assembled

[4] Robert Stradling and Meirion Hughes, *The English Musical Renaissance 1860–1940* (1993), 138, 139.

[5] John Carey, *The Intellectual and the Masses* (1992), 21.

[6] Ezra Pound, 'The New Sculpture', *Egoist* (16 Feb. 1914), quoted in Carey, *The Intellectual*, 72.

[7] See Ch. 2.

[8] Leonid Sabaneev, 'Music and the Economic Crisis', *Musical Times*, 75 (1934), 1076, 1077.

in Berlin at the Radio Exhibition one year earlier. Depicted are two electric pianos, an electric cello, an electric violin, two 'theremins', a broadcast microphone, a 'trautonium', and a 'hellertion'. A respectably attired audience looks on. In 1934 the *Musical Times* published a detailed prophecy, based on this photograph and influenced by Wells's *The Shape of Things to Come.*

> . . . almost all the instruments were able to deal with intervals even smaller than quarter-tones: so far from developing acuteness of the listener's ear, however, this led in most instances to a growing casualness of intonation on the part of the performers. . . . As to the effect of electric music on the profession, it was found that the variety of tone and power obtainable from a few instruments was equal to that of an orchestra of about thirty players. Inevitably there was a serious growth of unemployment.[9]

Could technology really be on the side of the musician?

The publisher Ernst Roth thought so. 'It takes many brains and many hands to carry music to the masses,' he writes in his autobiography, before supplying a detailed list. Concert promoters, producers, recording engineers, and film directors choose music for particular projects; concert agents and administrators must negotiate about artists and venues; engineers must design and build radios and gramophones; printers have to make tickets and posters, while a press officer must arrange for their dispatch; and, of course, music publishers must print the music and extract royalties. 'There is no end to what has to be done if music is to be available like drinking-water in a large city, and its material usefulness ensured.'[10]

Its material *usefulness*? Roth was, after all, a publisher: promoting music to performers and audiences was his job. But he was also a cultured musician with established European pedigree—one traditionally less egalitarian than Roth here allowed. In his eyes, music was not autonomous; here was a view which neatly divided composers into two distinct groups—those who wrote in an Ivory Tower and those who wrote for the people.

Composers and performers began to recognize that the current was changing. But such recognition came sooner for some than for others. In the 1950s—as this chapter's epigraph attests—the composer Richard Arnell felt sure enough of an empathetic audience and comfortable enough with the notion of recording technology to devise an opera on the subject, although its unhappy ending was perhaps a gritty moral. Two Grand Old Men of British music, Arthur Bliss and Vaughan Williams, and one Bright Young(ish) Thing, William Walton, wrote symphonic film scores in the 1940s—Vaughan Williams remarking that writing for film was excellent discipline for any composer. Yet many others were unconvinced by the positive side of technology—even when confronted with LP-driven revivals of Mahler, Bruckner, and early music.

[9] Adam Creevy quoted in 'Feste', 'Looking Ahead II', *Musical Times*, 75 (1934), 118.

[10] Ernst Roth, *The Business of Music* (1969), 39.

In this regard, Benjamin Britten was a little unusual. From an early age he demonstrated an enthusiasm for the developing technology. His schoolboy diary is filled with references to recordings or broadcasts he had listened to. At the end of his life he noted (with a nostalgist's eye) the importance of gramophone and radio in his musical education, listing his ten favourite records and the reason for their place in his affections. Brahms's Double Concerto, with Thibaud and Casals, was onc, sincc 'wc had this rccording at Gresham's, and I used to devise methods of getting hold of it'.The Scherzo of Mahler's Fifth Symphony was another—Britten having heard it 'on the radio from Hilversum in the early thirties; this started a passion for Mahler'; while for a long time, Stravinsky's own recording of his *Symphony of Psalms* was his 'favourite record'.[11] Moreover, Britten was usually quick to notice and act on sudden changes in recording technology. When LPs were introduced in the late 1940s, the composer royalty that had been established for the much shorter 78s was invalid. Britten was one of six co-signatories of a letter to *The Times*, which noted that

> the advent of long-playing records and tape recordings has entirely changed the situation in recent years and we contend that the provisions of section 8 of the [new Copyright] Bill should be confined solely to records whose playing time does not exceed that of the average record available before the long-playing record was introduced—namely, eight minutes or four minutes a record side. This would leave the composer free to agree with the manufacturers of these longer records an equitable royalty commensurate with the playing time of the record.[12]

Keeping abreast of technology ensured that composers avoided being exploited.

It was not only radio, film, and scratchy 78s that were transforming British music in Britten's lifetime. The arrival of the Arts Council in 1945—via several wartime experiments—put patronage into the hands of the government, which had its own aspirations for British cultural identity. The reopening of Covent Garden in the same year represented a serious attempt to develop and sustain a grand-opera tradition in a country without one. A revival of interest in festivals moved music away from metropolitan centres. Improvements in recording technology—most notably the arrival of the LP and of stereo—greatly intensified this mass industry.

Britten was involved in these new market articulators from their beginnings—often influencing their shape and potency. Inevitably his own music was moulded in the process. These two broad, inclusive statements are the basis of this book. Where other musicians spoke of the disastrous consequences of change, Britten

[11] Britten to Amis, 16 Oct. 1973. BPL, BBC Correspondence, 1973. The Mahler performance, with the Concertgebouw Orchestra conducted by Bruno Walter, was broadcast on 4 Oct. 1934.

[12] Britten (*et al.*) to *The Times*, 3 Apr. 1956. His co-signatories were Vivian Ellis, Arthur Benjamin, Howard Ferguson, Peter Racine Fricker, and Billy Mayerl.

quickly established relationships with the agents of change. The first of these was with publishing—a prerequisite for any *professional* composer. Britten's dealings with Oxford University Press (and its newly formed music department) and with Boosey & Hawkes in the early 1930s taught him much about markets, royalties, and the economics of music (Chapter 1). In the same period, Britten began exploring wider markets, via the BBC. His work was first broadcast when the Corporation was less than ten years old. The BBC was one of the chief disseminators of Britten's music, but, more importantly, it had a strong influence on the style, shape, and genre of his works in the 1930s (Chapter 2).

In 1946, one year after the enormous success of *Peter Grimes*, Britten formed his own opera company in collaboration with Glyndebourne's John Christie. His operas for this company and for the breakaway English Opera Group wonderfully illustrate the economics of genre, and paint a picture of Britten as impresario—a decidedly un-English role for a composer to adopt (Chapter 3). Overlapping with the works composed for the EOG were his grand operas *Billy Budd* and *Gloriana*. Written with Arts Council funding for Covent Garden, these two pieces pose a number of disturbing questions about varying official perceptions of British culture, and the role of the artist in this culture (Chapter 4).

The Aldeburgh Festival, established in 1948, increasingly became the principal forum for Britten premieres. As with the EOG, economic parameters shaped the product (Chapter 5). In the 1960s Britten retreated to Aldeburgh and new supply patterns developed: music was premiered at the Festival, broadcast by the BBC, published by Boosey & Hawkes or the new Faber Music, recorded by Decca, and quickly put on the market. The huge success of the *War Requiem* recording changed Britten's popular and critical reputation. Here was a potent symbol of the power of technology (Chapter 6).

Britten was, therefore, a modern, professional composer—much more so than Michael Tippett, his contemporary. Although his music *sounds* more modern, Tippett was far happier playing the Bohemian, only managing to get *A Child of Our Time* performed, and his reputation launched, once Britten had pulled the manuscript out from a desk drawer. This is both a wonderful image and an apt metaphor: Britten the opportunist and door-opener.

This approach to Britten's life and music only tells a small part of the story of this great musician. Moreover, it threatens the notion of autonomy in music: surely the actual product is more important than the process? Of course it is, but ever since Philip Brett first wrote about *Peter Grimes*, this actual process has demanded and received careful attention.[13] Brett has looked for and identified aspects to

[13] See Brett, 'Britten and *Grimes*', *Musical Times*, 118 (Dec. 1977).

this process that are barely touched upon in this book. Yet the two approaches are complementary rather than contradictory.

In his 1997 Proms Lecture Brett spoke of both product and process: 'Britten's artistic effort was an attempt to disrupt the center that it occupied with the marginality that it expressed.'[14] It is an extraordinary sentence, in nineteen words saying so much about Britten, about the composer of *Peter Grimes*, *Billy Budd*, *Owen Wingrave*, and *Death in Venice*. In the same lecture Brett talked about a life of conflicts and paradoxes, of friends unceremoniously dumped and walks with the Queen Mother. But the basis of these paradoxes, he argued, was Britten's desire to subvert *and* educate. Pacifism was a zealous commitment of Britten's, but it was also a cypher for other passions that Britten could not then speak of—primarily his sexuality. For *Wingrave* to be broadcast on BBC television, its explicit message as shocking and unpalatable in the late 1930s, when much of Britten's ideas about art and society were formulated, as its *implicit* meaning was in the late 1960s when the opera was conceived, was a remarkable feat. Yet such subversion needs energy, commitment, and organization—of this Brett was certain:

> 'All a poet can do is to warn' is the conclusion of the Wilfred Owen epigraph on the cover of the score of the *War Requiem*. But in order to warn, or do anything else, the poet/artist has to be heard. What North America may have taught Britten and Pears, then, was that to work for centrality at home would ultimately be more artistically and therefore politically effective than marginality abroad—as a means of articulating a message to society from that margin where Britten, at least, alway imagined he lived, as countless tales of his depression and darkness attest.[15]

In order to warn, or do anything else, the poet/artist has to be heard. This is why Britten's 'centrality' was so vital: we are usually dismissive or suspicious of lone prophets. For a message to be received, it has to be well packaged. This was a lesson he learnt at Auden's feet and insistence in the 1930s. Auden moreover, picking up Wilfred Owen's baton that had been swept aside in the 'peace' and recriminations following the First World War, was certain of the responsibility of artists to use their position to warn or educate, especially in the lead-up to the Second World War:

> All I have is a voice
> To undo the folded lie,
> The romantic lie in the brain
> Of the sensual man-in-the-street
> And the lie of Authority
> Whose buildings grope the sky:
> There is no such thing as the State
> And no one exists alone;

[14] Philip Brett, 'The Britten Era' (1997). [15] Ibid.

> To the citizen or the police;
> We must love one another or die.[16]

The 'voice' and the 'lie' were intrinsic to Britten's music from the 1930s onwards. The discovery of that voice will not be explored in this book; the forums by which Britten made certain that this voice was heard will be. The organizations that are explored in the following chapters—the relationships that Britten forged with the brokers of power (the market articulators)—of course signify one composer's determination to understand and (as far as possible) control the market place. But they should also be thought of in terms of Britten's determination to use his voice to redress the marginal status assigned him by his sexuality, his pacifism, his politics, and his sensitivity to injustice.

[16] Auden, 'September 1939', in Edward Mendelson (ed.), *The English Auden* (1986), 397. See also Kildea, 'Britten, Auden and "Otherness"', in Mervyn Cooke (ed.), *The Cambridge Companion to Benjamin Britten* (1999).

Chapter 1

Carrying Music to the Masses

> There is no sign as yet of the one man who is both of sufficient character and sufficient inventive genius to alter the stream of music today definitely and conclusively. This is perhaps only to be expected; nature is not in the habit of throwing up a Titan every 50 years or so . . .[1]

> . . . I have completed the Canadian work which I suggested to you a long time ago and about which Heinsheimer has always seemed so keen. . . . I dare say you will hear from him direct whether he thinks it will suit the American market or not. You see how commercially minded I am growing.[2]

The last century was a good time for children of shopkeepers. Politicians, intellectuals, Olympic athletes, and musicians of every kind emerged from behind the most unlikely counters. Edward Elgar, for example, died in 1934, whiskered, well fed, ennobled, and financially secure. His humble Worcester background was usually hidden behind his considerable achievements, although it was given the occasional airing—the gesture of a self-made man. To Siegfried Sassoon, Elgar's appearance was that of a retired Victorian army officer, and his outlook that of an aristocrat—'the Duc D'Elgar'.[3] Although Elgar never became prime minister, the fate and fortune of one woman of background similar to Elgar's, he did once consider becoming a Tory candidate for parliament and he met with Edward VII's warm approval. He was appointed Master of the King's Musick in 1924—a suitably archaic title for a position occupied by this status-conscious composer. And Elgar was for a time a member of the Athenaeum, although it

[1] Arthur Bliss, 'Aspects of Contemporary Music', in Gregory Roscow (ed.), *Bliss on Music* (1991), 71.

[2] DMPR 734.

[3] Meirion Hughes, '"The Duc D'Elgar": Making a Composer Gentleman', in Christopher Norris (ed.), *Music and the Politics of Culture* (1989), 41.

should perhaps be noted that he left in protest over its admission of the Labour prime minister Ramsay MacDonald, a person with whom, according to the composer, 'no gentleman can associate'.[4]

News of Elgar's death on 23 February 1934 would have penetrated quickly the Athenaeum's unwelcoming façade, where members would have been sad at the loss of one of their own (his resignation notwithstanding), but glad, as old men often are, that they had outlived him. Both *The Times* and the *Daily Telegraph*—requisite constituents of the club's reading room—had charted Elgar's final illness with conscientious care, and their reports on the day following his death were no less comprehensive. Both papers printed Sir Henry Wood's declaration that Elgar 'was such a mighty figure that one cannot think of him dead. It is the greatest loss to music that could have possibly happened, and a loss from which this country will take many years to recover, for there is no one else to touch him.'[5] Here was one grandee's tribute to another.

Although Wood was clearly mistaken in his suggestion that Elgar's death symbolized the mortality of English music, his was a view shared by many. Adrian Boult, then head of the BBC's music department, commented (more in the style of a *Radio Times* advertisement than an obituary) that Elgar's death would be a tragedy for broadcasting, a 'movement that brings the finest music to the greatest number of people'.[6] Ramsay MacDonald, with a degree of irony that almost certainly would have been lost on the composer himself, sent a telegraph to Elgar's daughter offering his condolences. The king and queen did the same, assuring her of their sympathy and their belief that 'this country and the world of music have lost in him a great composer, whose work will be long remembered'.[7] And an imperialist representative of the younger generation proclaimed in a letter to *The Times* that 'we who knew not England in its happier days turn to Elgar for his nobility, his sympathy and sincerity, and, above all, for his

[4] Elgar to the Athenaeum [draft], 11 Dec. 1924, repr. in Hughes, '"The Duc D'Elgar"', 54.

[5] *The Times*, 24 Feb. 1934, 17. Wood's response in the *Daily Telegraph* differed in only two words.

[6] *The Times*, 24 Feb. 1934, 17. The BBC's music department delivered another curiously self-serving tribute one month later. 'At a moment when we have been reading some almost ludicrous attacks on British broadcasting, it is right, when remembering Elgar, that we should give honour where honour is due. The musical staff of the B.B.C. has from the first made a policy of presenting Elgar generously to the public. From the late Percy Pitt, who, like Elgar, was outside the official and academic world of music, but who recognised his genius from the first, to Adrian Boult, who has honoured himself in paying homage to his great contemporary, the musicians of the B.B.C. have never wavered in their confidence with regard to Elgar.' Filson Young, 'The World we Listen To', *Radio Times*, 16 Mar. 1934, 800. Yet Elgar's Cello Concerto, his last great work, was completed in 1919, three years before the formation of the British Broadcasting Company. Given this, the suggestion that the BBC had a courageous, somehow perspicacious attitude towards the firmly established, 65-year-old Elgar is a little misplaced. See Jennifer Doctor, *The BBC and Ultra-Modern Music, 1922–1936* (1999).

[7] *The Times*, 24 Feb. 1934, 12.

essential goodness',[8] a view held by those of older generations as well, who had seen Elgar as a tangible symbol of England's former greatness.

Another member of the younger generation, Benjamin Britten, shied away from the autopsies and obituaries penned by many musicians and public figures. In his diary he did note the death of the older composer, but with gnomic brevity—'Elgar dies'. Britten was far more preoccupied with the first performance of his virtuosic choral variations, *A Boy was Born*, which had taken place that day.[9]

The coincidence of these two events—the death of the old and the 'birth' of the new, coming together with all the symmetry of classical mythology—precipitated an important psychological change in British music. Although rhetorical—Britten's own death forty years later would prompt a similar inquest into English music—the loss of a composer of Elgar's stature (compounded by the deaths of Holst and Delius later that year) and the need for a replacement was keenly felt in many British music institutions. These crudely articulated feelings were part of a wider 'turn' in British music: old markets were collapsing and new ones were emerging, while others, managing to straddle the 'old' and the 'new', were surviving. The rise of radio and the 'talkies' and sudden demise of the silent cinema, for example, immediately altered the market place for music: bonfires of piano sheet-music bore witness to the collapse of the piano culture which had been granted a new life and purpose in the era of silent film, anticipating by only a few years similar fires, but with more sinister intent, in Germany. But the talkies brought with them new opportunities. Incidental music for silent films had required a composer (dead or alive), and anything from one to twenty performers in each cinema. With the 'talkies', the labour pattern changed. Composer, arranger, conductor, and orchestra made the construction of each film score labour-intensive, but each showing of a new film was automated, mechanized, and economical.[10] The involvement of composers and performers in this new technology immediately widened the complicated debate on royalties, copyright, and performing right. And radio took on the 'talkies' in the 1930s, creating even more opportunities for composers, performers, and music managers, while also influencing genres and techniques.

A number of the institutions involved in this turn in British music were associated with the premiere of Britten's *A Boy was Born*. Britten's relationship with

[8] Clive Nicholson, *The Times*, 26 Feb. 1934, 10.

[9] Britten's diary, 23 Feb. 1934. Britten's comment on his opus 3 was: 'My "Boy was Born" goes infinitely better than rehearsals . . . It goes down pretty well.'

[10] I am much indebted to Cyril Ehrlich's pioneering studies of the economics of the British music industry: *The Music Profession in Britain since the Eighteenth Century: A Social History* (1985); *Harmonious Alliance: A History of the Performing Right Society* (1989); *The Piano: A History* (rev. edn., 1990); and *First Philharmonic: A History of the Royal Philharmonic Society* (1995).

each of these organizations established him as a professional composer, in circumstances far removed from Elgar's own rise to professional status. Contracts, copyright, performing right, the concept of intellectual property, and broadcasting had all been introduced or had changed markedly since Elgar's clumsy negotiations with Novello at the end of the nineteenth century. Relevant institutions of the day—Oxford University Press, Boosey & Hawkes, the BBC, the Performing Right Society, theatre and film companies, and Glyndebourne, making its debut in this tumultuous year—were consumers or monitors of vast quantities of music; Britten's involvement with them was assured because he was capable of supplying the goods within the allotted time. His growing awareness of the economics of music in the period 1934–9 influenced the scale, genre, instrumentation, and content of his music; it continued to do so for most of his career. With the deaths of three of England's Grand Old Composers, changes in the music industry were of course to be expected. But Britten's progression from amateur to professional status, from composer of juvenilia to creator of mature works that quickly entered and have remained within concert repertory, was an important part of this change.

Dots on Paper

Leisure patterns were long ago changed beyond recognition by the printing press and publishing, its favoured child. Five hundred years before Britten's birth, block-printed playing cards appeared in Europe—a modest gesture, certainly, in the history of printing (where technology quickly became *relatively* sophisticated and ambitious), but nonetheless a potent symbol of things to come. Only thirty years before the printing of these playing cards, Chaucer had written *The Canterbury Tales* for a very small readership; fifty years after the introduction of these cards to civilized European parlours and their less civilized equivalents, Chaucer's work was published in England by William Caxton on his new press. Here was a far more significant milestone in the printing revolution: large numbers of consumers could be entertained or enlightened in their own homes rather than at a public gathering. There were still controls over consumption—literacy and wealth for example—but parameters had shifted, and control was in different hands. Moreover, the appearance of *The Canterbury Tales* in print after its author's death foreshadowed issues of intellectual property and ownership, which would not be resolved until the twentieth century, and even then remained vulnerable to the vicissitudes of technology.

The revolution in music was no less significant. Printing eventually made music a mass product. The consumer was often also the performer although, ironically, the new technology in time encouraged the consumer to act as music analyst, critic, and philosopher. But the principle of 'dots on paper' (rather than the quite distinct issue of the performance of these 'dots') remained remarkably stable from the time of the first printed music to the early 1930s: selection and dissemination shaped demand.

The selection and dissemination of Britten's music had begun in the early 1930s with the publication of his Three Two-part Songs, but the process was refined with *A Boy was Born*. Britten commenced work on this piece in late 1932, composing on 25 November the theme which formed the basis for the subsequent variations.[11] At this time he was an unhappy student at the Royal College of Music, confident in the knowledge that his new piece would not be performed in a College concert. The work was finished in May 1933, seven months before Britten sat his ARCM. Soon after it was finished he played it through to Hubert Foss, the young head of Oxford University Press's music department, who, according to Britten, rather liked it.[12] Foss was an interesting character. In 1919, as a 20-year-old pianist, he began working for the Press in a moderately humble capacity, yet was appointed head of the new music department when it was formed in 1923. His youth, and the department's financial structure and short history, influenced Britten's negotiations with OUP. The Press was—and is now—a hybrid organization: part university department, part business. It had no shareholders, but neither did it have limitless funds from a paternal university. Although the purpose of an academic press ought to be the accumulation of prophets rather than profits, OUP's own benevolent instincts did not enjoy a free rein; commercial viability was an important editorial consideration. But commercial viability, as far as composers were concerned, was a difficult proposition. Financially, the new department was best equipped to establish contracts with relatively unknown composers, but these brought with them neither established business links nor a large appreciative public. More firmly established composers were usually already contracted to other firms, on more attractive terms than those that OUP could offer. The difficult task of building up a music catalogue within these constraints was Foss's responsibility, but his progress was marked by an alternating recklessness and caution more common in new businesses than their older competitors.

With prescience, luck, and opportunism, Foss rapidly expanded the new department in its first decade, publishing over two hundred works per year.[13] His view on this expansion was outlined in *Music in My Time*—an autobiographical

[11] Britten's diary, 25 Nov. 1932.

[12] Britten's diary, 2 June 1933.

[13] *Oxford Music: The First Fifty Years '23–'73* (1973), 6. This was part of a deliberate policy to make the largest possible music list in the shortest possible time. Humphrey Milford, head of OUP, once said that Foss, fulfilling his quest, came closer than any one person to ruining the Press. See also Duncan Hinnells, *An Extraordinary Performance: Hubert Foss, Music Publishing, and Oxford University Press* (1998).

amble around some of his musical associates—published, somewhat precociously and true to form, in 1933 when he was only 34 and when the Depression made paper scarce and biographical ambles luxurious. In it he argues that the music publisher's responsibilities are onerous, since the avenues by which a composer might reach the public are so few. Describing many of the works currently published as 'nothing but youthful indiscretions pressed upon the public so that the composer may get himself known',[14] Foss noted:

> The public is so often quoted as the final judge of musical merit that one asks how music that is played to the public is first judged worthy of so being played. It is judged from a reading of the score. Now, indisputably, even a modern score can be satisfactorily read; but it is equally obvious that the same mental effect cannot be obtained from a reading as from a performance. The difficulties are not only those of time and detail, but of purely aural effect, of space and acoustics, of physical reception by an independent organ, of appeal to the other men around the hearer who with him make up the audience. I point the finger not at the selector, but at the principle of selection. . . . Yet who can judge the public's mind?[15]

Here judgement of 'the public's mind' is partly glorification of the publisher's role, partly justification of past decisions; nothing as subjective as personal taste would be at home in this manifesto. Publishing is presented as democratic rather than autocratic, communal rather than personal. Hidden somewhere in all this is the acknowledgement that consumer tastes were forecast as much as sampled, and that any youthful indiscretions pressed upon the public were part of the selection and dissemination process, the shaping of demand.

Many of the British composers signed up by Foss in the department's first decade were at first far from the public's mind, even without him considering the role of the interpreter in influencing public perception—an especially significant factor in Britten's later career. Foss did, however, have his successes: Vaughan Williams, who was already 50 when some of his Whitman songs were published by the Press, was one of these, and the gentlemen's agreement he made with Foss ensured that OUP thereafter handled his music—which was greatly beneficial to the finances and prestige of the young music department. William Walton, whom Foss befriended in the early 1920s and whose music he started publishing soon after, was another of the publisher's successes, and the growing stature of this composer in the late 1920s must have encouraged Foss's belief in his own instinct, which complicated his dealings with Britten in the mid-1930s.

Britten's Three Two-part Songs—his first project with OUP—were accepted almost a year before his play-through of *A Boy was Born*.[16] Apart from these

[14] Hubert Foss, *Music in My Time* (1933), 90. [15] Ibid. 89.

[16] These songs were published separately in 1932 and not joined as a single publication until 1970. The 1970 title, however, is used here.

songs, Foss had seen a 'good many' of Britten's compositions—probably his *Phantasy* in F minor for string quintet, a String Quartet in D, Twelve Variations for piano, *A Hymn to the Virgin*, *The Birds*, two psalms, and his adventurous foray into a foreign language, the *Quatre chansons françaises*.[17] The selection of the part-songs was in many ways obvious: conventional rather than experimental, they could be published as part of the series Oxford Choral Songs which had been in existence since 1923—a series with existing markets and minimal financial risk, the ideal vehicle for the choral music of an unknown composer. But Foss rejected several works, which have since been issued by other publishers—admittedly in the light of Britten's mature reputation, or since his death, a period marked by active promotion of all of his music by the Britten Estate Limited, and the at times indelicate search by performance organizations and recording companies for splinters of the true cross. But the rejection of *The Birds*—a simple but beautiful song, of which Britten remained fond—and of the effective *A Hymn to the Virgin* was perhaps a portent: was Foss's analysis of OUP's established markets entirely accurate (there were still art-song and church-music cultures in England at this time), and was his instinct for quality music well tuned?[18]

In practice, Foss's commune had many members, and he did not rely solely on his own instinct. OUP's chain of command owed more to the civil service than a university department—at least an Oxford University department in the 1930s. Recommendations were sought, submitted, and frequently acted upon. One adviser was the composer, conductor, member of the BBC Music Advisory Committee, and editor of the Oxford Choral Songs series William Gillies Whittaker. His reaction to Britten's songs was, for the most part, positive. He did, however, consider the accompaniments too difficult and expressed doubts about the range of the first two songs: 'Will you ask the composer if he thinks a tone lower would be possible for the first? The second I certainly think ought to be a tone lower. . . . If it is for young peoples [*sic*] voices, say secondary school girls, F sharp and G are too high for the upper line, and F sharp much too high for the lower. It would cause strain.'[19] Foss promised to recommend the songs for publication subject to Britten's undertaking the changes suggested.

Whittaker's letter highlights a number of important points. First, in the 1930s (and still today) the music-production culture favoured the distributor, not a new composer. Selection, contracts, terms, and the absence of benevolence required patience and acquiescence (in equal measure) from the composer. Second, Whittaker's remark about the range of the songs and the difficulty of the

[17] Britten's diary, 29 Feb. 1932. The String Quartet in D was revised by Britten in 1974 and published by Faber Music the following year.

[18] Foss's reluctance to consider Britten's other works is discussed later in this chapter. See Stephen Banfield, *Sensibility and English Song* (1988) for an analysis of the English art-song culture.

[19] Foss to Britten, 29 Apr. 1932. BPL, OUP Correspondence, 1932–49.

accompaniment was not without basis. There certainly would have been some school choirs competent enough to perform the songs as they stood, but this rather ignored the rationale of the series: it was committed to attracting and supplying a mass market—not simply because of the near-religious fervour surrounding community singing and in education at this time, but because of the profit to be made from this market. It was a lesson quickly learnt by the composer.

Britten was not keen on editorial interference and sought counsel in his mentor and former teacher Frank Bridge. The older composer advised that Whittaker's comments must be 'tactfully considered', simply because it 'is the way the world wags'.[20] Although his complaints to Bridge may have been sincere, Britten had revised the second of the songs on 26 May and resubmitted them all to OUP two days later, nearly six weeks before hearing from Bridge.[21] It is unlikely, therefore, that he seriously entertained thoughts of declining Foss's offer. Foss meanwhile advised Humphrey Milford to accept them.[22]

By the time Britten came to submit *A Boy was Born* to OUP, these part-songs had sold reasonably well (Table 1.1)—one reason why negotiations were much smoother the second time around. Britten was still correcting proofs to the songs as late as October 1932, so this first royalty account deals with a period of only five months or so. These figures must be interpreted carefully: the round figures of American sales were obviously to an agent, and since later royalty accounts do not indicate further transatlantic trade for the choral songs it seems unlikely that they found an American market. All of this, though, was in the future, and the total 'sale' of almost 900 copies by mid-1933 was an impressive bargaining counter for Britten's negotiations over *A Boy was Born*.

Britten's strengthening relationship with the BBC soon became an equally impressive tool for negotiations.[23] Although performance and publication of music are two distinct operations, the BBC's involvement in *A Boy was Born* demonstrates the symbiotic relationship between 'dots on paper' and performance of these same dots. The Corporation's music department expressed an interest in broadcasting *A Boy was Born* at around the time Britten was discussing the work with Foss; each suitor was spurred on by the advances of the other. The importance of this was demonstrated a little later, when the premiere was postponed. Foss wrote to the BBC:

[20] Bridge to Britten, 7 July 1932. BPL, Bridge Correspondence.

[21] Britten's diary, 26 May 1932. Britten also dropped the title 'Studies in Canon' since he thought it sounded 'too fearsome'. DMPR 251. Ironically, Bridge also advised Britten not to 'bother about rushing the M.S. back to the O.U.P. There isn't a furious hurry—not really, I feel sure.'

[22] Milford had been responsible for OUP's first music publishing endeavours in 1923, and he kept a watchful eye on the more formal arrangements established two years later.

[23] Britten's involvement with the BBC is studied in detail in Ch. 2.

Table 1.1 OUP royalty account, year ending 31 March 1933: Oxford Choral Songs[a]

Sales	Printed	Sold		Presented	Stock	Royalty	
		Britain	USA			Britain	USA
No. 168 (4*d.*) 'The Ride-by-nights'	2,500	156	200	351	1,793	2*s.* 7*d.*	3*s.* 4*d.*
No. 169 (3*d.*) 'The Rainbow'	2,504	49	200	355	1,900	7*d.*	2*s.* 6*d.*
No. 170 (5*d.*) 'The Ship of Rio'	2,552	88	200	356	1,908	1*s.* 10*d.*	4*s.* 2*d.*

[a] OUP Royalty Account. BPL, OUP Correspondence, 1932–49. Copies listed under 'Presented' were given to various performance groups or conductors for promotional purposes. In 1970 these three songs were combined in a single volume and published under the title Three Two-part Songs.

It came as rather a shock to me, after the trouble we had been put to over Britten's work, to hear from him that the performance is now postponed till February. Surely the first argument against such postponement is that it is not very sensible to perform a Christmas work in February, and it seems to me rather rough luck on the boy that his first performance of his first important work should be given such an unfortunate position. Is this decision irrevocable or can something be done to keep it in its first place? I can easily get the copies out in time for your rehearsals if you will tell me when you are starting.[24]

Foss evidently had made a special effort to get the work ready for the BBC. The chronology makes it quite clear that the normal publishing time was reduced in this instance. Britten played through *A Boy was Born* to Foss in early June 1933; preliminary negotiations between publisher and composer continued until late July; the first performance was planned for November 1933, which left under three months to produce copies in time for rehearsals. This reduction in publishing time was possible because Foss removed several links in the chain of command which had been in operation for the three part-songs—a significant endorsement.[25] A tight publication schedule resulted: on 11 August the printers Henderson & Spalding issued an estimate of £123 for 1,000 copies, £150 for 2,000.[26] This estimate was considerably more than the cost of producing Britten's three part-songs, but the prospect of a BBC performance helped

[24] Foss to Dalmaine, 25 Sept. 1933. BBCWAC, Composer file, Benjamin Britten, 1933–44. The BBC replied on 29 Sept., stating that the Corporation wished to reserve Britten's work for a public contemporary concert, the first available one being in February.

[25] There are no letters or memoranda at either OUP or the Britten–Pears Library to suggest otherwise.

[26] OUP, Britten Correspondence, 1934–75.

override this consideration, since the first proofs were available for correction a little over one month later, just when Britten and Foss learnt that the BBC planned to postpone the first performance.[27]

The Economics of Genre: Performance

The BBC's easy advocacy of *A Boy was Born* resulted from three factors: the work's merit, its performance forces, and the culture of criticism which had built up around the young Broadcasting Corporation. Complaints that the BBC broadcast too much music without any particular musical pretensions were common in most of the major British newspapers at around this time and partially precipitated the BBC's Festival of British Music in January 1934. Adrian Boult described the works included in the Festival as the sum of British endeavour over the previous thirty years. An editorial in the BBC's magazine, *Radio Times*, concurred: the Festival included 'the best of contemporary British music in a comprehensive survey. The programmes are made up entirely of items by British composers and are as completely representative of the nation's endeavour *as circumstances allow*'.[28] Equipped with such a generous escape clause, the BBC was able to rebut the accusations of one listener who was astounded at the complacency of the Corporation's public statements, and horrified at most of the works included in the Festival.[29] But although British music was fortunately more than a sum of the parts included in the six broadcasts (works by Ethel Smyth, R. O. Morris, Alexander Mackenzie, Joseph Holbrooke, Eugene Goossens, Rutland Boughton, E. J. Moeran, and Patrick Hadley, for example), the Festival was a demonstration of the BBC's support for British music and an indication that the Corporation at least listened to criticism even if it could not necessarily be called to account for it.

In its goals the Festival wasn't an absolute success. Rebellion turned to mutiny when Constant Lambert, a composer represented in the series, asserted that works were chosen in deference to the feelings of composers rather than listeners: 'Either we can produce good music or we can't. If we can, then let it be played in company with the great masters.'[30] Fortunately the influential Percy Scholes came down on the side of the BBC, employing an unusual combination of jingoistic terminology and gastronomic metaphor to remind listeners that, while on the continent composers have reacted violently against older harmonies

[27] Britten's diary, 24 Sept. 1933. [28] *Radio Times* (29 Dec. 1933), 935. My italics.

[29] *Radio Times* (2 Feb. 1934), 305.

[30] Constant Lambert, *Sunday Referee*, 7 Jan. 1934, quoted in Nicholas Kenyon, *The BBC Symphony Orchestra* (1981), 93. Kenyon argues that the Festival was devised simply to appease members of the Music Advisory Committee. See Ch. 2 for a full discussion of the various BBC music advisory groups.

and forms, 'our boys seem to have kept their heads. . . . The Irishman said he preferred onions to strawberries because they were "more expressive"; some of those Continental cooks give us whole meals of onions, whilst ours use them as a reasonable seasoning.'[31]

Britten's 'reasonably seasoned' *A Boy was Born* was almost certainly helped by this climate, receiving, among other things, a lengthy preview in the *Radio Times*. This high-circulation weekly journal—kept by the wireless set for daily consultation—was initiated in September 1923 and had by the 1930s become a powerful medium through which the BBC could counter criticism that appeared both in daily papers and in music journals. Biographies of BBC staff, descriptions of how programmes were constructed, letters to the editor, programme details, and articles of general interest filled its pages. Much of this was written in a defensive, opportunistic manner. Edmund Rubbra's preview of *A Boy was Born* was decisive and positive, occupying a large proportion of the two-page section 'Notable Music'; Havergal Brian's preview of Egon Petri playing Busoni's Piano Concerto was relegated to second position.

In addition there was genuine enthusiasm for Britten's work on its own merits. The composer first played it through to three members of the music department in June 1933, two weeks after playing it to Foss.[32] Britten, in a rather paternal mood, noted in his diary that they 'seem to like my "Boy"',[33] and Victor Hely-Hutchinson's own report of this meeting supports the composer's assessment. After describing the *Phantasy* as 'individual and interesting, though not remarkably striking', he turned his attention to *A Boy was Born*:

> The other work which he played was a new set of choral variations for eight-part chorus and a small chorus of boys (unaccompanied). I was very greatly impressed with this work. It was beautifully written, very varied and dramatic and perfectly logical. I think we certainly ought to do it. There are one or two points in it where I feel that a little revision might profitably be given, but my impression may have been due to the fact that it was being played through on the piano and not performed on the medium for which it was written.
>
> I asked Mr. Britten tentatively and unofficially about the first performance, and he said that Mr. Kennedy Scott was interested in it but had not yet heard it. I suggested to him that, if convenient to him, he might give us the option of the first performance.

He concluded his memo with a nicely prescient touch: 'I do whole-heartedly subscribe to the general opinion that Mr. Britten is the most interesting new arrival since Walton, and I feel that we should watch his work very carefully.'[34] Hely-Hutchinson was no mindless bureaucrat. A composer himself whose slight

[31] Percy Scholes, 'British Music in our Century', *Radio Times* (5 Jan. 1934), 8.

[32] Britten's diary, 16 June 1933.

[33] Ibid.

[34] BBC memo, BBCWAC, Composer file, Benjamin Britten, file 1a, 1933–44. The memo was possibly addressed to Adrian Boult.

reputation today rests on seasonal performances of his *Carol Symphony* (described by Britten as 'utter bilge'[35]), he joined the staff of the BBC in 1926, became head of music for the midlands regions in 1933, and was appointed Professor of Music at Birmingham University in 1934. His view of Britten was refreshingly unpatronizing and his one adverse comment—the suggestion of revisions—was quickly diluted.[36] Instead, Hely-Hutchinson made every attempt to cultivate Britten. A concert broadcast, a first performance, and a glowing epithet were all offered. Anonymous reading-panels were neither expected nor asked to pass judgement on this new work. Even the BBC's competition fell into line: Charles Kennedy Scott turned down an offer of the first performance on the grounds that the work was 'ineffective, too difficult, & not "cantabile" enough'.[37]

Kennedy Scott was right on one point: *A Boy was Born* is extremely demanding. Unaccompanied, chromatic, virtuosic, innovative, and with as many as nine vocal lines, even a professional choir could expect to be taxed, with around four people per part and with limited rehearsal time. Britten had little experience in making music readily performable or well suited to a particular ensemble. Most of his juvenilia was written for his own technical development rather than for immediate performance—although the allocation of opus numbers in a rather idiosyncratic manner does suggest an eye for posterity. Initially the constraints and practicalities of performance were not important compositional influences (for example, his piece of 1923 deliciously scored for piccolo, flute, bassoon, cornet, violin, and double bass), although a trend away from the Utopian to the utilitarian is easy to observe. The genres and forms tackled in 1932 were more practical than those of 1925.

There is a strong link between particular biographical events and the music Britten composed as a boy and adolescent. In a later BBC radio talk Britten rather charmingly explained this link:

> I had started playing the piano and wrote elaborate tone poems usually lasting about twenty seconds, inspired by terrific events in my home life such as the departure of my father for London, the appearance in my life of a new girl friend or even a wreck at sea. My later efforts luckily got away from these emotional inspirations and I began to write sonatas and quartets which were not connected in any direct way with life.[38]

Britten's many works for the piano began appearing after he commenced lessons with Ethel Astle in 1920 or 1921. There is nothing surprising in his choice of instrument for these early works: a piano was readily available and since he was

[35] Britten's diary, 22 Dec. 1932. Britten heard the symphony in a broadcast performance.

[36] Although he may not have agreed with Hely-Hutchinson at the time, Britten did later revise the work.

[37] Britten's diary, 26 June 1933.

[38] This talk was subsequently published. Britten, 'How to Become a Composer', *The Listener* (7 Nov. 1946), 624.

yet to learn harmony and orchestration in any systematic manner, pieces could be improvised on the keyboard and then committed to paper. Many of the piano works completed—and a similar number of those left incomplete—were not given titles. Various shades of 'Allegro' were popular designations. At first there is carefree allocation of specific genre titles to the most unlikely recipients—a Symphony in F major/minor for violin, cello, and piano, for example. But as Britten's own piano skills and repertory grew, traditional forms came to predominate. Once he had passed the Associated Board Grade VIII piano exam with Honours in 1926, more and more Toccatas, Suites, and Sonatas appeared—forms he would have encountered amongst piano repertory at his level.

Britten's orchestral output increased markedly in 1925 after hearing Bridge's *The Sea* at the 1924 Norwich Triennial Festival in November. This performance of *The Sea* was not so much a stylistic influence: its scale and Britten's then idiosyncratic approach to orchestral writing ensured this. But it did awaken in the young composer a taste for orchestral music, hitherto almost completely dormant, and subsequently explored in nearly forty orchestral works in the period 1925–6. There were other influences at work in this period. In 1925 Britten composed a number of fugues: he was growing more sophisticated in counterpoint and harmonic language. Most pieces now received a specific formal title: Sonata, Trio, Overture, Canon, Rondo, and Suite were popular choices. Composition lessons with Bridge in 1928 and 1929 resulted in fewer works but higher standards; Bridge's demands for disciplined writing also changed the type of composition. Large orchestral pieces decreased significantly in number (four in 1928, none the following year) while the number of songs and works for small instrumental ensemble increased. Gresham's School provided performers and a captured audience, which probably explains the greater number of instrumental and chamber works produced during the period 1928–30.[39] The discipline and discouraging environment of the Royal College of Music, where Britten studied from 1930 to 1933, reduced the quantity and altered the type of music he wrote. Songs and chamber works increased in number, possibly composed with an eye to RCM concerts before he became disenchanted with the limited performance opportunities afforded within the College.

Yet although a trend towards more 'practical' music is identifiable in Britten's juvenilia, this was not always because he tailored works for the performers available. His song output, a major component in his late juvenilia, reflects the composer's love of literature rather than any regularity of song recitals—his mother's informal performances notwithstanding. Britten's growing sophistication in literary taste in the late 1920s, within the confines of

[39] Some of Britten's chamber works were definitely performed in a concert at Gresham's in March 1930.

English pastoral poetry, led to a rise in the number of vocal works composed.[40] Similarly, he wrote a large number of string quartets in 1927, at least partly as a result of the genre's demand for clarity of harmony and voice-leading, at a time when he was quickly developing his own harmonic language under Bridge's watchful eye.

The most striking change in Britten's patterns of composition occurred in the early 1930s, when he began dealing with OUP and the BBC. Both organizations made the young composer more closely aware of the relationship between music and its exponents. For *A Boy was Born*, it was agreed that the BBC's professional Wireless Singers would be expanded from forty to sixty or seventy.[41] The BBC's willingness to incur this extra cost demonstrates its commitment to contemporary music, but Britten could not expect to be similarly indulged elsewhere: chances for this work to be performed outside the BBC were limited. The piece's difficulty made it either unfeasible or unattractive to amateur choirs, while the professional choir was a rare phenomenon in England in the 1930s. After *A Boy was Born*, though, Britten wrote far more with his eye on the potential performers and market.[42] *Holiday Diary* (1934) was composed at the suggestion of his publisher—by then Ralph Hawkes, after machinations which will be detailed below—and performed by Betty Humby, an acquaintance of Britten and the future Lady Beecham; *Friday Afternoons* (1934) was composed with school students of Britten's older brother, Robert, in mind; the Suite for violin and piano (1934) was first performed, in part, by friends of Britten; Sophie Wyss inspired a number of vocal works in the mid- to late 1930s; and all of Britten's incidental music was written for specific theatre or film projects.[43]

The eventual broadcast of *A Boy was Born* on 23 February 1934 was overshadowed by Elgar's death, although it did receive a certain amount of critical attention. Ferruccio Bonavia in the *Daily Telegraph* commented that the 'ingenuity of the writing is striking, even when, as in the first variation, the effect of surprise begins to wear thin before the end is reached',[44] while M. D. Calvocoressi in *Musical Opinion* reiterated a criticism that had been freely applied to Britten's music at the Royal College, and one that would plague him over the coming years: 'it seems to me that now and then he avails himself of his technical efficiency a trifle ostentatiously.'[45] Yet the work had been well previewed and reviewed, and Britten himself had been happy with the performance. The

[40] See Kildea, 'Britten, Auden and "Otherness"', in Mervyn Cooke (ed.), *The Cambridge Companion to Benjamin Britten* (1999), 36–53.

[41] Britten to Benbow, 24 Jan. 1934. BBCWAC, Composer file, Benjamin Britten, file 1a, 1933–44.

[42] This is discussed in detail in Ch. 2.

[43] A more concentrated example of Britten composing for local forces is the Aldeburgh Festival, which is discussed in Ch. 5.

[44] Ferruccio Bonavia, *Daily Telegraph*, 24 Feb. 1934, 6.

[45] M. D. Calvocoressi, *Musical Opinion* (Apr. 1934), quoted in DMPR 330.

relationship between the BBC and Britten that had begun with the broadcast of his *Phantasy*, Op. 2 in August 1933 was consolidated, and future collaborations seemed assured. For the first time in his life Britten had access to a performance forum—at least one consisting of professional musicians and attracting very large audiences.

The Economics of Genre: Publishing

Immediately following the broadcast of *A Boy was Born* Britten announced that he was 'compelled to find a job' due to his 'straitened circumstances'.[46] He was not alone: in 1934 the official rate of unemployment was nearly 17 per cent, following the 1932 peak of 22 per cent.[47] For those directly concerned, the effect of cyclical unemployment and obsolescence through technological advancement was truly devastating. Moreover, the overall psychological impact of the Depression (at its height in Britain in 1931) was immense, while suspension of the gold standard in 1931 resulted in abundant economic analyses and theories for recovery. For most people the impact was less theoretical: priorities were retaining or finding jobs, feeding families, salvaging businesses. Arguments for the accountability of government expenditure, similar to those which dogged the BBC, were aggravated because of these conditions. Similarly, accountability in private business practice discouraged risk-taking and to some extent initiative.

Music was not protected from this environment, and its difficulties had been much worsened by the coincident demise of silent film, the consequently huge redundancy of cinema musicians and the devastating effects on music publishing.[48] The economics of publishing and performing new compositions created certain demands relating to genre; large orchestral works were thought uneconomic, yet, at the same time, the public was supposed not to favour chamber music. The demands created by publishing and performing were quite distinct, yet certainly not independent of one another. With professional orchestras, the larger the instrumentation the more expensive the work was to perform. To a

[46] Britten to J. F. R. Stainer, 15 Apr. 1934, DMPR 334. Britten's letter to Stainer was an acknowledgement of the latter's congratulations on the broadcast of *A Boy was Born*. Although the seriousness of Britten's financial circumstances cannot be dismissed (his father had just died), the letter was probably written in the hope that the Mendelssohn Foundation, which Stainer represented, would extend his grant once it expired. This Foundation was established in 1848 to fund composers and performers. Britten was awarded a partial grant in 1932 and 1933. The suggestion, however, that he be appointed Mendelssohn Scholar for six months from 1 September 1935 was rejected by Britten. For a full account of this see DMPR 254.

[47] A. H. Halsey, *British Social Trends since 1900* (1988), 174.

[48] Edwin Evans states that in 1928, 75 to 80 per cent of paid musical employment was provided by the silent cinema. 'Music and the Cinema', *Music and Letters* (Jan. 1929), quoted in Ehrlich, *The Music Profession*, 199.

lesser degree, this also applied to production costs of publishing it; but the specific demand for all newly published works was that they first found a market and then, most importantly, repeat performances.

The BBC upset traditional economics of performance. Since professional choirs and orchestras were salaried within the BBC, the logistics of performance within the Corporation depended less on the orchestral forces of a work (unless it needed augmentation) than whether it could be performed on the number of rehearsals it was prescribed; difficult modern works were clearly at a disadvantage in a system where rehearsals were set, almost regardless of the repertory performed. Britten's *Sinfonietta* for ten instruments had been abandoned in such circumstances when, in February 1933, Edward Clark and the composer agreed that it would not be ready for that afternoon's broadcast.[49] Yet without BBC resources, performances of large or difficult works were less feasible for a young composer, which in turn made them less feasible for a publishing company—never more so than against the economic backdrop of the early 1930s. Britten had already experienced this to some degree when Foss at first selected only his part-songs for publication, with their minimal financial risk, tangible appeal, and high potential sales.[50] For the most part Foss avoided works which, even though performable by amateurs, would have had difficulty finding markets and subsequent sales. Ironically, it was the part-songs that first made Britten aware of one of the most important aspects of genre economics for publisher and composer alike. Here he encountered problems with literary copyright, forcing yet another departure from the compositional practices that had developed through his juvenilia.

When Foss wrote to Britten in 1932 accepting his part-songs, he concluded with a discussion of royalties:

> I am afraid that you have chosen rather unfortunate poems for de la Mare always charges a high figure for permission to reprint, usually 2 to 3 guineas each in advance of a 5% royalty. I fear this will mean that we should have to offer you a very small royalty as clearly we have got to publish the works at a low price, if we do them at all.[51]

[49] Britten's diary, 5 Feb. 1933.

[50] These songs would most often be bought in sets of multiple copies.

[51] Foss to Britten, 29 Apr. 1932. BPL, OUP Correspondence, 1932–9. At most, Britten would have received a royalty of 5 per cent. In 1937, when Britten had established a reputation as a composer, OUP proposed to include 'The Ride-by-nights' in the Clarendon Song Book series, offering the composer a set fee of £1. 1*s*. 0*d*. Britten requested a payment per copy sold. OUP responded on 18 May 1937: 'We account to you for sales of your song on a royalty basis of 10%, less 5% to Walter de la Mare for the use of his words . . . were we to reimburse you for its inclusion at the rate of £1–1–0 per thousand copies we would really be paying at a higher rate—proportionate on the space occupied by the song in comparison with the size of the volume. Mr. de la Mare has accepted our proposal for a fee of £1–1–0 but should you still feel that you would prefer to receive a payment of so much per thousand, may I ask you to consider a rate based on the number of pages occupied, namely seven out of a total of eighty-one?' Britten then requested 10*s*. 6*d*. per thousand copies sold of the piano edition and the same amount per five thousand sales of the melody.

Walter de la Mare was much admired by Britten in this period: his juvenilia include eleven songs or choruses with words by the poet.[52] But de la Mare was not the only copyright author set by Britten in his youth. When he submitted *The Birds* to Boosey & Hawkes, he was told that the firm had published a setting of Belloc's poem once before and had had to pay a 50 per cent royalty to him ('I doubt if there is the remotest chance of our being able to mitigate these terms').[53] Indeed, of the seventy-four songs and choruses with identifiable authors, written before 1932, almost two-thirds would have been subject to copyright royalties had they been published.[54]

The conditions of copyright applying to Britten's works had been formalized in the 1911 Copyright Act. The original Berne Convention (1886) had brought together representatives from fourteen countries (not including the United States or Russia) who established certain guidelines for the protection of literary and artistic works. Among other things, restrictions over ready exchange of works in translation were introduced. But it was not until the revision of the Berne convention in 1908 that copyright protection was extended to cover a period of fifty years after the death of the author, a mechanism incorporated into Britain's 1911 Copyright Act.[55] Financial charges for setting words to music now endured long after the author's death.

Britten's modern if conservative literary taste did not at first give way to the commercial advantage of using non-copyright poetry. On 16 July 1932, soon after Foss's warning about de la Mare's likely royalty, Britten purchased a volume of poems by Robert Graves (1895–1985). He immediately set one of them, 'Lift Boy', as a companion piece for 'I lov'd a lass' (a poem by George Wither, 1588–1667), a song he had completed six weeks earlier, immediately after resubmitting his three part-songs to OUP.[56] On 12 October Britten showed the two completed songs to Foss, who rejected them—a curious decision, given their apparent suitability for the Oxford Choral Songs series.[57] Although his reasoning is a little difficult to divine, he almost certainly would have discussed with Britten the copyright on Graves's poem. One month later Britten bought

[52] Apart from the three part-songs, these were: 'Silver' (1928); 'The Quartette' (1929); 'A Song of Enchantment' (1929); 'Tit for Tat' (1930); 'I saw three witches' (1930); 'Vigil' (1931); 'Autumn' (1931); 'The Moth' (1931). Five of these songs ('A Song of Enchantment', 'Autumn', 'Silver', 'Vigil', and 'Tit for Tat') were compiled by Britten into a single volume (*Tit for Tat*) in 1968 and dedicated to Richard de la Mare, chairman of Britten's relatively new publishing company, Faber Music Ltd.

[53] Boosey to Britten, 17 Apr. 1935. BPL, Boosey & Hawkes Correspondence, 1935.

[54] Based on the catalogue of Britten's juvenilia, BPL. This total of seventy-four includes five biblical texts.

[55] Ehrlich, *Harmonious Alliance*, 12–13.

[56] Britten's diary, 16 and 18 July 1932; 2 June 1932.

[57] Britten probably composed the songs with this series in mind, flushed by his early success.

Ancient English Carols, which supplied most of the copyright-free texts for *A Boy was Born*.[58]

This piece marked the beginning of a long period in Britten's life where he avoided setting texts which would have incurred an author's royalty. It would be foolish to suggest that his desire to avoid royalty payments to authors (which were taken from his own royalties) completely overrode artistic principles, but there is no doubt in the early change in his habits—doubly surprising given his friendship with (and education at the hands of) that most modern and terrible of the *enfants terribles* W. H. Auden from 1935—and it is probable that this consideration continued to govern his output from 1934. Apart from his operatic collaborations and settings of poems written by close friends, in the next twenty years Britten was to publish only four works with texts by copyright authors (his attempt to include a setting of Irene McLeod's 'Lone Dog' in *Friday Afternoons* ended in a copyright impasse, and 'Begone, dull care' was set and substituted at the last moment).[59] 'In the bleak mid-winter' by Christina Rossetti (1830–94) was used in *A Boy was Born*; 'Jazz Man' by Eleanor Farjeon (1881–1965) is one of the songs in *Friday Afternoons* (1935); *Les Illuminations* is a setting of poems by Arthur Rimbaud (1845–91); and 'The Salley Gardens' by Yeats (1865–1939) is of course one of Britten's most famous folk-song arrangements (1941). Other miscellaneous folk-song settings had to wait until 2001 for publication (*Tom Bowling and Other Song Arrangements*) because Boosey & Hawkes was unable to negotiate an acceptable royalty with other parties for a number of the songs. In the remaining twenty years or so of his life Britten set more contemporary works that were protected by copyright: *Winter Words* (Hardy), canticles III (Sitwell), IV, and V (Eliot), and of course the Wilfred Owen poems used in the *Nocturne* and the *War Requiem*, but these were still outnumbered by many non-copyright poems. And dabbling with copyright authors in the late 1950s and early 1960s resulted in contrite letters of apology from composer to publisher. Novello extracted a percentage royalty and a one guinea fee for Britten's version of 'Sailor Boy' since it was based on a tune collected by a 'house' composer, Cecil Sharp.[60] Similarly, a Britten setting of 'The holly and the ivy' led to hasty negotiations with Novello, and caused the composer to pen the following note to his own publishing house:

[58] Britten's diary, 12 Nov. 1932.

[59] One work not included in this total is Auden's 'Out on the Lawn' which forms part of the second section of the *Spring Symphony* (1949). Britten and Auden's relationship had cooled considerably by this stage, but not to the point that commercial terms would dictate whether the former would set a poem by his estranged friend. More likely, this poem, with its combination of the political and the pastoral, both fitted the schematic design of the new symphony (acting as a chilling centre point), and served as a valedictory tribute to the Auden of the 1930s. Britten's problems with the copyright on the models for *The Rape of Lucretia* and *The Turn of the Screw*, as well as the problems with his proposed opera 'The Tale of Mr Tod', are discussed in Ch. 3.

[60] Britten to James, 22 Jan. 1959. BPL, Boosey & Hawkes Correspondence, 1959.

I am sorry I cause you so much trouble with my folk song arrangements. I am sure the steps you have taken about 'The Holly and the Ivy' are wise—it is always a weak position to have to appeal after the act; but I am afraid Messrs. Novello seem intractable to say the least. Anyhow, I promise you that in the future I shall never arrange a folk song without enquiring fully into its sources, and shall try to avoid anything which is copyright.[61]

And with this the gate was shut—rather too late and not properly secured, but shut nonetheless.

The Economics of Genre: Performing Right

Foss's reluctance to publish certain of Britten's works was not the only element complicating their relationship. Two works from 1934—the *Simple Symphony*, Op. 4, and the children's songs *Friday Afternoons*, Op. 7—chart the decline in Britten's relationship with OUP and his blossoming friendship with Ralph Hawkes. Foss accepted the *Simple Symphony* for publication on 30 July 1934, proposing to issue the work for sale, not just hire, and offering Britten a royalty of 12½ per cent on each copy sold. His acceptance of this work, however, was preceded by hesitation, as Foss made clear to Whittaker:

I have got to decide sooner or later whether to take up Benjamin Britten or not. At the moment I am letting certain works go, while retaining my hold, and am faced with the necessity to decide if I am going to publish the Oboe Quartet and (the work which I am sending you under separate cover) the 'Simple Symphony' for strings. . . . Will you give me your frank opinion, both of how much you like the work and how much you think others will?[62]

Whittaker's frank opinion was that the work was charming, and that it 'resolves itself into a commercial question for you'.[63] It was not a commercially intimidating proposal: the cost of publishing 350 full scores was estimated at £30, an extra £2 for 500 copies; each string part would cost £7 for 350 copies, £7. 10*s*. 0*d*. for 500. In all, the Symphony would be considerably cheaper to produce than *A Boy was Born*.[64] The commercial question resolved itself: 'I incline to accepting this', wrote Foss to Milford, 'in order to keep Britten. I believe it will get much performed.'[65]

Although history is on Foss's side, performances of the *Simple Symphony* were slow off the mark.[66] This was due entirely to yet another royalty, another

[61] Britten to James, 21 Feb. 1961. BPL, Boosey & Hawkes Correspondence, 1961. Similar promises were made after Boosey & Hawkes settled with other publishers over 'The Shooting of his Dear' (1958) and 'King Herod and the Cock' (1962).

[62] Foss to Whittaker, undated. OUP, Britten Correspondence, 1934–75.

[63] Whittaker to Foss, 28 June 1934. Ibid.

[64] Estimate of costs for the *Simple Symphony*, 13 July 1934. Ibid.

[65] Foss to Milford, undated [late June 1934]. Ibid.

[66] The *Simple Symphony* is today one of Britten's most recorded, performed, and popular works.

difference between the nineteenth and twentieth centuries in regard to the commercial affairs of composers. When the music division of Oxford University Press was formed in 1925, it did not join the Performing Right Society: like most publishers before 1914 (and several since), it considered that performing right was against the interests of the publisher. The principle of this royalty is simple: composers should be paid for each performance of their works—over and above the royalty they might receive for the sale or hire of scores. Technology muddied the relatively still waters surrounding the concert hall. Where once only major venues had hosted major works, gramophone, radio, and film now created new performance forums. Monitoring these performances and collecting the relevant fees (which now included those for mechanical reproduction) was neither straightforward nor consistently effective.

The PRS was founded in 1914 to do the monitoring and collecting. In its early years it found it hard to combat the central argument of dissenting publishers—that performing groups would limit themselves to works which were not subject to performing right, thus discriminating against the works and composers covered by the PRS. Although this argument weakened as more composers joined the Society, it was still a popular line of thought in the late 1920s. Foss had obviously discussed the issue of performing right with Britten early in their relationship. When he informed Britten that the conductor Hermann Scherchen planned a performance of his *Sinfonietta* in Strasbourg in early August 1933, he advised him that there was 'no question of a fee unfortunately, but I think you would be wise to lend him the score and parts'.[67]

In order to offer Britten attractive prospects, OUP needed to provide him with a viable alternative to the PRS. Foss addressed this in his early negotiations for a performance of the *Simple Symphony*.[68] In October 1934 he advised Britten to offer the work first to Leslie Heward (conductor of the City of Birmingham Symphony Orchestra) for a concert or broadcast, since it was possible that he would pay a performing fee of 5 guineas.[69] This was a considerable improvement on the view Foss had advocated only one year earlier. Britten concurred, and Foss sent the piece to Heward a few days later, maintaining that, as a 'world première', it was worth a performing fee of £5. 5*s*. 0*d*.[70] Heward thought not: 'If we were to stage the Last Supper with the original cast we should not get an extra £5 in our Sunday night house, so that is out of the question.'[71]

67 Foss to Britten, 20 June 1933. BPL, OUP Correspondence, 1932–9.

68 The first performance of this work was given by the Norwich String Orchestra, conducted by the composer, on 6 Mar. 1934. Foss's negotiations concerned its first performance following publication.

69 Foss to Britten, 13 Oct. 1934. OUP, Britten Correspondence, 1934–75.

70 Foss to Heward, 16 Oct. 1934. Ibid.

71 Heward to Foss, 24 Oct. 1934. Ibid. Heward showed himself to be none too fond of the work, adding a postscript to the letter: 'I think really it ought to have been left as little piano pieces & songs.

Wilfred Ridgway, conductor of the Birmingham String Orchestra, was second choice, and he was offered the 'première' for only £3. 3*s*. 0*d*. His response beautifully emphasizes the reluctance of music organizations to involve themselves in performing right if they could possibly avoid it and summarizes OUP's reputation was on this thorny issue. After expressing some enthusiasm for the piece (it was 'suitable for the Society's resources and likely to be attractive to our audiences'), Ridgway declared that 'the general opinion seems to be that a charge of £3–3–0, in excess of cost of purchase of score & parts, for performing right is an avoidable burden which the exigencies of concert giving today do not warrant our undertaking'. He raised one more point: wasn't OUP music free of additional performance charges?[72]

Ridgway's response had further implications: Foss had intended that the score and parts of the *Simple Symphony* should appear in early February 1935, but he decided to postpone publication until after the first performance, since 'once people can purchase copies, our performing fee goes west'.[73] Here was an unconscious admission that OUP could neither monitor performances nor extract fees on behalf of the composer. Foss's final efforts for a performance were thwarted when Boyd Neel turned down the work because of the proposed performing fee; Foss then informed Britten that he was publishing it immediately, thus 'throwing the work open to the public'.[74]

Negotiations over *Friday Afternoons* were no smoother. In August 1934, Britten informed Foss that the 'school songs' were almost finished and would be sent to him in a few weeks.[75] He probably submitted them on 20 September, along with his Te Deum in C—completed only a few days before.[76] Perhaps aware that their views on performing right were diverging, Foss offered to buy the Te Deum outright;[77] Britten instead negotiated a royalty of 10 per cent. That the Te Deum was accepted quickly is not surprising, given the established market for church music. Moreover, the unsigned contract for the work suggests that Foss was trying to emphasize that OUP could provide services equivalent to those offered by the PRS: a composer royalty of 10 per cent on each copy sold; a royalty on mechanical reproductions of 50 per cent; and an undertaking that the publisher was to be in charge of all performances, for which the composer would receive a royalty of 75 per cent of the fees charged, unless the performance was for gramophone or radio, in which case the composer would receive a

Why does Brittain [*sic*], who obviously has things to say, bother to say the same things twice? Tell him to write new things instead of dishing up old ones!'

72 Ridgway to Foss, 23 Jan. 1935. OUP, Britten Correspondence, 1934–75.

73 Undated memo. Ibid.

74 Foss's secretary to Britten, 16 Mar. 1935. Ibid.

75 DMPR 345.

76 Britten's diary, 17 Sept. 1934.

77 Foss to Britten, 6 Nov. 1934. BPL, OUP Correspondence, 1932–49.

royalty of 50 per cent.[78] This final undertaking—that OUP would be in charge of all performances—was in fact spurious in the case of the Te Deum. The church-music market operated on sales of multiple copies, and, as Foss had previously acknowledged, performance fees were impossible to extract on music sold, not hired, no matter how pious the purchaser. Moreover, the draft contract makes no mention of *petits droits*—'small rights' as opposed to the 'grand rights' of big theatre works—which OUP would have found impossible to monitor and collect.

The Te Deum's draft contract attempts to meet the points that Britten disputed in relation to *Friday Afternoons*. In December 1934 Britten was informed that OUP would publish the twelve songs.[79] On the same day, according to his diary, Britten and Foss had a 'real tussel' [*sic*] over performing right, which prompted the composer to consult Ralph Hawkes about the same problem immediately afterwards.[80] The following day Foss stated his precise views on Britten, OUP, and performing right. He would not cede to Britten the broadcast or mechanical rights (gramophone etc.) on the songs since 'the sales of the music on your own showing will hardly be a sufficient remuneration for the speculation on the outlay'. More to the point, 'I don't think that the performing rights question matters a rap as we should not charge for them anyhow, but I should be reluctant in principle to allow any Society whatsoever to have sole control of any part of any work published in this catalogue.' He then raised a number of points: was there any publisher who did not want a share in broadcasting and gramophone royalties? And did Britten realize that other composers affiliated to the PRS were published by OUP and found the arrangement advantageous since they took the 'lion's share' of any performing fees? Foss concluded his letter thus:

> I have a considerable belief in you as a composer as you know, and am anxious to encourage and help you all I can, but it must be apparent that a good deal of money will have to be laid out before a fortune is made on your compositions, and I feel you would be unwise to stress too much, at this stage, the importance of having your performing rights managed by only one central body.[81]

At Bridge's suggestion, Britten sought the advice, or rather the reassurance of the PRS: he had actually joined the Society three months earlier when Ralph Hawkes put the unsmoking gun in his hand, furnishing him with a PRS membership form along with terms for the publication of the *Sinfonietta* and the *Phantasy*—two works rejected by Foss.[82] He later informed Foss: 'I have cast my lot with the P.R.S., and I felt it right to stick to them.'[83]

[78] Te Deum contract, 26 Jan. 1935. BPL, OUP Correspondence, 1932–49.
[79] Foss to Britten, 19 Dec. 1934. OUP, Britten Correspondence, 1932–9.
[80] Britten's diary, 19 Dec. 1934.
[81] Foss to Britten, 20 Dec. 1934. BPL, OUP Files, 1932–9.
[82] Britten's diary, 15 Sept. 1934.
[83] Britten to Foss, 8 Jan. 1935. DMPR 360.

In his response to Foss's letter of 20 December, Britten had emphasized that it was a great mistake to separate performing and broadcasting rights but, since he had already submitted the songs, he would allow OUP to publish them. He further noted that all future works would be controlled by the PRS—leaving his relationship with OUP unsustainable.[84] Foss turned down the songs since, because of performing right, he was 'faced with the possibility of bearing a loss on these songs which I can never recover on other works of yours. In other words, by publishing them I should really be helping your future publishers and that hardly seems fair to us.'[85] Britten withdrew the songs and they were subsequently put out by Boosey & Hawkes—the firm that, for the next thirty years, acted as his exclusive publisher.

An Incidental Market?

Foss's attitude towards performing right was unfortunate—the tide was changing very quickly both inside and outside OUP. In January 1936 the Oxford Press actually became a member of the PRS, at the same time that Britten was signing an exclusive contract with Boosey & Hawkes. The economic historian Cyril Ehrlich attributes this change of attitude to the increasing complexity of performance fees in the light of new technology—particularly broadcasting.[86] Although this is contradicted by Lady Walton's unlikely assertion that OUP's change of heart and subsequent membership of the PRS was solely the result of her husband's efforts,[87] it is worth considering exactly why Britten and Ralph Hawkes were so aware of the potential of broadcasting—as both a performance forum and a source of revenue—while Foss remained so ignorant. In 1929 the BBC paid the PRS £45,000 to cover broadcast performances of music by Society members; in 1936 this increased to £121,926 and it was predicted that, under new terms then being negotiated, the figure would rise to £233,000 in the following year.[88] Even without knowledge of the actual figures, musicians were arguing for simple parity between the number of radio licences and the sum of performing right paid by the BBC. An alert publisher would have been aware of

[84] Ibid.

[85] Foss to Britten, 23 Jan. 1935. BPL, OUP Correspondence, 1932–9. In this, Foss was probably influenced by the poor sales of *A Boy was Born*—only eighty-seven copies had been sold in Britain by 31 March 1935. Foss, however, denied this in his letter of 23 January to Britten. 'You mustn't on any account imagine that I am disappointed with you or the work because "The Boy" has not sold. My railings are against the public and the musicians, and I am still unable to understand why an event of the importance of its creation should leave the practising musicians unmoved.'

[86] Ehrlich, *Harmonious Alliance*, 78.

[87] Susana Walton, *William Walton: Behind the Façade* (1988), 181.

[88] *The PR Gazette*, 1937, quoted in Alan Peacock and Ronald Weir, *The Composer in the Market Place* (1975), 81.

these arguments. The number of licences sold in 1924 was 2,614,324; twelve years later this figure had reached 7,359,327.[89] It is possible that Foss did not recognize the extent of the changes occurring around him; it is also possible that he really did believe that OUP could act as agent as well as publisher. It is most likely, however, that his interpretation of the Press's financial situation was such that incentives for performance rather than active discouragement were required. Performing right simply did not fit into this view.

Britten's enthusiasm for broadcasting grew out of its influential role in his music education. In the relative isolation of Suffolk, the BBC granted him access to music he would not otherwise have heard.[90] In the early 1930s he was quick to realize that the BBC had the performing forces and a publicly proclaimed policy on British music which could work to his advantage. Thirty years later Britten labelled the loudspeaker 'the principal enemy of music'—ideal for education and reiteration, nothing else—but it is safe to say that in the 1930s he was convinced of its economic importance to the composer and was determined to cultivate his connections with both the BBC and Boosey & Hawkes.[91]

Cultivating Ralph Hawkes proved simple, for he was anxious to reciprocate. In 1934 Hawkes was still a few years away from publishing, among others, Bartók, Stravinsky, and Copland (following Britten's suggestion), but the same instinct that would lead him to sign them up amid the devastation, upheaval, and opportunity of the Second World War was certainly active in the early 1930s. Britten's relationship with Ralph Hawkes and, to a lesser extent, Leslie Boosey, was immediately more positive than with Hubert Foss. Initially there were similarities in the mechanics of the two publishing firms—Boosey requested a simplification of the piano accompaniment to 'Lift Boy' and offered Graves the same royalty that Foss had paid to de la Mare for the Three Two-part Songs—but the new firm's approach to Britten's music was more inclusive, less piecemeal than OUP's. Britten was offered letters of introduction to foreign publishers;[92] casual work vetting scores;[93] encouragement and ideas for new works. Most importantly, Hawkes understood the commercial music world and was prepared to act as ad hoc agent on Britten's behalf. He was determined that Britten should be a *professional* composer and, moreover, was patient enough to

[89] *The PR Gazette*, 1937, quoted in Alan Peacock and Ronald Weir, *The Composer in the Market Place* (1975), 81.

[90] Britten's father was opposed to the gramophone and the wireless, so the young Britten did his listening at the homes of family friends and at Gresham's School.

[91] Britten, *On Receiving the First Aspen Award* (1978), 20.

[92] Hawkes to Britten, 16 Oct. 1934. BPL, Boosey & Hawkes Correspondence, 1934.

[93] Intriguingly, Britten was sent Shostakovich's opera *Lady Macbeth of the Mtsensk District* (1932) in this capacity, and paid 1½ guineas for his services. Hawkes to Britten, 21 Nov. 1935. BPL, Boosey & Hawkes Correspondence, 1935–41.

see this through.[94] With Hawkes's active encouragement, Britten worked with British film and theatre companies between 1935 and 1939—the year of his departure for America. As a result, Boosey & Hawkes became increasingly involved in the 'incidental' music Britten was writing for stage, screen, and radio broadcast—the histories of the publishing and theatrical institutions overlapping to a considerable extent.[95]

In his novel *Vile Bodies*—a romp through the hedonism of (southern) England in the late 1920s—Evelyn Waugh paints a marvellous picture of the burgeoning film industry. 'Now just you ask me anything you want about this film because I'm just here to answer,' the film director tells a bemused Adam Symes, the anti-hero of the story.

> 'Have you got my name? Have a card. That's the name of the company in the corner. Not the one that's scratched out. The one written above. *The Wonderfilm Company of Great Britain*. Now this film,' he said, in what seemed a well-practised little speech, 'of which you have just witnessed a mere fragment marks a stepping stone in the development of the British Film Industry. It is the most important All-Talkie super-religious film to be produced solely in this country by British artists and management and by British capital. It has been directed throughout regardless of difficulty and expense, and supervised by a staff of expert historians and theologians. Nothing has been omitted that would contribute to the meticulous accuracy of every detail. The life of that great social and religious reformer John Wesley is for the first time portrayed to a British public in all its humanity and tragedy. . . . Look here, I've got all this written out. I'll have them give you a copy before you go. Come and see the duel. . . .'[96]

Waugh delicately expresses or hints at a number of pertinent points: enthusiasm for the new technology; variety in documentary subjects tackled in early films; America's domination of this new industry; the precarious and transient nature of early film companies; and the curiously amateur deference towards supposed experts (the historians and theologians). Waugh also captures the excitement and spontaneity of film—its immediacy, its essentially democratic nature (here was a form of mass entertainment aimed specifically at the middle and lower classes),

[94] In an interview with Donald Mitchell in April 1975, the North American publisher Bailey Bird said that Hawkes's support of Britten in the 1930s and early 1940s was questioned by his colleagues. For years, at the end of the annual meeting 'the Chairman usually turned to him and said, "Well, Mr Ralph, I see we have spent so much money on Britten so far; when are we going to start getting some of this back? Do you have a report on Mr Britten?" On this occasion [1946, one year after *Peter Grimes*], however, it came to the end of the meeting and nothing happened, and the Chairman said, "Well, if there's no other business the meeting will be adjourned." So [Hawkes] said: "Just a minute, Mr Chairman. I haven't received my usual questions about Mr Britten this year."' DMPR 339.

[95] Britten's incidental music for radio, and the related issue of its influence on genre, is considered in greater detail in Ch. 2.

[96] Evelyn Waugh, *Vile Bodies*, 144. The book was published by Chapman & Hall on 14 Jan. 1930.

and its potential as educator and propagator, which made it attractive to leftish intellectuals. In this, Waugh could have been describing the General Post Office Film Unit, the youthful government-funded film company that was active in the 1930s, producing experimental and more utilitarian documentary films, attracting people such as the director John Grierson, the painter William Coldstream, and the sound engineer Alberto Cavalcanti.

Equally attractive as a sanctuary for left-wing intellectuals was the theatre. This art-form was greatly affected by the new medium of film—most particularly the 'talkies'—because of the competition it offered and the emancipation of visual imagery it inspired. The impact of film on theatre was almost immediately felt. In late November 1923, for example, a theatrical agent, with the dramatic flair expected from one in his profession, shot himself at the top of the dome of St Paul's Cathedral, leaving police and doctors with the particular difficulty of getting his body down the long, winding staircase. The cause of his depression was the advent of cinema and subsequent demise of his business. By the early 1930s interplay between the mediums was marked, and competition severe. But at least one theatre held its own. The Group Theatre of London—with its heady concentration of intellectuals, writers, directors, musicians, dancers, and designers—offered unique dramatic and socio-political commentary on British life, masquerading as entertainment. It was a characteristic product of its time, which Waugh might have been proud to invent.

Britten began his association with the Group Theatre and the GPO Film Unit in early 1935. In the course of the next four years, he was to write music for thirty-one films and seventeen theatre productions.[97] He also composed scores for seven radio productions—some of them substantial.[98] It was, therefore, a busy time for Britten, which best explains why between 1935 and 1939 the only 'serious' works completed were his Op. 7 to Op. 14 and a handful of smaller works. At the end of this period he lamented the fact that his art music had taken second place to his incidental music. To a friend he wrote that the reason he was going to America was 'to do some really intensive thinking & for me personally to do somework [*sic*] to please myself & not necessarily the BBC or [producer] Basil Dean!'[99] But this was still some years away.

Work on his first film, *The King's Stamp*, had a nice Waughian quality to it:

[97] John Evans, Philip Reed, and Paul Wilson (eds.), *A Britten Source Book* (1988), 131–53. Britten's incidental music, the topic of Philip Reed's doctoral thesis, is treated only summarily here.

[98] This figure deals with the period 1937–9 only. Britten wrote many more scores for radio dramas in Canada and America, and he resumed his work with the BBC in 1942. See Ch. 2 for details of the radio scores and Philip Reed, 'Catalogue Raisonné', in Evans, Reed, and Wilson, *Britten Source Book*, 130–65, for details of the other incidental scores.

[99] Britten to Mary Behrend, 17 Apr. 1939. DMPR 618.

I spend the whole blessed day slogging at the film music in my room—with a watch in one hand and a pencil in the other—trying to make what little ideas I have (& they are precious few on this God-forsaken subject) syncronize [sic] with the Seconds. Have a short break for a walk after tea . . . but otherwise I slog away until abt. 11.0 at night—trying to concoct some rubbish about a Jubilee Stamp.[100]

The 'rubbish' was in fact an effective score, written for two pianos, flute (piccolo), clarinet, and percussion (various instruments); some of the music Britten liked enough to reuse in later GPO scores. This is an important feature of the period—Handelian self-plunder resulting from limited time and resources. The GPO Film Unit and the Group Theatre could scarcely have provided a more effective apprenticeship. Britten later recalled this period: 'I had to work quickly to force myself to work when I didn't want to, and to get used to working in all kinds of circumstances. . . . I had to write scores not for large orchestra, but for not more than six or seven players, and to make these instruments make all the effects that each film demanded.'[101] Schoenberg differed *slightly* in his approach: 'I would be willing to write music for a film. . . . I would want $100,000 for the score. They must give me a year to write it and let me compose what I want. And, of course, I would have to say something about the story.'[102]

The most important element of Britten's apprenticeship, however, was political enlightenment. Rupert Doone, founder of the Group Theatre, saw his ensemble as a social force: 'Society must be changed if we want a living theatre. The theatre should suggest changes.'[103] The Group's 1935 production of Shakespeare's *Timon of Athens*—Britten's first theatrical collaboration—was full of such social commentary. James Agate in the *Sunday Times* considered the music ill-suited to the role: 'Timon bids the sun "draw from the earth rotten humidity", and Mr Benjamin Britten bids a concatenation of bassoon, oboe and clarinet . . . [to] echo this feat.'[104] But these were early days, and Britten's later collaborations with the Group Theatre brought him into contact with Brechtian ideas, the political commentary of German cabaret, the 'authentic rallying cries of

[100] Britten's diary, 1 May 1935. *The King's Stamp* was a short film about the creation of a postage stamp in honour of King George V's Silver Jubilee.

[101] Britten, 'How to Become a Composer', *The Listener* (7 Nov. 1946), 624. In this, he had an unlikely ally. In the same year Vaughan Williams wrote that 'film composing is a splendid discipline, and I recommend a course of it to all composition teachers whose pupils are apt to be dawdling in their ideas, or whose every bar is sacred and must not be cut or altered'. 'Film Music', *Film Music Notes*, 6/3 (1946).

[102] Bruno Ussher, 'Composing for the Films', *New York Times*, 28 Jan. 1940, quoted in Roy M. Prendergast, *Film Music* (1992), 47.

[103] Michael Sidnell, *Dances of Death* (1984), 132.

[104] James Agate, 'Hurly without Burly', *Sunday Times*, 24 Nov. 1935, quoted in Sidnell, *Dances of Death*, 134.

homo-communism',[105] the use of masks, and the quasi-Greek chorus, taken from Obey's *Le viol de Lucrèce* via Auden's *The Chase* and *The Dog Beneath the Skin*.[106] Moreover, Britten met many people who were to play important roles in his later life and music: the Communist poet Randall Swingler, singer Hedli Anderson, writer Montagu Slater, the director Tyrone Guthrie, composer Brian Easdale, the painter John Piper and his wife, writer Myfanwy. He saw his first homosexual couple, Doone and Medley, and witnessed ready acceptance and discussion of his sexuality in a manner unlikely to have been displayed in the waiting room of his father's Lowestoft dental practice. Most importantly, art and politics were discussed in the same breath: to these idealists, the function of each overlapped.

The result of Britten's association with these film and theatre companies was twofold: a heightened understanding of dramatic rhetoric and language, and the introduction of political idealism into his art music. On the former, Donald Mitchell makes the point that the 'sheer dramatic knack and flair that marked *Peter Grimes* must strike one not as qualities conjured out of the air but as manifestations of techniques that had been prepared over a long period in the often gruelling environment of a film studio, cutting-room or theatre pit'.[107] Part of the dramatic flair of *Grimes* is the musical rhetoric—the conscious use of sounds or music for persuasive effect. This had developed in the film studio. Particular forms such as the passacaglia and techniques such as leitmotiv were useful in film scores, since the first offered a slow build-up of tension and the second an analogue for recognition or association of ideas. Britten used both of these quite masterfully in *Grimes*. There were obvious technical limitations in writing for films. In 1933 the conductor Clarence Raybould, a later foe of Britten's, memorably described some of them:

> The musician is at the mercy of a well-meaning body of sound engineers who cannot yet reproduce the tone of a single violin adequately, let alone a mass of strings; whose idea of the characteristic tone of an oboe seems to be founded on toothcomb and tissue paper; and who, when criticised, think themselves unjustly abused because the banjo, the plucked string and the saxophone come off fairly well in recording.[108]

Although Britten's film scores do not revolve exclusively around those instruments that Raybould considered truthful in reproduction, he did tend to avoid or to use sparingly those instruments that recorded particularly badly (violins,

[105] Cyril Connolly on Communism as surrogate for homosexuality in Auden's *The Dog Beneath the Skin*, Sidnell, *Dances of Death*, 155. This technique of dramatic metaphor dominated Britten's treatment of homosexuality in his later works.

[106] Britten was clearly taken with this technique, calling Robert Speaight's performance as the Witness in the private performance of *The Dog Beneath the Skin* 'the best part of the show'. Donald Mitchell, *Britten and Auden in the Thirties* (1979), 119.

[107] Ibid. 30–1.

[108] Clarence Raybould, 'Music and the Synchronized Film', *Sight and Sound*, 2/7 (1935). The development of recording technology and its influence on music is discussed further in Ch. 6.

horns, and timpani, according to the film music historian Roy Prendergast), favouring unusual combinations of those that recorded well. Developing the facility of writing for these unusual combinations was excellent preparation for the chamber operas and the church parables. Similarly, the percussion writing in the 1935 score for the film *Coal Face* (including chains, coconut shells—which reappeared six years later in *Paul Bunyan*—a cup in a bucket of water, sandpaper, and a small drill), anticipated that of *The Young Person's Guide to the Orchestra* (1945) and *Noye's Fludde* (1958), while the somewhat gratuitous introduction of boys' voices to his score of *Telegrams* (July 1935) foreshadowed his lifelong fascination with the sound and company of trebles.[109]

Selling Britten

The introduction of political ideology into Britten's art music is much-travelled territory, but the effect of it on the composer's relationship with his long-time publisher has attracted fewer wayfarers.[110] Britten makes clear in his 1936 diary that he had Hawkes's support:

> 1936 finds me infinitely better off in all ways than did the beginning of 1935; it finds me earning my living—with occasionally something to spare—at the G.P.O. film Unit under John Grierson and [Alberto] Cavalcanti, writing music & supervising sounds for films (this one T.P.O. Night Mail) at the rate of £5 per week, but owing to the fact I can claim no performing rights (it being Crown property) with the possibility of it being increased to £10 per week or £2 per day; writing very little, but with the possibility & ideas for writing alot [sic] of original music, as I am going under an agreement with Boosey & Hawkes for a £3 a week guarantee of [future] royalties . . . [111]

Hawkes was, though, politically naive—at least as far as Britten's early programmatic music and wider literary-political trends were concerned. In thanking him for the dedication of *Our Hunting Fathers*—Britten's most overtly political work of the 1930s—Hawkes made it clear that he took the piece literally, missing any other messages or metaphors: 'It is very nice of you and I feel a little awkward in this respect, for I know nothing at all about hunting, neither am I a father but I will try to live up to it by learning more about monkeys and other hunting animals.'[112] He was a canny, prescient businessman, primarily interested in fostering his new composer's talents, with an eye on the long term. Yet considerations of

[109] Although Britten's score for this film exists, Brian Easdale was actually credited for the soundtrack. It is not clear why Britten's score was not used.

[110] See Mitchell, *Britten and Auden in the Thirties*, and Kildea, 'Britten, Auden and "Otherness"', in Cooke, *Cambridge Companion to Britten.*

[111] Britten's diary, 1 Jan. 1936. 'T.P.O.' was an abbreviation of 'Travelling Post Office', the apt working title of *Night Mail.*

[112] Hawkes to Britten, 21 July 1936. BPL, Boosey & Hawkes, 1936. See Mitchell, *Britten and Auden in the Thirties*, 19–49, for an analysis of the work's political analogies.

business and old-world patronage did not preclude Britten's political excursions, for over the next three years Hawkes also published, or considered publishing, other works containing a specific social or political message—the *Russian Funeral*, *On This Island*, *Advance Democracy*, and *Ballad of Heroes*. The publisher could hardly have remained blind to Britten's politics. His education, however, would also have grown observing sales trends in the early Britten–Boosey & Hawkes scores, and deriving the reasons for their success or otherwise in the market place (Table 1.2). The Boosey & Hawkes royalty statements were also Britten's first education in consumer taste.

Table 1.2 UK sales of selected Britten scores published by Boosey & Hawkes, 1935, 1939, 1940–2[a]

Score titles	1935	1939	1940	1941	1942
A Hymn to the Virgin	142	47	147	112	0
Sinfonietta, Op. 1 (miniature score)	24	9	26	58	112
'I lov'd a lass'	50	38	6	2	3
'Lift Boy'	72	10	11	0	0
Phantasy, Op. 2 (miniature score)	46	26	1	52	71
Phantasy, Op. 2 (parts)	0	15	8	11	30
The Birds	93	2	20	11	0
Holiday Diary, Op. 5	127	0	0	0	0
Suite, Op. 6	—	6	8	0	15
Friday Afternoons, Op. 7 (vol. 1)	—	13	2	8	9
Friday Afternoons, Op. 7 (vol. 2)	—	8	0	8	5
'Old Abram Brown', from *Friday Afternoons*	—	—	—	199	72
'Tragic Story', from *Friday Afternoons*	—	—	—	160	36
Our Hunting Fathers, Op. 8 (vocal score)	—	4	0	0	2
Soirées musicales, Op. 9 (full score)	—	13	0	18	27
Mother Comfort	—	0	0	19	0
Underneath the Abject Willow	—	0	0	6	0
Variations on a Theme of Frank Bridge, Op. 10 (full score)	—	16	0	41	10
On This Island, Op. 11	—	23	1	0	10
Piano Concerto, Op. 13 (two-piano score)	—	38	19	10	10
Advance Democracy	—	472	28	21	26
Ballad of Heroes, Op. 14 (vocal score)	—	316	9	24	104
Violin Concerto, Op. 15 (piano reduction)	—	—	18	22	3
Les Illuminations, Op. 18 (full score)	—	—	73	8	30
Les Illuminations, Op. 18 (miniature score)	—	—	0	0	60
String Quartet No. 1 in D, Op. 25 (miniature score)	—	—	—	—	49

[a] Boosey & Hawkes, Royalty Statements, 1935; 1939; 1940–2. BPL, Boosey & Hawkes Correspondence, 1935, 1939, 1940, 1941, 1942.

Hawkes did not originally envisage a particularly large market for Britten's scores. Initial print runs were small: 600 for *The Birds*, 500 for both *A Hymn to the Virgin* and *Holiday Diary*, 250 copies of the *Sinfonietta* and the *Phantasy* miniature scores, 250 sets of parts for the *Phantasy*, and 1,000 copies each of 'I lov'd a lass' and 'Lift Boy'.[113] The initial run of Britten's Three Two-part Songs, published by OUP in 1932, had been 2,500, and although the marketing strategy for these pieces (the Oxford Choral Songs series) was stronger than that in place at Boosey & Hawkes, Hawkes's approach to the house's new composer was practical if cautious.

The songs ('I lov'd a lass', 'Lift Boy', *The Birds*) and the piano suite *Holiday Diary* were assured of a better market than the *Sinfonietta* and the *Phantasy* because of their genre; they were priced accordingly (5*d*. for the two part-songs, 2*s*. for *The Birds*, and 2*s*. 6*d*. for the suite). Similarly, *A Hymn to the Virgin* could be expected to find its niche within the choirstalls of the Church of England, and was priced at 4*d*. All these works sold modestly well in their first year, benefiting from particular established markets, BBC broadcasts and the publicity surrounding Boosey & Hawkes's new composer. This publicity was driven, in part, by the large number of 'presented copies', issued to influential or interested parties by the publisher in its early years representing Britten. Over 200 copies each of 'I lov'd a lass' and 'Lift Boy', for example, were presented in 1935, while around 150 copies of *Holiday Diary* received similar treatment.

The sales figures for the *Sinfonietta* and the *Phantasy* are more interesting. Although a vigorous educational movement existed in England at the time, charged with the lofty aim of educating the masses in the complexities of serious music through dedicated literature, broadcasting, and the gramophone, the miniature score was then—and indeed remains—the property of the musically literate if not the serious scholar. Accordingly, initial print runs were small, and the price relatively high: 4*s*. for the *Sinfonietta*, 2*s*. 6*d*. for the *Phantasy*. Yet sales numbering twenty-four and forty-six respectively in their first year stand up rather well to the deliberately more popular songs.[114]

Generally, though, sales were slow. Mass-market works did better than Britten's absolute music, but not markedly so. Complex 'ideas' music at first fared no better: when *Our Hunting Fathers* was published in 1936, it did poor trade—although this may in part be explained by the critical mauling it received at the hands of hacks, immune or insensitive to its political message. But because of war, the market changed dramatically in 1939; the fate of Britten's works followed suit. Both the *Ballad of Heroes* and *Advance Democracy* did remarkably well *because* of their political message. Political movements have always had their

[113] Boosey & Hawkes, Royalty Statement, 1935. BPL, Boosey & Hawkes Correspondence, 1935.

[114] Sales of the *Phantasy* were possibly buoyed by its performance at the 1934 ISCM Festival.

songs, and *Advance Democracy*, an unaccompanied motet, was well suited to its purpose. The scale of *Ballad of Heroes*, however, prevented it from becoming a simple rallying call from the left; it is high-art Britten, literally a ballad (which, as most good ballads do, contains a moral just beneath its surface, in this case admonishment of those who stood at their doors ignoring the onslaught of Fascism). Moreover, the sales period listed for 1939 was considerably shorter than twelve months, since Britten received the first proofs of *Ballad* in mid-March.[115] Could war, as it had been for Elgar twenty-five years earlier, be good for sales of music with strong national programmatic content?[116]

Before 1939, however, the future of these 'political' works was not promising. Although Hawkes happily supported Britten in his endeavours, from 1937 he attempted to steer his charge in a more conventional direction. He encouraged the composition of a piano concerto for the BBC (and acted as intermediary);[117] he proposed a ballet for Sadler's Wells;[118] he pushed both the Violin Concerto and *Les Illuminations*;[119] he suggested, rather presciently, a work for children along the lines of *Peter and the Wolf*;[120] and he gently directed Britten towards opera, giving him a score of *Rigoletto* for Christmas 1938.[121] Less conventionally, Hawkes also offered Britten the opportunity of writing for the trumpets and trombones that had been crafted especially for the 1938 coronation, and whose future—even in a monarchy—seemed spasmodic at best.[122]

This change had come about because Britten's works were by now attractive to large performing organizations which favoured more conventional forms and genres. Although he still needed to earn a living from the composition of incidental music, Britten had to allow time for larger projects. The contacts that Hawkes arranged for Britten ranged from the conductor Serge Koussevitzky and the violinist Antonio Brosa to mandarins at the BBC and the Proms. When the British Council offered Britten a commission via his publisher, Hawkes demonstrated the extent and significance of his relationship with the young composer:

My own suggestion is that you go for the Symphonic Poem, for I think it would be a most useful work. Actually, we have no full scale orchestral work from you of this nature

115 Britten to Enid Slater, 13 Mar. 1939. DMPR 611.

116 In the First World War, sales of Elgar's patriotic scores (*The Fourth of August*, etc.) were high, falling away almost completely after the Armistice. See Kildea, *World War I and the British Music Industry* (1991), 87–90.

117 Hawkes to Wright, 14 Dec. 1937. DMPR 534.

118 Hawkes to Britten, 17 Dec. 1937. BPL, Boosey & Hawkes Correspondence, 1937.

119 Hawkes to Britten, 30 May 1939. BPL, Boosey & Hawkes Correspondence, 1939.

120 Hawkes to Britten, 17 Jan. 1941. BPL, Boosey & Hawkes Correspondence, 1941. Hawkes suggested a work with narrator—such as *The Young Person's Guide to the Orchestra* used four years later—and scoring that 'should be thought out in such a way that it can be adapted for a simple orchestra'—which was the principle behind the much later *Noye's Fludde*.

121 Britten to Hawkes, 29 Dec. 1938. DMPR 598.

122 Hawkes to Britten, 21 Apr. 1938. BPL, Boosey & Hawkes Correspondence, 1938.

and for performances elsewhere it would doubtless be most useful. On the other hand, perhaps an Overture might suit you better and I must leave this to you. I certainly do not favor [*sic*] a Symphony.[123]

The result—the *Sinfonia da Requiem*—was part symphony, part symphonic poem. The keyword in this communication is 'useful', suggesting the development of an overall marketing strategy for Britten's music. Moreover, by the time of this commission, Hawkes had seen some returns on his strategy from music dressed in more conventional clothing. The Piano Concerto, in 1939, was a child of the BBC. It was premiered at the Proms in a live transmission (the sound transmitted on both radio and experimental television), and given a repeat broadcast in December that year. Nearly forty piano scores were sold in 1939 (Table 1.2), a modest figure, perhaps, but likely to have been far greater in 1938, when publicity and initial performances would have generated much interest in the new work from serious musicians, some of whom were no doubt performers willing and able to take on the virtuosic piano writing.[124]

The complete vindication of Hawkes's structured policy for Britten and his music was, of course, *Peter Grimes*. In 1946 over seven hundred vocal scores of the opera were sold in Britain (an extra 1,400 scores had been printed since the the first run). More telling, perhaps, were the sales of *The Rape of Lucretia*: 671 vocal scores between the 12 July premiere and the end of 1946. These figures represent a great increase in the initial sales of a Britten work—only *Rejoice in the Lamb* and *A Ceremony of Carols* obtained higher sales in their first year: 1,166 and 1,514 copies respectively in 1943, a reflection of the size of the voracious English church-music market.[125] Britten had proved himself a serious composer, able to tackle all the forms and genres of contemporary art music. With Hawkes's support and encouragement he was then free to subject these same forms to experiment—as he did from the late 1940s onwards.

Most significant about the period 1934–9 is how quickly things changed. Perceptions, expectations, and technology all moved on apace once the funeral orations for Elgar, Holst, and Delius had been quietly filed away. Arthur Bliss's cheerless words in the epigraph deserve reconsideration here: 'There is no sign as yet of the one man who is both of sufficient character and sufficient inventive genius to alter the stream of music today definitely and conclusively.' Perhaps Bliss's score for Korda's 1935 film *Things to Come* was one prophecy too many, for the one man with the character and talent to alter the stream of British music was already shaking its foundations.

123 Hawkes to Britten, 23 Sept. 1939. BPL, Boosey & Hawkes Correspondence, 1939.

124 In most instances, as Table 1.2 shows, sales of a new work fell off dramatically in its second year on the market.

125 Royalty and Copyright statements, various dates. BPL, Boosey & Hawkes Correspondence, 1942–54.

Chapter 2

Britten and the BBC

> Your tweeny maid or cook-general may be addressing a meeting at the Albert Hall on 'How I would Govern Asia.' . . . You are enjoying, after long inductional training, an organ sonata by Sorabji. You cannot play it very well, as it is a trifle tricky, but you are revelling in a broadcast version from an organ with saxophones as pipes, and a jacquard-loom mechanism as interpretative artist. Your maid comes back tired, in spite of the ovation she has received, and says: 'Ere, I carn't abide that stuff; carn't yer switch over to Leipsic and get "Wink yer eye, Molly" which is real good music?' According to the democratic . . . idea, she is just as good a judge as you are, and there is no such thing as an educated musician, or a musician at all.[1]

> As broadcasting goes on, the technique of special composition for wireless will be explored more fully; but however thoroughly this art—in some aspects an entirely new one—is developed, the same root principles will always lie at the bottom of the best broadcast music: strong melody and simple texture.[2]

When Swinburne presented his socialist reverie to the Musical Association in December 1926, the British Broadcasting Company had only twenty-four days to live. The Crawford Committee, established in 1925 to evaluate the first few years of Britain's broadcasting monopoly, recommended in March 1926 that the Company become a Corporation, and that it be granted a ten-year charter. Evidence presented to the Crawford Committee by interested parties listed the many objections to broadcasting: fewer people attended fewer concerts; popular songs endured less than six months where once they had lasted twelve; orchestras in hotels were being replaced by wireless sets; and performers were fast becoming consumers—content to sit and listen to the radio rather than practise their art.[3]

[1] J. Swinburne, discussion following Percy Scholes, 'Broadcasting and the Future of Music', *PMA*, 53rd session (1926–7).

[2] 'Composing for Wireless', *B.B.C. Handbook 1929*, 167.

[3] Asa Briggs, *The History of Broadcasting in the United Kingdom* (1961), i. 344.

Outside the formal atmosphere of the inquiry, prediction and assessment of broadcasting was equally impassioned, if a little more imaginative, and lasted well into the 1930s. Swinburne saw the real value of broadcasting in giving news of football, racing, actresses' divorces and telling the time; 'Music is a mere by-product.'[4] The anonymous author of *Radio and the Composer* recalled with melancholy interest that the first piece of copyright music to be broadcast by the British Broadcasting Company in 1922 was 'Drake goes West!', taking composers' profits and incomes with him.[5] And in the language of prohibition, bootleg booze, and jazz, Thomas Beecham prophesied that in 'twenty years' time there will not be a single musical institution left in this country, except possibly organisations providing music inside a cellar in London. You will depend for every kind of music on the radio and musical reproduction by mechanical devices.'[6]

By 1930 Wellsian imagery was more or less ingrained in British middle-class consciousness, thus Beecham's and Swinburne's predictions of machine-dominated music-making should not be viewed solely as a product of the BBC (although the jacquard-operated saxophone pipes are more Waugh than Wells). To genteel sensibilities, technology was tolerated as long as it was servant rather than master. Yet for every criticism of broadcasting and its effect on British music, a well-constructed defence existed—usually supplemented by *gravitas*-inducing statistics. Far from ruining the livelihood of composers, the BBC supplied the Performing Right Society with 39 per cent of its total annual revenue in 1935, increasing this to 54 per cent over the next five years.[7] Neighbourliness in villages intensified as the radio became the altar at which tea was drunk and wrongs righted.[8] Education in schools and of adults was greatly enhanced by broadcasting. Instrumental playing was inspired rather than discouraged by radio: 'Do you know that since I have had this wireless, I have taken up my violin again?' one ex-soldier confessed, adding the modest disclaimer 'I know I shall never play as well as Kreisler . . .'.[9] And, neatly foreshadowing 1990s Blackpool Conference speeches by dewy-eyed Conservative MPs, broadcasting promoted a positive, family-based moral code: 'goodness knows the age needed something which would bring back the young people to their homes.'[10] In spite of the rhetoric, a serious message emerged: in less than ten years, broadcasting had markedly altered dissemination and reception of both popular and serious music. Although 'Wink yer eye, Molly' vied with Sorabji for wider attention, both

[4] Scholes, 'Broadcasting and the Future of Music', 24.

[5] *Radio and the Composer* (1935), 17.

[6] W. R. Anderson, 'Wireless Notes', *Musical Times* (Nov. 1934), 991.

[7] Paddy Scannell and David Cardiff, *A Social History of British Broadcasting* (1991), i. 181.

[8] Briggs, *History of Broadcasting*, i. 346.

[9] Scholes, 'Broadcasting and the Future of Music', 32.

[10] Ibid. 18.

were available to all who chose to listen.[11] The democratization of serious music—an art-form which had previously been the property of an educated elite—clearly was to affect young composers.

Percy Scholes predicted that broadcasting's influence would not be confined to the dissemination and reception of music. 'The introduction of new harmonies, new forms, new types of orchestration, is all dependent upon the receptivity of the mind of the audience, and with so much music going on, will development be very much speeded up . . . ?'[12] It was a significant point, although Scholes was blind to the immediate effects of broadcasting: the nature and limitations of radio technology were already encouraging experiments in form and orchestration. The BBC was to offer composers even greater opportunities in the 1930s—a professional orchestra, elevation in the status of incidental music, commitment to contemporary music—all of which would influence the composers working for the Corporation.

Britten was 8 years old when the British Broadcasting Company was formed.[13] The profound effect of radio on the composer's musical education is evident from the numerous and often enthusiastic references in his diary to broadcasts. Unlike older composers, Britten was aware of the power of radio for almost all his composing life, and for him efforts to exploit it came much earlier and more naturally than for many of his older colleagues. His negotiations with the BBC in the early 1930s led to involvement in radio drama, frequent appearances as performer or conductor, broadcasts of large-scale performances, live opera transmissions, and a number of commissions (and many more attempted ones). Although this delicate—never formulaic—relationship between broadcaster, composer, and popular reputation makes analysis difficult, it is nevertheless certain that, from its early role in educating the young Britten in the latest and the greatest music to its commissioning of the television opera *Owen Wingrave* in the late 1960s, the BBC exerted a strong influence on the composer and his music. The impact of broadcasting on the marketing of Britten's music is still significant today.

Policy, Genre, and Broadcasting in the 1930s

Britten's negotiations with the BBC over the first broadcast of *A Boy was Born* in February 1934 highlighted the cultural ascendancy of the new broadcasting medium.[14] The negotiations also illustrated a number of the Corporation's

[11] Although this particular battle did not last: in 1940 Sorabji forbade public performance of his music.

[12] Scholes, 'Broadcasting and the Future of Music', 23.

[13] The Company was founded in October and began transmitting on 14 Nov. 1922.

[14] See Ch. 1.

distinguishing features. The BBC's chorus and orchestral players were of a sufficient standard to perform difficult contemporary music; rehearsal time was *usually* adequate because of their full-time contracts—a situation almost unique in Britain. The *Radio Times* and *The Listener* allowed extensive proselytizing, although the vested interest of both publications in the BBC's success did result in frequent appearances of new wine in old skins. Contemporary music appealed to the music department's planners and conductors, and composers could submit scores for approval and performance; although this system, by its very nature, favoured some composers and styles at the expense of others (the decision-making body representing a fairly conservative line of thought), successful applicants often benefited from continuing patronage, although new works still had to be submitted and assessed according to ever-changing selection criteria, a source of considerable frustration for composers at the time. And the potential audiences for art music broadcasts, in the days when there were only a few radio channels, far outstripped that of any London season.

The negotiations over *A Boy was Born* also illustrated specific aspects of BBC music policy. Since the BBC's formation, criticism of its music policy had steadily increased (especially of the Corporation's approach to contemporary British music). This criticism was fuelled by the fact that the Corporation was funded principally by the licence fees paid by radio owners who demanded a say in their investment. Criticism was therefore heated, even surreal: 'Neither Reith nor Boult would deliberately push us into a cesspool or a madhouse; but they have no hesitation in muddying us up with the most rubbishy kinds of dance music, and putting our brains in the cages of a sort of riddle music which has no answer except a lemon.'[15] Yet criticism came from all sides: too little dance music, too many popular works, too many obscure works; most importantly, comment emerged from the general public and from within the BBC itself. These two very broad groups, with often differing perspectives, frequently attacked the BBC's promotion of British music. When in September 1934 the radio critic W. R. Anderson asked what was to be done with the 'unwieldy, unanswerable BBC', he outlined a very real concern at the time: who exactly was responsible for the music the BBC chose to broadcast?[16]

The development of the many BBC policies was by no means a simple process, complicated as it was by early and pressing concern about the role or function of broadcasting in Britain. John Reith, General Manager of the British Broadcasting Company from its formation in 1922 and then Director-General of the British Broadcasting Corporation from 1927, saw this function in terms of education rather than pure entertainment; according to Reith, to use 'so great a scientific invention for the purpose of "entertainment" alone' would be 'a prostitution of its

[15] 'Notes and News', *Musical Times*, 75 (1934), 446.

[16] Anderson, 'Wireless Notes', 811.

powers and an insult to the character and intelligence of the people'.[17] Despite its educationist pedigree, the BBC's role in contemporary music was criticized by the maverick British composer Rutland Boughton, who detected a continental bias that prevented the appropriate representation of British music, namely his own. Writing to programme builder Edward Clark in June 1934, Boughton stated:

> If you will refer to my previous letter you will see that you were invited to the recital (of my new opera) given yesterday, Friday. Of course, I am not surprised that you didn't come. The unfair treatment of my work by the BBC is apparently becoming obvious to the general musical public. As you have long been in a position where you could have corrected that treatment, I should prefer you no longer to make private & personal professions of interest in my work. It will survive the rubbish you chiefly have been instrumental in foisting on the London and wireless public.
>
> And now a good bye to you. I can't waste my time with a grievance because you are incapable of knowing music from muddle and muck.[18]

Even if Boughton's frequent outbursts were justified (and much of Clark's activity did centre around non-British music, in particular that of the Second Viennese School), Clark could certainly have disputed that Boughton was representative of contemporary British music. But a memo concerning music policy at the BBC in 1931–2 reinforces Boughton's complaint: '. . . obviously we shall want to do whatever important new English works are ready for next season . . . and of course any new work by Vaughan Williams would be included at the earliest date.'[19] Selecting 'important new English works' remained a contentious process: at best, the performance or broadcast of a new piece rested on the advocacy of BBC personnel and outside 'experts'; at worst, it depended on the taste of one person.

By the mid-1930s the music department used two panels to advise on music policy and to deliver recommendations on contemporary music submitted for performance and broadcast by the BBC. These were the Music Advisory Committee and the smaller, younger Music Programme Advisory Panel. The relationship between committee, panel, and music department was complicated; the panel was formed in April 1934 as a BBC response to the committee whose members, 'leading representatives of the British musical profession', spent most of their time attacking both policies and personnel of the department.[20] Boult had long recognized the limitations of the Music Advisory Committee, writing in 1933 that he enjoyed the meetings because he considered its members 'representative of the average or perhaps of the rather more stupid type of

[17] J. C. W. Reith, *Broadcast Over Britain*, 17, quoted in Briggs, *History of Broadcasting*, i. 250.
[18] BL, Add. MS 52256.
[19] BBC memo, BBCWAC, Music Policy, file 1a, 1930–43, R27/241/1.
[20] Scannell and Cardiff, *Social History*, 201.

professional'.[21] Since 1930 the eight-man committee had been complaining about the BBC's neglect of British music, in particular the established British music that this advisory committee represented.[22] The BBC's formation of the three-man panel, whose members were Arthur Bliss, Benjamin Dale, and Sidney Waddington, was an attempt to provide an alternative to the constant criticism presented by the larger committee by creating a more effective channel for the views of professional musicians on music programming decisions.[23] The music department quickly established a good working relationship with the Panel, although the self-advocacy displayed by committee members was not entirely eradicated. At a panel meeting in early November 1934, those present recognized that 'Many [new] works are unfortunately just too good to be rejected, yet not sufficiently so to have hope of success. Really good works could always be used, but their number was so very limited';[24] yet at the next meeting the panel approved *any* work by Bliss for performance in a contemporary music concert in January 1935; and on 5 February 1935 a sextet by Clarence Raybould, another member of the BBC music staff, was recommended for performance despite the panel's scarcely enthusiastic conclusion that 'the work, without having any particular musical pretensions, was not entirely unworthy'.[25]

A Boy was Born also illustrated one less obvious but fundamentally important feature of the BBC's programming: composers either had to produce scores and parts themselves, or pay for their production by professional copyists. Either expense or timescale, therefore, could militate against the performance of new large-scale work. And it is clear that Britten came to see this in the 1930s as a vital point. Later, in 1940, when he had been in America only a short time, he wrote of the endorsement and practical benefits of a printed score:

In America perhaps the printing of modern music has lagged behind performances, and in this respect the publisher seems scarcely to have realized that a printed work stands a much better chance of establishing itself in the regular repertory than a sometimes

[21] Memo from Boult, 12 May 1933. BBCWAC, Public Concert Policy, R27/432.

[22] Committee members at this time were Sir Hugh Allen (Chair), Dr E. C. Bairstow, Sir Walford Davies, Sir J. B. McEwen, Sir Landon Ronald, Colonel J. C. Somerville, Dr W. G. Whittaker, and the President of the Incorporated Society of Musicians.

[23] As Jennifer Doctor establishes, BBC motivation for forming this panel was also that Arthur Bliss had been offered and had declined the position of Assistant Music Director of the Corporation. A panel of programming advisers was thus deemed necessary. See Doctor, *The BBC and Ultra-Modern Music, 1922–1936*, 232–40.

[24] BBCWAC, Music Programme Advisory Panel Minutes, file 1a, 1934–6, R27/250/1, 10 Nov. 1934.

[25] BBCWAC, Music Programme Advisory Panel Minutes, file 1a, 1934–6, R27/250/1, 5 Feb. 1935. Raybould's Sextet in E flat was recommended for performance in a meeting on 4 Apr. 1939. BBCWAC, Music Programme Advisory Panel Minutes, file 2, 1938–9, R27/250/3.

illegible score, and parts that may not have been too well copied and have been thumbed and blue-penciled [*sic*] from Boston to Los Angeles.[26]

In the late 1920s the BBC made much of its commitment to young composers on this very issue:

As an example of the encouragement by the B.B.C. of young composers, one may quote the fact that it frequently pays for the cost of copying orchestral parts from the score of a new work—composers know how difficult it is to obtain performances without providing, at considerable expense, these parts—in order to perform it.[27]

By the early 1930s, though, any such commitment from the BBC had fallen away, and composers without a publisher were left susceptible to the high cost of producing performance material. Quite apart from the practical consideration of producing parts, the imprimatur of a reputable publishing house tended to align a work more closely to the music department's delicate selection criteria. This was a reciprocal matter: as Britten discovered with *A Boy was Born*, the BBC's own 'imprimatur' could greatly raise chances of the work's publication.

The blurred distinction between 'serious' music and 'incidental' music (the elevation of the genre) was a feature of Britten's output in the 1930s. Britten's limited composition time in the years after he left the Royal College of Music made such 'blurring' a necessity, yet it was the BBC that made a virtue of this necessity. As early as October 1935, the Corporation's Music Programme Advisory Panel suggested that a work based on Britten's music for the GPO film *The King's Stamp* be included in a contemporary music broadcast.[28] And in 1937 the same panel approved a proposed series of five programmes featuring music specially written for films by composers such as Britten, Benjamin, and Bliss (the 'doyen of British film composers', who unfortunately missed both the meeting and his colleague's laudatory display).[29] In order to put into context Britten's meteoric rise through the ranks of the BBC in the late 1930s, it is important to note that in 1936 Britten was not held in high esteem by all the Corporation's departments. Although he was commissioned in 1936 to compose incidental music for a feature based on King Arthur, it was only after at least Bax and Boughton—and probably Herbert Murrill—had turned down the offer.[30] When Hawkes suggested a fee of £100 to cover broadcasting and recording rights throughout the BBC, the Features and Drama Executive responded coolly: 'I agree entirely with Music Ex. when he says that if Rutland Boughton was

[26] Britten, 'An English Composer Sees America', *Tempo* 1/2 (American edn.) (Apr. 1940), 2.

[27] 'Broadcasting and the Composer', *B.B.C. Handbook 1928*, 89.

[28] BBCWAC, Music Programme Advisory Panel Minutes, file 1a, 1934–6, R27/250/1, 1 Oct. 1935. Britten had arranged this suite, at the BBC's suggestion, in July 1935. Britten's diary, 24 July 1935.

[29] BBCWAC, Music Programme Advisory Panel Minutes, 1936–7, R27/250/2, 15 June 1937.

[30] BBCWAC, Music Programme Advisory Panel Minutes, 1936–7, R27/250/2, 1 Sept. 1936.

willing to accept £100, Britten ought to take less. Britten is a very young man, and I cannot believe his name means anything to the public—I am afraid I had never heard of him.'[31]

The King's Stamp was Britten's first incidental score—written for the GPO Film Unit—and had been completed only a few months before it came to the attention of the music panel. Although the BBC's broadcast proposal came to nothing (Britten makes no reference to any such performance in his diary), Britten reused material from this score in other GPO films. Like the Music Programme Advisory Panel, Britten was well aware of the potential spill-over from his incidental music into his serious compositions. His *Soirées musicales* (1936) and *Matinées musicales* (1941) both took music from his score for Lotte Reiniger's silhouette film *The Tocher* (1935), an advertising feature detailing the considerable merits of the Post Office Savings Bank.[32] For the film, Britten composed fourteen small fragments—each eight to twenty seconds long—based on music by Rossini, scoring them for flute, oboe, clarinet, two percussionists, piano, and boys' voices. The later works were larger in scale, but the fragmentary nature and origins of the incidental music directly influenced Britten in his choice of genre for *Soirées* and *Matinées*—namely the suite. Britten had written a number of orchestral and instrumental suites as a boy, but it was not a genre he employed again until his Suite, Op. 6, for violin and piano, written at exactly the same time as the score for *The Tocher*. It is a genre Britten returned to frequently in his art music after the war, and it owed more than a little to his earlier experience in writing incidental music, where short, contrasting movements, often with programmatic or illustrative character, are juxtaposed, with considerable dramatic effect.

Further examples of art music based on incidental scores are easy to identify. 'Funeral Blues', one outstanding piece in Britten's score for Auden's and Isherwood's play *The Ascent of F6* (1937), was soon afterwards rescored for solo voice and piano as one of the *Cabaret Songs*. The other three cabaret songs explore a style that had received little attention within Britten's output of art music, and which must be viewed as a direct consequence of the composer's technique developing through incidental music; the intended audiences of these theatrical endeavours, and their links with popular and European political culture, encouraged Britten in his popular-music excursions. Similarly, material from Britten's music for Priestley's *Johnson over Jordan* (1939) was used in the third variation of his work for piano (left-hand) and orchestra, *Diversions* (1940). In other instances, the material migrating from incidental into art music remained more or less intact. Music from Britten's score for the radio feature *King Arthur*

[31] Memo from R. Burns, 13 Apr. 1937. BBCWAC, Contributors File, Copyright, Benjamin Britten, 1937–62.

[32] The concept and institutions of savings had been severely undermined by the Depression, which gave rise to a number of films on this very theme in the 1930s.

appeared in two of his later works. An orchestral scherzo became the 'Dance of Death' in *Ballad of Heroes* (1939), and other material supplied the theme of the revised Impromptu of the Piano Concerto (1945).[33] The transition from *King Arthur* to *Ballad of Heroes* was relatively simple because of the former's scale: double winds, four horns, three trumpets, three trombones, tuba, timpani, two percussion players, harp, strings, and chorus. More significantly, the borrowing suggests that music for medieval pageantry was not at all incompatible with contemporary political events in Europe (one narrative aspect of *Ballad of Heroes*), showing Britten's programmatic intent as splendidly adaptable.

Other plunderings were more shameless and, significantly, often premeditated. Britten viewed such borrowing as simple redistribution of material, giving long-term potential to music which would otherwise survive only the length of a play's season, a film's vogue, or the brief life of a radio broadcast. It was an indication of Britten's commercial acumen as much as a solution to the plight of an over-busy composer. Ralph Hawkes encouraged such activity, often requesting that Britten send in his incidental scores so that their suitability for adaptation and publication could be ascertained.[34] But the shift from this approach to the composition of an incidental work with the expectation of life beyond the circumstances of its commissioning required two things: the luxury of a relatively long period of composition, and an experimental approach to traditional genres (the fragmentary nature of much incidental music limited its potential as serious music), which was only really possible within the BBC. Britten conceived *The Company of Heaven*, a 1937 BBC radio drama, as a serious, publishable work from its inception. He informed Hawkes immediately after commencing work on it that he was unwilling to sign away any publishing rights for it because he felt that 'a short choral work could easily & quite profitably be made out of it for you. When it's done I'll show you & see what you think.'[35] Certainly the generous orchestral forces permitted in BBC commissions encouraged such effortless interchange (*The Company of Heaven* is scored for soprano and tenor soloists, SATB choir, timpani, organ, and strings), and Britten was well aware of the publishing and marketing potential of a 'short choral work' in pre-war England. But the constrictions of a BBC programme—no matter how experimental its approach to any genre—were to influence greatly the form of Britten's final product. With poems liberally interpolated, Britten's music was compartmentalized, and so required a sense of overall unity.

[33] The BBC had also investigated the possibility of a suite based on Britten's music for *King Arthur*. Raybould quashed the suggestion: 'It is not at all probable, in its present state.' Memo, 14 May 1937. BBCWAC, Composer file, Benjamin Britten, file 1a, 1933–44.

[34] For example, see Britten's letter to Hawkes, 28 July 1937, which discusses the possibility of publishing material from *The Ascent of F6*. DMPR 497–8.

[35] Britten to Hawkes, 6 Aug. 1937. DMPR 499. *The Company of Heaven* was eventually published in 1990.

Britten's solution to this problem may have been at the expense of the actual programme. Its producer, Robin Whitworth, thought the completed music erred too much on the side of the 'absolute' and relegated the prose and verse to a position of secondary importance.

It was intended to be a Feature programme conveying a coherent and continuously developing line of thought, conveyed primarily by words but with music sometimes emphasizing the thought and sometimes playing a main part in its conveyance. The orchestra seems to have appreciated this better than Britten, who, . . . instead of troubling to understand the programme . . . ploughed his own furrow, and provided . . . a straight-forward musical entity.[36]

The piece can in no way be considered a 'straight-forward musical entity', although Whitworth's point that the music came out of it all better than the words certainly has validity. The work's posthumous publication suggests that Hawkes, too, found it unsuitable. Like *The Heart of the Matter*, a sequence of Sitwell's poems and Britten's music which the composer devised for the 1956 Aldeburgh Festival, *The Company of Heaven* was an unholy marriage of words and music, and clumsy progeny resulted. Britten confessed in his diary that he didn't really understand the programme: 'What interests me is that I have nice words to set.'[37] From a musical point of view, he was undoubtedly successful: according to Britten, the orchestral players considered it the best incidental music they had ever performed.[38] Indeed the motivic interaction between movements, the cyclic conception of the work, and the incorporation of hymn tunes into the orchestral texture were techniques that Britten turned to again and again throughout his career.

The problems encountered in *The Company of Heaven* were not enough to deter either producer or composer. After a six-month break, Britten began work in 1938 on *The World of the Spirit*, a Whitsun programme of words and music. The scale of Britten's score was much more ambitious than that of its predecessor: double winds, four horns, two trumpets, three trombones, tuba, timpani, percussion, harp, organ, strings, and chorus. Although it was composed in less than two months, it is again probable that Britten intended the work to have life beyond the BBC. Britten told Hawkes in early May 1938 that he had nearly finished the 'big B.B.C. Holy show' and that it might be of some use to him.[39] He also gave the work a specific genre title—an oratorio, and one in the 'grand style', he proudly informed Kenneth Wright, a central figure in the BBC's music department, in late May.[40] The religious nature of the programme was underlined through Britten's use of the plainsong 'Veni creator spiritus'

[36] DMPR 499. [37] Britten's diary, 29 Sept. 1937. [38] Ibid.

[39] Britten to Hawkes, 5 May 1938. DMPR 556.

[40] Britten to Wright, [postmarked 28 May 1938]. DMPR 558.

(another technique to which Britten returned) and the broadcast was considered successful enough for it to be repeated the following year. But problems of cohesion still existed, and the hybrid nature of the work made it unsuitable for publishing in its current form.[41] When Britten next returned to the idea of a religio-dramatic narrative, his solution was to avoid spoken text and to link sections with quasi-recitative. The dramatic unity and success of the result—*Saint Nicolas* (1948)—is without doubt. Although the works commissioned by the BBC were not published during Britten's lifetime, they represent an important stage in his development as a composer. The scores contained experiments in musical and dramatic ideas, the effects of which reappear consistently in later concert and stage works. Most importantly, by eroding the distinction between functional and autonomous music, Britten was evolving a new style of 'incidental expression'—an elevation of the genre. This crossover—combining the features of apparently incompatible genres—is also an important feature of Britten's later works.

The second characteristic of much of Britten's serious music in the 1930s—its chamber quality—similarly owes much to the composer's incidental scores, the music he heard broadcast in the 1920s as he developed his own musical vocabulary, and his growing relationship with the BBC as a composer in his own right. In the late 1920s and early 1930s in Britain chamber music was not a particularly popular genre, regarded by many as elitist, austere, and exclusive to the cognoscenti. With more than a hint of red rags and bulls, the BBC set out to develop, almost invent, public taste for classical, British, and contemporary chamber music. This last category was, perhaps, the most contentious and misunderstood, partly because the BBC often used the term 'chamber music' interchangeably with 'contemporary music', thereby fuelling public antipathy towards the genre, or at least what audiences understood to be the genre. As ever, the *Radio Times* was a forum for the various arguments:

> It has been in my mind for some time past to write to you on the subject of the almost universal condemnation of Chamber Music, which puzzles musicians and bewilders your musical director. From time to time I have arguments about it with people who took no interest in music and knew nothing about it until they obtained wireless sets, and I ask them whether they like *Andante Cantabile* by Tchaikovsky, the Beethoven setting of *The Lost Chord*, and one or two other well-known things, and always receive a surprised answer in the affirmative. When I tell them that these are examples of Chamber Music I am scorned, and informed that Chamber Music is that awful noise like cats squealing that they hear on the wireless, labelled 'Chamber Music' in the programme. Now the fact is that the programme compilers are to blame for this; they reserve the description 'Chamber Music' for the music of modern 'advanced' composers and very rarely apply it to the Chamber Music of the classical or more orthodox

[41] It was eventually published in 2001.

composers whose compositions are almost always described simply as trios, quartets, or quintets.[42]

Early series of BBC contemporary chamber-music concerts did reinforce this unfortunate public misassociation of terms. Music by Bartók (then demonized in Britain), Berg, Hindemith, Schoenberg, Stravinsky, and a few contemporary British composers was performed. Scholes later recalled that in one such series of contemporary music concerts, broadcast live from a public concert hall in London, his presence often accounted for a quarter or a fifth of the whole audience and never less than a thirtieth.[43]

Yet despite public antipathy, the BBC considered the rationale for its chamber-music crusade in the 1920s to be sound, and, as the above letter to the *Radio Times* suggests, remnants of this outlook survived into the 1930s—notwithstanding the incredible changes to policy and programming within the BBC following the 1930 formation of the BBC Symphony Orchestra.[44] Moreover, the Corporation considered that there were technical and philosophical arguments that supported its stance on chamber music, even above the musical arguments in its favour:

> When Broadcasting was invented it was realised by the programme builders that here was its most potent ally, for Broadcasting . . . is essentially an intimate thing, as is Chamber Music, and that there could be no more enjoyable way of listening to it than by overhearing it, as it were, relayed by a microphone from its performance inside the four walls of a studio.
>
> Broadcasting favours Chamber Music in still another way. By its nature it is essentially the most simple in texture of all concerted music, and there is probably nothing more perfect in wireless musical transmission than the sound of a well-balanced String Quartet or Trio. Additional instruments such as a Clarinet or a Flute or a Piano well played and blended do not add in complexity so much as to greatly affect this unique efficiency in reproduction.[45]

The public remained unswayed by such arguments, bemoaning the educationist approach of the young Corporation. Moreover, where were the well-balanced

[42] F. J. Hargreaves, 'Listeners' Letters: Chamber Music', *Radio Times*, 34 (4 Mar. 1932), 578, repr. in Doctor, *The BBC and Ultra-Modern Music*, 120. The prejudice remained for many years. R. J. E. Silvey, head of the BBC's Listener Research Unit, much later noted that no chamber music series ever attracted a large audience—until the 'fatal words' were left out of the billing, and the series was titled 'Music in Miniature'. R. J. E. Silvey, *Who's Listening?* (1974), 113.

[43] Percy Scholes, *The Mirror of Music*, vol. ii (1947), 797n.

[44] See Doctor, *The BBC and Ultra-Modern Music*, 199ff. and 378–89. One aspect of Doctor's argument is that, since orchestra members were salaried within the BBC, it was cheaper to programme orchestral concerts than chamber concerts with outside musicians. This financial and artistic freedom did considerably alter the balance of orchestral music and chamber music in the BBC's output, but it would be wrong to suggest that the 1920s drive on behalf of the latter was simply financially motivated.

[45] 'Chamber Music in Broadcasting', *B.B.C. Handbook 1928*, 97.

string quartets of Haydn, Mozart, or (young) Beethoven, to counter any suggestion that chamber concerts were a purely modern phenomenon? A survey of over one million *Daily Mail* readers in February 1927, in a period before alternative programmes on different radio signals were available, indicated that nearly 20 per cent preferred 'variety and concert parties' to any other type of programme. Other listeners hinted at international conspiracies: 'Because we won't swallow whatever the Extremist [Music] Department of the BBC chooses to perform (or to let its foreign friends try on us, as on the dog) we are treated as naughty children.'[46]

Britten cultivated his own mission for chamber music in the 1930s, buoyed by the contemporary European sounds and sonorities he was then hearing and had heard broadcast in the previous decade, and most probably aware of the public arguments for and against it that simmered away, now and then finding expression in daily newspapers and weekly magazines. There are again two strands of his output to consider—his incidental scores and his art music; again, the distinction is not always clear. Although his first nineteen opus numbers (1932–9) include a piano concerto, the vocal and orchestral *Our Hunting Fathers* and *Ballad of Heroes*, and the *Variations on a Theme of Frank Bridge*, much of Britten's work in this decade was of chamber proportions or was heavily indebted to the textures and sonorities of chamber music.[47] Limited economic means naturally restricted the scope of much of the incidental theatre and film music—apart from one or two big film companies, the BBC alone could commission larger scores—but chamber works and song also preponderated in Britten's art music, and the relationship between this and his incidental scores makes an interesting study in the composer's development.

There were two features of Britten's life in the 1930s that particularly influenced his 'serious' composition: he was extremely busy earning a living as a composer of incidental music, which restricted the scope of undertakings outside his regular employment; and he came into contact with a number of talented performers and writers, which resulted in fruitful collaborations—very much a feature of Britten's post-war life. Even more importantly, Britten's incidental music represented a refinement of his programmatic music skills. This, combined with the composer's developing political sensibilities (which found expression in a proliferation of vocal works), marked the 1930s as a period of real transition for Britten—from a composer of absolute music to one who wrote complex programmatic scores. The vast majority of his juvenilia (up to his

[46] 'Letter to the Editor', *Musical Times* (May 1931), 444–5. The Corporation's evangelism on this issue in the late 1920s can be discerned by examining the breakdown of programming in 'typical' weeks in October 1927, 1928, and 1929: the percentage of broadcast time allocated to chamber music grew from 0.6 to 3.1 and then again to 3.3 (see Briggs, *History of Broadcasting*, ii. 35). In these same weeks, orchestral music occupied 10.1 per cent, 5.6 per cent, and 7.4 per cent of total programme time.

[47] The *Sinfonietta*, although large-scale in conception, is undoubtedly a chamber work.

Sinfonietta, Op. 1, of 1932) are without programmatic content, and in this he was partly influenced by the current European vogue, accessed primarily though radio broadcasts and his fast-growing collection of miniature scores. Many are also large in (intended) scale—a concerto for violin and viola, ballet scores, songs with orchestra, symphonic poems, a symphony. There were other important influences on the composer between 1933 and 1938—his publishers and his teachers all had specific ideas on the sort of music Britten should be composing—but this change from 'absolute' to programmatic, and from large- to small-scale, owed much to Britten's work with the BBC, the GPO Film Unit, and various theatre companies.[48]

Britten's diary in this period details his blossoming relationship with the BBC, one in which chamber and programme music played a huge role. Leslie Woodgate was keen to perform any choral work by Britten following the success of *A Boy was Born*, which he had conducted, thereby demonstrating how vital it was for a young composer to receive the support of a 'BBC conductor'. The *Sinfonietta* was scheduled on 29 June 1934 in the second contemporary concert in one season to feature his work—an almost unheard of phenomenon for a British composer—as a result of similar enthusiasm for the composer by other members of the music department (in this instance Edward Clark). A full-time job in the Corporation was discussed in early 1935 during several meetings involving Britten, Boult, and Woodgate.[49] Clark put forward Britten's name to Cavalcanti in April 1935, which resulted in Britten's full-time employment with the GPO Film Unit.[50] Britten's *Phantasy* and *Simple Symphony* were both broadcast in mid-1935, and his *A Hymn to the Virgin* was performed under Woodgate's direction in October. In December Britten discussed his future compositions with Wright and Clark,[51] heard another broadcast of *A Boy was Born*, and came to realize that performances of his music, outside the BBC, were thin on the ground.[52] This of course intensified Britten's relationship with the Corporation.

All of Britten's works broadcast by the BBC in this period, however, were old—composed before the first performance of *A Boy was Born*. As with Tavener or Górecki in the early 1990s, the success of one composition led to demand for other works—perhaps of less merit. Britten's Suite, Op. 6, for violin and piano, however, was written after the broadcast of *A Boy was Born* and was the first in a succession of small-scale works produced during the following three years—works which were quick to write and cheap to rehearse and perform. Begun in

[48] Although the music written for the BBC represents the pinnacle of Britten's incidental scores, it was a logical development of the techniques assimilated in writing music for film and stage, and the three are equally important—indeed, difficult to separate—in any examination of Britten's art music.

[49] Britten's diary, 8 Feb. 1935.

[50] Britten's diary, 27 Apr. 1935.

[51] Britten's diary, 2 Dec. 1935.

[52] Britten's diary, 1 Jan. 1936.

November 1934, the Suite was ready in its original three-movement form by 17 December, when it was performed by Henri Temianka and Betty Humby at the Wigmore Hall. Britten met Clark on the day of the performance, and it is unlikely that the work was not discussed.[53] Britten added two movements over the next few months—a period of regular meetings between the composer and BBC personnel—and the complete work was performed by Britten and Antonio Brosa (alongside Beethoven's Violin Sonata, Op. 30 No. 3, and various songs with the soprano Sophie Wyss, indicative, perhaps, of a move away from the 1920s typical and demonized chamber-concert menu) in a BBC broadcast on 13 March 1936.[54] Britten's fee for the performance was 10 guineas.[55] A few days before this broadcast, the first performance of Britten's *Russian Funeral* had taken place. This march for brass and percussion, composed in a matter of days, was included in a concert presented by the London Labour Choral Union. Its life beyond this performance was determined by the brass band experts at Boosey & Hawkes. Submitted soon after its premiere, the score was 'carefully considered', before being rejected as insufficiently 'melodious to appeal to the bulk of such bands'—its political feathers left unruffled, even unnoticed. Furthermore, the experts thought that 'the whole style of the composition is unsuitable as a Brass Band piece generally'.[56] It was published after the composer's death.

Two Insect Pieces (for oboe and piano), *Lullaby for a Retired Colonel* (for two pianos and very much made to order), *Temporal Variations* (oboe and piano), and *Reveille* (violin and piano) belong to the same period. Like *Russian Funeral*, these works share a number of characteristics: they were composed relatively quickly; they coincided with Britten's steadily intensifying relationship with the BBC's music department; they were usually broadcast by the BBC soon after completion; and none received an opus number from the composer or was published until after his death. This last point suggests that, with limited time and with pressures from the GPO, Britten was content to cultivate a performing profile within the BBC by providing a steady trickle of smaller, even minor, pieces, at the expense of composing music of lasting significance. The BBC was not the only party scurrying for other works.[57]

From 1936, however, Britten became more concerned with the creation of large-scale works of lasting significance. He was still extremely busy as a jobbing

[53] Britten's diary, 17 Dec. 1934.

[54] The work was performed by Frederick Grinke and Britten in the 1938 ISCM Festival in London, where it caught Bliss's ear and was subsequently recommended for a further broadcast.

[55] BBC Contract, 17 Jan. 1936. BBCWAC, Artists File, Benjamin Britten, file 1a, 1933–44.

[56] Ruch to Britten, 12 May 1936. BPL, Boosey & Hawkes Correspondence, 1936.

[57] Hawkes requested a copy of *Temporal Variations* after it received a positive review in the *Daily Telegraph* following its Wigmore Hall premiere. He did not, however, proceed with publication. It was not published until 1980. Hawkes to Britten, 16 Dec. 1936. BPL, Boosey & Hawkes Correspondence, 1936.

composer, yet with a reputation in this area secured, he became more selfish about his own art music. The first hint of this was in mid-1936 when Britten completed his opuses 8 and 9. The former—*Our Hunting Fathers*—was independent of the BBC, having been commissioned by the Norfolk and Norwich Triennial Festival (the work was broadcast in April 1937, seven months after its premiere at Norwich). Frank Bridge's relationship with the Festival helped secure the commission for the young composer, and the involvement of the London Philharmonic Orchestra allowed Britten the full and highly professional orchestral forces previously denied him through circumstance.

Britten's Op. 9, though, his *Soirées musicales*, owes much to the BBC's performance environment at the time. Its expedient adaptation of an existing collection of pieces, based on music by Rossini and composed for film, is consistent with the composer's and broadcaster's quest for new works, and its moderately large orchestral forces made performance outside the BBC unlikely (Britten hedged his bets by writing an arrangement for small orchestra simultaneously, an indication that he was well aware of the difficulties in obtaining performances of large-scale works). The piece was broadcast two months after completion, repeated four months later, and given a BBC Prom performance on 10 August 1937. According to Britten's diary, this performance was not well received, an extraordinary reaction given the deliberately popular nature of both the piece and the presumed taste of the Prom audience.[58] Yet the work's ultimate success was primarily due to the BBC. Between January 1937 and March 1945, *Soirées musicales* was broadcast around twenty-five times; its closest competitor from Britten's catalogue, the *Simple Symphony*, received only four broadcasts in approximately the same period.[59] Britten spoke of the success of *Soirées* in March 1943, when writing its companion piece, *Matinées musicales*: 'I am afraid it'll never be as popular as Soirées—but it may give that a rest from time to time . . .'.[60]

At the time of the second broadcast of *Soirées musicales*, Britten and Auden began work on a song collection. Although not an orchestral work, the composition and performance of *On This Island* further illustrate the strength of the composer's relationship with the BBC. Sophie Wyss showed Kenneth Wright—then BBC Assistant Director of Music—two of the songs which eventually formed part of the collection, but he considered them too insubstantial to be broadcast on their own:

> They are lovely little songs, but from the point of view of 'Contemporary Concerts' not quite of the style and weight people will expect. I was wondering therefore if you have anything in mind, or could tackle anything in the nature of a big song for Miss Wyss

[58] Britten's diary, 10 Aug. 1937.

[59] BBCBH, Third Programme, Broadcast Record File, Britten. These figures do not distinguish between broadcasts on the Midland, South, or Central services before the war.

[60] Britten to Stein, [postmarked 8 Mar. 1943]. DMPR 1117.

which could be added to these two as an interesting first performance from your pen on that occasion. We should be honoured to include it.[61]

Britten replied on 14 September, agreeing with Wright and informing him of two further songs he planned to add to the set. He concluded the letter casually: 'By the way, I think the publisher wants to print them pretty soon. Do you want first performance reserved for you?'[62] To a certain degree this was skilful bluster on Britten's part, but this style of negotiation with someone of Wright's seniority did represent a considerable shift in only a few years; Britten's contact with the BBC music department occurred at a high level and allowed both composer and Corporation to develop a strategic approach to the exploitation of each other's goods or services. Wright was, indeed, honoured to present the premiere.

It was against this background that Wright planned a major Britten performance—the composer's proposed piano concerto. Next to a symphony, a piano concerto was possibly the most difficult project Britten could have undertaken. Its traditions were generally redolent of old-world Romanticism, associated with the cult of the virtuoso, and towering in the hierarchy of genres attached to established and successful composers; in undertaking one, Britten could expect close public and critical scrutiny of his efforts. Both he and Hawkes felt this strongly: the publisher's 1937 Christmas present to his young charge was a selection of piano concerto scores. Britten appreciated the hint, promising to try to emulate the masterpieces.[63] The BBC's involvement in the concerto antedates the composition; on 14 December Hawkes informed Wright that Britten planned to write a piano concerto, although before this time the work seems to have been discussed only in the most non-committal manner. Wright contacted Britten immediately, requesting the premiere for a Prom concert the following season with the composer as soloist.[64] For a composer whose concert works, according to Boyd Neel, were little known outside the BBC, the engagement was clearly extremely lucrative. But there were mixed blessings: Prom audiences had certain expectations of programmes and performers. Although Henry Wood had always included new works in his programmes—a tradition retained when the BBC took over the administration of and financial responsibility for the Proms in 1927—the series remained essentially 'populist'. Ticket prices were

[61] Wright to Britten, 10 Sept. 1937. BBCWAC, Composer File, Benjamin Britten, file 1a, 1933–44. Britten himself (sardonically) considered the songs 'far too obvious & amenable for contemporary music'. Britten's diary, 19 Nov. 1937.

[62] Britten to Wright, 14 Sept. 1937. BBCWAC, Composer File, Benjamin Britten, file 1a, 1933–44.

[63] Britten to Hawkes, 30 Dec. 1937. DMPR 537.

[64] Wright to Britten, 14 Dec. 1937. BBCWAC, Composer File, Benjamin Britten, file 1a, 1933–44.

kept extremely low, especially in the promenade section of Queen's Hall, and performances of popular war-horses continued a tradition of democratizing high culture. In 1938, the year of Britten's concerto, there were performances of all the Beethoven and Brahms symphonies, two symphonies by Haydn and three by Mozart, three by Sibelius, two each by Schubert, Dvořák, and Tchaikovsky, and one each by Dyson, Franck, Mendelssohn, Moeran, Rachmaninov, and Vaughan Williams. There were twenty-nine concertos for one or more pianos, ten for violin (including the Brahms Double Concerto), and fifty separate orchestral or vocal excerpts from Wagner operas.[65] Outside these genres, less mainstream works were programmed, but this only reinforced the dominance of the piano concerto within the Proms' cultural profile.

Britten was well aware of the Prom audience's expectations of genre. He was also considerably restricted in the time available to work on the piece; serious composition began in February 1938, which left him only six months to complete (and learn) the concerto, as well as compose the ambitious radio incidental score for *The World of the Spirit*. The pressure of time is not insignificant: in his incidental music such pressure often resulted in large-scale borrowing from other scores. In his art music, Britten was more circumspect; but, as noted above, part of his score for *King Arthur* found its way into the revised version of the Piano Concerto, and it is not inconceivable that, because of time limitations, some of the ideas for this 'populist' work may have originated in (or been intended for) one of Britten's many incidental scores.

Britten was 'elated' by the finished concerto.[66] After the first rehearsal he informed Bridge that the work 'certainly sounds "popular" enough', a line taken by Alan Frank in his *Radio Times* preview: 'Britten holds the view . . . that the music should be attractive to listen to: he dislikes this business of dividing music up into light and serious compartments . . . All this is by way of preparing you for my view that this new Piano Concerto . . . derives in spirit from Tchaikovsky and perhaps Liszt.'[67] It was a safe pedigree for a Proms piano concerto (both of Tchaikovsky's concertos and one of Liszt's were programmed in the same season), but likely to antagonize critics who viewed Britten's technique as somewhat facile. Constant Lambert's review of the premiere in *The Listener* was mostly positive, commenting on the rousing reception provoked by both soloist and composition, but worried that Britten was in danger of turning out 'one show piece after another, [and] of being more concerned with texture than with content'.[68] The critic of *The Times* also applauded the concerto's form and texture before questioning its content. But he described the writing for both piano and

[65] David Cox, *The Henry Wood Proms* (1980), 332–9.

[66] Britten to Hawkes, 4 July 1938. DMPR 569.

[67] Alan Frank, 'New Concerto', *Radio Times* (12 Aug. 1938), 16.

[68] Constant Lambert, *The Listener* (25 Aug. 1938), 412. Quoted in DMPR 579.

orchestra as brilliant, and noted popular reaction to the work.[69] William McNaught in the *Musical Times* dismissed the virtuosic piano part as 'rapid splashwork',[70] and, in the terms of a Victorian manual of etiquette, Ferruccio Bonavia in the *Daily Telegraph* admonished Britten for his orchestration: 'It may be fashionable to use and abuse percussion instruments; but the result lacks finesse . . .'.[71] Yet Britten had set out to compose a coruscating showpiece. He had intended a brilliant texture for the traditional form, and 'splashwork' is quite an apt description for the piano writing in the first movement. Lisztian facility is present in the writing, and the concerto is determinedly 'popular'. Britten fulfilled all his intentions—intentions moulded by the circumstances of the work's composition—and was baffled by the critical response: 'I can't see anything problematic about the work. I should have thought that it was the kind of music that either one liked or disliked—it is so simple—& cannot make out why it is that they have to hunt for programmes & "meanings" and all that rot!'[72] He was accurate in his assessment of the work—people did seem either to like it or dislike it. But he did eventually come to see problems with it, and revised it in 1945. Britten later said that he had been told so often that the concerto was no good that he had come to believe it himself.[73]

The Piano Concerto is the first in a line of large-scale explorations of traditional genres—a shift from Britten's composing patterns of the previous few years. Only three months after its premiere Britten began work on his Violin Concerto—also a genre that celebrates the cult of the virtuoso and one that occupies a principal position in the hierarchy of established genres. *Ballad of Heroes*, for tenor or soprano, chorus, and orchestra was written in a few weeks in 1939, designated an opus number (14), and performed in a 'Festival of Music for the People'. *Les Illuminations*, Op. 18, *Canadian Carnival*, Op. 19, *Sinfonia da Requiem*, Op. 20, and *Diversions*, Op. 21, for piano (left hand) and orchestra all followed in the next two years. Each consolidated the move away from chamber music, reversing a four-year trend in Britten's output. Regardless of critical reaction to the Piano Concerto and the works that followed, the BBC's support for Britten before the war did not waver, leaving him in the relatively privileged position (for a British composer) of being able to write large-scale works with the certainty of professional performance. If there are facile elements in Britten's early excursions into large forms, they are only part of a developing full-orchestra language, which found perfect expression in *Sinfonia da Requiem*. Without the opportunity to hear these pieces in professional performances, Britten's development would have been slower and less assured.

[69] *The Times*, 19 Aug. 1938. Quoted in DMPR 579.

[70] William McNaught, *Musical Times*, Sept. 1938, 703. Quoted in DMPR 578.

[71] 'F.B.', 'Playboy of Music', *Daily Telegraph*, 19 Aug. 1938. Quoted in DMPR 577.

[72] Britten to Mary Behrend, 26 Aug. 1938. DMPR 576.

[73] DMPR 66.

Creating and Losing an Audience

Since performances of Britten's music outside the BBC were few, Hawkes was well aware that the main opportunities for building the composer's reputation must continue to be with the Corporation. The publisher's modest dealings with it in 1935 concerning Britten—about copyright, scores, and parts—developed into a more entrepreneurial role during the following two years. The importance of this new symbiotic relationship was understood by composer, publisher, and broadcaster alike—a mixture of the professional and more friendly relationships shared by the key players. In January 1938 Wright actively promoted Britten's music to the conductor Bernard Herrmann, then associated with the American Columbia Broadcasting System.[74] One month later he informed Britten that he had arranged a performance of *Variations on a Theme of Frank Bridge* under Scherchen in Vienna, and, in order to cultivate the interest in the piece expressed by Sacher and Ansermet, he asked that Hawkes pay for a private recording.[75] Wright also asked for a private recording of the Piano Concerto, a work he planned to promote to the directors of the Baden-Baden Festival (prompting him to enquire whether Britten conformed strictly to the Nazi stipulation of Aryan).[76] In April 1939 the BBC broadcast the first complete programme of Britten's music (a week before the composer and Pears left for America), including the first performance of two songs from *Les Illuminations*.

Hawkes treated these premiere broadcasts seriously. He was in contact with Wright while the Piano Concerto was still being written, coordinating an extensive publicity campaign, which involved the resources of both the BBC (*The Listener*) and Boosey & Hawkes.[77] He also acted the role of unofficial contemporary music agent for the BBC. Following his return from America in April 1938, Hawkes promised to show Wright a number of new works, the result of his travels. Formalizing the relationship between the two men and the organizations they represented, Hawkes wrote that he was 'much indebted to you for the kind work that you do when you go abroad and you may rest assured that I shall do my best to arm you with as much propaganda as possible in this direction'.[78] And to Britten, the distinction between the two organizations slowly blurred—

[74] Wright to Herrmann, 14 Jan. 1938. BBCWAC, Composer File, Benjamin Britten, file 1a, 1933–44.

[75] Wright to Britten, 23 Feb. 1938. Ibid.

[76] Wright to Hawkes, 15 July 1938. Ibid. Britten's response, on 1 September, discounted Wright's efforts in this particular case: 'Yes, as far as I know, there has been no Semitic ("Semitic", I believe, being considered the opposite of "Ayran"!!) blood in our family. But I shouldn't bother about anything in Germany for me or the Concerto—because, even if you succeeded in getting a date for me there, I don't feel I could accept it.'

[77] Hawkes to Wright, 11 Apr. 1938. BBCWAC, Composer File, Benjamin Britten, file 1a, 1933–44.

[78] Hawkes to Wright, 19 Apr. 1938. Ibid.

action for one so often satisfying the other. Britten invited Wright to hear his cabaret songs in a run-through for Hawkes, a procedure copied on a number of occasions.[79] And echoing his publisher's words, Britten thanked Wright for his efforts on his behalf: 'I think you are rendering a great service to music by your grand propaganda methods.'[80]

As the relationship between composer, publisher, and broadcaster intensified, so too did the need for a firm contractual arrangement. In March 1937 Hawkes drafted the following contract for 'proposed commissions to . . . Mr Benjamin Britten to compose certain works for the B.B.C.': no assignment of a work's copyright or performing right could be made to the Corporation; responsibility for the preparation of parts must lie with the BBC; and should Boosey & Hawkes either publish the commissioned work or accept it for publication before the first performance, the BBC should be prepared to pay the normal hire charge for such a work (no distinction was made here between hand-copied and engraved orchestral parts).[81] The contract's inflexible terms—very much in favour of the publisher—suggests that Hawkes was aware of Britten's potential as much as the BBC's, and was keen to capitalize on both from the very beginning, although this in no way lessened his enthusiasm for or genuine belief in Britten's music.

The power of this composer–publisher–broadcaster triumvirate is made obvious in comparison with the contrasting case of Michael Tippett. In 1939, when Britten's reputation was beginning to expand beyond the BBC, Tippett's works were rejected by OUP, Boosey & Hawkes, the British section of the ISCM, and by the BBC itself.[82] The Corporation had deliberated over a number of Tippett scores in the late 1930s. In March 1938 Wright had asked Bliss for an appraisal of Tippett's 'Symphony No 1 in B flat', adding the scarcely encouraging postscript: 'A quartet by Tippett was given in the Studio some time ago, and it impressed most of us as being sour without conviction, and quite lacking in personality or charm.'[83] Another score was rejected by the Music Programme Advisory Panel in 1940.[84] Unlike Britten, neither of his contemporaries Elisabeth Lutyens and Grace Williams (Britten's college friend) received BBC performances of their works without first submitting the scores for approval. Moreover, even works by

[79] Britten to Wright, 16 Jan. 1938. DMPR 543.

[80] Britten to Wright, 1 Sept. 1938. BBCWAC, Artists File, Benjamin Britten, file 1a, 1933–44.

[81] Hawkes to Candler, 4 Mar. 1937. BPL, Boosey & Hawkes Correspondence, 1937.

[82] Ian Kemp, *Tippett: The Composer and his Music* (1984), 51.

[83] Wright to Bliss, 31 Mar. 1938. BBCWAC, Music Programme Advisory Panel, file 2, 1936–40. This work was never published, and the title 'Symphony No. 1' was applied to another work written in 1944–5. Tippett's submission of this early symphony to the BBC five years after its composition is rather curious. He later considered his String Quartet No. 1 (1934–5) to be his first real composition, yet his attempts to attract BBC patronage led to the submission of a work which even he valued less than a quartet dismissed as 'sour without conviction'.

[84] Dale to Vowles, 27 June 1940. BBCWAC, Music Programme Advisory Panel, file 2, 1936–40.

Schoenberg and Webern were subjected to the panel. It is important not to build up a picture of the BBC in the 1930s as a monolith quite incapable of discerning good music from bad; Lutyens and Tippett were late starters, while public acceptance and understanding of music of the Second Viennese School was scarcely widespread. Yet the BBC was the largest supplier of art music in Britain, and certain bureaucratic mechanisms were developed to deal with supply, which were 'corrupted' by the favourites and tastes of individuals within the organization.

In May 1939, before the outbreak of war, Britten and Pears followed Auden and Isherwood to America. This move signalled the beginning of a change in Britten's standing within the BBC, although the process was by no means simple. Once war was declared, the role and profile of radio increased as the public sought news and moral support. Accordingly, in November 1939, Boult produced a wartime 'Music Policy' for the BBC. The most significant acknowledgement in his statement was that without an alternative broadcasting programme (the national and regional programmes became one at the beginning of the war), it was necessary for 'every concert to appeal to an infinitely wider audience'. This, he continued, would mean shortening programmes, and rigorously ruling out the mediocre—presumably a concession to the highbrow rather than the low-brow listener.[85] The policy statement further noted that efforts were to be made to include international artists as soon as possible, and that the 'evacuation' of the BBC Symphony Orchestra from London, apart from establishing a new audience base, must not interrupt the regularity of its concerts. Boult also listed 'public psychology' as one of the 'recent modifying influences' on policy: 'The prevailing psychological conditions are an extremely difficult factor to explain in terms of policy. In general, the tendency is towards an increased proportion of the great classics, as this literature contains the finest and most inspired musical thinking.' Boult conceded that this could easily go too far, but was certain that the importance of 'keeping abreast—if not in advance—of the musical world becomes even more necessary if music is to hold its place as a cultural force rather than a mere spiritual sop'.[86] Bach cantatas, Handel anthems, Bach, Beethoven, Mozart and Schubert masses, and Romantic symphonies were all listed as examples of the most inspired musical thinking. But keeping abreast—or in advance—of the musical world was difficult: contemporary music was to be reduced to a monthly broadcast, rubbing shoulders in the same concert with 'masterpieces of old music'. Such changes in policy came under attack in a letter to the journal *Author* in 1940, its signatories including Austin, Bantock, Dunhill, Ireland, Lambert, Smyth, and Vaughan Williams. Their complaint was that the BBC had abandoned most contemporary British music from the beginning of the war, except for that of a few individuals, with the programmes by and

[85] Boult, 'Music Policy', 14 Nov. 1939. BBCWAC, Music Policy, file 1a, 1930–43, R27/245/1.
[86] Ibid.

large 'given over to the foreigner!'. The letter stressed that 'genuine music' by British composers should receive a larger share of broadcasting time than it then attracted; as a national institution, the BBC was obliged to promote native composers, and the progress of music in Britain depended on it.[87] In the very least, the letter was evidence that composers viewed the role played by the Corporation in the success or failure of contemporary British music as crucial—ever more so during a war in which British identity and sovereignty were under attack.

Britten was not included in Boult's 'cultural force' for most of the time he was living in America. According to broadcasting records held at BBC Radio Three, between May 1939 and April 1942—Britten's 'American period'—he was represented by seventeen BBC broadcasts of his orchestral works; yet ten of these were of *Soirées musicales* (the relatively light nature of *Soirées* made it perfect for the prevailing broadcasting restrictions).[88] But the change in Britten's status was not simply the product of reduced programme time and content. During the war the BBC exhibited unguarded hostility towards those with 'suspicious' politics. Conscientious Objectors were banned from working for the BBC until March 1941, which excluded many of the most talented artists working in the 1930s. Alan Bush, the Communist musician who had first conducted *Russian Funeral* and who had organized the 'Festival of Music for the People' in which *Ballad of Heroes* was premiered, suffered the ignominy of a total ban—only rescinded after Vaughan Williams's wide public campaign in his support. It is probable that Britten himself was censored just before the outbreak of war. When the score of *Ballad of Heroes* was submitted to the BBC in late April 1939—five days before Britten's departure for America—an unidentified member of the Corporation noted that the music department had received reports of the first performance, and that no plans were made for the work's inclusion in future programmes.[89] Since the musical substance of the piece is on a par with that of *Our Hunting Fathers* (which had been broadcast with little attention given to its rather obscure political message), and is superior to many of the other works broadcast as a result of the BBC's (or more specifically Wright's) enthusiasm for Britten, the rejection surely rested on *Ballad*'s overt political content.

Once war had begun, prejudice towards Britten quickly grew. In September 1940 Ernest Chapman of Boosey & Hawkes informed Erwin Stein, a pupil of Schoenberg and subsequently an editor at Boosey & Hawkes and close friend of Britten, that the Royal Philharmonic Society had turned down the new Violin

[87] Kenyon, *The BBC Symphony Orchestra*, 164.

[88] The method of logging performances was rather primitive and was almost certainly not accurate. Figures listed, therefore, must be considered the minimum.

[89] Chapman to Miss Wright, 24 Apr. 1939. BBCWAC, Composer file, Benjamin Britten, file 1a, 1933–44.

Concerto because of the composer's domicile abroad. 'I am afraid there have been similar hints from other quarters about Britten recently and it seems as though it may become difficult to keep up his performances.'[90] In the same month Hawkes wrote to Britten: 'As I have only been back a few days, I have not yet seen anybody that you know but I have seen evidence of a situation which I think I must bring to your notice immediately. There is no doubt at all that we are going to have difficulty in getting performances of your works and caustic comment has been passed on your being away.'[91] Britten responded by telling Hawkes not to press his works at all: 'If people want to play them over there, they will, but I don't want you to embarrass yourself in any way.'[92] This type of public antagonism was originally directed towards Auden and Isherwood, and included questions in the House of Commons. But the climate soon came to include Britten, too. An article in the *Musical Times* attacked both Britten's music (even though the composer was never mentioned by name) and his politics:

> Why should special favour be given to works which are not of first rank when they come from men who have avoided national service, and when so many British artists have suffered inroads upon their work so as to preserve that freedom which, musically, they have not yet enjoyed to the full? It is not encouraging to see others thriving on a culture which they have not the courage to defend.[93]

In 1942 Britten returned to England to face an increasingly hostile BBC. Certainly he still had his advocates within the Corporation: Julian Herbage, an old hand in the BBC music department, was present when Britten played through new works to Hawkes a few days after arriving back in England, and was greatly impressed by the *Sinfonia da Requiem* and the *Seven Sonnets of Michelangelo*. He wrote to Boult that 'one looks for most important if not great things from him in the future'.[94] Laurence Gilliam, head of the features department, wrote on Britten's behalf to the Conscientious Objectors' Tribunal in July 1942, explaining that Britten had been commissioned to write incidental scores for a number of 'important broadcast programmes' and that plans for future programmes 'of national interest' had already been made.[95] But Gilliam's enthusiasm for Britten's involvement in such programmes met with opposition from those who considered Britten's 'exile' in America a cowardly and anti-British

[90] Chapman to Stein, 6 Sept. 1940. Lewis Foreman, *From Parry to Britten* (1987), 234.

[91] Hawkes to Britten, 26 Sept. 1940. BPL, Boosey & Hawkes Correspondence, 1940.

[92] Britten to Hawkes, 7 Oct. 1940. DMPR 867.

[93] E. R. Lewis, 'English Composer Goes West', *Musical Times* (June 1941), quoted in DMPR 870.

[94] Herbage to Boult, 23 Apr. 1942. DMPR 653.

[95] Gilliam to Objectors' Tribunal, 6 July 1942. BBCWAC, Composer file, Benjamin Britten, file 1a, 1933–44.

act; any jealousy of Britten's success and any resentment of his homosexuality could now be expressed in terms of nationalism. The Controller of Programmes issued a music policy statement in March 1942 which conceded that 'political considerations' might affect the BBC's attempts to achieve the best possible broadcast of worthy music with the largest possible audience.[96]

By July 1942 veiled threats had become blatant obstructionism. In 1942 Britten was invited to compose incidental scores for the joint BBC–CBS radio programmes referred to by Gilliam in his letter to the Objectors' Tribunal. Each programme in this series written by Norman Corwin was intended to foster Anglo-American relations, an important consideration at that stage of the war. Under the general series title 'An American in England', listeners could find out about 'Women of Britain', 'London to Dover', or rationing in England. Gilliam first checked whether author and producer had any objections to Britten's involvement in the project, reassuring them that the composer's line was 'anti-killing but anti-fascist in all other respects', which those who had fought in the Spanish civil war may have found hard to take.[97] Both author and producer agreed on the composer's participation, but Boult 'somewhat violently implied that he considered Britten's employment for the Corwin programmes to be unfortunate'.[98] Boult's objection was overruled.

Britten's role in the radio feature *The Rescue* elicited more prejudice. In April 1943 Britten agreed to compose music for the programme on the understanding that he would conduct it. In September 1943 Dennis Wright, unaware of this agreement, invited Adrian Boult to conduct the BBC orchestra for the four-day rehearsal period and then the broadcast. Boult declined, declaring himself antagonistic towards the composer and his work—a view long reciprocated by Britten who considered Boult a terrible conductor and the complete antithesis of Frank Bridge, who Britten felt should have been appointed chief conductor of the BBC Symphony Orchestra when the post went to Boult in 1930. The awkward, sometimes antagonistic, relationship between the two men underpinned some of Britten's negotiations with the BBC. Clarence Raybould, chief assistant conductor of the BBC Orchestra, was then asked to conduct by Bliss; although he expressed the same opinion of Britten as Boult, he agreed so that the work would remain under the direction of a staff conductor.[99] Dissatisfied with Bliss's reasons for supporting Raybould, Britten announced that he would complete the score, but would take no further part in the production.[100] One reason

[96] 'BBC Music Policy', 6 Mar. 1942. BBCWAC, Music Policy, file 1a, 1930–43, R27/245/1. The Director of Music, the Deputy Director of Music, and Arthur Bliss contributed to this policy statement.

[97] Gilliam to Murrow, 9 July 1942. BBCWAC, Composer file, Benjamin Britten, file 1a, 1933–44.

[98] Memo, 22 July 1942. Ibid.

[99] Memo from Bliss, 25 Oct. 1943. Ibid.

[100] Britten to Bliss, 27 Oct. 1943. Ibid.

for Bliss's advocacy of Raybould became obvious two days later: he asserted that the orchestra resented Britten because he was a Conscientious Objector. Edward Sackville-West disagreed: 'I entirely disbelieve Bliss's assertion that the orchestra resent your being a C. O. That Boult does so is probably true; but that is immaterial: he has nothing to do with it.'[101] Richard Howgill, the Assistant Controller (Programmes), washed his hands of it: 'The Music Department should solve the difficulties with Britten for which they seem to be responsible on account of certain personal opinions being allowed to become too widely spread.'[102] Whether it was personal prejudice or general malice, there is no doubt that Britten's status within the BBC presented a sorry contrast to that of those halcyon pre-war days.

Britten's political attitudes also restricted broadcast performances of his art music. Boosey & Hawkes sent Raybould a copy of Britten's *Matinées musicales* for consideration. Raybould replied that the score was 'of no interest to me because of the composer's personal view and behaviour, I was going to say politically, but expand this to "nationally". I have the utmost contempt for the whole gang of young people who are dodging the country's call.'[103] Raybould's position at the BBC was one of some influence—through his radio dramas, his involvement with the Music Advisory Committee, and as one of the main staff conductors. Moreover, his command over orchestral programming was large. His obstructions and Boult's attitude therefore restricted the broadcasts of Britten's music between 1939 and 1942, and in some cases beyond.

Rehabilitation

Britten's few BBC champions, primarily Kenneth Wright and Herbage, and the positive result of his Tribunal hearing initiated a slow rehabilitation of the composer within the Corporation. It was by no means instantaneous: in the three years between Britten's return from America and the end of the war, there were thirty-five broadcasts of his orchestral works—double that for his American period (also three years), although his stable of works was now bigger (including *Matinées musicales*, which accounted for eight of the broadcasts). But Britten's new musical partnership with Pears—celebrated in a Wigmore Hall recital on 23 September 1942 and exploited by the Council for the Encouragement of Music and the Arts (CEMA) during the remaining war years—fulfilled exactly the BBC's quest for outstanding British artists, and BBC engagements for the pair provided a forum for the composer's music. However, programme content in the mid-1940s provoked a periodic BBC complaint:

[101] Sackville-West to Britten, 30 Oct. 1943. Ibid.

[102] Memo, n.d. [early Nov. 1943]. Ibid.

[103] Raybould to Stein, 12 July 1943. Ibid.

> Our music planning has completely come adrift—whether deliberately or accidentally—from the Beethoven–Brahms–Tchaikovsky standards . . . The BBC is not against experiment in music. It acknowledges its duty to the new or less-played composers. But none of these considerations must be allowed to cause it to abandon the traditional standards. They form 80 per cent of the main strands of the public's appreciation of Symphonic Music. We must return to them at once.[104]

It was an old conflict—to what extent to answer public demand—and shows how far the BBC had moved from its early days under Reith. The formation of the Listener Research Unit in 1936 pre-empted the real change in function that the BBC would undergo during the war—from educator to morale booster. Criticized from the outset as the 'most devoted believer in one-way conversation that the world has ever seen',[105] the BBC began systematic surveys of listeners' habits, likes, and dislikes. The effect of these findings on programmes was slow (in 1953 a music programmer had to request access to the reports[106]), but the concept of demand—personified in listener research—did affect all BBC departments. In the music department, listener research often uncovered villains in programmes broadcast. In 1942 a sales ledger clerk, one of nearly five hundred listeners questioned on BBC music policy, stated 'I can't stand composers like Britten, Bax, Walton and the rest. For sheer, crude, brutal, unmelodious music theirs is about the giddy limit.' The pedigree of his judgement was then established: 'Walton's "Scapino" for example; I prefer "Tiger Rag" to that.'[107] This same clerk's specific reactions to the balance of BBC music programmes contributed to the information presented in Table 2.1.

Although the results are meaningful only in the context of figures detailing the existing balance of music in the schedule, they nonetheless raise a number of important points. The symphony still reigned supreme. At the beginning of the war, the number of symphony concerts had been cut, in line with the BBC Symphony Orchestra's move from London, and the immediate practical difficulties of mounting large-scale performances. Without the necessary infrastructure (studio, library, artists, etc.), live performances were almost completely dropped from the schedules, replaced by cinema organ music and poorly chosen art music. This prompted complaint from Vaughan Williams, which Boult rebutted by pointing out that between 2 and 11 September 1939, eleven symphonies by major composers had been broadcast. 'I admit that many of them were at impossible times to listen, but rightly or wrongly, we have assumed . . .

[104] Memo from Herbage, 15 Jan. 1945. BBCWAC, Music Policy, file 1b, 1944–7, R27/245/2.

[105] William Beveridge in a 1935 radio talk, quoted in D. L. LeMahieu, *A Culture for Democracy* (1988), 281.

[106] BBCWAC, H.M.'s Monthly Meetings, Minutes 1951–8, file 1b, R27/197/2, 2 Mar. 1953.

[107] Broadcast Music Policy, Listener Research Report, 1 Apr. 1942. BBCWAC, Audience Research Special Reports, R9/9/6. *Scapino*, Walton's orchestral work, was composed in 1940, only two years before the survey was conducted.

Table 2.1 BBC music programme balance, 1942: survey of listeners' requests[a]

Genre	Increase (%)	Satisfied (%)	Decrease (%)
Symphony concerts	58	40	2
Chamber music	38	51	11
Instrumental recitals	36	55	9
Longer choral works	33	45	22
Grand opera	33	50	17
Organ recitals	21	50	29
Light orchestral concerts	15	38	47
Other choral music	15	52	33
Light opera	10	55	35
Song recitals (men)	8	45	47
Song recitals (women)	4	41	55

[a] Broadcast Music Policy, Listener Research Report, 1 Apr. 1942. BBCWAC, Audience Research Special Reports, R9/9/6.

that most of Britain had gone on to a shift system . . .'.[108] The request for more chamber music is an unexpected reaction from fans of 'Tiger Rag' (55 per cent of those surveyed, however, thought chamber music was most appropriate after 10.00 p.m.), although it should be remembered that Myra Hess's extraordinary wartime recitals had helped change remaining public prejudices towards the genre. The ease with which singers filled programme time is reflected in the overwhelming desire for fewer song recitals. But next to an appetite for grand forms and genres—the almost clichéd Beethoven–Brahms–Tchaikovsky standards used as a benchmark by many within the BBC by 1945—the most consistent response to each question was support for the status quo. When asked whether broadcasts contained too little or too much familiar classical music, 45 per cent of respondents were satisfied with the way things were, 28 per cent thought there was too little, while 27 per cent thought there was too much. Of the latter, seven out of every nine thought there should be more contemporary music. It was an encouraging climate for Britten's music; his return to the BBC schedules from late 1942 onwards should be viewed in this light.

Britten's move to large-scale genres, and the post-war formation of the Third Programme (the BBC's highbrow music and arts channel), ultimately affected his return to prominence in BBC schedules. Practical restrictions remained for the duration of hostilities, but political considerations slowly dissipated. His reputation—like that of other pacifists—benefited from a moderately low

[108] Boult to Vaughan Williams, 26 Oct. 1939. Foreman, *From Parry to Britten*, 224.

profile. His performances in factories and jails contributed markedly to his rehabilitation. But it was the success of *Peter Grimes* in June 1945 that cemented the rehabilitation process: the BBC's early support for Britten—like Hawkes's—was vindicated.

The BBC's display of favour towards Britten following *Grimes* was not unequivocal: Herbage thought the opera full of 'too much intellect and far too little heart', and that it wouldn't enter the repertory.[109] But Hely-Hutchinson, recently appointed Director of Music, demonstrated his personal support for the new bright young thing of British music when discussing Vaughan Williams's *Sir John in Love*. Opposed to a broadcast of the complete opera, Hely-Hutchinson viewed the presentation of part of it with misgivings, on grounds of the comparative treatment of Vaughan Williams and Britten.

> This [difference] will be accentuated if we do 'The Rape of Lucrezia' [*sic*] complete—and I think it very improbable that we shall be allowed to do 'The Rape of Lucrezia' unless we do it complete.
>
> Of course I entirely agree that we can never be accused of neglecting Vaughan Williams, but this is a question of the comparative treatment of the 'doyen' of English composers and a young and brilliant composer. [110]

It was far removed from the 1931–2 policy statement that any new work by Vaughan Williams would be included in the schedules at the earliest date, and although Vaughan Williams was considered primarily a composer of symphonies rather than operas, the shift in ground is considerable.

Britten's own perception of his relationship with the BBC seems to have been less rosy than the reciprocal view. On 1 July 1946 Britten dined with Erwin Stein from Boosey & Hawkes and Etienne Amyot from the BBC to discuss plans for the formation of the Third Programme. According to Amyot:

> the first half of the dinner was a tremendous attack against the BBC by Britten, which threatened at moments to become quite hysterical. He said he had no faith in the new programme and that, though we might for a week or two spend a lot of money and time in trying to get the things we wanted, the Service, like the Home and the Light, would disintegrate by Christmas and be indistinguishable from either A or B. . . . But towards the end of the evening he was infinitely more amenable, and I found, by ignoring Stein completely and concentrating entirely on Britten, that I was able to change his point of view; so much, that he said he would very much like to write a Festival Overture for our opening concert on 29th September . . .[111]

[109] Memo, 8 June 1945. BBCWAC, Composer file, Benjamin Britten, file 1b, 1945–50.

[110] Memo from Hely-Hutchinson, 8 Apr. 1946. BBCWAC, Music Policy, file 1b, 1944–7, R27/245/2.

[111] Amyot to Barnes, 2 July 1946. BBCWAC, Composer file, Benjamin Britten, file 1b, 1945–50.

Britten's *Occasional Overture* was broadcast on this occasion, earning Britten's prompt request that it never be performed again. But more important than Britten's climb-down is the fact that discourse between composer and broadcaster was so direct, a return to his pre-war channels of communication. Britten complained quite a few times of being neglected and misunderstood by the BBC; the Corporation took each complaint seriously, sending out a pacifying force armed with statistics, commissions, or expressions of goodwill.

To the writer John Moris, by the time of the Third Programme's inception, the BBC's programmes had become conciliatory: every pill was coated with sugar, and any item thought unpalatable was rendered 'either in a tone of apology or with the horrible cheeriness of the scout-master, the padre, or the matron of an expensive nursing home'.[112] The Third Programme would not compromise or make concessions to popular taste—it was, therefore, a terribly important innovation for British composers.[113]

Britten remained well represented in the schedules of the Third Programme. Amyot considered that Britten's music and the goals of the Third Programme ('to project all that is fine in contemporary art') were totally compatible.[114] Britten received the offer of many commissions for occasional works, most of which he declined. And despite the Programme's sometimes discouraging policy on studio opera—primarily because of expense—the Controller of the Third Programme stated that Britten's operas should have a regular place in the schedules.[115] They did: the Third Programme fought the Home Service for the first broadcast of *Albert Herring*;[116] the first Covent Garden performance of *Peter Grimes* was planned for broadcast;[117] in 1947 the Programme agreed not to present further outside broadcasts of either *Albert Herring* or *Lucretia*, but to arrange instead studio performances the following summer;[118] four broadcasts of *The Beggar's Opera* were planned for one week in 1948;[119] and each of Britten's operas in the 1950s was broadcast and quickly repeated. When Murrill protested that the Third Programme was over-playing Britten's operas, a view shared by some other composers at the time, he earned rebuttal from a department which did

[112] John Moris [ed.], *From the Third Programme* (1956), pp. v–vi.

[113] See Humphrey Carpenter, *The Envy of the World: Fifty Years of the BBC Third Programme and Radio 3 1946–1996* (1996).

[114] Amyot to Bass, 26 July 1946. BBCWAC, Artists File, Benjamin Britten, file 1b, 1945–7.

[115] BBCWAC, Minutes of Third Programme, Music Meetings, file 1a, 1946–9. R27/200/1, 26 Jan. 1949.

[116] BBCWAC, Home Service Music, file 2, 1947–8, Minutes, 4 Feb. 1947.

[117] BBCWAC, Minutes of Third Programme, Music Meetings, file 1a, 1946–9. R27/200/1, 20 Aug. 1947.

[118] Minutes, 10 Sept. 1947. Ibid.

[119] BBCWAC, Home Service Music, file 2, 1947–8, Minutes, 28 Mar. 1948.

not 'feel this to be a real danger at present in view of the unique position of Britten in contemporary English Opera'.[120]

The Third Programme's enthusiasm for Britten's music was only partially matched by other sections of the BBC. In 1951 Britten complained that the Home Service did not broadcast his works, and that the omission was a deliberate policy.[121] Murrill's response was that if a particular composer received lavish representation in the Third Programme, he or she could expect less attention from the other services.[122] Britten's complaint suggests that he was well aware that his public profile in the late 1940s and early 1950s depended to a large extent on the BBC. Each broadcast of one of his operas brought his name and music into the public domain, but it also brought in much-needed funds for the fledgling Aldeburgh Festival. Britten was frank about this: both he and the Head of the Transcription Service understood that broadcasts taken from the Festival encouraged artists to accept the low fees offered since broadcast fees increased their income, profile, and market value.[123] Britten later directly cooperated with the BBC in mounting a performance of Buxtehude's *Last Judgment*, making it quite clear that its inclusion in the Festival depended entirely on a BBC broadcast of the work and the consequent fees.[124] It was a mutually profitable situation—one which developed from the first broadcasts of English Opera Group performances.

A high profile on the Third Programme, however, did not necessarily indicate a high profile in Britain: the channel was quickly identified as specialist and attracted an accordingly small audience. But the Third Programme reinforced Britten's reputation with specialist audience and critics alike. The BBC no longer influenced Britten's style or genre as it had so persuasively in the 1930s, but in the 1940s and 1950s, before Decca began recording and releasing Britten's works soon after their completion, the BBC played an important role in keeping his music in the public domain. In his eyes this reinforced the validity of his post-war activities (he considered himself a musician for the people), although it did fuel resentment and contribute to the sharp change in his critical reputation in the early 1950s. Even in the 1960s, when much contemporary music moved in quite a different direction from that which Britten pursued, the BBC continued its support. In 1963 it broadcast approximately forty hours of his music; in

[120] BBCWAC, Minutes of Third Programme, Music Meetings, file 1a, 1946–9. R27/200/1, 2 Feb. 1949.

[121] Wellington to Murrill, 19 July 1951. BBCWAC, Composer File, Benjamin Britten, file 2, 1951–62.

[122] Murrill to Wellington, 30 July 1951. Ibid.

[123] Memo from M. A. Frost, 13 May 1957. BBCWAC, Outside Broadcasts—Sound, Aldeburgh Festival, file 1, 1955–8. See Ch. 5.

[124] Ibid.

the same year, Tippett's music took up just over ten.[125] Clearly the many musicians—including Beecham—who predicted that broadcasting would destroy the live concert and the composer's livelihood could not foresee the mutually profitable relationship that was possible between radio and the musician.

[125] In 1969 this rose to over fifty-seven hours, although this declined steadily over the following five years, ending up on thirty-four hours in 1974. This was partly to do with the phasing out of regional broadcasting. A blip in this pattern of decline occured in 1973 when the BBC broadcast over fifty-one hours of Britten's music; this total was buoyed by first broadcasts of *Death in Venice*.

Chapter 3

The Impresario and the English Opera Group

> The history of opera in this country is curious and complicated; it is also very characteristically English in its mixture of amateurish enthusiasm, professional indifference, occasional bright ideas without the least sense of planning for the future, commercial routine and—from the general public—complete ignorance and bewilderment.[1]

> For Britten himself, this triumph meant something more than the immediacy of being an internationally recognised composer. It meant for him that he was now willing in himself, and, indeed, determined to be, within the 20th century, a professional opera composer.[2]

While touring Canada with the English Opera Group in 1957, Britten was asked by a music critic to describe the difference between *The Rape of Lucretia* and *The Turn of the Screw*. 'The title is different, and the story', replied Britten. 'Oh yes, of course, but the music, Mr. Britten—what would you say was the difference between the music of "The Rape of Lucretia" and "The Turn of the Screw"?' 'The notes are the same, but they are in a different order.'[3] The comparison between the two works is a profitable one, although not in the sense intended by the music critic, nor in Britten's precise if dismissive reply. *The Rape of Lucretia*, Britten's first opera after *Peter Grimes*, owed its presentation at Glyndebourne in 1946 to private patronage. Britain then was just beginning to explore the institutionalization of national culture through its new Arts Council. The premiere of *The Turn of the Screw*, presented by the English Opera Group in Venice less than ten years after Glyndebourne's *Lucretia*, was supported by the Arts Council and the Venice Biennale Festival. The period separating these two operas was

[1] Edward J. Dent, *A Theatre for Everybody* (1945), 55.
[2] Michael Tippett, 'A Tribute to Benjamin Britten', *The Listener* (16 Dec. 1976), 791.
[3] General Manager's report on visit to Ontario. BPL, EOG Correspondence, 1957.

one of intense change: private patronage gave way—however incompletely—to a government-subsidized market economy. The influence of this evolving cultural environment on Britten's music was considerable.

In 1945 flesh was added to the skeletal (wartime) Council for the Encouragement of Music and the Arts (CEMA) to form the Arts Council of Great Britain. Its involvement in the work of the EOG raised significant issues concerning, initially, the economics of state patronage: Britten was required to put a price on a commodity that had been considered priceless only a few years earlier. This economic self-assessment had its problems—not least with the flawed estimates of costs involved in presenting Britten's new operas from 1947 onwards—but economic arguments were soon supplanted by ethical ones (the duty of the state to fund the arts), and documentation charting the complicated relationship between the Arts Council and the EOG suggests a strong connection between genre and the economics of performance, of which Britten was certainly aware. By the end of the 1950s, Britten's and Pears's desire to distance themselves from the general administration of the Group was patent, and in 1961 the EOG came under the auspices of Covent Garden. For the Group during its first ten years, though, Britten composed four chamber operas: *The Rape of Lucretia*, *Albert Herring*, *Let's Make an Opera*, *The Turn of the Screw*.[4] He also made realizations of two other operas: Gay's *The Beggar's Opera* and Purcell's *Dido and Aeneas*. The background to these works offers a significant insight into Britten's compositional methods and illustrates how increasingly he came to be influenced by the economics of genre.

The Glyndebourne English Opera Company

Despite the financial and artistic success of the 1945 Sadler's Wells season of *Peter Grimes*, the opera antagonized many within the company. Edmund Donlevy, who played the part of the apothecary Ned Keene, regretted the elements of 'quarrelsomeness, overweening ambition, envy, fear of unemployment, hysteria . . . which have appeared in so many guises during the last six months or so and which have done more to damage the artistic standard of the company's work than anything else could possibly have done'.[5] In late July 1945—six weeks after the premiere of *Peter Grimes*—Britten informed Pears that a new opera company, run by the composer and his associates, would open at Dartington in May or June 1946.[6] Imogen Holst was then Director of Music at Dartington and had

[4] *The Rape of Lucretia* was composed for the Glyndebourne English Opera Company—a direct forerunner of the English Opera Group whose history will be considered in this chapter.

[5] Undated and unaddressed letter from Edmund Donlevy. Sadler's Wells Archive, Opera 1937–52, Staff Contracts, Correspondence, Salaries.

[6] Britten to Pears, [?22 July 1945], DMPR 1269.

met Britten and Pears as a result of their wartime involvement with CEMA. The proposal was attractive for Dartington: Holst admired Britten's music, and the company would bring much prestige to the college. For Britten, the attraction lay in the fact that the ensemble was to operate without the restraints of the traditional and conservative management he had encountered at Sadler's Wells. Soon after, however, the wealthy John Christie offered the company both financial security and a home at Glyndebourne—an offer quickly accepted.

It was a mutually beneficial arrangement. Christie viewed the proposed company as a means by which he could reopen Glyndebourne, which he had closed at the end of the 1939 season for the duration of the war.[7] Britten's company was not Christie's first attempt at reopening his house: in 1945 he had begun negotiations with Thomas Beecham and the Philharmonia Orchestra. Plans were devised for a 1946 season of *The Magic Flute* and *La Bohème* (with the scoutmasterly possibility of 'knock[ing] together a third opera in no time' should the two works be insufficient) with Beecham conducting for no fee.[8] With tedious predictability quite lost on Christie, negotiations with Beecham completely broke down; no further plans for a 1946 opera season were made until the Britten proposal appeared.[9] Admittedly, Christie viewed Britten's proposed company with more enthusiasm than its product—dreaded *contemporary* opera—and this was a later source of tension between the directors. Since its inception in 1934, Glyndebourne's repertory had consisted almost entirely of Mozart operas (Donizetti's *Don Pasquale*, and Verdi's *Macbeth* in its first professional English production were the exceptions). Although the scale of the proposed contemporary opera was comparable with that of the works produced at Glyndebourne before the war, the style was clearly not. But Christie was determined that his pre-war investment in the opera house—something around £100,000—should not be wasted, and, with a combination of flair and *faux*-altruism, plans for the new company went ahead.

Christie's own plans, however, were not entirely self-centred. He considered post-war England's music to be of a very low standard, and that only he had the knowledge and resources to rectify this. In an interview with members of the Arts Council in July 1946, Christie stated that 'the whole of the orchestral work in London is lamentable from the London Philharmonic Orchestra downwards'. The Arts Council wrote a comprehensive report on its outspoken pupil:

> He talks of starting his own orchestra or, in fact, two orchestras, one for Mozart and a larger one for general music. He also talks, if he can see no other way of improving the

[7] Christie organized a provincial tour and short London run of *The Beggar's Opera* in 1940, but he did not mount a season at Glyndebourne.

[8] Spike Hughes, *Glyndebourne* (1965), 154.

[9] Rudolf Bing report, undated. GFO, Glyndebourne Society Ltd. Beecham was notorious for his grand plans, generous financial support, and cheeky inability to conform to expectations.

musical standard of this country, of running his own Opera and, if necessary, of building a new Opera House. . . . He threw in the remark that chamber music was not all that it should be. Finally, to get back to Covent Garden, he says that as regards the actual forthcoming productions, they are going to make one very fatal mistake. Instead of bringing entire Opera Companies from the Continent and sending them back again after they have done their season, what ought to be done is to bring over the best individual talent to play with English players and teach them the tricks of the trade.[10]

By the standards of pre-corporate-trouble-shooting and multinational consultancy, it was an impressive tirade; clearly the town was not big enough for both Christie and Beecham, who spoke from remarkably similar platforms. Although not always blessed with facts (Covent Garden's plans by this stage were centred on the formation of a permanent English opera company) or solutions ('chamber music was not all that it should be'), the analysis contained some salient points from a scarcely disinterested party.

The timing of Christie's meeting with the Arts Council helps to explain his vitriolic attack on what were, even then, the Council's sacred cows: Covent Garden and one of the London orchestras. Glyndebourne's battle to attract Arts Council funding had finished—bitterly and essentially unsuccessfully—two weeks earlier; rather than the grant mooted by the Council when the company was first discussed, Glyndebourne was eventually offered limited guarantee against loss on the tour of *Lucretia*, but not on its season at Christie's house. The importance of this short-lived company lies not in its effect on *Lucretia*—a work which remained modestly immune to the changing constituents of the company's subsidy. Rather, the significance of the dialogue between Glyndebourne and the Arts Council (and a detailed understanding of it) lies in the precedent established for state funding of a small opera company. When the English Opera Group rose from the wreckage of the Glyndebourne English Opera Company, it inherited a funding mechanism that had been constructed in the previous year in circumstances quite removed from those in which the new company now found itself. This then affected the shape and style of the operas composed by Britten in the following years.

Eric Crozier first met representatives of the Arts Council in November 1945 to discuss the possible formation of a company that would present a short season of opera and drama in England and Europe. By January 1946, when Crozier resumed his correspondence with Steuart Wilson, the Arts Council's Music Director, the proposal had been modified considerably: drama would be omitted 'for the first year'; only one opera would be presented in the first season (*The Rape of Lucretia*); and the company would be based at Glyndebourne with Britten, Crozier, Dorothy Elmhirst (from Dartington), John Christie, and

[10] Memo from E.H.P., 3 July 1946. ACGB, Music Department M/1—OP/1 1945–55.

Rudolf Bing as directors.[11] Crozier made one fundamental error in his January letter to Steuart Wilson (compounded later by Christie's casual references to the building of new opera houses, and his unsuccessful attempt to buy the freehold of Covent Garden): he mentioned large sums of money without blushing, creating the impression of dilettante directors. Wilson's offer from the previous year—£5,000 if an equal amount could be found independently—was no longer required: 'the Glyndebourne Organisation have accepted full responsibility for the scheme, financially and otherwise.'[12] According to Crozier, the cost to Glyndebourne—including production expenses and a playing season of fifteen weeks—would be around £20,000 (the four-week tour of the continent was to be under the auspices of the British Council). The role of the Arts Council would be to guarantee the company against losses up to £5,000.[13] The letter concluded with the hope that the 'first production of Benjamin Britten's opera may create a demand for a kind of opera that is presentable within comparatively narrow economic limits'—presumably an exceptionally high demand, given the costs involved.

Wilson's marginalia to Crozier's letter illustrate his immediate reaction to the proposal, on which he remained moderately intractable during the following months of negotiations. Next to the list of proposed directors, Wilson noted that Customs and Excise would probably object to Crozier and Britten, since they were interested parties (this concerned Glyndebourne's exemption from Entertainment Tax). He also wrote that a guarantee against loss would be appropriate only if more than one opera were produced. And he added that a guarantee for the tour could be considered, but not for the full period outlined by Crozier.[14] Although Crozier was asking for the minimum of Council support, he was also offering far less than had been listed in the original proposal. Wilson's considered response to the proposal highlighted the change in the Council's stance.[15]

Negotiations—of sorts—continued until June, only one month before the premiere of *Lucretia*. An indication that the Council was close to providing some support came with its request in early June for detailed estimates of income and expenditure. Again, Glyndebourne waved around figures that were much too large; Bing's estimates of income were naive, while expenditure—according to Mary Glasgow, secretary-general of the Arts Council—was 'alarmingly high' (Table 3.1).

[11] Crozier to Wilson, 18 Jan. 1946. ACGB, Glyndebourne Correspondence, 1945–6. Bing had been manager of Glyndebourne before the war. He became the first director of the Edinburgh Festival in 1947 before being appointed General Manager of the New York Metropolitan Opera, a position he held from 1950 to 1972.

[12] Crozier to Wilson, 18 Jan. 1946. ACGB, Glyndebourne Correspondence, 1945–6.

[13] Ibid.

[14] Marginalia, ibid.

[15] Wilson to Crozier, 31 Jan. 1946. Ibid.

Table 3.1 Production expenses (estimate), *The Rape of Lucretia*, 1946 (£)[a]

Board and residence for company of 25 for 7 weeks	700
Fares	45
Rehearsal salaries	
12 Orchestra (2 weeks)	480
16 Singers (5 weeks)	480
Music staff and stage management (6)	436
Artistic management (4)	635
Office (4)	184
Stage (17)	480
Other rehearsal expenses	190
Scenery, costumes, wigs, shoes, helmets, etc.	2,700
Music hire	120
Preliminary advertising, printing, etc.	300
General administration expenses (over 8 months)	400
Insurances	100
Theatre light	50
London box office (20 weeks)	200
Sundries	200
Total	7,700

Weekly running expenses

Production expenses 1/11th	700
Singers' salaries (16)	530
Orchestra (12)	350
Conductor, producer, stage manager and assistant coach	70
Wardrobe mistress, stage foreman, props master, electrician	35
Hire, insurances, general overhead	55
Weekly advertising	60
Transport (company of 38)	50
Sundries	50
Total	1,900

[a] Bing to Glasgow, 11 June 1946. ACGB, Glyndebourne Correspondence, 1945–6.

Spread over eleven weeks, the weekly running expenses of £1,900 (incorporating production costs) would indeed come to the £20,000 first mentioned by Crozier in January 1946. This was expensive for a single opera: in 1947 the English Opera Group was to seek £12,000 working capital to form an entirely new company, to produce two operas, and to buy back from Christie the rights, sets, and costumes for *Lucretia*. A further comparison is found in the 1949 *Arts*

Enquiry, which lists the average cost of a production at Sadler's Wells as £3,000.[16] Similarly, in 1952 John Denison informed Rudolf Bing (by then at the Metropolitan Opera) that the cost of a single opera production at Covent Garden could be from £7,000 to £15,000—this for a large theatre, chorus, and orchestra.[17] But these comparisons were still some years away. Covent Garden, however, obliged with something much closer, with which the Arts Council would have been intimately acquainted. *Carmen*, performed a few months after *Lucretia*, had a production budget of £7,022 (including £2,826 on costumes, £2,721 on scenery, and £225 on props)—almost £700 less than that for *Lucretia* (Table 3.1).[18] This is an alarming comparison, given the different scale of the two operas. In this period it did cost more to run Covent Garden than the Glyndebourne English Opera Company, but not remarkably more. The average weekly running cost of Covent Garden was around £5,707—but this included the cost of the ballet corps. Without the ballet, the amount was probably closer to £4,000.[19] This figure does not include individual production expenses, but does incorporate £850 for soloists, £1,560 for the orchestra, £615 for the chorus, advertising, and royalty expenses, and the wages of stage hands, electricians, and wardrobe personnel. Although similar in total, Glyndebourne differed from Covent Garden in including administrative costs within its production budget. The difference between expenses of the two companies, however, was not commensurate with the difference in their size. Next to Covent Garden, Glyndebourne was spending too much money for a company of its proportions, a point not lost on Wilson and Glasgow.[20] Furthermore, incorporation of administrative costs into the Glyndebourne production budget does suggest that Christie viewed *Lucretia* as the vehicle through which his opera house and company could be rebuilt.

Bing's estimated income from *Lucretia* was equally high. He talked confidently of capacity audiences for the Sadler's Wells season and the tour, reaping (after royalties and commissions) £16,500 for the Glyndebourne English Opera

[16] *Arts Enquiry* (1949), 80. This presumably does not include the company's running costs. The *Arts Enquiry* was a widespread investigation into the state of all the arts in Britain.

[17] Denison to Bing, 6 Oct. 1952. ACGB, Opera 1951–2, OP/6. See Table 4.5 for production costs of various Covent Garden operas.

[18] ROH, Covent Garden, File 148.

[19] ROH Trust, 22 April 1947, Minutes, 1946–51. The figure of £5,707 is the average of the six weeks prior to 22 April. The figure of £4,000 is gained by removing expenses directly associated with the ballet, and reducing certain costs (by less than half) since they would have been shared by the two companies. The first opera season at Covent Garden opened in January 1947 with *Carmen* (*The Fairy Queen* was first presented in December 1946—outside the opera season because of its masque-like qualities). Other productions in the first season included *Manon*, *The Magic Flute*, *Der Rosenkavalier*, and *Turandot*, although these last two operas were not produced until after 22 April, and formed no part of the weekly average discussed in the letter of this date.

[20] See Ch. 4 for an analysis of post-war Covent Garden.

Company.[21] Bing obviously wanted to reassure the Council that its guarantee would never be called upon; but underlying this is his confidence in a new opera by the composer of *Peter Grimes*. This confidence in the product—later recognized as misplaced because of its innovative scale and nature—probably influenced the significant shift from a request for funding from the Arts Council to the lesser commitment of a guarantee against loss; with long-term commercial exploitation of *Lucretia* expected, profit rather than mere survival was predicted.

The Arts Council was somewhat quicker than Bing to see holes in such economic rationale. An internal memo established that, at its Sadler's Wells season, the company would need to take £2,633 per week to stay within the budget estimates:

> The Sadlers' [*sic*] Wells Opera at their best, have played to about £2,100 [per week]. I would imagine that this Company would average £2,000 (their share £1,500). At the Cruikshank theatres, they need £2,900 a week to get out, which, judged by Sadlers' Wells finance, is a large figure to ask. Should they play to an average of £2,000 weekly, they would lose £600 per week. If the whole season (four weeks Sadlers' Wells and five weeks tour) is taken at an average of £2,000 a week, the loss will be about £5,000. If the takings are less than £2,000 on the average, the tour will be pretty disastrous. I think it fairly certain that, if the Arts Council gives a guarantee of £3,000, the whole of it will be called upon . . .[22]

It was a remarkably prescient analysis—all the more potent for Bing's ignorance of the sums involved. More significant was the Council's willingness to provide a guarantee, knowing that it was likely to be required.

In June 1946 the Arts Council formally offered Glyndebourne limited guarantee against loss of £3,000 for the nine-weeks tour of *Lucretia*. 'In offering assistance to the tour of "The Rape of Lucretia"', Glasgow remarked, 'the Arts Council express[es] the hope that the programme of the new Company performing may be enlarged and that this production may mark the beginning of a long-term policy.'[23] Wilson had argued for this amount, and not for the £5,000 first 'promised' in 1945, in a letter to Glasgow. 'Is it fair to Sadler's Wells and Covent Garden seasons of opera to diminish their quota . . . by so large a proportion for one venture? . . . Failing much better evidence and figures from Bing I should advise that £3,000 should be our top limit.'[24] This was again significant as far as future funding was concerned: without a secure, long-term policy, without

[21] Bing to Glasgow, 3 June 1946. ACGB, Glyndebourne Correspondence, 1945–6. Bing further states that a possible one-week extension of the tour would bring in a further £1,500 for Glyndebourne.

[22] Bandstone to Glasgow, 13 June 1946. ACGB, Glyndebourne Correspondence, 1945–6.

[23] Glasgow to Bing, 18 June 1946. Ibid.

[24] Wilson to Glasgow, 12 June 1946. Ibid.

Christie's personal wealth, and with the spectre of Covent Garden looming large, the English Opera Group was to inherit a considerable handicap.

The bitterness provoked by the reduced sum of the guarantee and by the negotiations between Glyndebourne and the Arts Council seeped into print. Britten was pressed by Christie to write to *The Times*; his letter appeared on 11 July:

Sir,—Two leading members of the Arts Council have now stated that Glyndebourne is 'lending' or 'letting' its opera house for the production of *The Rape of Lucretia*. This is a complete misrepresentation of facts. When some eight months ago the Glyndebourne management became aware of my plans for opera I was approached by Mr. Bing, Glyndebourne's general manager, and was offered the production of my new opera at Glyndebourne for the reopening of the Glyndebourne festival—an offer which I gladly accepted. The engagement of all artistic personnel, and the whole organization of the production, carried out in closest collaboration and agreement with myself, was and is in the hands of the Glyndebourne management, who are presenting the opera and are financially and otherwise solely responsible for it.[25]

'The purpose of this letter', Britten added, was 'to inform the Arts Council, who from the start were asked to collaborate . . . of the facts'. The timing of the letter gave its content extra sting: it appeared one day before the premiere of *Lucretia*. When challenged by Wilson, Britten became even more antagonistic:

My letter to the Times was caused by intense surprise that two important members of the Arts Council were in possession of either wrong or no information of the facts concerning the re-opening of Glyndebourne with my new opera. The two members will, I am sure, have no wish to conceal their identity. Their two statements were obviously made in good faith.

I do not, I am afraid, understand your remark about 'confusion over finance'. To me the matter is quite clear. I understand that some time ago you told Eric Crozier that the Arts Council would be prepared to put up £5,000 for our plans if an equal amount were forthcoming from other sources. We could then neither find the money, nor a theatre or organisation which was prepared to undertake the work until Mr. Bing heard of our plans, and immediately offered us Glyndebourne's resources & facilities. I do not think that offer was made because £5,000 had been promised from the Arts Council, but it was made from that knowledge. After the Arts Council's offer was not kept, it did not affect Glyndebourne's plans and, as you know, negotiations went on for a long time with the Arts Council.

Finally the outcome was, as far as I know, that the Arts Council has now offered a guarantee which would operate and be calculated only after Glyndebourne had lost £700 per week. I must endorse Glyndebourne's attitude in the matter & cannot help feeling that Glyndebourne isn't the only loser in the complete collapse of collaboration with the Arts Council.[26]

[25] Britten to *The Times*, 11 July 1946.

[26] Britten to Wilson, 16 July 1946. ACGB, Glyndebourne Correspondence, 1945–6.

It is possible that Britten was not informed of the delicate talks between the Council and Glyndebourne—his composition schedule was tight enough to warrant this, although in subsequent years a tight schedule did not preclude Britten's direct involvement in the administration of the EOG. Crozier later said that neither he nor Britten was aware of the costs involved in staging *Lucretia* at Glyndebourne, and that they both took this ignorance with them into their new company.[27] But Britten, whether through ignorance or knowledge, was being wilfully obstructive, and was drawn into political mud-slinging by Christie. Britten had neither the facts on his side, nor the moral high ground. Sir Ernest Pooley, Chairman of the Arts Council, was understandably negative in his response to Britten's letter: if it was 'intended to attack publicly the Arts Council, or some of its members, you cannot expect our mutual relations to be very cordial'.[28] Vaughan Williams identified himself as one of the Arts Council members under attack for his ignorance of the negotiations, earning a consolatory letter from Wilson with the apposite remark 'Pity Ben should write to the Times when he should have been attending to his score!'[29] To Britten himself, Wilson wrote, 'My own feeling is that we want you to write the music and leave to the rest of us who cannot do that, to organize finance. . . . Anyway there is the opera!—and I do not think that our arguments will prevent it being a success.'[30]

The opera was considered a success, but certainly not an unmitigated one. Expectations of the work were high, and the reopening of Glyndebourne after the war guaranteed an audience—70 per cent of seats were sold within the first three or four days of tickets going on sale.[31] George Barnes of the BBC informed Bing in October that the listener research report on the first broadcast of *Lucretia* 'confirmed our anxiety to give a second performance, [and] we would have gladly made the space available on almost any date'.[32] Critical response, however, was mixed—the libretto and the Christian epilogue attracting much criticism. William Glock, later Controller of Music at the BBC, thought the ending 'appalling', and Duncan's libretto too prone to versification. Desmond Shawe-Taylor, in the *New Statesman*, cited one example (later deleted) of this versification: 'All authorities agree that the Etruscan conquest of Rome dates from 600 B.C.—that is, approximately', which could almost be read as a bad parody of Auden's verse writing. Shawe-Taylor went on to criticize Britten's handling of the rape scene: 'One does not, of course, demand a crude Straussian representation of the lustful crime, but the violence of rape must surely be

[27] Kildea interview with Crozier, 11 Apr. 1994.
[28] Pooley to Christie, 18 July 1946. ACGB, Music Department M/1—OP/1 1945–55.
[29] Wilson to Vaughan Williams, 18 July 1946. ACGB, Glyndebourne Correspondence, 1945–6.
[30] Wilson to Britten, 18 July 1946. Ibid.
[31] Bing to Downes, 24 Apr. 1946. GFO, *The Rape of Lucretia*, 1946.
[32] Barnes to Bing, 28 Oct. 1946. Ibid.

matched by some sort of musical violence, and I cannot think that this was the moment to launch the two commentators on a figured chorale.'[33] The *Evening Standard* was more enamoured of Duncan's contribution—'Not for him the drawing-room comedy with its cocktail wit or tea cup pleasantries'—but disliked what it perceived as the *Madama Butterfly* conclusion to the opera ('It only needed Tarquinius to return with a Roman wife and the parallel would have been complete').[34] It is fair to say that the more controversial elements of the opera detracted from the dramatic potency of the work; many critics pounced rather than pondered. But in doing so, they left unconsidered the brilliant and innovative features of the opera and its score.

Duncan, though, later acknowledged the preciousness of parts of his libretto. In 1969, he asked Britten for a further revision of the opening chorus:

> I am at the moment thinking of 'the prodigious liberality of selfcoined obsequious flattery.'!! This silly mouthful was, as I've confessed somewhere (if not to you?) a sort of tease when I wrote it (you'd been telling me that even a telephone Directory could be set). . . . & so I wrote those lines as a challenge, expecting you to throw them out. To my dismay, you weren't tripped up at all & later Peter coped with them too—& the 'joke' rebounded in my own face. But perhaps I've been hanging on this hook of my own making long enough? Would you consider cutting both 'prodigious liberality' & 'selfcoined'? Then the line would read 'pay his way with obsequious flattery'. But don't worry if this change upsets yr musical fabric, I'll have to wear my own red nose.[35]

Both Duncan's red nose and the phrase remained. But as an illustration of Britten's compositional process, the letter should not be undervalued. In the introduction to the libretto of *Lucretia* Britten made much of the composer–poet relationship. 'Many people think that composers can set any old kind of poetry to music . . . But I believe that if the words of a song match the music in subtlety of thought and clarity of expression it results in a greater amount of artistic satisfaction for the listener.'[36] A few years before this he had rejected Auden's 'Christmas Cantata' because of its unwieldy language. But Duncan's libretto is full of awkward, ornamental poetry, which Britten set rather than rejected; the words were anything but as subtle and clear as the music. Britten's judgement—so sure in *Grimes* and subsequent operas—deserted him. And if Duncan viewed parts of the libretto as a joke, or at least Britten as the butt of one, the composer–poet relationship cannot have been as close as Britten thought.

The *Lucretia* tour was a financial disaster. Audiences were small—mostly, Crozier alleged, because there was little advertising, and the 'magic name' of

[33] Shawe-Taylor, 'The Rape of Lucretia', *New Statesman* (20 July 1946).

[34] *Evening Standard*, 13 July 1946. This paper had, two days previously, printed the scoop that Glyndebourne tradition would be reversed and that 'Beer will be served'.

[35] Duncan to Britten, 14 Nov. 1969. BPL, Duncan Correspondence, 1969.

[36] Benjamin Britten, 'Preface', *The Rape of Lucretia* (1946).

Glyndebourne held scant sway in the provinces.[37] Aksel Schiøtz, who shared the role of the Male Chorus with Pears, wrote to Moran Caplat from Edinburgh saying that the audience at one performance had been very enthusiastic ('almost Glyndebourne-like'), but that the '"gentlemen of the press" seem to be against everything which is not Bohème'.[38] Bing recorded a loss on the tour of £3,137, and the whole of the Arts Council guarantee was called up as a result.[39] Although this loss was not quite that predicted by the Arts Council in June (partly because the financial capacity of a week at Glyndebourne was greater than calculated, and partly because the Council insisted that Christie absorb all the production costs rather than include a proportion of them in the running costs of the tour), it was close enough to exonerate the Council should it accuse Glyndebourne of ignorance in its business dealings.

The loss on the tour damaged Christie and Britten's relationship, but not as irreparably as Humphrey Carpenter suggests.[40] In early October Britten told Peter Diamand—the impresario responsible for the company's visit to Holland—that they were splitting from Glyndebourne,[41] although in late September Bing was unsure of any definite plans.[42] Moran Caplat had written to Glasgow on 30 August saying that Christie was adamant that negotiations over the past should not be allowed to jeopardize the future; his salvage operation was under way.[43] Letters between the parties in 1947 and 1948 demonstrate that Glyndebourne was keen to maintain a connection with the EOG; when Crozier made it known in late 1947 that the EOG did not wish to perform at Glyndebourne in 1948, Bing stated his regret, but promised to reopen discussions at any stage.[44]

The relationship between the various directors was probably exacerbated by Christie's and Bing's distaste for touring (outlined in a letter to Glasgow in December 1946)—although it is equally likely that Britten clung to the issue as a supposed indication of irreconcilable differences, thus forging a path towards his coveted autonomy. If there were any differences, they were kept from the cast: Margaret Ritchie (Lucia) wrote to Bing on 2 November asking 'What can this be about "deteriorated relationships" between Glyndebourne and Ben? I had until your letter came thought all was most amicable between you. Indeed I

[37] Kildea interview with Crozier, 11 Apr. 1994.

[38] Schiøtz to Caplat, 13 Aug. 1946. GFO, *The Rape of Lucretia*, 1946. Caplat joined the staff of Glyndebourne in 1945 and was appointed General Administrator in 1949, a post he kept until 1981.

[39] Arts Council Finance Officer to Bing, 12 Dec. 1946. ACGB, Glyndebourne Correspondence, 1945–6.

[40] Carpenter, 240.

[41] Ibid. 244.

[42] Bing to the cast of *Lucretia*, 26 Sept. 1946. GFO, *The Rape of Lucretia*, 1946.

[43] Caplat to Glasgow, 30 Aug. 1946. ACGB, Glyndebourne Correspondence, 1945–6. Caplat also pointed out that the loss on the tour thus far (including the appropriate portion of the production expenses) was £4,500.

[44] Bing to Crozier, 17 Dec. 1947. GFO, Selection of Minutes and Agenda Papers for Glyndebourne Society Ltd, 1945–9.

remember Ben saying with infinite pleasure that John was prepared to back him "through thick and thin".'[45] But by this stage, Britten and Crozier had already met with Wilson to discuss a new company, quite separate from Glyndebourne.

Albert Herring and the New English Opera Group

'Despite the total failure of our previous relations, Britten & Crozier called on Oct 13th to ask advice about the setting up of a new company intended to be the owner of its own rights and productions.'[46] The total capital they sought was £12,000; this included the £1,000 needed to buy back the sets and costumes of *Lucretia*, and the rights, which Christie held until October 1947.[47] The proposal envisaged a company of twenty-four singers and an orchestra of twelve. Wilson prevaricated, stating that the Arts Council could not commit itself to funding non-existent companies, although in his internal report of the meeting he recorded that 'Britten's music is an important thing. Should he have to make a company to exploit it? At present only Glyndebourne could . . .'.[48] The question was rhetorical: if existing conventional avenues such as Glyndebourne and Sadler's Wells were closed to Britten's operas, a new company was the only alternative. In late December Wilson advised Anne Wood, a friend of Pears's from the BBC Singers, brought in as General Manager of the new company, that he would recommend to his executives that the English Opera Group be awarded a grant of not less than £3,000 and closer to £5,000, which was his estimate of the shortfall, as suggested by the submitted proposal.[49] The former figure was approved by the Executive Council, although Wood was informed by Wilson in April 1947 that the formality of an application was required before the funds could be released.[50]

The grant of £3,000 was inadequate for the EOG's purposes—largely because the Group failed to attract contributions from other sources—but the Group did not realize this until late 1947. Although it is possible that Wilson had originally pleaded for a grant of £5,000, as he stated in his letter to Wood, the lesson of Glyndebourne's perceived fiscal irresponsibility most likely provoked a cautious response. The grant also illustrates an important bureaucratic perception of post-war contemporary British music: although the product was seen as important, the Council's priorities were conservative. Their cautious approach was to some

[45] Ritchie to Bing, 2 Nov. 1946. GFO, *The Rape of Lucretia*, 1946.

[46] Memo from Wilson, 2 Dec. 1946. ACGB, Minutes and Correspondence of the EOG.

[47] At this meeting Britten and Crozier mentioned a figure of £10,000, although when the EOG prospectus was issued in early 1947 the sum was listed as £12,000; possibly the Group had become aware of the Arts Council's intention of providing £3,000 rather than the £5,000 as mentioned in a letter to the EOG in late December.

[48] Memo from Wilson, 2 Dec. 1946. ACGB, Minutes and Correspondence of the EOG.

[49] Wilson to Wood, 30 Dec. 1946. Ibid.

[50] Wilson to Wood, 22 Apr. 1947. Ibid.

extent conditioned by the concept of the impractical 'struggling artist' which had survived the war, and which ironically was propagated by the national body formed, in part, to change this.

The EOG grant illustrates other aspects of the Council's perception of the commercial and cultural role of Britten's music in English society. Although the Arts Council provided £3,000, a quarter of the EOG's starting capital, music and opera grants in the year to 31 March 1948 amounted to £193,440; of this, £98,000 was allocated to Covent Garden and £23,000 to Sadler's Wells.[51] Sadler's Wells is the more relevant comparison because of its size and the scope of its aims, but also because of the iconic nature of Covent Garden; yet Sadler's Wells was less committed to British opera than it was to more commercially viable ventures. The Arts Council was soon to grapple with 'positive discrimination' for British music, but in culturally bleak post-war England it was not yet easy to allocate funds to projects lacking obvious commercial appeal, on the argument that they would define and promote a British cultural identity. It was considered far more important to encourage institutions to develop by enabling them to mount works with mass appeal. In 1947–8 grants to Covent Garden and Sadler's Wells increased by approximately 75 per cent and 55 per cent respectively over the previous year.

There is one further aspect of the EOG's grant to be considered. When William Fell, Arts Council representative in Cambridge, requested extra Arts Council funding in early 1947 to allow the Group to present a season in Cambridge, Wilson replied that no more money could be allowed, and his secretary added that 'The impression I got from Mr. Wilson was that the costs of this Company are too high, and that they must learn to cut their cloth accordingly'.[52] By the end of the year Wilson's assessment of the Group's costs proved correct, but in mid-1947 the EOG interpreted its position quite differently. An estimate of its expenses and receipts for the coming seasons at Glyndebourne, The Hague, Amsterdam, and Lucerne, listed production costs at £8,000 and receipts, including the Arts Council grant and private donations, at £7,050—a manageable deficit.[53] Yet at the end of 1947 production expenses totalled £23,200, which was over three times the June figure (Table 3.2). Lack of experience had combined with facile optimism to produce hopelessly inaccurate estimates. Receipts for the European tour were considerably smaller than for Glyndebourne,[54] and Crozier lamented that despite financial support from the British Council for the Group's tour, the venture lost the EOG around £3,000 for the twelve performances.[55]

[51] *The Arts Council of Great Britain Annual Report 1947–48*, 22.

[52] Wilson's secretary to Fell, undated [late April/early May 1947]. ACGB, Minutes and Correspondence of the EOG.

[53] BPL, EOG, General Files 4, 1947.

[54] BPL, EOG, Cash Book, 1947.

[55] Eric Crozier, *Aldeburgh Festival Programme Book*, 1948, quoted in Carpenter, 253.

Table 3.2 Summary of income and expenditure of the English Opera Group, 1947–1949[a]

Year	Expenditure (£)		Income (£)	
1947	Running expenses	23,200	Ordinary income	19,300
	Production expenses	4,500	Arts Council grant	3,000
	Management and sundry	3,300	Donations	3,700
			Loss	5,000
	Total	31,000	Total	31,000
1948	Running expenses	13,300	Ordinary income	14,500
	Production expenses	5,400	Arts Council grant	5,000
	Management and sundry	4,500	Donations (film rights)	3,000
			Loss	700
	Total	23,200	Total	23,200
1949	Running expenses	13,000	Ordinary income	14,100
	Production expenses	3,500	Arts Council grant	3,000
	Management and sundry	2,700	Guarantees paid	2,000
	Profit	1,400	Donations	1,500
	Total	20,600	Total	20,600

[a] Compiled from information in a letter from Lawrie to Pooley, 17 Nov. 1950. BPL, EOG, General Files 4, 1950.

Although an underestimation of expenses is understandable in the first season of any artistic venture, the deficit was to cast a long shadow over future seasons.

Table 3.2 requires careful interpretation. James Lawrie, the experienced and diplomatic chairman of the EOG, sent these figures to Sir Ernest Pooley, intending them to paint a dark picture of Arts Council ambivalence against a backdrop of sagacious financial management and artistic integrity within the EOG. This backdrop is partly true for 1948 and 1949, although figures have been tidied up to make the record of management seem better than it actually was.[56] In spite of the sanitized accounts, the Group's total running costs in 1947 are not only extraordinarily high compared with its own assessment of June 1947, but are still greater than its expenditure in the following years. The budget figures are also nearly three times the amount sought by the directors when they formed the company—a fact of limited significance until the implications are considered: had the directors managed to raise the £12,000 working capital originally

[56] The deficit for 1947 listed by Lawrie is £5,000 compared with £6,000, which was the figure recognized at the time in the EOG's internal accounts. Although a profit of £1,400 may have been made on activities in 1949, the balance sheet for this year records a bank overdraft of almost £3,600.

sought, rather than the £7,000 they achieved, the accounts for 1947 would almost have balanced, even if that capital had been used to pay off the deficit rather than being invested in assets for the company's future use.

The deficit was the culmination of a number of factors, although the 1947 Glyndebourne season was not one of them. The terms negotiated with Christie for *Lucretia* had been generous: 60 per cent of takings, and a free rehearsal period (with the exception of overtime staff wages).[57] Although in 1947 Covent Garden seated four times as many people as Glyndebourne, the financial capacity of the two venues was approximately the same, because of contrasting ticket prices.[58] With a financial capacity of approximately £1,000 per performance, the economic potential of the Glyndebourne season for the EOG was considerable; the Group received over £5,000 for ten performances of *Albert Herring* and two performances of *Lucretia*.[59] These receipts suggest an audience totalling at least 70 per cent capacity, an excellent figure for a new British opera, but not particularly surprising in view of the peculiar social environment of Glyndebourne, with its established and conservative audience, often more interested in being seen than in the actual opera or production. Christie allegedly greeted friends at the first performance of *Albert Herring* by saying 'This isn't *our* kind of thing, you know'.[60]

The provincial tour of the two operas and the short season at Covent Garden compounded the economic problems of the European tour. Although the Group had negotiated a guaranteed minimum in several of the venues, the figure agreed upon was far less than the cost of performance. Artists' wages for the seasons in Newcastle, Bournemouth, and Oxford were £1,125, £1,348, and £1,345 respectively, but the Group's share of receipts was only £700, £810, and £1,143.[61] Those who had been disappointed with *The Rape of Lucretia*, Britten's first operatic venture after *Grimes*, were more than ready to despair at *Herring*. Despite positive public reaction, the opera was labelled by critics variously as a 'charade' and 'a diverting piece on the second plane', and the composer 'a first-rate opera talent going partly to waste'.[62] These reviews had immediate influence on Peter Diamand, who had booked *Herring* for a season in Holland; after reading Frank Howes in *The Times*, Diamand attempted to cancel his booking.[63] The impact of the critics on regional

[57] Directors' Meeting, 11 Feb. 1947. ACGB, Minutes and Correspondence of the EOG.

[58] Eric Walter White, *The Rise of English Opera* (1951), 204. This was not the case with *The Rape of Lucretia*. The financial capacity for this production was £618 owing to the revised prices set by Glyndebourne for a new opera outside the conventional Glyndebourne Festival.

[59] BPL, EOG Cash Book, 1947.

[60] Eric Crozier, 'Staging first productions 1', in David Herbert (ed.), *The Operas of Benjamin Britten* (1979), 29.

[61] BPL, EOG Cash Book, 1947.

[62] Frank Howes, *The Times*, 21 June 1947; William McNaught, *Manchester Guardian*, 21 June 1947; Ernest Newman, *Sunday Times*, 29 June 1947. Quoted in Carpenter, 252.

[63] Ibid. 253.

audiences is less tangible, but not negligible. Crozier, who credited Christie with the phrase 'charade', viewed *Albert Herring* as the final breakdown in the relationship between Britten and Glyndebourne. 'After all, it takes place in a shop; I don't know if he [Christie] had ever been in a shop.'[64]

But if costs were high in the Group's first season, so were receipts. Ordinary income, generated from box-office receipts and broadcast fees, was significantly higher in 1947 than in the following years (Table 3.2). Debt would curtail the EOG's activities in later years, but it is tempting to view 1947's high ordinary income as the result of an extended season planned by optimistic EOG directors, ignorant of the economics of opera. This was partly true: the directors had hoped that long seasons would generate large income, although by late 1947 they could see that the result was clearly not as they had anticipated:

> Mr. Crozier stressed the point that takings were generally disappointing and did not meet the Company's running costs, quite apart from paying off any proportion of production costs. The result of this was that whereas we had hoped to gain by performing as long and as often as possible, in practice the Company lost on every performance given. Some of the loss had been offset by profits to the Company on broadcasts and recording, and by the profits (amounting to something over £1,000) from the Glyndebourne season of 3½ weeks.[65]

Income from broadcasts and recordings was considerable. The Third Programme broadcast two Glyndebourne performances of *Albert Herring* and one of *Lucretia*. In addition, a recording of an *Albert Herring* rehearsal was broadcast twice in the run-up to the first performance, and a discussion between Britten, Crozier, and Piper on 'How to Make an Opera'—a significant conversation given Britten and Crozier's *Let's Make an Opera* only two years later—was also broadcast at the time of the premiere.[66] In all, the broadcasts and recordings netted the Group nearly £4,500,[67] and 'brought the Company a substantial profit over and above what had to be paid out in fees to the performers'.[68]

For all such economic uncertainty, the EOG enjoyed significant financial advantages over many conventional opera companies. Although hire of music and payment of performing right still applied, these fees, minus commission, were eventually returned to Britten; as music director of the EOG, he usually compensated for this expenditure by not charging the Group for his services, or

[64] GFO, recorded interview with Crozier, Nancy Evans, and Alan Blyth, 17 Apr. 1992. In the same interview, Crozier states that Christie found the dress rehearsal audience 'very vulgar' because it laughed 'long and loud' at the opera.

[65] Directors' Meeting, 13 Oct. 1947. ACGB, Minutes and Correspondence of the EOG.

[66] General Meeting, 15 July 1947. ACGB, Minutes and Correspondence of the EOG. Although recorded in the minutes under this title, the BBC title was 'An Opera is Planned'.

[67] BPL, balance sheet 1947. Takings (£14,857) subtracted from ordinary income (£19,300).

[68] General Meeting, 15 July 1947. ACGB, Minutes and Correspondence of the EOG.

by charging very little. Occasionally, in the best traditions of Thomas Beecham and Balfour Gardiner, Britten made cash donations to the Group.[69] Furthermore, it was always possible to pay soloists less than they would have received from established companies, because many of the singers wished to be associated with a project in which they believed. 'We are a happy Group and work well together with a fanatical devotion to Ben,' wrote Margaret Ritchie, the schoolmistress Mrs Wordsworth in *Albert Herring*.[70] It was a fertile combination—limited finances and the cult of the guru—and was later subtly exploited.[71] But in the company's first season, salaries were unrealistically high. While rehearsing *Lucretia*, Emelie Hooke (Female Chorus) and Denis Dowling (Junius) received a weekly wage of £6 (plus free board and accommodation); and Joan Cross (Lady Billows) and Peter Pears (Albert) each received £32 for the first three performances of *Herring*.[72] Pears had received half this for three performances of *Peter Grimes* only two years before,[73] and although that was with an ensemble emerging from a war-restricted economy, it was possibly a better model for a new company in its first season than that adopted.

Albert Herring was the first of Britten's operas to be 'commissioned' by the EOG, and it wears an optimistic face. The orchestra of thirteen is identical to that used for *Lucretia*—single winds, horn, string quartet, double bass, harp, percussion, piano (played by the conductor)—reflecting an economy of resources and a recognition that the two operas would be in repertory together and should sensibly employ identical orchestras. Such economy was not applied to the singers, and two separate casts existed for the repertory operas. *Herring*'s cast of thirteen is larger than that for *Lucretia*, but it is unlikely that Britten could have created the bustling village environment with fewer characters. In this sense the choice of *Albert Herring* as the EOG's first new work owes something to Britten's emancipation from the restrictions of Sadler's Wells and Glyndebourne, whilst initially retaining the financial security of the latter; it was to be four years before Britten would write another opera with the promise of such security.

Begging for Opera

By mid-July 1947 the artistic directors of the EOG had practically decided that Britten would 'rearrange' John Gay's *The Beggar's Opera* for production in the

[69] He also made donations to the Aldeburgh Festival. See Ch. 5.

[70] Ritchie to Wilson, 27 June 1947. ACGB, Minutes and Correspondence of the EOG.

[71] When an amalgamation between the EOG and Covent Garden was discussed in 1954, David Webster of Covent Garden stated that he 'had heard that the Group paid very low fees and questioned whether that could continue if the Group was officially part of Covent Garden'. Memo by Douglas, 11 Mar. 1954. BPL, EOG Correspondence, 1954.

[72] BPL, EOG Cash Book, 1947.

[73] Sadler's Wells Opera Salary List, week ending 23 June 1945. Sadler's Wells Archive.

following season. 'It was unlikely that any composer could have a new opera ready in time for the 1948 season, but we should still hope to put on a new opera in 1949 by some composer other than Mr. Britten.'[74] By January 1948, when Britten commenced work on the score, the opera, which had originally been chosen for reasons of expediency, was now required to be a commercial success: the EOG was £6,000 in debt.

There was every reason for the EOG's artistic directors to think that *The Beggar's Opera* would succeed where *Albert Herring* had not. Nigel Playfair's 1920 production of Austin's realization of the work had offered all the appeal of a West End musical, with audiences to match. It was performed 1,463 times, and frequently revived later in that decade and in the early 1930s.[75] A new production was created for Glyndebourne in 1940; although it failed to repeat the success of the early 1920s, it once more brought the opera into the public eye. Concurrent with this revival, Edward Dent made his own realization of the score for Sadler's Wells, where Tyrone Guthrie was then working.[76] Guthrie was to be Britten's choice for collaborator, once he had committed himself to arranging a new version of the opera.

The story of *The Beggar's Opera* is less complicated than that of *Lucretia* or *Herring*. Although Guthrie and Britten were keen to reveal the darker elements of the opera, which had been lost in the frippery of Playfair's production, the directors of the People's Palace saw this as no obstacle to commercial success and in February chose the unfinished work to reopen the theatre in October: the combination of Britten's talent and Gay's plot assuaged any doubts. Not everyone would have been sanguine at the prospect of Britten realizing the opera. The concept of authenticity in early music, already emerging in England during the 1930s, became a stronger, if slow-fused, force after 1945: Britten's approach to this complicated and contentious issue—established in his 1940s folk-song arrangements and realizations of Purcell songs—was directly opposed to the teachings of scholars such as Dent or Thurston Dart. In spirit, Britten was much closer to Wanda Landowska who, in explaining her approach to Bach, said 'little do I care if, to attain the proper effect, I use means that were not exactly those available to Bach'.[77] To Britten, 'effect' was more important than so-called 'authenticity', yet his slightly dismissive tone in the introduction to the Boosey & Hawkes edition of *Orpheus Britannicus* suggests that he was well aware of the growing arguments for the latter. Presenting the work as a 'performing edition for contemporary conditions', Britten and Pears castigated past editions for

[74] Directors' Meeting, 15 July 1947. ACGB, Minutes and Correspondence of the EOG.

[75] The normally cynical and cold-hearted Evelyn Waugh attended this production six times in 1920.

[76] Eric Walter White, *Rise of English Opera*, 152.

[77] Wanda Landowska, *Landowska on Music* (1964), 356.

lacking the 'Purcellian spirit', before asserting that, as in Purcell's time, the figured basses had been elaborated in a 'personal way'. 'But it has been the constant endeavour of the arranger to apply to these realizations something of that mixture of clarity, brilliance, tenderness and strangeness which shines out in all Purcell's music.'[78]

There were commercial considerations in all of this; would Britten both antagonize serious musicologists and forfeit the popular appeal of the work by realizing it in his 'personal way'? Britten dismissed the serious musicologists—for their ideas and possibly for the patently small section of the market that they represented. Yet in dismissing one party, he was not necessarily embracing the other. The composer Herbert Murrill, Head of Music at the BBC, a few years later pinpointed the commercial and musical issues at stake:

> If the musical output on the various Services were fully interlocking (and assuming Light, Home and Third to have equal coverage) I believe it would be right to suggest that the Beggar's Opera would be more acceptable to Light and Home listeners in Austin's or Dent's edition and that the vastly more debatable Britten realisation be given on Third. Similarly with his arrangements of Folk Songs and old melodies: Warlock, Keel, Sharp and others are musically excellent and unquestioned: the more experimental settings of Britten would seem more suited to Third. Purcell realisations in Britten's hands have become matters of argument and contention in the musical world and are in some quarters actively disliked. If the enjoyment of Purcell's music in, say, the Golden Sonata or the Queen's Epicedium is the reason for broadcasting it, the older realisations are better. If an examination of the principles governing thorough-bass and its realisation are intended, Britten's editions will provoke discussion. Therefore, generally, I think we would suggest the more normal realisations on Home and Light, and Britten's realisations on Third . . .[79]

If Britten's 'abnormal' realization of *The Beggar's Opera* was thought more suitable for the deliberately elitist Third Programme, would it ever attract popular audiences, and in doing so solve the problem of the Group's deficit?

Sir Michael Balcon, an independent film producer associated with the Rank organization, was confident that it would, and halved the EOG's deficit by purchasing the film rights. These rights were to include an option on the use of designs, freedom to study the production in detail, and access to the advice of the artistic directors.[80] Although the film was never made, Balcon's initial enthusiasm for the project was genuine: in March 1948 Crozier reported to the directors that agreement between the various parties was imminent, and that 'Boosey & Hawkes as well as Mr. Britten had now offered to make over their respective

[78] *Orpheus Britannicus*, ed. Benjamin Britten and Peter Pears (1948).

[79] Murrill to Wellington (Controller, Home Service), 30 July 1951. BBCWAC, Composer File 2, Benjamin Britten, 1951–62.

[80] Directors' Meeting, 13 Oct. 1947. ACGB, Minutes and Correspondence of the EOG.

financial share to the English Opera Group who would thus get the total sum of £3,000'.[81]

Boosey & Hawkes duly made its contribution to the EOG, but the process provoked a certain amount of friction, which left Britten in no doubt that his publisher, or more specifically Boosey, was severely critical of the Group's business dealings.[82] The publisher's share of the film rights was £1,000, about which the EOG was not at all happy. Following some quick foot-work, Crozier in mid-February was able to inform Britten that Boosey was prepared to recommend to his Board that the Company either lend or give the £1,000 to the EOG, but that it might be repaid from Britten's future royalties. Crozier rather dangerously passed on Boosey's view that if the EOG were to collapse, it would rid Britten of a major distraction and would thus allow him to compose more music.[83] Britten wrote to Boosey and received a defensive reply, which conceded that the EOG could retain the £1,000, and which left little doubt that publisher had been mauled by composer for his views. Once opened, the subject was not contained:

> Now, my dear Ben, I have never been 'venomous' about the EOG. I know how dear it is to your heart and I appreciate its artistic value and what it has done. I must confess that I have had a feeling that you have been asked to bear more than your full share of the burden in many directions in keeping it going; but there comes a time when one may be simply throwing good money after bad, and before I saw this year's programme I admit I felt that the contribution you were making together with the share that I knew you want us to forego was only doing this very thing.[84]

It was a responsible reply from a caring, if interested, party. As a gesture of goodwill, the donation demonstrates Britten's status in the eyes of his publisher, though Boosey, like Wilson before him, continued to feel a certain unease. After seeing the programme for 1948, Boosey was 'not more sanguine, that would be too strong a word, but less disturbed about the future, since it seems much more possible to calculate the actual money required to run the scheme than has been the case heretofore'.[85]

This was not an entirely accurate assessment, but the directors were too busy trying to cover the deficit to quibble. As with many of the brilliantly named characters in this new operatic realization, penury bred inventiveness. Lawrie, hoping that Danny Kaye's 'brilliant take-off of a German singer' might lead him to support the art-form he parodied so successfully, wrote to the comedian outlining the immediate need for £5,000, and the long-term need for a similar amount.[86] More successful, if less inspired, was the request in mid-1948 for loans

[81] Directors' Meeting, 9 Mar. 1948. ACGB, minutes and correspondence of the EOG.

[82] In 1947 Hawkes had actually been invited to become a founding director of the EOG.

[83] Crozier to Britten, 16 Feb. 1948. BPL, Crozier Correspondence, 1948.

[84] Boosey to Britten, 24 Feb. 1948. BPL, EOG Correspondence, 1948.

[85] Ibid.

[86] Lawrie to Kaye, 17 Feb. 1948. BPL, EOG General Files 4, 1948.

from people connected with the Group. Britten, Lawrie, John Piper, Basil Wright, and even Mrs Wright (senior) were part of a small coterie who contributed £3,800 to EOG finances.[87] But by mid-1948, with the production of *The Beggar's Opera* in hand, this was absorbed (probably precipitated) by the current season's expenses rather than the previous year's.

The Group's efforts to economize and capitalize are discernible in Table 3.3, a budget compiled in early May 1948 projecting expenditure and income for the imminent Cambridge season. The inflated artists' fees for one week of the previous season would now cover total running costs in the first week of the opera's run (week ending 29 May). The artists' rehearsal salaries in each of the two weeks leading up to the opera (£306) were shared by twenty-three singers, and would have included subsistence allowance, since the company was by then based in Cambridge. And in order to combat the vagaries of attendance that had affected receipts in the previous year, the EOG received a set fee. Although at £1,250 it was higher than the average return on the previous year's regional performances, it made little impact on the EOG's overdraft, which stood at over £8,000 after the first week of *The Beggar's Opera*. Clearly the opera would have to be further exploited if production costs were to be recouped.

Opportunities for exploitation over the next month were limited—not so much in number but in financial potential. Costs were covered for performances of *Albert Herring* at the first Aldeburgh Festival in early June, but the financially precarious nature of this new venture allowed nothing more.[88] The fee for performances in Holland (£900) was absorbed entirely by travel expenses and salaries; remuneration for performances at the Cheltenham Festival was £300 short of the total costs for the week; travel to Belgium consumed the entirety of the fee for performances in late July; and a return to Cambridge, again for a week of performances and £1,250, contributed another £300 to the Group's mounting deficit.[89]

These attempts to exploit the opera established that the product, as it stood, was not financially viable: expenditure continually exceeded income. Despite initiatives to cut costs, the size of the cast ensured that little or nothing of the set fee survived the deduction of the artists' fees, let alone other production expenses. Setting a higher fee in England was a wise precaution, but if a percentage system was in operation above this set fee, audiences were never large enough for it to be invoked. The opera was not a commercial success, and many considered that it was Britten's score more than anything that limited the number of performances in the years following. In 'personalising' the work Britten made it genre-specific—more opera than musical—and lost the simplicity and ambiguity that had traditionally attracted non-opera audiences. He kept songs that

[87] BPL, EOG General Files 4, 1948. [88] See Ch. 5.

[89] BPL, EOG General Files 4, 1948.

Table 3.3 English Opera Group, estimated balance sheet, May 1948 (£)[a]

Receipts	Expenditure		Totals	Overdraft
	Outstanding bills	768	768	4,102
	Week ending 8 May (London)			
	Artists' salaries	250		
	Stage staff salaries	36		
	Management salaries	38		
	Rent rehearsal room	10		
	Travel to Cambridge	40		
	Production expenses	50		
	Management expenses	20	444	4,546
	Week ending 15 May (Cambridge)			
	Artists' salaries	306		
	Stage staff salaries	40		
	Management salaries	38		
	Rent	10		
	Production expenses	100		
	Management travel and expenses	20		
	Orchestral rehearsal expenses	172		
	Insurance	50	736	5,282
	Week ending 22 May (Cambridge)			
	Artists' salaries	306		
	Stage staff salaries	60		
	Management salaries	38		
	Production expenses	100		
	Management travel and expenses	20		
	Orchestral rehearsal expenses	300	824	6,106
	Week ending 29 May (Cambridge)			
(Cambridge fee)	Total running costs	1,400		
1,250	Production expenses	2,000	3,400	8,256

[a] BPL, EOG General Files 4, 1948.

Austin had excised; introduced ensembles where Gay had solos; wrote choruses where there were none, sometimes loading them with rhythmic complexities. For his now standard 'repertory' orchestra, he made an exceptionally clever realization, using a harmonic language far removed from that of Gay's original. Britten's conception of the work was truly operatic, and drew upon an even more traditional concept of opera than that of his two previous stage works.

Many critics were sensitive to the paradoxical score: the music critic of the *Birmingham Weekly Post* stated that the work was 'one for connoisseurs. The music composed by Benjamin Britten lifts the well-known airs on to a grand opera plane.'[90] To the music critic of *The Times*, the question was not how much modernism a diatonic tune would hold but whether the jewel would still sparkle.[91] The critic of the *Evening News* adapted this idea for his own readers, spurning such a highbrow metaphor along the way: 'It is brilliantly done. The only question is whether it ought to be done at all. It would be an ingenious literary experiment no doubt to rewrite "Baa Baa Black Sheep" in the style of T. S. Eliot, but one suspects that some of the simple charm of the original would be lost.'[92] And Charles Stuart in the *Observer* warned that there were few things Britten hadn't done with Pepusch's 'untouchable' tunes. 'Those for whom the Frederic Austin-Lovat Frease [*sic*] version at Hammersmith is still a green and sacred memory will regard the whole business as a personal affront.'[93]

Guthrie, who had antagonized Britten and Pears during rehearsal with his criticisms of the singer ('You look as if you're doing Stainer's *Crucifixion* on skates at Scunthorpe'[94]), contributed little to the opera's libretto. The text was taken entirely from Gay's and Pepusch's third edition, except for 350 words of Guthrie's own. Functional rather than inspired (Beggar: 'Hurry! Hurry! Change the scene! The customers are waiting!'), they nonetheless formed the basis of Guthrie's request for a share of the royalties. Britten's offer of 10 per cent of his share was double what Guthrie had suggested,[95] although irony may have been intended: the offer was made in late September, by which time Britten was probably aware that 10 per cent of his share would never amount to very much.

Making an Opera

In July 1948 Britten told a correspondent for the journal *Stage* that he was working on a children's opera: 'There are too few operas . . . which are designed not only to appeal to children, but to be within their range of performance and production.'[96] Britten and Crozier had first discussed the possibility of writing a work for children in February 1947,[97] yet they did not agree on a subject until well over a year later. Although works such as *Friday Afternoons* (1935), *A Ceremony of Carols* (1943), and *The Young Person's Guide to the Orchestra* (1945) had

[90] *Birmingham Weekly Post*, 1 Oct. 1948.

[91] *The Times*, 28 May 1948.

[92] *Evening News*, 19 Sept. 1948.

[93] Charles Stuart, 'The Beggar's Opera', *Observer*, 12 Sept. 1948. 'Frease's' real name was Fraser.

[94] Carpenter, 267.

[95] Guthrie to Britten, 3 Oct. 1948. BPL, Guthrie Correspondence, 1948.

[96] 'Opera for Children', *Stage* (15 July 1948).

[97] Carpenter, 273. In an unpublished article, 'The Little Sweep' (1993), Crozier says that the collaboration began in autumn 1946. The later date is taken from Crozier's unpublished autobiography, written before the 1993 article, and is more likely.

shown Britten's interest in working with children and his credentials as an educationist, there is no doubt that the composer would have been attracted to an opera that would be quick to write and cheap to perform, and have a potential audience larger than that of his other operas (children, after all, would have to be taken to the opera by adults).

Britten began work on the composition sketch in April 1949 and finished it in two weeks; at the time he was under considerable pressure to complete his *Spring Symphony*, then planned for a performance in Tanglewood in the summer. The idea of dividing the opera into two parts—the first an explanation of some technical aspects of writing and staging an opera, and the second the opera itself—probably came from a series of films made by the Ministry of Education in the 1940s. One of these, a film on ballet, explored the development of ideas for a ballet, the rehearsal of the actual choreography, and then the ballet itself. Crozier saw this film in July 1948 and wrote to Britten about it a few days later. There was a possibility that the Ministry of Education would commission a short opera for this very series, but Crozier's insistence that this should be written for film alone was impracticable as far as the EOG's finances and repertory were concerned, and was not pursued. Nor was Crozier's suggested synopsis—coyly entrenched in the middle-class England of vicars, choir-boys, and the Oxford–Cambridge boat-race—which demonstrated the composer's admirable judgement. The plot centred on two villages, each with 200 inhabitants or so, and

> a keen rivalry between their teams of bell-ringers and their choirs of boys, and with an annual competition organised by their respective vicars for bell-ringing, singing and sports, which could include everything from darts in the local pubs to a miniature Oxford–Cambridge boat-race (in compliment to the vicars) between the village choirs on the river joining the two places.[98]

The prize for the winning village? A supper hosted by the losing village. The story of the sweep boy, based on Blake's poem 'The Chimney Sweeper' from his *Songs of Innocence*, was chosen soon after.

The background to the opera's composition was once more one of financial adversity. The EOG had recorded a bank overdraft of £5,400 at the end of 1948, which had led to extended negotiations with the Arts Council. Writing without the knowledge of the EOG directors, Crozier sent a devastating appraisal of the Council's operations to Eric Walter White, the Council's liaison officer for the EOG. 'It seems that the Arts Council is compelled to . . . support only those enterprises that are spectacular in intention, certain of wide publicity and likely to be immediately popular . . .'.[99] Invoking a complaint that has remained a yardstick in criticism of the Arts Council, Crozier expressed a fervent personal protest against a policy which 'doubles the large Covent Garden subsidy of

[98] Crozier to Britten, 2 Aug. 1948. BPL, Crozier Correspondence, 1948.

[99] Crozier to White, 21 Feb. 1949. BPL, EOG General Files 4, 1949.

£60,000 in the current year and threatens to halve the small English Opera Group subsidy of £5,000, which pampers the successful at the expense of the struggling venture.'[100] Embarrassed about the possibility of antagonizing the Council, James Lawrie intervened, requesting that White ignore the letter. Although Crozier's distress over a cut in the EOG's grant was based on unofficial information, it was proved correct one month later. Asked why the Group was offered only £3,000—£2,000 less than the previous year—White asserted that the Council did not have the facilities to offer the full amount.[101] And although Crozier had been incorrect about a doubling of the Covent Garden grant, the truth would have offered him even less comfort: Covent Garden's grant of £145,000 was increased to £170,000 in 1949–50.[102]

Aware that the grant's reduction would be viewed with little enthusiasm by Barclays Bank, whose correspondence with the Group was by then persistent in its content and volume, Oliver Lyttelton, Chairman of the EOG, requested that the Council guarantee a minimum grant of £3,000 for the following year, 'irrespective of the programme undertaken'.[103] A guarantee of at least £3,000 was provided, although the proviso—or more accurately lack of proviso—suggested by Lyttelton was rejected.[104] Lawrie had to take action over the dilemma: the grant could be used to appease the bank or finance new productions, but not both. Reduced seasons and minimal expenditure for the next eighteen months were accepted by the Board as essential for the Group's survival.

Britten was conscious of the EOG's perilous footing when he began work on *Let's Make an Opera*. Two very different production budgets for the opera (Table 3.4), one made in November 1948, the other in March 1949, suggest that Britten's conception of the opera changed as a result of the Group's finances.

It is possible that costs in the first budget were inflated in an attempt to obtain more money from the Council, although this is unlikely: past experience had shown that expensive production estimates rarely improved the strained relationship between patron and client. It is more likely that Britten's own approach to the work changed in the course of four months. For an orchestra to require six rehearsals, as indicated in the pre-composition budget, Britten must have been planning to compose a difficult score. For professional singers to need four weeks to rehearse their parts, and children eight weeks, Britten must have envisaged quite difficult or elaborate roles. And the allocation of nearly £900 for sets and costumes suggests a plan for the opera quite different from the eventual production. In spite

[100] Ibid.

[101] Minutes of Directors' Meeting, 18 Mar. 1949. ACGB, Minutes and Correspondence of the EOG.

[102] *The Arts Council of Great Britain Annual Report 1949–50*, 26.

[103] Lyttelton to Glasgow, 19 Mar. 1949. ACGB, Minutes and Correspondence of the EOG.

[104] Minutes of Directors' Meeting, 25 Mar. 1949. Ibid.

Table 3.4 Budgeted production costs (£) of *Let's Make an Opera*, November 1948 and March 1949[a]

	1948	1949
1. Professional singers		
Four weeks at £15 each per week	240	
Two weeks at £12 each per week		120
2. Designer's fee	120	50
3. Scenery	500	40
4. Fifteen costumes	375	150
5. Producer	100	
Three weeks at £15 per week		45
6. Orchestra rehearsals:		
Six at £25 each	150	
Two at £18 each		36
7. Conductor		
Four weeks at £25 per week	100	
Two weeks at £20 per week		40
8. Fares and transport		40
9. Music coach		10
10. Props	60	
11. Rehearsal of children, over eight weeks	320	
Total	1,965	531

[a] Compiled from information in a letter from Sweeting to White, 25 Nov. 1948. ACGB, Minutes and Correspondence of the EOG; and BPL, EOG General Files 4, 1948 and 1949.

of the simple story and the intended audience, the earlier budget suggests a complex work—more like *The Beggar's Opera* than *Paul Bunyan*.

The uncomplicated show that Britten completed is slightly out of character. His previous works for children retain the harmonic language and approach to melody employed in his works for adults. And *Noye's Fludde*, Britten's next children's opera, is far more complex in concept and music than *The Little Sweep*. Wary of the accusations of elitism that had plagued his realization of *The Beggar's Opera*, and keeping the EOG's penury in mind, Britten wrote an unambiguous 'hit'. Furthermore, without chorus, with minor principals played by children at little or no cost, with an orchestra of seven and only one set, the hit was undoubtedly Britten's most cost-effective work for stage.

The opera received excellent reviews and houses in its first season. Even Frank Howes in *The Times* was appreciative, although he threatened to cross from appreciation to condescension with his opening line 'Once upon a time lived an unhappy little boy called Sam'.[105] Ironically, the work's success undermined

[105] Carpenter, 276.

aspects of its financial potential. For its December season at the Lyric Theatre, Hammersmith, two casts were needed to provide the eight performances each week. In order to explain the double casts, Elizabeth Sweeting, the General Manager of the Group, asserted that the professional singers had commitments of their own to fulfil during the busy Christmas season, and to maintain a 'high standard of performance, it had been essential to give both casts performances, rather than use one cast with understudies only'.[106] Child labour laws would also have affected casting and performance of the opera. Even so, it was considerably cheaper to run than its predecessors (Table 3.5).

One contentious expense during the season was the performing right and hire fee (Table 3.5). Reference to Boosey & Hawkes's share in the opera's royalties cunningly appeared in an article at the time, its source anonymous, hinting at supposed exploitation. Erwin Stein, Britten's principal contact at Boosey & Hawkes, offered to discuss the matter with the publishers, and for the last three weeks of the season (from after Christmas into the first half of January) publisher royalties were waived. When Britten's next opera for the EOG was ready for performance, the composer negotiated with his publisher over this issue, achieving exclusive rights for the Group for a set period.[107]

Table 3.5 Running costs (£) of *Let's Make an Opera*, Lyric Theatre, 1949[a]

Costs	Week ending					
	19 Nov.	26 Nov.	3 Dec.	10 Dec.	17 Dec.	31 Dec.
Management expenses	2	5	5	5	5	3
Insurance	4	4	4	4	4	4
Salaries	575	551	559	548	572	581
Living bonuses		7	3	3	3	3
Stage hire	5	4	4	4	4	19
Stage expenses	4	2	3	6	11	8
Comp. tickets	16	7	7	7	11	4
Hire of electrics					2	2
PR and hire	92	92	92	92	92	
Piano expenses					4	9
Gratuities					8	
Total	698	672	677	669	716	633
Receipts	675	675	675	675	675	728

[a] BPL, EOG General Files 4, 1949. Figures have been rounded off to the nearest pound.

[106] Minutes of Directors' Meeting, 22 Dec. 1949. BPL, EOG General Files 4, 1949.
[107] The opera *The Turn of the Screw* is discussed later in this chapter.

The entire season, including one week in Cambridge and one in Brighton, reaped a profit of £265: it was the first of Britten's operas to be self-supporting. The point was not lost on the Group's management: Elizabeth Sweeting, whose role it was to pacify the ever-anxious Barclays Bank, wrote to Lawrie saying that 'now that we have a regular money-maker in the Children's Opera, it would be disastrous to be treated too severely by the bank at this stage'.[108] This was a novel situation for the EOG. And for the first time since the Group had burnt its fingers with *Albert Herring*, the new General Manager, when he opened negotiations with the Lyric Theatre in March 1950 for a Christmas season of the opera, asked for remuneration on a percentage basis rather than for a set fee.[109]

Let's Make an Opera was revived frequently during the 1950s. Norman Del Mar, the conductor on many of these occasions, 'wasn't sure that in the end we didn't go on doing it too long'.[110] Initially there was no tangible reason for restraint, and plenty for exploitation. Regional opera tours remained expensive, and it soon became obvious that opportunities for profit were limited; a four-week tour in November 1950 lost the Group £437, against the budgeted deficit of £110. Yet a London season of the opera immediately following this tour resulted in a profit of £329, commensurate with the estimated £336. Despite losing over £1,000 on a 1951–2 season at the Lyric Hammersmith, attendance was comparable with that in the opera's first season.[111] And although a run at the Royal Court Theatre in 1955–6 resulted in a profit of only £105, receipts in the final three weeks averaged £1,500. It was the closest thing to a money-maker that the EOG would ever produce.

The Festival of Britain

In 1851 England had mounted the Great Exhibition. Its aim was to display the work of many prominent British and foreign manufacturers and artists—'the beneficial effects of which are not for our own day only, but "for all time"'.[112] Although such benefits were not apparent in every exhibit (a 'Group of Stuffed Cats', for example, five drinking tea and the sixth playing a harpsichord, ambitiously listed as a 'foreign industrial product'[113]), the Exhibition soon became a symbol of England's industrial and economic hegemony—in Thackeray's words, a display of England's 'arms of conquest . . . the trophies of her bloodless war'.[114]

108 Sweeting to Lawrie, 8 Nov. 1949. BPL, EOG General Files 4, 1949.
109 Minutes of Directors' Meeting, 1 Mar. 1950. BPL, EOG General Files 4, 1950.
110 Carpenter, 277.
111 BPL, EOG account books (salaries) 1947–57, excluding 1948 and 1950; BPL, EOG General Files 4, 1952.
112 *The Crystal Palace and its Contents* (1851), 196.
113 Ibid. 206.
114 Thackeray, quoted in 'United Kingdom', *Encyclopaedia Britannica*, xxix. 85.

Yet many thought that these 'arms of conquest' were exploited with little skill over the next fifty years: an uncited manufacturer, concerned with the implications of free trade, warned other industrialists that 'the day is not far distant, when instead of looking to foreign countries to take your goods, you will have to look at home to find *some remedy for the poverty which the increasing power of production is fast bringing upon our country*'.[115] But the threat seemed idle when seen against the splendour and promise of Britain's achievement.

The contrast between 1851 and 1951—the year of the Festival of Britain—could scarcely have been greater. Rationing, in place until 1950 (and even after this date for some commodities), appeared symbolic of Britain's economic position at the time: cautious and constrained. The Festival of Britain, a celebration of the hundredth anniversary of the Great Exhibition, was a deliberate attempt to regain the initiative displayed at the Crystal Palace—a gesture from Attlee's Labour government. At the time it seemed moderately successful in the arts, with increased government expenditure on art, drama, and music, and the construction of new buildings to house them. Apart from the buildings produced for the occasion, though, the Festival's long-term impact was negligible, hampered somewhat by the change of government immediately afterwards, and by a change of direction during Churchill's third term of office.[116] But initially the Festival was intended to inaugurate a new age—one of confident assertion rather than austerity.

In the lead-up to the Festival year, the EOG's leitmotiv returned. Although there was to be no new opera from Britten, and a year of limited undertakings (centred on Aldeburgh and an inevitable season of the children's opera), Lawrie, Clark, and Britten met representatives of the Arts Council on 17 November 1950, to argue 'the urgent need for further financial assistance if the company were to avoid being put into immediate liquidation'.[117] For once the plea was successful—but this was because of the imminence of the Festival of Britain. In addition to the £3,000 already allotted, the EOG was promised a special Festival grant of £5,000 and an advance of £5,000 on the following year's grant.[118] The £10,000 still left the Group £5,000 short of their estimated expenditure for 1951, but promises of financial support from Boosey & Hawkes, and a pruning

[115] *The Disastrous consequences which are likely to arise to the manufacturing trade of this country from the carrying out of the proposed Great Industrial Exhibition of all nations in 1851* (1850?), 14.

[116] Lawrie wrote to Douglas on 9 Nov. 1951: 'I am extremely disturbed about the probable attitude of the new Government to expenditure on such awful unnecessary things as Art. I think you and the Executive Committee ought to make all your future plans on the assumption that we may receive nothing at all from the Arts Council in future. I don't want to be too gloomy, but I don't care much about the temperature in Whitehall insofar as I can gauge it.' BPL, EOG General Files 4, 1951.

[117] Directors' Meeting, 17 Nov. 1950. ACGB, Minutes and Correspondence of the EOG.

[118] Pooley to Lawrie, 22 Nov. 1950. BPL, EOG General Files 4, 1950.

of the budget, brought income in line with expenditure—if solely for 1951. The terms and circumstances of the Council's offer, however, suggest a degree of prejudice against Britten. On enquiring whether the £10,000 was conditional on the implementation of all the Group's plans, Lawrie was informed that the Council hoped the EOG would be in a position to perform several of the works in its repertory, but that it realized that 'its offer would put the Group in a position where it would be forced to effect various economies and, in the case of new productions, it considered that, if possible, priority should be given to Brian Easdale's "The Sleeping Children"'.[119] Britten, who had never been favoured with such 'positive discrimination', now saw it being applied to Easdale: his opera received Council support simply because it was a new British work by someone other than Britten.[120] As such Easdale's opera was an expression of the Council's supposed desire for diversification, very much in line with the original aims of CEMA, but not entirely convincing when compared with the level of funding for Covent Garden, which greatly reduced money available for other projects.

Britten had always been sensitive to the possibility that the EOG might be criticized for performing a repertory consisting entirely of his own works. The EOG's prospectus included 'other composers' in its plans; the directors spoke in 1947 of their desire to stage an opera by 'some composer other than Mr. Britten';[121] at a meeting in February 1949 between the directors of the EOG and the Arts Council it became clear that 'the Group was mindful of the fact that, as regards opera, they had so far produced the works of only one composer. They were anxious to broaden their activities';[122] and in April 1949 the Group made plans to perform works by composers other than Britten in the Festival year.[123] Britten's sensitivity was not misplaced. In June 1952 a pious Mr Stoney wrote a letter to the editor of *Musical Opinion*, criticizing the EOG's record:

> On its establishment in 1947 ... [the EOG] secured Arts Council support and, moreover, asked for contributions from the public to further a policy which included the statement that 'it is part of the Group's purpose to encourage young composers to write for the operatic stage'. Yet, in the five years that have ensued, only one new opera has been produced—Brian Easdale's 'The Sleeping Children'—apart from the operas of Benjamin Britten, who is one of the English Opera Group's Artistic Directors. On the other hand, Lord Harewood stated in the May, 1951, issue of *Opera* that the E.O.G. 'has given no less

[119] Pooley to Lawrie, 25 Nov. 1950. BPL, EOG General Files 4, 1950.

[120] On 1 March the Arts Council had offered the EOG £2,500 to mount *The Sleeping Children* and to repeat it in the Festival year. Ibid.

[121] Directors' Meeting, 15 July 1947. ACGB, Minutes and Correspondence of the EOG.

[122] Memo concerning meeting between Lyttelton, Lawrie, Crozier, Pooley, Denison, and White, 25 Feb. 1949. ACGB, Minutes and Correspondence of the EOG.

[123] Directors' Meeting, 12 Apr. 1949. Ibid.

than 488 stage performances of the four operas by Benjamin Britten, which are included in its repertory'.[124]

Correspondence in *Musical Opinion* ensued: the EOG maintained that the Arts Council grant barely covered overhead costs; in reply, Stoney asked whether it would cost more to put on an opera by Walton, Lambert, Rubbra, Berkeley, or Tippett, 'instead of a whole covey of operas by Mr. Britten?'[125] Stoney's argument hit out in all directions, finding villains in Covent Garden, the Arts Council, and the EOG, and although it post-dates the EOG's attempts to commission operas from other composers, it epitomizes a growing resentment of Britten's success in the early 1950s.[126] The Britten Festival, mounted by the EOG as part of the Festival of Britain, seemed only to fuel this prejudice. Britten's determination that works by other composers should be performed by the EOG in 1951—Easdale's *The Sleeping Children*, Purcell's *Dido and Aeneas*, and Holst's *The Wandering Scholar*—owes something to these criticisms.[127]

For both the EOG and the Festival of Britain, the Britten Festival symbolized British artistic achievement. Lawrie, the Chairman of the EOG, had first hinted at the benefits that the smaller festival would bring to the larger in a letter to the Arts Council in 1950. He stated that without the EOG's involvement there would be no performance of a Britten opera until September, and that there should be no need to point out what a curious anomaly this would appear to a foreign visitor, 'whose idea of British opera is likely to be bounded by the name of Britten, although if he happens to be a musicologist, it may include as well the name of Purcell, whose "Dido and Aeneas" will also be in the Group's repertory'.[128] Even so, the Britten Festival was an ambitious undertaking; a three-week season, seven operas each week, a complex rotation of artists in performances of *The Rape of Lucretia*, *Albert Herring*, *Let's Make an Opera*, and a double-bill of Monteverdi's *Combattimento di Tancredi e Clorinda* and Purcell's *Dido and Aeneas*. *Dido* served a number of purposes. Since most of Britten's energies were absorbed in the composition of *Billy Budd* and its eventual performance at Covent Garden, *Dido* countered any thoughts that Britten might be neglecting the EOG.[129] Basil Coleman has written of the Group's dependence on Britten, and of the divided loyalties that this provoked in the composer;[130]

124 A. Stoney, 'Letter to the Editor', *Musical Opinion* (June 1952), 525.

125 Basil Douglas, *Musical Opinion* (July 1952), 615. A. Stoney, *Musical Opinion* (Aug. 1952), 675.

126 See Ch. 6.

127 The different phases of critical reaction to Britten and his music are discussed in Ch. 6.

128 Unattributed letter [probably Lawrie] to the Arts Council, undated [*c.*1950]. ACGB, Minutes and Correspondence of the EOG. The author's appointment of musicologists as Purcell's custodians highlights the incredible pioneering attitude Britten had towards his older idol, and how much circumstances have changed since then.

129 *Billy Budd* and *Gloriana* are considered in Ch. 4.

130 Basil Coleman, 'Staging first productions 2', in Herbert, *The Operas of Benjamin Britten*, 37.

two years without a new Britten work would have disappointed the company, especially since it was not involved in *Billy Budd* and could claim little of the composer's attention in late 1951. Perhaps remembering the response to his realization of *The Beggar's Opera*, Britten treated *Dido and Aeneas* in a less 'personal' manner. He focused primarily on solving problems in the dramatic construction of the work and on creating a continuo part from Purcell's figured bass, rather than making an elaborate orchestral score. On the whole, the opera was therefore cheap to realize, rehearse, and perform—an important consideration, given the Group's financial position and the composer's workload. And *Dido* added another composer's name to the Group's repertory, even if it was one only to be 'recognized by musicologists'.

According to the 1950–1 Arts Council Annual Report, 'the Britten Season, despite the great personal prestige of the composer, was not, financially, the success which had been hoped for'.[131] Critics, however, reacted favourably: reviews of the first production of *Dido* complimented Britten on his realization, especially in relation to his new ending to the second scene. And reviews of *Albert Herring* and *The Rape of Lucretia* were generally positive—though the critic of the *Yorkshire Observer* suggested that *Lucretia* was hardly 'suitable fare for a festival'.[132] But the Arts Council report undervalues the financial success of a season that did more than break even. Although Douglas complained of 'wretched houses' in the first week,[133] the EOG's receipts for the three weeks—box-office takings, minus the commission taken by The Company of Four which produced the run—totalled just over £6,000. A fee for broadcasts in the second week brought the total profit to £1,140.[134] Expenses comprised primarily running costs, and thus this listed profit did not take into account all the production costs of *Dido*, which would be levelled against future productions. Although it was only with *Let's Make an Opera* that receipts started to equal running costs, for this to occur in a whole season of Britten operas was no small achievement. It is possible that the EOG was originally hoping for a far greater profit from the season, expecting large, patriotically minded audiences. This was unlikely, given the attendance record in the first four years of the Group's existence, and several budgets predicted a loss of £1,500 on the season.[135] More likely, the EOG was wary of boasting of its financial survival to the Arts Council, in case this affected future negotiations. The Britten Festival contributed to a general income for the Group in 1951—including the Arts Council grant—of nearly £23,000. This figure was the highest in the Group's history, and was partly responsible for an excess of

131 *The Arts Council of Great Britain Annual Report 1950–51*, 6.

132 See Eric Blom in the *Observer*, 6 May 1951; Scott Goddard in the *News Chronicle*, 2 May 1951; the *New Statesman and Nation*, 19 May 1951; and *Yorkshire Observer*, 12 May 1951.

133 Douglas to Lawrie, 7 May 1951. BPL, EOG General Files 4, 1951.

134 BPL, EOG General Files 4, 1951.

135 BPL, EOG General Files 4, 1950.

income over expenditure—£361—for the first time in the EOG's experience.[136]

The Sorry Tale of Mr Tod

Britten was still working on *Billy Budd* when he articulated his thoughts about two new operas. The first was a children's opera based on Beatrix Potter's *The Tale of Mr Tod*, to be scored for soprano, tenor, baritone, and bass soloists, and possibly six children. The second was a larger-scale opera based on Henry James's *The Turn of the Screw*. 'Of the two he would find "The Tale of Mr. Tod" more congenial after the strain of finishing "Billy Budd"', a decision the EOG left to the composer.[137] Britten chose the former, aware that *Budd* would occupy his time until December, and conscious of the economic arguments in favour of children's opera.

Plans for the new opera had advanced moderately by November 1951. A librettist had been chosen (William Plomer) and was working on the story; designers were selected; a probable orchestra outlined (flute, oboe, clarinet, violin, viola, cello, piano, and percussion—its expanded size over *Let's Make an Opera* an anticipation of economic well-being); and a performance of the opera proposed for Aldeburgh in May and Cheltenham in July, with a subsequent run in London's West End—a significant indication of the Group's aspiration for the new work.[138] During this planning, however, Britten became aware of the issue that would eventually force him to abandon the opera—that of copyright. In general, Britten had avoided the problem of author's rights in most of his previous operas by collaborating directly with librettists and using source material that was without copyright restrictions. Britten's previous difficulty with dramatic copyright had been in 1946 when André Obey's *Le viol de Lucrèce* was used as the basis of his new opera, without permission being granted or a royalty discussed; hasty negotiations followed and litigation was avoided. Prior to this, however, Britten had avoided copyright authors for eleven years.

As soon as Britten expressed his intention to adapt *The Tale of Mr Tod* for the stage, his publisher commenced negotiations with Frederick Warne & Co., who held the copyright of the Potter story. They requested a royalty of 10 per cent on retail sales of the published music, and 25 per cent of the proceeds on both performing and mechanical rights. Ernst Roth from Boosey & Hawkes, ever in his element, wrote to Britten on 30 May telling him that a royalty of 2½ per cent on

[136] BPL, EOG Annual Accounts 3, balance sheet 1951.

[137] Minutes of meeting of Executive Committee, 12 May 1951. BPL, EOG General Files 4, 1951.

[138] Minutes of meeting of Executive Committee, 19 Nov. 1951. Ibid.

music sales and 10 per cent for performing right was all the copyright holders should expect, and that he had informed them of this.[139] Surprisingly, given Britten's earlier experience of such claims, the composer continued with his plans for the opera, incorrectly assuming that the problem would be resolved. Roth attempted to clarify the situation with the copyright holders soon after the first performance of *Billy Budd*, and in its reply of 19 December the company made it clear that the royalty terms stipulated by Roth were unacceptable. Citing the disproportion between the royalty for the librettist and that for the Potter copyright owners, the company stated that the emphasis in the royalty should be on the writer of the original story, and not on the librettist. 'Whilst we appreciate the outstanding abilities of Mr. Benjamin Britten as a composer, we must also remind you that Miss Potter's books are classics of the nursery, and are probably the greatest stories for children that have ever been written.' The letter concluded with unerring logic: 'A work which combines an outstanding composer and an outstanding author should be recompensed to the author in equal proportion.'[140] Money spoke as cogently as Roth did, and the opera was dropped.

In late December, when these negotiations were breaking down, the 1951 Christmas season of *Let's Make an Opera* was just beginning at the Lyric Theatre, Hammersmith. It was, in one way, a test: how was the opera holding up? It was actually holding up very well, doing brisk business over its four weeks: average takings were comparable with those of the 1949 Lyric season, when the opera was new and the work's concept innovative.[141] The children's market was showing no signs of tiring. Britten therefore was keen to capitalize on this niche and, following the recent copyright difficulties, his attempts to avoid an unoriginal libretto took on truly cosmic proportions in the following months. 'Tyco the Vegan', with an original libretto to be written by Plomer, was sufficiently developed by March 1952 for Britten to request of his librettist an audience song which would implore the children to return to earth, presumably from the planet Vega. Concurrent with this request, however, was Lord Harewood's suggestion of an opera for the 1953 coronation of Princess Elizabeth. Neither subject would entail copyright restriction. Yet it was *Gloriana*, with its dramatic plot and established deadline, that soon came to occupy Britten's time and affection.

The Turn of the Screw

The composition of *Gloriana* effectively ruled out the possibility of a new Britten opera for the EOG in 1952. Although Pears protested at the abandonment of

[139] Roth to Britten, 30 May 1951. BPL, Boosey & Hawkes Correspondence, 1951.

[140] Warne & Co. to Roth, 19 Dec. 1951. Ibid.

[141] BPL, EOG Accounts and Salaries, 1951–2.

established plans,[142] to curtail the EOG's activities was appropriate and advisable: Arts Council funding for 1952 had been absorbed by the Group's 1951 programme, and in order to maintain their now happier relationship with the bank, it was good sense for them to exploit existing operas in 1952, rather than to create new ones. Britten said that he was confident that he would be able to complete both *Gloriana* for Covent Garden and a new opera for the EOG for 1953—possibly motivated by Pears's antagonism towards the coronation opera.[143] Given the copyright difficulties he had faced with *The Tale of Mr Tod*, his choice of Henry James's *The Turn of the Screw* is curious: it was still in copyright. Britten possibly (and naively) hoped that American copyright rules would not affect him or would be easily dealt with. More likely, though, was that his choice of James's story probably resulted from his intense preoccupation with the subject.

Britten's interest in Henry James dated from the early 1930s. He had become acquainted with *The Turn of the Screw* in a BBC broadcast on 1 June 1932 and had read the novella itself six months later. Britten found the work 'glorious & eerie', an 'incredible masterpiece',[144] but seems not to have considered it as the basis of an opera until the early 1950s. Myfanwy Piper, wife of the artist and EOG designer John Piper and eventual librettist of the opera, suggested it to Britten because of the composer's interest in the corruption of innocence, and because she found the novella's prose so 'densely musical'.[145] Of more interest to the composer than the 'musical prose' (which would anyway have to be adapted for a libretto) was the ambiguity of the story, which resembled that which Britten had exploited in *Grimes*, in *Billy Budd*, and, to some extent, in *Gloriana*. Were the ghosts real, or were they a projection of the governess's insecurity and infatuation? Had Quint pursued sexual relations with Miles and with the previous governess? Or even, as suggested by one recent critic, was Miles projecting his own homosexuality onto Quint, and did he die because in denouncing Quint he was denouncing his own nature?[146]

The novella's ambiguity was one of the copyright issues that first surfaced in November 1953. Although Britten had decided in January 1953 that the opera would not be ready until 1954—thereby having to elicit gracious postponement from the Venice Biennale Festival, which had planned a 1953 premiere—Piper continued work throughout the year, in consultation with Britten. It was not until November that an attempt was made to procure the rights of the story—a

[142] See Lord Harewood, *The Tongs and the Bones* (1981), 135. *Gloriana* is discussed in detail in Ch. 4.

[143] Pears was ambivalent about playing the role of Essex and was disappointed that plans for the EOG were to be interrupted. See Ch. 4.

[144] Britten's diary, 6 and 7 Jan. 1933.

[145] Carpenter, 337.

[146] Mansel Stimpson, 'Drama and Meaning in *The Turn of the Screw*', *Opera Quarterly*, 4/3 (Autumn 1986), 82.

considerable oversight on Britten's part. The first response was not promising. Isador Caplan, Britten's solicitor from the mid-1940s, wrote to the American lawyer Edward Roth on 20 November, who in turn contacted Mr Reynolds, the solicitor representing the James estate.

> Mr. Reynolds would not open his files to examine the contracts in order to determine whether or not the operatic rights had already been granted. His attitude is that the determination of whether or not such rights had been granted, would be a matter for his counsel, which would entail the expenditure of time and money, and unless that were financially worth while, he would not undertake to do it. Furthermore, and quite apart from contract, he would not grant the operatic rights to anyone over the objection of either Twentieth Century Fox or the present grantee of the dramatic rights since he felt that both of these firms had dealt very handsomely with him and he would not want to do anything to disturb the existing amicable relationship.[147]

So Britten had to overcome Reynolds's carefully nurtured philistinism and the plenipotence of a Hollywood film studio in the 1950s; he would also have to fight for the right to exploit the very ambiguity that he found so attractive in the story. Reynolds informed Caplan that 'the original book had certain overtones which were objectionable to the heirs and that in previous contracts, they had made stipulations limiting the treatment of the original story so as to eliminate these overtones.'[148] This extraordinary statement was presumably a reference to James's homosexuality, which had hitherto been kept firmly behind the closet door. Eliminating these overtones would involve Reynolds reading the new material, a task that he was unwilling to undertake because of the paucity of monetary returns likely from the allocation of operatic rights. Prior to this, Britten had argued in favour of defining some of James's ambiguity: the ghosts were taken from the governess's mind—possibly their sole domain in the novella—and would appear as characters in their own right, thus allowing the children to collude with objects from the spirit world.[149] But Britten's final product treads a very fine line: the collusion is explicit about nothing other than a recognition—an acceptance of the ghosts' existence. When it came to setting other ambiguous parts of the novella, Britten was even more careful. Acting on Pears's interpretation of the book, he wrote to Piper on 26 April stating that the draft libretto, with its intimation that Quint had 'made free' with Miles, should be altered so that Quint's 'freedom' was confined to the former governess, all within the far more acceptable realm of heterosexuality.[150] Britten eventually changed his mind, but retained James's quaint expression ('made free'), which was ambiguous enough to leave its exact nature to the audience's imagination, hoping that this would not antagonize Reynolds. Producers of the opera have

[147] Roth to Caplan, 23 Nov. 1953. BPL, EOG General Files 4, 1953. [148] Ibid.

[149] Harewood, *The Tongs*, 139.

[150] Britten to Piper, 26 Apr. 1954. BPL, Piper Correspondence.

subsequently 'made free' in their interpretation of this point (Jonathan Miller took this even one step further, suggesting an incestuous relationship between Miles and Flora[151]), but the actual libretto is intentionally vague on this issue.

Negotiations with Reynolds continued throughout the composition of the opera, and for some time after its completion. The lawyer Edward Roth formed the impression that Reynolds was resentful because Britten had written the work without first obtaining the rights.[152] This was certainly possible, since negotiations were never smooth. Permission from Twentieth Century Fox was forthcoming, but only if the work was presented on the 'legitimate stage', and was not recorded, filmed, or televised.[153] Caplan advised the Group not to contest this immediately, since recording companies had shown little interest in the other Britten operas, and the restrictions did not seem to include direct broadcasts.[154] Reynolds, informed of this decision by Twentieth Century Fox, granted permission for ten performances of the opera in Venice, 'and no other rights'.[155] Reynolds's bellicose stance owed something to the fact that the US copyright for *The Turn of the Screw* expired at the end of 1954, and with it his Indian summer. The British copyright on the work still had ten years to run, so Caplan requested that further negotiations be opened with Reynolds on the basis that the Group had been approached by Decca to record the opera while it was in production in London in October, and that ten performances, confined to Venice, would preclude any serious exploitation of the new work.[156]

Although various specific rights were allocated during the next six months, it was not until 21 June 1955 that Caplan discovered a way to circumvent Reynolds's control. Acting on the advice of a professor of English, Caplan moved to terminate all copyright negotiations since it was impossible to prove that the opera's libretto was based on the novella and not on a serialization of the story that had appeared before the publication of the book, and over which Reynolds had no control.[157] This left only the rights owned by Twentieth Century Fox, and in October 1955 Caplan reported that all forms of exploitation of *The Turn of the Screw*, except for film and broadcasting, would be covered fully by an agreement then being considered by the studio.[158] Since the London office of Twentieth Century Fox was aware of the broadcasts of the opera that had already taken place, yet had not acted to question or oppose them, the EOG decided that it was unlikely that this right, though not granted, would be policed.[159] It is probably no coincidence that when Britten next based an opera

151 Carpenter, 339. 152 Roth to Caplan, 23 Nov. 1953. BPL, EOG General Files 5, 1953.

153 Litchfield to Caplan, 28 Jan. 1954. BPL, EOG General Files 5, 1954.

154 Caplan to Douglas, 28 Jan. 1954. Ibid. This was a very liberal reading of the rights.

155 Reynolds to Selig, 26 Feb. 1954. Ibid. 156 Caplan to Selig, 14 Apr. 1954. Ibid.

157 Caplan to Gishford, 21 June 1955. BPL, EOG Correspondence, 1955.

158 Minutes of Directors' Meeting, 19 October 1955. BPL, EOG General Files 4, 1955.

159 Ibid.

on a James novella (*Owen Wingrave*), he did so after the British copyright had expired.

Critical reception of the Venice performances was mostly positive. Felix Aprahamian in the *Sunday Times* described the opera as the peak of Britten's achievement, while Colin Mason in the *Manchester Guardian* called it a 'masterpiece'. Praise was not unanimous; perhaps not surprisingly for an Italian critic and musician, the composer Riccardo Malipiero complained that the orchestra lacked weight owing to its size.[160] Britten had once again used an ensemble of thirteen; despite the generous terms of the Festival commission, the opera would soon have to earn its own living, and in repertory with the other chamber works. This factor, and the financial history of the EOG, had influenced Britten's negotiations with Boosey & Hawkes over *The Turn of the Screw*. With the distribution of the royalties for *Let's Make an Opera* firmly in his mind, Britten negotiated with Anthony Gishford (Boosey & Hawkes) that Clause One of his current contract should be waived; the composer would no longer be bound to submit the work to his publisher, who in turn would not be bound to decide within three months whether he would publish the work. Exclusive performing rights could then be allocated to the EOG for a mutually agreed period, which was financially advantageous for the Group.[161] The EOG drew up a contract with Britten and Piper whereby the composer was to receive 6 guineas per performance in England (£100 per performance in Venice) and half of all performing fees received by the Group for broadcasts or television performances (then an optimistic clause); Piper would receive 3 guineas per performance in England (£50 in Venice) and a quarter of the revenue generated from radio and television broadcasts.[162]

Any financial advantage for the EOG flowing from Britten's arrangement with his publisher was undermined by the Group's season at Sadler's Wells in October 1954 (Table 3.6). The programme offered mixed fare: both *The Beggar's Opera* and *The Rape of Lucretia* preceded the London premiere of *The Turn of the Screw*, of which, rather cautiously, only four performances were presented. A double-bill consisting of Arthur Oldham's *Love in a Village* and Lennox Berkeley's *A Dinner Engagement* was the fourth production in the season.

There are few surprises in Table 3.6, although noteworthy is an audience of 83 per cent for *The Beggar's Opera* on 9 October, and one of 60 per cent for the double-bill on 15 October. Apart from the reception of *The Turn of the Screw*, the Group considered the season a disaster, and concluded the year with a deficit of

160 Carpenter, 359–60.

161 Gishford to Britten, 2 Apr. 1954. BPL, Boosey & Hawkes Correspondence, 1954.

162 BPL, EOG General Files 5, 1954.

Table 3.6 Receipts of Sadler's Wells season of the English Opera Group, October 1954, represented as a percentage of the theatre's financial capacity[a]

The Beggar's Opera	4 October	52
	9 October	83
	13 October	64
	16 October	37
	Average	59
The Rape of Lucretia	5 October	37
	12 October	51
	14 October	49
	Average	46
The Turn of the Screw	6 October	73
	8 October	87
	11 October	93
	16 October	100
	Average	88
Love in a Village/A Dinner Engagement	7 October	44
	9 October	24
	15 October	60
	Average	43
	Season average	61

[a] Compiled from EOG accounts. BPL, EOG General Files 5, 1954. The percentage of the theatre's financial capacity must not be confused with a percentage of the theatre's seating capacity; the former does not take into consideration the scale of ticket prices: box-office receipts could have been made up of many tickets at the cheapest rate, or fewer at the most expensive rate.

£2,000.[163] With minimum effort, and flouting all previous procedures, the EOG procured a 'retrospective grant' from the Arts Council to cover this loss.[164]

Although the deficit owed something to the high production costs of the new opera, it was also the result of poor attendance—which tells us something about public perception of Britten's music at this time. The high costs are easier to explain than this shift in audience appreciation. Lulled into a false sense of security by the Biennale Festival's fee, the Group allowed a period of several weeks for coaching, a full month of rehearsals, and a great enough financial incentive for the singers to forgo all other engagements during the rehearsal period.[165] Almost

[163] Lawrie to Williams, 16 Nov. 1954. BPL, EOG Correspondence, 1954.

[164] Directors' Meeting, 20 Dec. 1954. ACGB, Minutes and Correspondence of the EOG.

[165] Coleman, 'Staging First Productions 2', 37.

£10,000 was spent fulfilling these commitments and covering running costs in Venice—considerably more than the production and running costs of Britten's previous operas.[166] Any hopes that there would be surplus funds to invest in the Sadler's Wells season were soon lost.

Reasons for poor attendance are less clear. In his request for a retrospective grant, Lawrie cited a bus strike as one justification for the often negligible audience, although he also suggested that 'misjudgment in the planning of the programme' probably contributed to limited attendance.[167] The Group's principal misjudgement became evident only with hindsight: *The Turn of the Screw* could easily have sustained more than four performances, although it was an untested commodity when the season was planned and as such posed something of a risk. The other misjudgements suggest ignorance of audience expectations. In May, when it looked as though there would not be enough funding to include *The Beggar's Opera* in the Sadler's Wells season, John Denison, who had taken over from Eric Walter White the position of Arts Council Assessor of the EOG, proposed that the Group increase the number of performances of *The Turn of the Screw*. Demonstrating curious reliance on the supposed popularity of *The Beggar's Opera* ('it was the most likely [out of the works in the season] to be popular at the box office'[168]), the EOG declined. In the event, although *The Beggar's Opera* had the second highest average for the season, it was not a particularly impressive total. Similarly, *The Rape of Lucretia* was considered one of Britten's most popular operas, and its poor record in the Sadler's Wells season alarmed the directors; average receipts were disarmingly similar to those of the double-bill—works that would never breach the theatre's fire regulations. As a result, it was ten years before *The Beggar's Opera* was revised, and five years for *The Rape of Lucretia*; both revised productions appeared within the confines of the Aldeburgh Festival.

It was perhaps natural that audiences would eventually tire of *Lucretia*, an opera that had been presented in London approximately every two years since its composition. But the next two seasons of *The Turn of the Screw* suggest that London audiences at the time were being over-exposed to Britten's music—an extraordinary response to this work, given both its novelty and its subsequent reception and introduction to international operatic repertory. The season at the Scala Theatre in September 1955 was a natural attempt to exploit the new work.[169] The fortnight was shared between *The Turn of the Screw*, *Let's Make an Opera*, and a double-bill consisting of *A Dinner Engagement* and Walton's *Façade*. Receipts for the children's opera were only 55 per cent of capacity; those for the double-bill 59 per cent; while those for *The Turn of the Screw* were just 68 per cent

[166] Douglas to Britten, 27 May 1954. BPL, EOG Correspondence, 1954.

[167] Lawrie to Williams, 16 Nov. 1954. Ibid.

[168] Douglas to Williams, 6 May 1954. Ibid.

[169] Minutes of Artistic Directors' Meeting, 7 Oct. 1954. BPL, EOG General Files 5, 1954.

1. Recording *Peter Grimes* for BBC TV at Snape Maltings Concert Hall, February 1969

6. The catalogue of Britten's Published works issued by Boosey & Hawkes in 1939

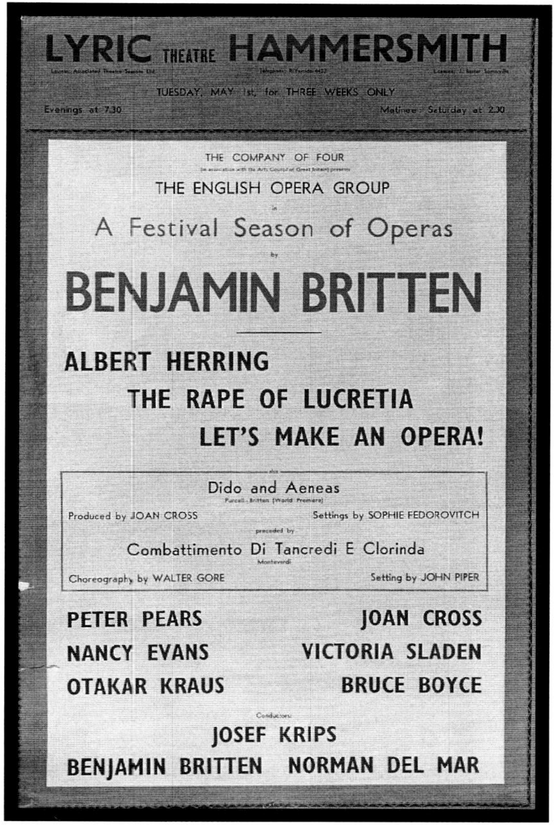

7. Publicity for the 1951 'Britten Season' at Lyric Theatre, Hammersmith

of capacity, 20 per cent less than the average figure in the previous year.[170] One year later, the response was even less enthusiastic (Table 3.7).

The average of receipts for the whole season was 42 per cent of the theatre's financial capacity; having budgeted on 66 per cent, the Group suffered a net loss of £1,100 for the two weeks.[171] Finding solace in artistic integrity rather than audience figures, the directors confidently assured everyone that '*The Turn of the Screw* remained the highest achievement of the season'.[172] It was not revived again until five years later at Aldeburgh, which suggests the directors assumed that, for whatever reasons, the opera's appeal was transient. The EOG finished the year with a deficit of £3,500, its first of this size for some years. Talk of liquidation was accompanied by a return to the frenzied correspondence with the Arts Council that had dominated the Group's early years. Britten reacted accordingly: he began work on another opera for children, *Noye's Fludde*, a year later, happy to re-enter a market that had hitherto treated him well financially and which allowed him to write for performers and audiences with whom he felt some affinity.

Table 3.7 Receipts of Scala Theatre season of the English Opera Group, 26 September–6 October 1956, represented as a percentage of the theatre's financial capacity[a]

The Turn of the Screw	26 September (without Britten)	22
	28 September (without Britten, Pears, Vyvyan)	23
	29 September	39
	1 October	46
	3 October (without Pears)	42
	5 October (without Pears owing to illness)	59
	Average	39
Venus and Adonis, Façade, Sāvitri	27 September (with Sitwell)	58
	6 October (matinée with Sybil Thorndike)	32
	Average	45
Venus and Adonis, Ruth	2 October (world premiere of Berkeley's *Ruth*)	60
	4 October	30
	6 October	35
	Average	42
	Season average	42

[a] BPL, EOG General Files 5, 1956.

[170] BPL, EOG General Files 5, 1955.
[171] Directors' Report for 1956. BPL, EOG Correspondence, 1956.
[172] Ibid.

Following the increasingly poor response to *The Turn of the Screw* in England, Gishford suggested to Britten in November 1956 that the exclusivity agreement should be terminated.

I put to him my own feeling that by October of next year the Group is likely to have derived all the benefit it can from the exclusivity of this work. Speaking as its publisher, I think that a further year and three months from that date, as was provided for in the exchange of letters, would redound more to the disadvantage of the work than to the advantage of The English Opera Group. There will of course be no question of its further use being denied to the Group and personally I do not think that its inclusion in the Group's repertory will be in any way invalidated by the fact that it is generally available.[173]

It was an accurate assessment of the situation, and in January 1957 Britten capitulated. The agreement had not been as successful as the Group had anticipated; certainly avoidance of publisher royalties meant considerable savings for the EOG, but it also deprived the composer and the librettist of the royalties that would have resulted from wider exploitation of the work.[174] The fact that no other companies in England were presenting the opera did not encourage a high rate of bookings for the EOG production. And the EOG, along with Britten and Piper, were asked by Boosey & Hawkes to contribute to legal fees from copyright negotiations; these fees would probably have been absorbed by the publisher alone, had a conventional composer–publisher contract been in place.[175] Termination of the exclusivity agreement was the final acceptance that *The Turn of the Screw* had not been the financial success in England that the EOG had hoped for.

The English Opera Group celebrated its tenth birthday in both 1956 and 1957—symbolic of tentative origins in Glyndebourne, under a different name, in 1946. It was a time of retrospection for the Group and its critics. Although positive in his article in the *Observer*, Eric Blom's subtle condescension was characteristic of many critics' view of the EOG. 'If the artists can be called stars, they are not planets, but a constellation, casting a mild light but a steady one, illuminating and reflecting each other.'[176] The EOG was not amateurish, but neither was it 'real' opera, with real opera stars and powerful, simple plots: English verismo had a long way to go. Critics nonetheless wished the Group a happy future, naively predicting stability. But, as on many occasions in its ten-year history, when the economics of opera had dictated the Group's fortunes, the EOG was changing once more; Britten's future operatic works were to change with it. From Britten's perspective, the difference between *The Rape of Lucretia* and *The Turn of the Screw* may have been in the title, the story, and the order of the notes, but in the history of the EOG, the former had initiated a certain style, which was closed by the latter.

173 Gishford to Douglas, 13 Nov. 1956. BPL, EOG Correspondence, 1956.

174 Embarrassed at this, Britten extracted £100 from Boosey & Hawkes for Piper.

175 Minutes of Directors' Meeting, 31 Jan. 1956. BPL, EOG Correspondence, 1956.

176 EOG press sheet. Ibid.

Chapter 4

The Arts Council's Pursuit of 'Grand Opera'

> It will be the first task of Fascism in the cultural plane to elevate the public taste by releasing the national culture from the tyranny of commercial standards. Gone is the old aristocracy, which in the 18th century—to their honour!—patronised such men as Dryden, Pope, and Samuel Johnson. Fascism must take over this duty of patronage, and with as generous a hand.[1]

> Poor old English opera. For so long the play-ground of amateurs and dabblers.[2]

By drawing heavily on an article in the *Fascist Week* in support of his call for a British Ministry of Fine Arts, Henry Welsh added an unexpected voice to a then familiar argument. Where successive governments had ignored the value of British arts, Fascism could offer Sir Oswald Mosley, founder of the British Union of Fascists, with his assured cultural pedigree. Where Viscount Snowden ('with whom we have little in common') had failed in his attempt to fund grand opera in England in the early 1930s, the 'Fascist scorpion will be more grievous than the Snowden whip, and the Philistines will be belaboured into building for us one of the finest opera houses in the world'.[3] The year 1934—in which talk of Fascism infiltrated the bucolic pages of the *Musical Times*—was in fact Fascism's 'Indian Summer' in Britain; events in Spain only two years later were to turn public opinion against the Fascist cause, its doctrine largely discredited. Significantly, the extreme right's advocacy of a British Ministry of Fine Arts, balanced on the left by Communism's 'Art for the People', helped to keep the argument for state patronage beyond the pale of mainstream politics. Yet, in a

[1] Alexander Raven, 'Fascism and Culture', *Fascist Week*, 22, quoted in Henry Welsh, 'Letter to the Editor' ('A British Ministry of Fine Arts'), *Musical Times*, 75 (1934), 448.

[2] Tippett to White, 23 Nov. 1949. ACGB, Music Department, 1945–55.

[3] Welsh, 'Letter to the Editor'.

little over ten years, the British government would claim to be creating one of the finest opera companies in the world, financed by the Arts Council, Britain's newly formed ministry of arts. The move into the political mainstream was neither smooth nor certain, and this uncertainty never more obvious than in the Council's early policies on opera in Britain. Opera was to be 'grand'; but, with too little money and without a firm British precedent, the Council's task was never easy. Covent Garden and Sadler's Wells were both courted by the new Council, their cautious insistence on the traditional and the large scale of their operations reinforcing the Arts Council's (at first) narrow vision of British culture.

Britten's own vision of culture in his homeland in the late 1940s differed markedly from the Arts Council's. His four chamber operas after *Peter Grimes*—*The Rape of Lucretia* (1946), *Albert Herring* (1947), *The Beggar's Opera* (1948), *Let's Make an Opera* (1949)—had stood far outside the Council's aspirations, and had attracted relatively little financial support. Yet *Billy Budd* (1951) and *Gloriana* (1953), composed on a scale considerably different from their predecessors, were supported by the Arts Council through commission fees and lavish Covent Garden productions. Britten's relationship with the Council during the creation of these two works (and the events they celebrated—the Festival of Britain and the coronation of Elizabeth II) raises a number of important questions: had Britten previously been marginalized as an opera composer because his views on British opera, as expressed in his dramatic chamber works, conflicted with those of the Arts Council? Was the composition of *Billy Budd* and *Gloriana* a conscious attempt to break free from this 'marginal' status? And, paradoxically, would Britten have attracted more financial support, and more productions of his works in Britain, had he never developed chamber opera but instead continued to write music drama on the grandest scale?

A Budget for Music

In his 'Outline of a Master Plan for the First Five Years' of the new Arts Council, Steuart Wilson, its music director, modestly proposed to 'help in the establishment of "Opera in English" as the basis of the Covent Garden season'.[4] Underlying Wilson's unassuming proposition was an important principle: the Arts Council saw the formation of a permanent (not seasonal) new opera company as its primary responsibility. Both John Maynard Keynes (Chairman of the Arts Council and the new Covent Garden Trust) and Wilson had served on the committee deciding the future of the theatre at Covent Garden,[5] and although

[4] Music Panel Paper No. 1, 23 June 1945. ACGB, Sec. 46–76, Box M.21, Advisory Panel on Music, Minutes.

[5] Frances Donaldson, *The Royal Opera House in the Twentieth Century* (1988), 41.

an 'arm's-length' policy would exist, at least initially, between funding body and recipient, this 'personal responsibility' for the new child at Covent Garden would result in a relationship pointedly different from that between the Council and its other clients. Although it was unspecified in his master-plan, Wilson viewed opera in 'grand' terms: large orchestra and chorus, famous (international) conductors and soloists, and spectacular productions of works from the operatic canon. The Council's ambition for 'Opera in English' did not negate the grand scale envisaged: post-war euphoria ensured that Covent Garden would stand as an expression of nationalist achievement as much as the home of a new opera company; opera in the vernacular was a fundamental part of this expression. As Frances Donaldson notes, 'Opera in English' was, by 1945, already a crusade: an English 'style' of opera could only be realized if libretti were written in or translated into the national tongue.[6]

Despite the crusading spirit, the arguments for and against opera in the vernacular were scarcely well defined. Edward Dent, a contributor to the Sadler's Wells publication *Opera in English*, was not at all sure that nationalism would be enough to turn the public away from the prevailing (pre-war) conception of 'grand' opera: 'Opera to be "grand" had to be foreign, and it followed that English opera, unable to afford real "grandeur", had to be shabby, dowdy, and provincial.'[7] In the same book, Tyrone Guthrie asserted that it was a common thing in England to hear people of 'taste and education' declare that they preferred to hear opera in a language they did not understand.[8] The allure of the unknown should not be underestimated; yet, like the directors of Sadler's Wells, who optimistically planned to channel profits from the sale of *Opera in English* into a fund for commissioning new English operas, Covent Garden and the Arts Council were certain they could convince audiences that a thorough understanding of libretto and drama was not necessarily a bar to grandeur and enjoyment.

The Arts Council's £25,000 grant to Covent Garden in 1945–6 may have been based on an estimate formulated as early as March 1944. Mary Glasgow, writing to Keynes on 29 March of that year, referred to Leslie Boosey's efforts to obtain the lease of Covent Garden and administer the theatre, stating that Boosey had estimated the total cost ('assuming not a penny were taken') to be in the region of £25,000.[9] Boosey was prepared for his firm to put up all the money immediately necessary for the opening, 'but if the thing is to develop on the grand non-profit-making national scale which he visualizes, they would want

[6] Ibid. 47. [7] Edward Dent, 'The Future of British Opera', in *Opera in English* (1945), 31.

[8] Tyrone Guthrie, 'Introduction', *Opera in English* (1945), 8.

[9] Glasgow to Keynes, 29 Mar. 1944. ACGB, Sec. 54–0.2.b, Opera and Ballet Sub-Committee, Minutes Oct. 54–Dec. 57, Papers Oct. 54–7.

guarantees from other sources for the future'.[10] Boosey & Hawkes soon took responsibility for rent, rates, insurance, and the salaries of the administrative staff of the theatre, the Covent Garden Opera Trust, and the small stage staff.[11] With rent at £10,500 a year, Boosey's estimate for total administrative costs was probably close to the mark. Yet, although the Arts Council's 'pound for pound' financial support of Covent Garden and its abandonment of the simple, retrospective 'guarantee against loss' system was of the greatest significance, the grant of £25,000 was totally inadequate compared with the needs of a new national company performing throughout the year. The effect on the hierarchy of Arts Council music funding across the board was considerable.

By October 1945, soon after the Covent Garden Trust had taken control of the theatre, Wilson's 'five-year plan' had on it considerably more flesh, and it provides a clear indication of the Council's priorities (Table 4.1). With an unlisted ½ per cent contingency, implementing the plan depended heavily on the attached proviso: 'Mr. Wilson said that the actual sums of money were not stated because the main point was the relative importance of each section. . . . One pocket might be used to fill another in case of over-estimating or under-spending.'[12] Not surprisingly, the Industrial Concerts—a relic of morale-boosting wartime policies and the recipient of the same amount of Council funding as Covent Garden—soon gave way to new calls on the Council's funds.

Although the Covent Garden Trust promoted its new opera company on very English lines, it deferred to European models on the issue of state subsidy. Comparisons, often ill-informed and always unfavourable, were circulating well before the new company's first production. The Arts Council collected data of comparative subsidies in other countries—perhaps with the intention of pressing the government for more money—and would have taken scant comfort in the knowledge that the Teatro Colón in Buenos Aires, a company cited as comparable to Covent Garden in its general expenses, received the equivalent of £300,000 in 1948.[13] If anything, this knowledge worsened the situation for other groups vying for Council funds: it made both the Arts Council and the Covent Garden Trust determined to put their national opera house on a similar level of funding.

It was against this backdrop that Britten sought funds for the English Opera Group. The criteria for the EOG's grant were quite different from those for Covent Garden. Since Wilson's plan included funding for only the two large opera

[10] Glasgow to Keynes, 29 Mar. 1944. ACGB, Sec. 54–0.2.b Opera and Ballet Sub-Committee, Minutes Oct. 54–Dec. 57, and Papers 54–7.

[11] Donaldson, *Royal Opera House*, 42.

[12] Minutes of Music Panel, 25 Oct. 1945. ACGB, Sec. 46–76, Box M.21, Advisory Panel on Music, Minutes.

[13] 'Subsidies to Foreign Opera Houses', ACGB, Music Department, 1945–55, Opera 1946–9. Grants in other cities to their main companies included Prague: £250,000 (1947); Paris: £300,000 (1946); and Brussels: £70,000 (1947).

Table 4.1 Proposed music expenditure—proportions of the Arts Council's total annual budget, 1946–51[a]

Opera	%
Covent Garden	20
Sadler's Wells	4
Orchestras	
Existing	
A.	9.5
B.	5.6
Chamber	3.2
String	3.2
New formations	
N.E.	4.3
East Anglia	2.7
Wales	6.4
Yorkshire	1.1
Concerts	
Industrial	20
General (including rural)	8
Chamber music groups	4
Grants	
National Federation of Music Societies	4
Committee for the Promotion of New Music	0.4
Rural Music Schools Council	0.8
Croydon Corporation	0.8
Performing Right Society	1.5

[a] Minutes of Music Panel, 25 Oct. 1945. ACGB, Sec. 46–76, Box M.21, Advisory Panel on Music, Minutes. Table does not include money allocated to the construction and maintenance of buildings. Class 'A' orchestras were those in full association with the Arts Council (the London Philharmonic Orchestra, the City of Birmingham Orchestra, the Liverpool Philharmonic Orchestra and the Hallé Orchestra). The class 'B' group consisted of the Scottish Orchestra, the Reid, and the Northern Philharmonic.

companies, money was theoretically unavailable for other groups. The Council dealt with this by invoking a system of guarantees against loss, rather than conditional grants, and by demanding innovative programming—rescinding guarantees if this innovation was not forthcoming. Although it did not have any significant effect either way on the actual grant, a direct correlation between rhetoric and programming soon developed. The Council often found itself unable to fund or guarantee a programme that 'varied from the original proposition' in the same way that it might 'look indulgently' on performances of a certain work. For the EOG, programmes were continually juggled somehow to bring the Group's (often inaccurate) production estimates into line with the unwritten criteria of the Council. Touring the provinces, however expensive, was welcomed because it helped deflect the criticism that the Council was prone to favour central London; any reduction of the EOG's touring plans as a result of economic stringency always resulted in muddier rhetoric. Before long, the Council considered the EOG to possess a 'definite though limited value as an experimental opera company', though it was uncertain that chamber opera would ever appeal to composers other than Britten.[14] By 1948 the Group's special character—and thus its marginalization—was accepted and sustained by Britain's central arts funding body.

Equally, the EOG was somewhat scarred by its original association with Glyndebourne—lavishly funded as it was by its owner John Christie. Insulated by his money and isolated by the conviction that he was the only person in England with the ability to run an opera company, Christie was probably not the best person to establish a working relationship with the new Arts Council. Disastrous diplomatic relations between the two organizations, combined with the lack of any spare Council funds, meant that Glyndebourne's grant of £3,000 in 1946 acted merely as a guarantee against loss on the nine-week tour of *Lucretia*; the opera gained no financial support from the Council for its season at Christie's country house. Moreover, Britten's 1946 letter to *The Times* implied strong allegiance to Christie in his battle for Arts Council funds.[15] Despite deterioration in the relationship since then, both parties had proved that it was possible to tour a new opera for nine weeks at a loss of £3,000. Although it was not quite the model Crozier and Britten had in mind for the new English Opera Group, the tour of *Lucretia* provided a tangible link between opera and expenditure, in an area largely alien to both the Council and Covent Garden in their early years. It is not really surprising that the Council saw the EOG as a natural extension of the Glyndebourne English Opera Company—despite having nothing of Glyndebourne's capital or assets—and funded it accordingly. The Council's £3,000 grant to the EOG in 1947, as was explored in Chapter 3, was only the beginning of an uneasy relationship between the two parties.

A Further Budget for Music

By November 1948 it was clear to Wilson that the original budget for music in Britain was inadequate, and that Covent Garden was both principal cause and

[14] 'Some Notes on the Arts Council's Policy for Opera and Ballet' in a letter from White to Pooley, 11 Nov. 1948. ACGB, Music Department, 1945–55.

[15] See above, p. 82.

casualty. With a deficit of £118,000 in 1948–9 (£58,000 more than its initial grant), the opera house was a serious financial liability to the Council. Wilson blamed the Covent Garden Trust for settling originally on £25,000 when it should have 'thought in terms of at least £100,000 for a subsidy'—a figure that had been discussed by the Trust and promptly dismissed by Maynard Keynes, the brilliant and cultured economist, by this stage ennobled.[16] Wilson's estimates for the following season were prefaced by conjecture. The purpose of Covent Garden, he argued, was to present grand opera from the conventional repertory; Sadler's Wells was ideal for a different type of opera at much lower cost; the English Opera Group stood for the exploration of new themes in unconventional productions, with short tours owing to limited appeal. Wilson's conclusion was that if a comprehensive budget for the support of opera was needed, the figures would approximate as follows:[17]

	1948–9 (£)	(1947–8)
Covent Garden	120,000	(98,000)
Sadler's Wells	25,000	(23,000)
Sadler's Wells Ballet School	5,000	(5,000)
English Opera Group	5,000	(3,000)
Intimate Opera	1,000	
Glyndebourne	10,000	
Total	166,000	

This estimate represents a far higher capital outlay than that of the Council's first budget, but the hierarchy of Wilson's original five-year plan was maintained: Covent Garden still received an 'allocation' of five times the amount offered to Sadler's Wells.[18] In this 'rifling of one pocket to fill another', two figures stand out. An increase in the EOG grant from £3,000 to £5,000 would barely cover the Group's deficit, let alone provide for the innovation expected of an experimental opera group, with its 'limited value'. Yet Glyndebourne, with its very high costs and its 'scale of prices . . . [putting] them out of reach of the ordinary

[16] Steuart Wilson, 'A Budget for Music', 25 Nov. 1947. ACGB, Sec. 54–0.2.b, Opera and Ballet Sub-Committee, Minutes Oct. 54–Dec. 57, Papers Oct. 54–7.

[17] Ibid. At the time of this document Wilson listed the 1947–8 grant for Covent Garden as £60,000 and Sadler's Wells as £18,000. The supplementary grant of £38,000 for Covent Garden was intended to reduce the deficit (£20,000).

[18] The 1949 Arts Enquiry established that average production costs at Covent Garden were £7,000 per opera compared to £3,000 at Sadler's Wells. At this time, Covent Garden employed 300 people compared to Sadler's Wells's 150; the difference in costs between the two orchestras amounted to £1,000 per week. *The Arts Enquiry: Music*, 80.

public, even if the public had time to go to Glyndebourne',[19] was to be rewarded with a grant of £10,000. Although Christie did not receive this funding (his fractious personality and 'his' new Council-supported Edinburgh Festival probably contributed to this), Wilson's budget suggests that the elitism of Glyndebourne was somehow more attractive to the Council than that of the EOG. At least it produced mainstream opera to capacity audiences.

At around this time, Michael Tippett wrote to Eric Walter White criticizing the conception of national opera shared by Covent Garden and the Arts Council. Tippett's concern was that if Covent Garden 'goes on whoring after expensive (or from the press publicity end, psychologically extravagant) productions, instead of getting down to building a Volkstheater tradition of good solid work on little money, then it may well kill the goose that lays the eggs'. Stating that both he and Vaughan Williams had put this 'gloomy view forward prophetically' at an early panel meeting, he went on to say:

> What we need in England is not really yet a glamorously expensive national semi-international opera-house—but a long-scale policy like that which made our Ballet. A state-supported school and hard work. In my humble opinion old V[aughan].W[illiams]. and I were sounder than Sir Steuart and [David] Webster [Managing Director Covent Garden]. The Arts Council muffed its chances of laying the real foundations down for a national opera. I'm so afraid that if the financial squeeze comes about in months or years, that the Arts Council will lop off grants proportionately—probably stemming Sadler's Wells again without really bringing a sense of reality into the Garden play-ground. Poor old English opera. For so long the play-ground of amateurs and dabblers.[20]

Although it prompted an unattributed Arts Council comment 'most of this, I think is sound sense', the letter attacked the basic purpose of Covent Garden and the designs of the Council: both groups *were* attempting to create a glamorously expensive national semi-international opera house. And complaints about amateurs and dabblers were legion: Webster's management; various soloists; opera in English. The average audience attendance in the most expensive seats for twelve consecutive performances of opera in late 1947 was 35 per cent in the stalls, 27 per cent in the stalls circle, and 25 per cent in the grand tier—Covent Garden was not yet a Mecca for the wealthy or the glitterati.[21] The Council's attempts to fill these seats—thus saving the goose and its eggs—became a preoccupation over the next few years. Webster's unrepented sentiment before the 1947–8 season—that 'it seems incredible that certain sections of the public view opera in English as inferior to opera in foreign languages'—slowly went the way of bad

[19] Steuart Wilson, 'A Budget for Music', 25 Nov. 1947. ACGB, Sec. 54–0.2.b, Opera and Ballet Sub-Committee, Minutes Oct. 54–Dec. 57, Papers Oct. 54–7.

[20] Tippett to White, 23 Nov. 1949. ACGB, Music Department, 1945–55.

[21] Steuart Wilson, 'A Budget for Music', 25 Nov. 1947. ACGB, Sec. 54–0.2.b, Opera and Ballet Sub-Committee, Minutes Oct. 54–Dec. 57, Papers Oct. 54–7.

Puccini translations. The whole process of redefining Covent Garden resulted in an even narrower concept of grand opera, and Britten's attempts to become part of this operatic culture became even more difficult.

Tippett was not a disinterested party; he prefaced his assessment of the problems at Covent Garden by noting Webster's interest in his new work *The Midsummer Marriage*, and was hopeful that a performance would follow. The opera was not to be performed for almost six years, and in a very different Covent Garden. Britten's own thoughts on opera in England were canvassed six months later by a special Arts Council committee. Formulated when he was working on *Billy Budd*, they define a link between the opera fringe (Britten and the EOG), and the opera establishment (Covent Garden and the Arts Council).

Billy Budd and Grand Opera

In a manner reminiscent of the denouement of a Poirot mystery, the Arts Council set itself the task in 1950 of 'solving' England's opera problem. 'What we are trying to do, Mr. Britten, is to make up our minds what are the real requirements in regard to opera and ballet during the next five years, and what funds will be needed to sustain them on the basis of building up a national opera and a national ballet.'[22] The gravity of the whole approach can be gauged from the panel's membership: Sir Ernest Pooley (Chairman of the Arts Council), Ifor Evans, Lord Esher, the composer Dr T. Wood, W. E. Williams, John Denison (music director of the Arts Council), and Eric Walter White. Like Britten, others consulted by the panel had their own axes to grind, and the exercise became a non-too-subtle form of lobbying. But the panel's language and questions, and Britten's answers, illustrate the divergent view of opera held by the two parties.

'I am very ignorant about what you do, Mr. Britten: do you only produce your own operas, or do you produce other people's operas as well?'[23] It was perhaps a mistake for the panel to show too much deference to Lord Esher. But in doing so, it displayed its own vulgarity as much as Esher's. Britten was asked to comment on whether it mattered if an opera singer could act if he or she could sing as well as Melba; would English composers contemplate writing smaller operas, 'what I might call the opera comique standard'?; was large-scale opera more difficult to compose than small-scale?; wasn't *Peter Grimes* intended for a full-sized orchestra?; could the public be persuaded to attend EOG performances all the year round if the repertory remained as it was?; and, Lord Esher enquired, couldn't Britten's chamber operas be performed at Covent Garden if

[22] Sir Ernest Pooley, Consultation with Mr. Benjamin Britten, 5 July 1950. ACGB, Sec. 54–0.2.b, Opera and Ballet Sub-Committee, Minutes Oct. 54–Dec. 57, Papers Oct. 54–7.

[23] Ibid.

he just rescored them for a larger orchestra? Significantly, this issue of size dominated the interview, and most questions displayed an often conscious prejudice against chamber opera. Wood asked the composer whether he thought there was growing demand for chamber opera; when Britten agreed but did not explicate, Wood pressed the point by saying 'as opposed to the more grandiose grand opera', gently presenting the two forms as incompatible. Britten, perhaps disingenuously, conceded the existence of some opposition to the genre, 'but if a person is moderately disposed towards opera and modern opera in particular, I do not think there is any initial resistance to us'. But his disingenuousness probably backfired: the Arts Council had not displayed a partiality towards modern opera before then, and it was not a policy likely to fill seats at Covent Garden.

The panel's apparent ignorance of Britten's output is alarming, considering the Arts Council's important role in selecting works and ventures to support. Yet there is reason to suspect that Britten's own views on opera had undergone subtle transformation since his post-*Grimes* shift from large-scale opera. By stating to the panel that he could see himself writing 'one big opera to, say, six small ones',[24] Britten was readmitting grand opera to the fold, if infrequently. In reality, the readmittance became more of a fond embrace: even including the three small-scale church parables composed in the 1960s, the proportion of 'small' to 'large' in Britten's remaining operas is almost one to one. This is significant, because large-scale opera was at this stage beyond the scope of the EOG and would result in the composer's working with the type of company that had prompted the formation of the Glyndebourne English Opera Company. But the composition of large-scale opera, and the subsequent move to the larger opera companies, was the logical result of the frustration Britten felt while running an organization that spent so much of its time with its head only just above water. This frustration was to prompt the EOG's amalgamation with Covent Garden in 1960.

The commissioning of *Billy Budd* occurred in this environment: a composer moving away from chamber opera and an Arts Council drawing no closer to it. The Council's commissioning scheme for the Festival of Britain—a celebration of the hundredth anniversary of the Great Exhibition of 1851, of which *Budd* was one result—helps to illustrate the music department's conservative view of genre. The Arts Council promoted two commissioning schemes for the Festival of Britain—operatic and orchestral. The music department's 1951 Festival subcommittee began work on the orchestral project in late 1948. At a meeting of the full panel on 5 November, it was agreed to recommend a number of proposals to the Council. Bliss or Walton should be asked to write a large choral and orchestral work, lasting forty-five minutes and to be performed at a special concert given by massed choirs assembled from all parts of Britain; performance of the work at

[24] Sir Ernest Pooley, Consultation with Mr. Benjamin Britten, 5 July 1950. ACGB, Sec. 54–0.2.b, Opera and Ballet Sub-Committee, Minutes Oct. 54–Dec. 57, Papers Oct. 54–7.

provincial centres, on a smaller scale, was considered mandatory. A Festival Psalm, to be staged in a thanksgiving service at St Paul's Cathedral, should be commissioned from Rubbra or Finzi. With the precedent of Handel's *Water Music* firmly in mind, Gordon Jacob should be asked to compose a serenade for military band, designed for performance outdoors, 'in or around boats'. Constant Lambert was to write a Festival Overture; Bax a piano concerto; Vaughan Williams a simple broad unison song 'for use in youth clubs, schools, Women's Institutes, etc. and for rural communities in general'; and Thomas Wood should be invited to write a part-song for male voices and brass band, 'intended for use more particularly in mining and other industrial areas where these resources are available'.[25] A march for military band ('on the lines of Walton's "Crown Imperial"') would also be required.[26] With each composer type-cast, and with most suggested genres reflecting England's late Romantic artistic values—pastoral, industrial, and imperial all vying for attention—the hundredth anniversary of the Great Exhibition was not only to be celebrated, it was to be celebrated in true 1851 style.

At subsequent meetings it transpired that most invitations had been accepted by the intended composers; the panel's reaction to those refusing is as illuminating as its original choice of works and musicians. In place of an overture, Lambert proposed a setting of Coleridge's poem 'Fire, Famine and Slaughter'—hardly a paean to post-industrial ideals—which was dismissed by the panel as 'unsuitable'. Vaughan Williams declined the commission of a broad unison song—despite his credentials as a champion of rural values—and the panel approached Sir George Dyson. Bax prevaricated about writing a piano concerto, so the panel decided to invite—and in this order—either Britten, Ireland, or Rawsthorne to compose the work. Britten was too busy with *Budd*, while Ireland, who wanted to compose an orchestral work, challenged the panel's determination that 'a piano concerto was in fact the work required'. Rawsthorne's very fine Piano Concerto No. 2 was the result. The Council's desire to control every aspect of the pieces commissioned is obvious; the insecurity of the music department's first years was to be stabilized by a conservative stable of works, each with the Council's imprimatur, and each forwarding the cause of English culture amidst post-war gloom.

The Council's regressive view of new music—with its emphasis on familiar forms and genres—was not confined to the orchestral commissioning scheme. The Opera and Ballet Panel met in June 1948 to discuss opera commissions for

[25] Music Panel Meeting, 5 Nov. 1948. ACGB, Sec. 46–76, Box M.21, Advisory Panel on Music, Minutes. Present at the meeting were Mary Glasgow, David Webster, Audrey Mildmay, Frank Howes, Lennox Berkeley, Percy Heming, James Lockyer, Thomas Wood, John Denison, Eric Walter White, M. J. McRobert, E. L. Horn, and Mona Tatham.

[26] Ibid., and Minutes of Music Panel Meeting, 6 Oct. 1949. ACGB, Advisory Panel on Music.

the Festival. 'Of the composers whose works might be suitable for production on the grand scale at Covent Garden in 1951, Benjamin Britten and William Walton are the obvious choices.'[27] Walton was busy with a BBC commission, which left Britten—a composer supposedly committed to the plans and scale of the English Opera Group. According to the minutes of the meeting, Britten was already considering a new grand opera for production in 1951, to be written for large orchestra, full chorus, and six to eight principals. A composition timetable is even listed: autumn 1948 to summer 1949—composition of libretto; autumn 1949 to autumn 1950—composition of score; winter 1950/1—copying of parts.[28] The timetable was probably provided by Eric Crozier, and it indicates that both he and Britten were told of the Council's plans for 1951 some time before the meeting. A measured game ensued, with Britten pretending that he was in a position to mount this new opera without the collaboration of the large companies. David Webster, who was also present at the meeting between Crozier and members of the opera panel, played along, offering the composer Covent Garden for the first performance of his new grand opera in 1951. Britten replied, equivocally, that he certainly intended to write a big new opera which should be ready in time for the Festival.[29] Despite his cool response (and Britten was not impressed by standards at Covent Garden at the time), there is little doubt that the composer seized the opportunity offered by the Festival. In his 1950 interview with the Arts Council panel he conceded that his chamber operas were 'totally unsuitable to be played at Covent Garden'.[30] If responsibility for production were to be taken away from the EOG—which had an overdraft of £8,000 at the beginning of June 1948—a large-scale opera would be required.[31] By the time the panel met on 22 June, Britten had discussed with E. M. Forster the possibility of collaborating on a new opera, and Forster's own views on opera—similar to the Arts Council's lofty aspirations—thus combined with economic factors to make the composition of a large-scale work the logical consequence.

The chronology of *Billy Budd* from here is complicated, reflecting Britten's continued attempts to maintain the situation in his favour. The commission was offered in November 1948, but Britten four months later had still not responded formally.[32] A draft contract was sent to him in May 1949 giving him total freedom as to the libretto and choice of librettist, although the Arts Council did

[27] Opera and Ballet Panel Meeting, 22 June 1948. ACGB, Opera and Ballet Panel and Standing Committees for Opera and Ballet, Minutes and Papers Feb.–Dec. 1948.

[28] Ibid.

[29] Carpenter, 270.

[30] Sir Ernest Pooley, Consultation with Mr. Benjamin Britten, 5 July 1950. ACGB, Sec. 54–0.2.b, Opera and Ballet Sub-Committee, Minutes Oct. 54–Dec. 57, Papers Oct. 54–7.

[31] See Ch. 3 for further details of the EOG's financial situation at this time.

[32] White to Britten, 27 Nov. 1948 and 26 Mar. 1949. ACGB, Festival of Britain 1951, Box 10a, Festival Brochures and Programmes.

specify that he 'arrange the musical disposition of the score and the mise-en-scène so that the opera is suitable for production at the Royal Opera House by the Covent Garden Opera Trust'.[33] Britten's response was to suggest that the opera might be more suitable for Sadler's Wells, to which the Council replied that although it had intended the new work for Covent Garden, it might consider either a production by Sadler's Wells or one as part of the Edinburgh Festival.[34] Finally, Britten informed White that he could not tie himself 'to where it will be done for reasons you already know'; he did, however, favour Sadler's Wells, '<u>if</u> . . . given a free hand re casting, [and] size of orchestra', but he could not guarantee that the work would be completed by 1951 without a commission. The terms were left open, although Covent Garden did eventually present the premiere.[35]

Britten's formative relationship with Sadler's Wells and his attitude towards Covent Garden in the late 1940s partly explains his somewhat paranoid approach to the commission. Crozier had written to White about this as early as July 1948, stating that any new opera would be staged by the EOG in association with the chorus and orchestra of Covent Garden, under the direct artistic control of the EOG.[36] The conditions were not practicable, yet Crozier ensured they were taken seriously by including the threat that 'it may be possible to obtain a private commission for Ben's next opera that would be considerably greater than any commission the Festival of Britain could offer'.[37] To finish the letter casually with the disclaimer that the idea for a private commission 'may come to nothing' in no way weakened this counter-threat, and the subsequent negotiations were influenced by the possibility that this new *Grimes* might go elsewhere.

But there was further upset from other factors beside Britten's experience with Covent Garden and Sadler's Wells. Britten's previous three operas had all been small in scale, and much negative critical response had been directed precisely at their size and allegedly limited scope, which was a view matched neatly by the Council in its 1950 interview with Britten. With a large work, Britten would be returning to 'centre stage' from the more marginal operatic position he then occupied, under the watchful eye of critics expecting another *Grimes*. Britten's need to control production of the new work—apart from keeping the opera in England—was as much recognition of this emergence from the operatic wilderness as tacit acceptance that the British public's view of opera was closer to the Arts Council's than to his own. The contrast between the Council's persistence in establishing a new grand opera company and its recurring apathy towards the work and the future of the EOG is extraordinary. Yet the Council

[33] White to Britten, 13 May 1949. Ibid.
[34] White to Britten, 31 May 1949. Ibid.
[35] Britten to White, [received] 13 Oct. 1949. Ibid.
[36] Crozier to White, 5 July 1948. Ibid.
[37] Ibid.

saw *Budd* as its own opera as much as Britten's, adding another established genre to its shopping list of English culture.

Eric Walter White previewed *Billy Budd* in *The Listener*, with the pride befitting a modern-day patron of the arts. The new work was Britten's 'maturest opera to date, one that in skill of construction, psychological subtlety, and theatrical effectiveness can without exaggeration be compared with the later works of Verdi'.[38] Others not involved in the opera also previewed or reviewed it, including Stephen Williams in the *Evening News*:

> One always resents having it dinned into one's ears that a new work is a masterpiece before it has been performed; and Benjamin Britten's 'Billy Budd' was trumpeted into the arena by such a deafening roar of advance publicity that many of us entered Covent Garden on Saturday (when the composer conducted the first performance) with a mean, sneaking hope that we might be able to flesh our fangs in it.[39]

That Williams retracted his fangs and labelled *Budd* a 'masterpiece' in no way compromises the fact that the opera did receive an enormous amount of advance publicity—more than for any of Britten's previous operas—and most of it predicted a great operatic triumph. A London premiere explains much of this, but not simply because of Covent Garden's proximity to Fleet Street; after five years of 'provincial' opera, Britten and his distinguished librettists were writing a major work for England's major opera company. The composer had come home. The BBC responded with a live broadcast of the first performance, although this was no new policy: the Corporation had also broadcast the premieres of *Lucretia* and *Albert Herring*. And in a year when newspapers either aligned themselves with the goals of the Labour-devised Festival, or criticized with zeal (Beaverbrook's *Evening Standard* and *Daily Express*), any specially commissioned element of the Festival could expect close scrutiny.

This scrutiny resulted in very mixed critical reviews of the first performance. The *Sunday Times* reported that enthusiasm for the new opera recalled the premiere of *Peter Grimes*—a view that Crozier supported.[40] Perhaps predictably, given his cosy relationship with the Aldeburgh Festival, Kenneth Clark told Forster that *Budd* was 'one of the great masterpieces that change human conduct', although the future author of *Civilisation* was clearly no slouch in the area of cultural criticism.[41] The distinguished critic Ernest Newman, however, wrote a review in the *Sunday Times* which was at once highly disparaging about Britten's return to grand opera and wholly prescient about the changes that the composer would later effect in the work:

[38] Eric Walter White, '*Billy Budd*', *The Listener* (22 Nov. 1951).

[39] Stephen Williams, *Evening News*, 3 Dec. 1951.

[40] *Sunday Times*, 2 Dec. 1951.

[41] Carpenter, 300.

The action would have gone better into two acts than four; by that means we would have been spared a good deal of repetition and padding and one or two scenes that are too 'operatic' in the unflattering sense of the term, the worst example being the ensemble of the ship's company in praise of Captain Vere at the end of the first act. I could imagine something of this sort happening on the deck of HMS Pinafore, but hardly on that of HMS Indomitable.[42]

Other critics also disliked the end of Act I, but few accused the work of being 'too operatic'. Its supposed tunelessness and lack of conventional forms, the extraordinary absence of women, the weak characterization, and the dramatically flawed prologue and epilogue—all registered complaints, no matter how far of the mark they appear today—ensured that, to many critics, *Budd* was not 'operatic' enough—at best, a partial success. Because of the enthusiasm with which the opera was anticipated, the result was bound to disappoint, and it is this feeling of disappointment that comes over most strongly in many reviews. Britten had let them down. After studying the vocal score of *Budd*, the usually prescient Desmond Shawe-Taylor wrote an enthusiastic preview in the *New Statesman*, but then watered this down after the first performance with the confession that the 'opera as a whole does not quite fulfil the hopes I had built on it'.[43] Shawe-Taylor, an admirer of Britten's music, did not escape unassailed: in a letter to Lennox Berkeley two weeks after the premiere, Britten dismissed the critics as 'vermin', and denied that they had much effect on public opinion, except on 'those dreary middlebrows who don't know what to think till they read the *New Statesman*!'[44] Before the London premiere, Webster had enthusiastically planned a Paris season of *Budd*, through which he expected to introduce the opera into the dizzy heights of the canon. The opera was duly presented there in May 1952, but critical reaction was even more tepid than it had been five months earlier. Three other presentations followed in 1952, but it was not until Britten's 1960 revision of the opera (repackaging it into two acts and effecting some of the other changes outlined in Newman's review) that interest in the work slowly rekindled.[45] A BBC broadcast of the new version in 1960 was followed by a 1964 Covent Garden production. If not quite rivalling the Savoy's great nautical opera in performance figures, *Billy Budd* has been presented by one of the major international companies every few years since. This product of the Arts Council's vision of grand opera now sits close to, if just outside, the operatic canon. There can be no doubt, however, that it is one of Britten's greatest works.

[42] Ernest Newman, *Sunday Times*, 9 Dec. 1951.

[43] Desmond Shawe-Taylor, *New Statesman* (8 Dec. 1951), quoted in Carpenter, 301.

[44] Britten to Berkeley, quoted in Carpenter, 300.

[45] Paradoxically, interest in the original four-act version has recently grown, promoted by Donald Mitchell, with performances at Covent Garden and in Vienna, among other places, and in a recording conducted by Kent Nagano.

A Coronation Opera

If the Arts Council's conservatism was exhibited in Festival commissions, it played an even more obvious role in the coronation. To celebrate the new Elizabethan age, the Council decided to commission from leading British composers and poets a collection of short a cappella pieces.

> The poets and composers are invited to approach their problem by choosing some aspect of contemporary Britain which they feel moved to treat in a spirit of acceptance, praise, loyalty, or love. Humour need not be excluded, but it is advisable to keep in mind the bearing of the individual part upon the whole . . . an item of brittle, sardonic, or satirical wit will be out of place and damaging to the general effect.
>
> So much for the manner. For the matter, the term 'contemporary Britain' should be understood in the widest sense, as including, for example, celebration of the countryside or city; the courage, skill or character of the people; the nobility or charm of their traditions and customs in public or private life; their jealously guarded and ancient liberties; their religious faith or tolerance. A search for modern parallels with the age of the first 'Oriana' may prove fruitful: the continuing spirit of discovery; the renascence of music or of the arts as a whole, loyalty to the monarchy, and compliment to the first lady of the land.[46]

In between the above draft and the formal commission, the a cappella pieces had become madrigals, and the collection 'An Oriana Garland' or 'A Garland for the Queen'. It was a regressive view—reinforced by the reference to the Oriana madrigalists—and one to which the ten poets responded with alarming ease. Swans, hollow reeds, fountains of sweetness, birds at dawn, emerald fields, and gabled roofs litter the poems; spring and summer have precedence over autumn and winter; bold children run by wild brooks. Walter de la Mare suggested that devotion to England should be set 'on the memory of your past', while Clifford Bax, taking to heart the Council's perceived renascence of the arts, noted that 'Elizabeth, Anne and Victoria brought | An age of style and of noble thought. | So may you do, and may all the arts | Burgeon from loving and loyal hearts.'[47] The composers—the great and the good of the land—employed various Tudor music techniques, and the collection was produced in time for the Coronation.

Both Walton and Britten declined the Council's invitation to contribute to the 'Garland'. Walton objected in principle to a poem that would contain no brittle, sardonic, or satirical wit—'all my best sides'.[48] Britten protested that he was far too busy with *Gloriana* to take on more work.[49] Although the Arts Council had not directly commissioned the new opera, it supported the first

[46] Arts Council Music Panel memo, undated. ACGB, Festival of Britain 1951, Box 10, Festival Brochures and Programmes.

[47] *A Garland for the Queen*, 10–14. Ibid.

[48] Walton to Denison, undated. Ibid.

[49] Britten to Denison, 9 Nov. 1952. Ibid.

production at Covent Garden via a supplementary grant of £15,000—an extraordinary sum given the piecemeal approach to support the Council offered the EOG.[50] Despite mixed critical reaction to *Billy Budd*, David Webster displayed his enthusiasm for a new opera by Britten as early as April 1952, when he assured Britten that if 'the Treasury does not fork out direct [for the new production], Cov. Gard. will find the money'.[51] More important than the Council's supplementary funds is its outlook on the coronation: was this representative of public and critical expectation of a 'Coronation Opera', and did it affect Britten in his approach to the new work?

Britten went into the composition of *Gloriana* with a rather narrow brief. Lord Harewood recounts how, on a skiing trip in March 1952, Britten discussed various 'national' operas: *The Bartered Bride* for the Czechs, *Manon* for the French, *Die Meistersinger* for the Germans, and *Boris Godunov* for the Russians. 'For the Italians undoubtedly *Aida*, said Ben. "It's the perfect expression of every kind of Italian nationalist feeling, national pride—but where's the English equivalent?" "Well, you'd better write one."'[52] National opera was not a new subject in England; twenty years earlier Vaughan Williams had described *Die Meistersinger* as the perfect representation of national spirit. 'Here is no playing with local colour, but the raising to its highest power all that is best in the national consciousness of his own country. This is universal art in truth, universal because it is so intensely national.'[53] Yet to accept that a 'national consciousness' exists and to elevate it to the highest power requires more than a little dabbling in local colour—something Britten had studiously avoided in his previous operas (except perhaps in *Albert Herring*, where it was dressed up in satire); but he would soon have to deal with it in *Gloriana*.[54]

Lytton Strachey's *Elizabeth and Essex* gave Britten a debatable start. Certainly Elizabeth I, against a backdrop of Tudor mystery, pageantry, heightened royalty, and—not least—splendid costumes, was the perfect embodiment of the Council's image of the coronation. And, if still a little early for positive feminist deconstruction, the powerful sovereign in Strachey's story would appeal to

[50] ROH, Covent Garden, Board Meeting Minutes, 1950–6, 17 Mar. 1953.

[51] Britten to Plomer, undated. Philip Reed, 'The Creative Evolution of *Gloriana*', in Paul Banks (ed.), *Britten's Gloriana* (1993), 19.

[52] Harewood, *The Tongs*, 134.

[53] Ralph Vaughan Williams, *National Music and Other Essays* (1972), 72–3.

[54] In his operetta *Paul Bunyan*, Britten had attempted to create a nationalist work out of a mythical American figure, with only limited success. The ragbag of genres brought to the operetta by composer and poet (Auden) may have been in line with its creators' commercial aims, but it undermined any sense of dramatic unity, and these two Englishmen were left unable to articulate convincingly this American legend. Typical of the critical response was that by Robert Bagar, writing with dedicated apathy in the *New York World-Telegram*, who decided that the opera was full of 'singing trees, singing geese, singing cats, a singing dog', and that the 'sets were O.K., and the costumes, ditto. The orchestra played decently more often than not.' Quoted in DMPR 917.

those who expected much from the new Elizabethan age. But Strachey's story deals essentially with the decline of a sovereign and the emotive corruption of her power. And giving this story 'local colour'—and in a form recognizable to Her Majesty's subjects—would not come easily to Britten. Although *Billy Budd* was an attempt at writing a more conventional form of opera (the all-male cast notwithstanding), even one of its librettists had despaired over aspects of the musical construction. In a letter written in early December 1950, Forster informed Britten that Claggart's monologue 'O beauty, O handsomeness' was his most important piece of writing and that he did not think the composer had made it sufficiently important musically:

> I want *passion*—love constricted, perverted, poisoned, but nevertheless *flowing* down its agonising channel; a sexual discharge gone evil. Not soggy depression or growling remorse. I seemed to be turning from one musical discomfort to another, and was dissatisfied. I looked for an aria perhaps, for a more recognisable form. I like the last section best, and if it is extended so that it dominates my vague objections may vanish. 'A longer line, a firmer melody'—exactly.[55]

It was a slightly more sophisticated version of one critical response to the opera—that Britten had been 'daring enough to compose a score without one whistleable tune'.[56] Britten responded in *Gloriana* with elaborate 'pastiche' (Ernest Newman's term and one that Britten abhorred) or a 'revitalization of older forms and styles' (the critic of the *Birmingham Post*). The courtly dances—which include a Coranto, a Pavane, a Morris Dance, and a Galliard—self-consciously refer to old styles of music, in both title and content. And the choral dances—including 'Time and Concord', 'Country Girls', 'Rustics and Fishermen'—idealize a pastoral England. The dances are the most obvious indication that Britten 'packaged' *Gloriana* into recognizable forms. But he went much further, composing orchestral preludes, finales, and arias with abandon not seen since *Peter Grimes*. Throughout, Britten divided each scene with appropriate labels: 'Entrance of the Queen', 'The Queen's Announcement', 'Lady Essex's Pleading'; or (and more importantly given their specific genre-titles) 'Raleigh's Song', 'Cecil's Song of Government', 'Second Lute Song', 'The First Duet for The Queen and Essex', 'The Dressing-Table Song', or even simply 'Duet' and 'Double Duet'. It was Britten's most conventional operatic structure—almost a number opera—and owed much to the predominantly negative critical response to *Budd* and the composer's determination to tap into the national consciousness—to produce a truly 'national' stage work.

[55] Mervyn Cooke and Philip Reed, *Benjamin Britten: Billy Budd* (1993), 61.

[56] Stephen Williams in the *New York Times*, reprinted in Donald Mitchell and Hans Keller, *Music Survey* (1981), 392.

More significant than the above indications of genre conformity is the opera's masque in Act II—Britten's concession to pageantry, and one linked with Establishment expectations of the work. The Board minutes for 16 September 1952 suggest that Covent Garden originally saw the coronation gala along traditional lines: excerpts from opera and light opera, dancing from the ballet corps, and perhaps some orchestral music.

Mr Webster said that the date appointed for the Gala Performance was 8th June. The board discussed the programme to be given at this performance. In view of the special circumstances attending the commissioning of the new Britten opera ('Gloriana') it was agreed that this must be the work to be performed. It was anticipated that the opera would contain scope for dancing, but as this was regarded as most important, it was generally agreed that the matter should be discussed urgently with Mr. Britten. It was further suggested that it would be welcome to the Ballet Company (who had always hoped for a ballet by Mr. Britten) if the ballet sections of the opera were self-contained and capable of being performed separately. Finally it was agreed that the first performance of the new opera should be given before the Gala Performance.[57]

Two points emerge from this: first, although the Board was determined to present the premiere of *Gloriana* before the gala performance ('the kind of audience that one attracts on such an occasion is on the whole not the type one wants for a first performance', Webster wrote presciently[58]), it was Britten who objected. At a Board meeting in October it was reported that 'Mr. Britten would very much prefer the first performance to be given on the Gala night, because the opera was written as an offering to the Queen'.[59] Britten's stubbornness here is difficult to understand; even the Queen Mother had commented on the deadening effect of the presence of the royal family at premieres. After Constant Lambert's ballet *Tiresias*, first produced in 1951, she had assured Webster that she was 'sure this Ballet will have a much greater success at subsequent performances. It is most interesting but we do not bring the kind of audience that responds well to a first performance of this kind.'[60] Britten's desire to play a role in this important event—either because in doing so he would create a national opera, his own *Boris Godunov*, or because it allowed him closer access to the upper echelons of British society—ultimately prevailed over common sense, and the premiere of the opera was held on the gala night.

The second important point to emerge from the minutes is that although work on the libretto had commenced some months earlier, Britten had probably only

[57] ROH, Covent Garden, Board Meeting Minutes, 1950–6, 16 Sept. 1952.

[58] Webster to Viscount Waverley, 25 July 1952. ROH, Covent Garden, C.G. Gala Performance Item 59/4a, General Correspondence.

[59] ROH, Covent Garden, Board Meeting Minutes, 1950–6, 21 Oct. 1952.

[60] Webster to Viscount Waverley, 25 July 1952. ROH, Covent Garden, C.G. Gala Performance Item 59/4a, General Correspondence.

just begun sketching the music around the time of the September Board meeting, and thus composition of the opera coincided with demands from Covent Garden for greater involvement of the ballet company. But this was a contentious suggestion; Frederick Ashton rightly maintained that the type of dances suitable for an opera with an Elizabethan theme would not display the virtuosity of the ballet corps at its best. The Board concluded that a separate ballet would have to be performed on the night of the gala.[61] Britten's mortified response was almost identical to that of the Composer in Strauss's *Ariadne auf Naxos*: 'you know that only over my dead body, & dead opera too, will there be a ballet before Gloriana that night. Let them prance on their points as much as anyone wants after—but not before.'[62] Sensing that there would be few wanting a ballet at the end of the evening—least of all Her Majesty, for whom this might be a 'severe strain'—the Board decided that the 'least unsatisfactory' solution was that the ballet company should appear only in the opera, and that Britten should do everything possible to incorporate special music for dancing.[63] The resulting masque, with its fair share of point-prancing, is the least successful aspect of the drama. Although noble in its intention to show a loving and much loved queen, the masque is disproportionately long, and the narrative impetus established in Act I dissolves uncomfortably. The similarity between the music, words, and style of the masque and the Council's Oriana Garland was probably no coincidence. Britten's concession showed dubious judgement.

Covent Garden's concession—that the premiere of *Gloriana* should occur on the night of the gala—was equally questionable. As a result, the audience included thirty-one members of the royal family, fifty-seven members of the royal household, one hundred and thirty-six ambassadors and ministers, ninety-nine Cabinet and Shadow Cabinet Ministers, seventy-three delegates from the Commonwealth Prime Ministers' Conference, thirty members of the Colonial Office, twelve Commonwealth Parliamentary Delegates, thirty people under the auspices of the Lord Chamberlain's Department for Visiting Foreign Royalty, thirty members of Covent Garden's staff, and eighty guests of Covent Garden and the Arts Council.[64] Of the 1,000 seats in the orchestra stalls, circle, and grand tier, almost 600 were occupied by people on Covent Garden's Debrett-esque invitation list.

The pompous Tory MP-cum-music critic Beverly Baxter described the scene:

> Just in front of us sat Sir James Dunn and his nice wife and, leaning out of a box, was that elegant Montrealer J. W. McConnell. I rather think that George Drew was among the

[61] ROH, Covent Garden, Board Meeting Minutes, 1950–6, 25 Sept. 1952.

[62] Britten to Webster, 20 Nov. 1952. ROH, Covent Garden, Benjamin Britten Correspondence.

[63] ROH, Covent Garden, Board Meeting Minutes, 1950–6, 20 Jan. 1953.

[64] Letter to Viscount Waverly [probably from Muriel Kerr], 10 Apr. 1953. ROH, Covent Garden, C.G. Gala Performance Item 59/4a, General Correspondence.

political nobs, but, at any rate, Louis St. Laurent was undoubtedly sitting close to Premier Bob Menzies of Australia. . . . Mr. Speaker Morrison of the British House of Commons looked apprehensive. In private he plays both the fiddle and the bagpipes but how would he respond to this new cacophonous music of the ultramoderns? The only politician who seemed unworried was Premier Nehru of India. He has lived so long on the edge of a volcano that even Britten's music would be unlikely to frighten him.[65]

It was first-night parading at its worst. If Baxter was indicative of the degree of sophistication in the theatre that night, the opera was clearly in trouble. Not surprisingly, the masque and the courtly dances, treated in isolation, were an immediate success with this audience and with many critics. But the sum of the parts did not necessarily make a whole. Those who applauded the pageantry detested the spoken epilogue, where the dying queen recalls people and events in her past. Even Donald Mitchell, Britten's closest critical ally, thought it 'problematic'. But fifty years on, the epilogue stands as an innovative and masterful conclusion to the (revised) opera.[66] Cinema has transformed opera and theatre techniques in the last few decades, and ready acceptance of these new techniques—and of the 'bleakness' ('inappropriate') and 'chilliness'[67] of the epilogue—confirms Britten's dramatic prescience rather than any misjudgement. Indeed, when twenty-five years later Eva Peron died on stage in Lloyd Webber's *Evita*, it was an almost exact replica of Queen Elizabeth's death in *Gloriana*.

The first-night response to *Gloriana* ensured that the opera would not immediately receive the nationalist laurels that Britten and Harewood had so desired. Applause of the eminent and dignified audience was muted by white gloves and even, perhaps, some ignorance of how to behave At The Opera. And while critics were quick to applaud individual scenes, they were even quicker to disparage the supposed consequent disruption of dramatic purpose. 'As a pageant, as a piece of stage colour and production . . . *Gloriana* succeeds. As an opera it is a dead loss' was a typical verdict.[68] Some audience members agreed:

I believe a great many other people feel as I do that it was a great mistake, a really lamentable mistake, to choose a work of Benjamin Britten's for last night's Gala at Covent Garden. . . . I imagine all the statesmen and potentates present must have been entirely unimpressed, if not thoroughly bored, by the whole performance . . .[69]

Not so. Seymour Egerton of the establishment Coutts Bank wrote Wood an appreciative letter the day after the gala: 'not only was the decor magnificent but

[65] Beverly Baxter, 'The One Sour Note of the Coronation', *Maclean's Magazine* (1 Sept. 1953), 53–4.

[66] Revisions included the excision of various characters from this epilogue, but the principle remained the same.

[67] Antonia Malloy, 'Aspects of the First Critical Response to *Gloriana*', Banks, *Britten's Gloriana*, 63.

[68] 'E.S.', '*Gloriana*', *Music and Musicians*, 1/11 (July 1953), 3.

[69] Gilbert Talbot to the Directors of the ROH, 9 June 1953. ROH, Covent Garden, C.G. Gala Performance Item 59/4b, General Correspondence.

all the arrangements for arriving and departing could not have been bettered.'[70] It was a popular theme in thankyou letters at the time: 'We all enjoyed Gloriana itself very much, but I think that we will treasure most the memory of the occasion itself. In these days when even the best seats in the house are apt to be graced only by lounge suits, it was nothing less than thrilling to see Covent Garden look as it does in one's dreams.'[71] The dreams came at a price: £1,660 spent on internal temporary renovations; three swags of red and white roses for the royal box at £15 each; fifty-four magnolia garlands at £4 each; a rose de Meux garland for the queen's powder room at 7*s.* 6*d.* per foot; and two oval mirrors for the royal retiring room, each decorated with (unspecified) green foliage at 5 guineas a piece.[72]

Britten hid behind inaccurate box-office figures: to Plomer he wrote that 'Gloriana came to a triumphant, & temporary, conclusion I gather last Saturday. It has been an enormous success, from the box office, having on average beaten all other operas there this season.'[73] In reality, apart from *Wozzeck* and *Figaro*, *Gloriana* was the season's worst-performing opera—a pattern repeated during Covent Garden's tour to Bulawayo in late 1953. The Board expressed concern at the 'bitter nature' of the critical and public reception of the work. 'It was felt that, while the work had undoubtedly been rushed, it contained much fine music.'[74] Some Board members extended this into an indictment of a libretto ill-suited to a gala occasion; the expectation that Britten would compose another *Merrie England*—and the sense of failure when he did not—was clearly not confined to the gala audience. Rather illuminatingly, the Chairman of Covent Garden hoped that 'those who appreciated and understood the work would find a means of expressing their views, for he feared that its unfavourable reception might react adversely upon the Arts Council as well as upon the Royal Opera House'.[75] Britten's brief love affair with these two august bodies was over, and reconciliation was some years off.

Britten revised the epilogue of his 'slighted child' (his own term), and sanctioned performances of the opera without the masque. Although subsequent productions have tended to retain it, Britten's ambivalence towards the scene suggests that critics may have come close to the mark. Indeed, without incredibly careful handling, the masque can seem like a pretty ritual, adding little to the narrative and taking much from the drama.[76] Britten's antagonism towards any kind of gala performance lasted well into the 1970s, when he refused to launch

[70] Egerton to Wood, 9 June 1953. ROH, Covent Garden, C.G. Gala Performance Item 59/4b, General Correspondence.

[71] N. E. Martin [Cabinet Office] to Wood, 9 June 1953. Ibid.

[72] Estimate by Constance Spry (florist), undated. Ibid.

[73] Britten to Plomer, July 1953. Banks, *Britten's Gloriana*, 46.

[74] ROH, Covent Garden, Board Meeting Minutes, 1950–6, 16 June 1953.

[75] Ibid.

[76] The same criticism is often made of the rituals in Birtwistle's operas.

Death in Venice on such an occasion.[77] Yet the failure of the opera in 1953 should also be viewed in terms of the cultural climate. To Robert Hewison, who has analysed *Gloriana* in terms of 1953 English culture, 'the darkness at the close of *Gloriana*, even the failure of the first night, shows that Britten was more in touch with his time than the pomp and circumstance of a Royal gala might lead us to suppose'.[78] It is more probable that, like the Arts Council, audiences would have preferred babbling brooks, sleeping swans, and bold sunrises to a portrait of a bald and dying queen at the end of her reign; fifty years after the first performance, at the end of another Elizabethan period (but with a somewhat more tarnished image of royalty prevailing), the extraordinary success of the *Gloriana* revivals, and the incredible poignancy of the opera's final scene, do tend to support this view.

A Case for Grand Opera

Like *Gloriana*, Britten soon became Covent Garden's 'slighted child'. The composer retreated to the security of Aldeburgh, while Covent Garden's enthusiasm for Britten's works was replaced by a dispassionate assessment of the difficulties involved in performing them. Yet when Sadler's Wells proposed a production of the coronation opera in 1966, Covent Garden responded in a rather territorial manner, as Pears made clear:

> I hear that you want to put pressure on Ben to withdraw his agreement to the Sadler's Wells 'Gloriana'. . . . The work is in the public domain. There has been no talk of 'Gloriana' at the Garden for ages—there is no sign of it for the next two years. Sadler's Wells offer[s] him a firm immediate date with the producer of his choice and the Elizabeth of his choice (who in three years may well be past it). Why should he wait? Gloriana was a so-called 'flop' at Covent Garden for two reasons: first, because of the Comedy of the first night and the shock at not having a 1953 Merrie England, and second, more important, because it is <u>not</u> a Covent Garden opera. Ben is incapable of writing 'grandiose', both sound-wise and stage-wise, and Gloriana is in fact much more likely to come off in a smaller theatre than Covent Garden.[79]

Sadler's Wells won the day, and the company's season of *Gloriana* helped the opera along its rather long road to rehabilitation.[80] More interesting than Pears's evaluation of the opera's premiere is his impassioned but nevertheless inaccurate assessment of Britten's *métier* as an opera composer. Although at the time of Pears's letter both he and Britten were involved in the second of the intimate

[77] ROH, Covent Garden, English Opera Group Ltd. Board—Minutes 1960–72, 14 Dec. 1972.

[78] Robert Hewison, 'Benjamin Britten and the *Gloriana* Story', in Banks, *Britten's Gloriana*, 15.

[79] Pears to Webster, 22 Apr. 1966. ROH, Covent Garden, Benjamin Britten Correspondence.

[80] The launch of this rehabilitation was the 1963 performance at Royal Festival Hall to celebrate Britten's fiftieth birthday, on the day President J. F. Kennedy was shot.

church parables, Covent Garden, from the mid-1940s up to 1953, sustained unshaken confidence in the composer's ability to write grand opera. Indeed, this enthusiasm for Britten's music, alongside many economic and social arguments, suggests that Britten—notwithstanding his attraction to chamber sonorities and his desire to write for Peter Pears, whose voice was not best suited to grand opera in the conventional sense and theatres—might have been better served, from the pont of view of opera infrastructure and public taste in Britain, had he never composed chamber opera, but instead had continued to write grand opera for England's grand opera house.

The success of Sadler's Wells's 1945 foray into contemporary English opera had been remarkable. Britten's withdrawal of support from Sadler's Wells in 1945 and Covent Garden's ideological quest for national opera had ensured a relatively fluent introduction of *Peter Grimes* into the larger company's repertory. Even before this introduction was completed, Webster was negotiating with Britten for a new large-scale opera for Covent Garden's 1947–8 season. In November 1946 the ROH Trust discussed the possibility of performing *Lucretia*, a proposal that was dropped because Christie's ownership of the performing rights lasted until October 1947. 'The alternative would be a new work by Mr. Britten. There was general support for this proposal which it was felt might establish a connection which would be useful in later years.'[81] The Trust's intention was clear, and Webster was asked to pursue the suggestion with Britten. His goodwill is evident in the resulting letter: all details of casting and design for the new production would be decided in consultation with the composer; *Peter Grimes* would be in the theatre by the second season; Britten would receive total cooperation from Covent Garden in his new opera company—including use of the theatre, production staff, and even artists.[82] Webster's determination to form a close collaboration with Britten, along nineteenth-century Italian lines, was without doubt. And even though Britten's reservations about established opera companies—even barely established ones—must already have been known to Webster ('We realise from all that you said how intent you are in maintaining the freedom and independence that you feel you need for yourself and the people immediately collaborating with you'[83]), he was obviously not aware of how much time Britten would put into the newly formed English Opera Group.

The commercial success of Covent Garden's *Peter Grimes* can only have increased the company's enthusiasm for Britten's music (Table 4.2). Although respectable (even enviable for a modern English opera), an average attendance at *Grimes* of 66 per cent in 1947–8 had further significance: fourteen performances of *Grimes* were given—the highest number of any opera that season, and a large

[81] ROH, Covent Garden, ROH Trust—Minutes, 1946–51, 22 Nov. 1946.

[82] Webster to Britten, 25 Nov. 1946. ROH, Covent Garden, Benjamin Britten Correspondence.

[83] Ibid.

Table 4.2 Audience attendance figures, *Peter Grimes*, Covent Garden 1947–1954, as a percentage of seating capacity[a]

Date		%	Date		%
1947	6 November	67		1 November	48
	11 November	59	1949	14 January	93
	13 November	68		3 March	74
	28 November	87		14 October	73
	9 December	75		9 November	58
	13 December	67		1 December	73
1948	1 January	88		30 December	50
	6 January	82	1950	17 February	84
	12 March	78		4 May	70
	17 March	43	1953	14 November	86
	17 April	76		16 November	67
	26 April	29		20 November	59
	6 May	50		24 November	44
	22 May	52		4 December	55
	5 October	55		9 December	73
	23 October	79	1954	20 April	47

[a] ROH, Covent Garden, Misc. Book 25. In this book paying attendance at each opera is listed. The table represents these figures as a percentage of the theatre's seating capacity. Alterations to this capacity over the period covered have been included in the equation. Figures represent paying audience only.

number over which to sustain high attendances—playing to a total paying audience of 18,606. Its closest rivals as far as number of performances is concerned were *Tristan* (with Flagstad) and *La traviata* (with Schwarzkopf); each of these received ten performances and attracted a total paying audience of 18,910 and 18,790 respectively. And on average attendance alone, *Grimes* beat *Turandot*, *Der Rosenkavalier*, *Il trovatore*, and *Rigoletto*: not only was Britten's first major opera competing with some of the stars of the operatic canon, but in some cases it was actually winning.

Average attendance for *Peter Grimes* increased over the two subsequent Covent Garden seasons (70 per cent in 1948–9 and 68 per cent in 1949–50). As a result, *Grimes* did better at the box office than *Fidelio* and *Boris Godunov*, although figures for the later seasons are less impressive than for 1947–8, when far more performances of the opera were given. Regardless of this, *Grimes* was financially, critically, and artistically viable for the Royal Opera House—no small consideration in the company's first years of economic stringency and organizational mayhem—and Britten himself was seen as a composer worth cultivating. This cultivation took a number of forms over the years following: pleas for a new opera regardless of the Festival of Britain commissioning scheme; requests for collaboration with John Gielgud on a production of *The Tempest*; attempts to book Britten to conduct a number of performances of *Peter Grimes*; and even the suggestion that Britten should be appointed music director of Covent Garden. Britten declined these offers and more, but the goodwill remained obvious and, some time after the failure of *Gloriana*, became mutual.

At the same time as Covent Garden's successful first production of *Peter Grimes*, the English Opera Group presented a short season at Covent Garden of Britten's first two chamber operas. Despite the Opera Trust's assurance of amity, this season was the first and last appearance of the EOG at Covent Garden; public reaction to *Lucretia* and *Albert Herring* in this theatre was not at all encouraging (Table 4.3). Britten later labelled *Lucretia* his most popular chamber opera, yet it averaged an audience attendance of only 53 per cent at Covent Garden. The opera was then only one year old and exhibiting nothing of the staying-power of *Grimes*. Even though *Albert Herring* attracted larger audiences on average than *Lucretia* (58 per cent), the public response was in one sense more alarming; this was the opera's first London season, and it was attracting few of those who would come to *Peter Grimes* in the following months. Clearly, Britten's name (and indeed Pears's) was not enough to guarantee large audiences at the Opera House; the actual opera, its size, the company performing it, and the marketing/subscription mechanisms in place were important factors.

The success of *Grimes* and the mixed fortunes of the EOG coincided with Webster's suggestion that Britten should write an opera to be performed at Covent Garden in 1951. Although Britten's agreement was slow in coming, his authority within Covent Garden was never in doubt: 'as you know our views on

Table 4.3 Audience attendance figures, EOG season, Covent Garden, 1947, as a percentage of seating capacity[a]

Albert Herring		*The Rape of Lucretia*	
8 October	61	10 October	44
9 October	48	14 October	55
11 October	65	17 October	60
13 October	42		
15 October	60		
16 October	56		
18 October	73		

[a] ROH, Covent Garden, Misc. Book 25. Figures based on a seating capacity of 2,022, that used by Covent Garden in its 1947–8 attendance calculations for its own season. Figures represent paying audience only.

this matter [of casting] differ so strongly that before I commit myself to any production of a new work at Covent Garden I shall have to be very strongly assured that my demands will be met.'[84] Not least of the difficult requirements met for *Billy Budd* was the need for an all-male cast. Covent Garden's accession to Britten's demands—the expensive hiring of guest singers from outside the company, and flying in the face of audiences' conception of grand opera—was no empty gesture.

Despite the critics' mixed reaction, *Billy Budd* was enormously popular in its 1951 season—selling out for the first six performances (Table 4.4). Although Britten planned to fulfil his EOG commitments after the completion of *Budd* (including the commission for the Venice Biennale Festival), the opera's commercial success, and the composer's pleasant relationship with Covent Garden, must have made grand opera rather alluring. Writing to Webster after the premiere of *Billy Budd*, Britten emphasized his delight in the atmosphere and quality of the opera company. 'You said you hoped it was only the beginning of our collaboration, & so do I. I wish, when the alarms have somewhat died down, we could have a talk to discuss in what way I could be a help to you, because I most sincerely would like to be.'[85] The benefits of their continued collaboration would hardly be one-way, and the image here of a composer seduced by his grand-opera experience is hard to deny. Yet the commercial success of the opera was in fact limited: the final six performances in April and May 1952 attracted an audience average of only 55 per cent—a sorry contrast to the capacity audiences of the first six shows. The significance of this can scarcely be exaggerated. Britten and Covent Garden embarked on informal negotiations for a new opera in early 1952 with every indication that *Budd* would follow the commercial path paved by *Grimes*. By the time of the disastrous commercial result of the April/May performances, Princess Elizabeth had given her approval to the new project *Gloriana*, and Britten and Plomer had already committed themselves to it. Britten's new work was to be completed in the shadow of this neither critically *nor* commercially successful piece, and the pressure for conventional opera would have been high.

The audience response to the first season of *Gloriana* did nothing to encourage in Britten a long-term return to grand opera (Table 4.4). If not quite on the same scale as *Billy Budd*, the first run of *Gloriana* did reasonably well—an average attendance of 70 per cent, although this figure disguises some fairly undersubscribed performances. But most telling is the opera's rerun in January and February 1954, when audiences averaged only 36 per cent. Without the sustaining publicity of the first run of a new opera, *Gloriana* did miserable business. From Covent Garden's perspective, the coronation opera displayed the worst

[84] Britten to Webster, 27 Oct. 1948. ROH, Covent Garden, Benjamin Britten Correspondence.
[85] Britten to Webster, 9 Dec. 1951. Ibid.

Table 4.4 Audience attendance figures, *Billy Budd* and *Gloriana*, Covent Garden, 1951–4, as a percentage of seating capacity[a]

Billy Budd		*Gloriana*	
1 December 1951	86	8 June 1953	80
8 December	100	11 June	84
11 December	99	13 June	93
15 December	100	18 June	74
21 December	100	30 June	61
27 December	100	2 July	65
17 April 1952	67	4 July	46
21 April	51	7 July	52
26 April	50	9 July	53
1 May	63	11 July	73
8 May	49	29 January 1954	34
13 May	47	2 February	34
		16 February	39

[a] ROH, Covent Garden, Misc. Book 25. Figures for *Budd* based on a seating capacity of 2,018, that used by Covent Garden in its 1951–2 attendance calculations. Figures for *Gloriana* based on a seating capacity of 2,026 (1953), that used by Covent Garden in its 1952–3 attendance calculations; and 2,062 (1954), the figure listed in the 1957–8 ROH Annual Report. The remaining 14 per cent of the audience at the first performance of *Budd*, and 20 per cent at *Gloriana*, were most likely made up with people holding complimentary tickets. Figures represent paying audience only.

traits of its genre: expensive and indulgent (twelve trumpets for the gala night since, as Imogen Holst put it so succinctly and without even a trace of irony, 'what else were the taxpayers paying for'?[86]), but without the appeal to counter these two qualities.

Gloriana established that a correlation between production costs and popularity did not exist; only half of the £24,000 spent on producing the new opera (not running it) was recovered at the box office. It was also one of the most conspicuously expensive operas mounted by Covent Garden in its first fifteen years (Table 4.5). Certainly the supplementary grant from the Arts Council inspired the lavish spending on the production, but Covent Garden would have seen its outlay as investment in an opera that it was sure would capture the public's imagination and support, and thus remain in the company's repertory for years to come.

[86] Imogen Holst, diary entry, 30 Oct. 1952. Philip Reed in Banks, *Britten's Gloriana*, 35. Ironically, she was (perhaps consciously) revisiting Beecham's advice to William Walton when he was composing *Belshazzar's Feast*, that he might as well include a brass band in the score since the piece would only ever be played once.

Table 4.5 Production costs (£), Covent Garden Opera, December 1946–October 1955 (selected and rounded off)[a]

First performance	Opera	Costumes	Scenery	Props sundry	Miscellaneous	Music	Fees	Rehearsal expenses	Design and production expenses	Total
12 Dec. 1946	*Fairy Queen*	3,816	2,126	208	43	678	1,285	—	—	8,156
14 Jan. 1947	*Carmen*	2,826	2,721	225	19	71	920	240	—	7,022
22 Apr. 1947	*Rosenkavalier*	3,988	1,875	415	59	848	668	—	—	7,853
29 May 1947	*Turandot*	6,214	2,045	1,631	79	65	1,085	560	—	11,679
31 Oct. 1947	*Rigoletto*	1,015	1,545	106	266	10	620	205	40	3,807
6 Nov. 1947	*Grimes*	1,057	829	1,161	80	758	1,150	38	—	5,073
21 Jan. 1948	*Meistersinger*	1,327	174	337	15	404	368	798	—	3,423
19 Feb. 1948	*Tristan*	88	241	228	47	15	300	410	—	1,329
12 May 1948	*Boris Godunov*	7,121	5,674	765	250	16	525	330	272	14,953
15 Oct. 1948	*La Bohème*	592	183	231	25	48	—	9	—	1,088
29 Oct. 1949	*The Olympians*	5,384	3,604	931	447	3	500	1,097	98	12,064
21 Dec. 1950	*Queen of Spades*	11,484	4,183	798	191	261	1,575	479	—	18,971
26 Apr. 1951	*Pilgrim's Progress*	4,683	3,073	410	36	88	765	640	67	9,762
6 Aug. 1951	*Bohemian Girl*	7,723	5,162	613	78	734	1,400	3,477	467	19,654
1 Dec. 1951	*Billy Budd*	4,302	2,045	635	171	10	1,131	2,212	457	10,963
13 May 1953	*Elektra*	762	568	5	15	241	1,000	1,506	162	4,259
8 June 1953	*Gloriana*	16,784	3,922	271	31	21	1,400	1,560	—	23,989
3 Dec. 1954	*Troilus*	6,674	3,019	141	74	9	1,113	1,143	10	12,183
17 Jan. 1955	*Midsummer Marriage*	4,070	1,785	448	49	13	775	676	115	7,931
17 Oct. 1955	*Otello*	7,976	3,999	600	112	107	1,200	493	235	14,722

[a] ROH, Covent Garden, File 148.

Although the EOG was aware that popularity was not necessarily linked to high production expenses (*Let's Make an Opera*, for example), it lacked Covent Garden's buying power. The extravagance on a production might not have attracted British audiences, who were only just beginning to cultivate a taste for opera, while at the same time Britten and Covent Garden were still learning how to present it; audience figures demonstrate consistently high support for operas with big-name stars. Such a cast for one performance of *Die Meistersinger* in Covent Garden's third season attracted almost 20 per cent more than the average attendance at the same production with a different cast, in spite of the higher priced tickets.[87] Furthermore, Covent Garden was buying these stars—and indeed running the company—for far less than the Metropolitan Opera, for example. In 1952, when John Denison and Rudolf Bing compared costs of the two companies, Bing observed:

> It looks to me as if you were working there under slave labor conditions! Your average chorus salary of $28 [£9–10] per week compares with our weekly rate of $107.50. Your average orchestra rate of under $50 per week compares with ours of $153 per week. Apparently the more expensive of your new productions cost something like $40,000 while we must budget anything between $70,000–$80,000 for a new production....
>
> Of course your ticket prices are very much lower than ours. One guinea is approximately $3 while our top price so far was $7.50 and will this season go up to $8. Our cash loss of the past season was approximately $490,000 which covers a 22 week season in New York and a 7 week tour in the provinces....
>
> Now as far as solo personnel is concerned, we have quite a few singers whom we pay $500, $600, $700 and $800 per performance, while the vast majority would get anything between $200 and $500 per week, but there are only a few beginners who get less than $200 per week. In fact, our minimum union rate for solo singers is $175 per week.[88]

There are dangers in blanket comparisons between the two companies' operational costs in their own countries (for example, the Metropolitan's chief mechanic, chief electrician, and property master were each on a salary of approximately $16,000 per annum, which, as Bing pointed out, was on a par with the earnings of the British Secretary of State for Foreign Affairs), but the international nature of some commodities used by both companies permits some comparisons. The average cost of 'Guest Artistes' at Covent Garden in the year to 31 March 1955 for ordinary opera performances was £146 per performance; for the *Ring* in May 1955, the average was £922 per performance.[89] The cost of more expensive guests was usually covered by higher ticket prices and larger audiences. Yet, rather than exploiting Covent Garden's ability to hire opera stars relatively cheaply, thus ensuring the commercial success of the opera (admittedly some

[87] ROH, Covent Garden, Misc. Book 25.

[88] Bing to Denison, 8 Oct. 1952. ACGB, Music Department, 1945–55, Opera 1951–2.

[89] ROH, Covent Garden, File 190, Artists' Salaries 1948–70.

would have baulked at the thought of learning a new English work), Britten insisted on using singers from the EOG in his Covent Garden operas—none of whom, apart from Pears, had strong commercial appeal (or indeed, large voices). Joan Cross received only £50 per performance of *Gloriana* while Pears received £80; it was not much more than the fees both would receive for *The Turn of the Screw*, and is a striking indicator of the perceived commercial value of these two singers on the London operatic stage.

Britten was lucky to be composing opera in Covent Garden's early years of optimism and experimentation, but the company's youth meant that mistakes were made and opportunities lost. Britten's next venture with Covent Garden was the commercially successful ballet *The Prince of the Pagodas*, but his desire to return to the opera stage was obvious: 'I do hope we can meet before too long; don't think of me only as a ballet composer, will you?!!'[90] Webster didn't, and a few years later agreed to produce *A Midsummer Night's Dream*. Britten himself was more circumspect about this opera, 'which would be so written as to be suitable either in a small theatre (e.g. at Aldeburgh) or in a large theatre (e.g. at Covent Garden)'.[91] It followed the limited commercial success of *The Turn of the Screw*, and suggests that Britten was hedging his bets. But even with poor houses, Covent Garden's capacity ensured that its productions of Britten's operas played to far more people per performance than the EOG's performances in Aldeburgh and on tour, and were treated more seriously by music critics. And whatever the merits of Covent Garden's Britten productions, emerging public taste was for grand opera—as was that of this grand opera's sponsor, the Arts Council. Today, audiences throughout the world for *Grimes* outnumber those for the ensuing four chamber operas combined, and the Royal Opera, not small companies best suited for productions of the small-scale operas, continues to be the tarnished jewel in the Arts Council's crown. At a time when the economic reasons for mounting chamber opera are absolute, it is Britten's big operas—*Peter Grimes*, *Billy Budd*, *Gloriana*, *A Midsummer Night's Dream*, and *Death in Venice*—that opera companies, with their existing *and* surviving infrastructure, continue to promote.

[90] Britten to Webster, 18 May 1955. ROH, Covent Garden, Benjamin Britten Correspondence.
[91] ROH, Covent Garden, Opera Sub-Committee—Minutes 1951–9, 14 Oct. 1959.

Chapter 5

Aldeburgh's Court Composer

> And yet—there was something absurd about travelling so far to win success with British operas that Manchester, Edinburgh and London would not support. The cost of transporting forty people and their scenery was enormously high: despite packed houses in Holland, despite financial support from the British Council in Switzerland, it looked as if we should lose at least three thousand pounds on twelve Continental performances. It was exciting to represent British music at international festivals, but we could not hope to repeat the experiment another year.
>
> 'Why not,' said Peter Pears, 'make our own Festival? A modest Festival with a few concerts given by friends? Why not have an Aldeburgh Festival?'[1]

The above account of the Aldeburgh Festival's origins, if not apocryphal, is not without mythical tinges. Like most classical myths, it has appeared in many guises since its first publication in 1948—its portentous words given more significance as each year passed and the Festival's achievements increased in number and scale. Like many myths, the delineation between good and evil is clear: the artist on one side, an indifferent society on the other. And although protestations of modesty underpinned Pears's suggestion, the idea of a festival in a town without an opera house, in a county without extensive rail networks, and in a country then with few motor cars was almost hubristic—with Pears as the self-styled Icarus, joining feathers together with wax before flying towards the sun. Where once Arachne had spun herself into hubris, Pears and Britten counted seats and measured the stage of Aldeburgh's Jubilee Hall; this done to their satisfaction, and the economic rationale for a festival in place, the revenge of the insulted goddess (Athene) was surely only a season away.

Yet there was no nemesis; instead, the foundations of a remarkably successful, long-running festival were laid. But in laying them, Britten was tinkering with the traditional patterns of demand and supply; although his music remained on

[1] Eric Crozier, *Aldeburgh Festival Programme Book* (1948).

offer, purchasing it was made more difficult. Britten's work with the BBC in the 1930s had been an extension of a barely formulated socialism: the older methods of supplying a product to an elitist market had given way to the democratization of serious music. But the new festival would revert to elitist presumptions and practices. Its positioning demanded a specific audience—local or mobile—while the size of venues made tickets scarce and hierarchies of taste inevitable. Moreover, Pears's 'few friends' were anything but modest: Bream, Rostropovich, Vishnevskaya, Richter, and Britten (as performer) each built a lasting relationship with the Festival. The intimacy and flexibility of their involvement (where else would you find Britten and Richter playing piano duets?) gave Aldeburgh's Festival a flavour quite different from that of Salzburg or Edinburgh.

If this were a history of such festivals—Salzburg old and distinguished, Edinburgh young and innovative—it would have to be content with names and dates—a catalogue of often rich and famous musicians who performed; it might also attempt an analysis of the effects of these performances on concert repertory, performance practice, and, that elusive concept, the canon. But because the Aldeburgh Festival was, like Bayreuth, directed by a composer, its history must be more than a list of artists who would never be rich on its (financial) pickings. With new works written every year for Festival premieres, the relationship between the performance environment and the music composed must be considered. Did the audience at Aldeburgh bring with it new demands to which Britten responded, or was the reverse the case? Did the economics of the Festival limit the scope or dictate the type of composition, as it so obviously had with the English Opera Group? Moreover, did the invention of Festival traditions—in Hobsbawm's memorable phrase—influence the music Britten composed?[2]

Britain's Festival Culture

By the end of 1946 Britten's relationship with John Christie and his Glyndebourne Festival, which was idiosyncratically run and which prided itself on its independence, was troubled. Jealousy, intrigue, stupefaction, and hostility—neatly paralleling the onstage emotions of *Lucretia*—distracted Britten from his creative work. Throughout his stay at Glyndebourne, Britten remained ignorant of all but the most basic financial details of producing opera, although the lessons learnt from this company with its somewhat unrealistic conception of demand and supply would probably have been of little use. This changed very quickly: the composer's first year with the EOG (as outlined in Chapter 3) left him not only financially numerate but also too close to the *process* of opera to

[2] Eric Hobsbawm and Terence Ranger (eds.), *The Invention of Tradition* (1992).

compose truly autonomous stage works.[3] Quite apart from the opportunities for concert works and exhibitions offered by Pears's suggested festival, a new base for the EOG at Aldeburgh—neither immediate nor permanent as will be seen below—with guaranteed performances during the Festival, fees set by the Group's directors, and the theatre agent's commission (like Churchill) dormant, was clearly an attractive idea.[4] But if Britten's experience of touring the English provinces had taught him anything, it was that audiences did not always attend or applaud opera. How would a season in Aldeburgh succeed where those elsewhere had not?

Humphrey Carpenter, in his biography of Britten, is not without his own shades of mythogenesis. Writing on post-war music in Britain, he confidently states that in 1947 'festivals were springing up everywhere'.[5] Although the new Edinburgh Festival was on hand to support Carpenter's belief in a burgeoning interest in the arts, the size and aims of this Scottish event distinguished it from other British festivals, most of which owed their origins to polished notions of civic pride, the dawning recognition of tourism as a commercial industry,[6] and a pro-rural element to CEMA/Arts Council funding (though this was to diminish rather quickly). And Carpenter's quaint phraseology takes no account of the scale, complexity, and commercial implications of this phenomenon, with its new, and very un-British, packaging and marketing of 'the Arts'.

There were British pre-war precedents for the Aldeburgh Festival. Some had ridden on the coat-tails of the expanding industrial cities; new, local entertainment was required, with all the style but without the inconveniences of the capital. But the new provincial patrons were almost always middle or upper-middle class and were entertained accordingly: opera and symphonic music were perceived as de rigueur. Keeping up with the Joneses resulted in an audience and an income for these occasions. The Glastonbury Festival is one example. Founded in 1914 by the composer Rutland Boughton as an arena for performing his own music—notably *The Immortal Hour*—Glastonbury soon cultivated its own alternative chic. George Bernard Shaw saw in this Festival hope for 'The Music of the Future'; his article under that title of 1922 made this clear:

Glastonbury, steeped in traditions which make it holy ground . . . still has no theatre, no electric light, no convenience for Wagnerian drama that every village does not possess.

[3] Autonomy would come with *Billy Budd*, and to a lesser extent *Gloriana*, but these were not written for the English Opera Group (see Ch. 4).

[4] Following his massive defeat in the 1945 election, Churchill spent six years in opposition before returning to power in 1951, with pronounced repercussions for British culture and government funding thereof.

[5] Carpenter, 253. Richard Adams, in his study of almost 200 British music festivals, lists only two that originated in 1947—Stroud and Edinburgh. Adams, *A Book of British Music Festivals* (1986).

[6] The Cheltenham Festival, for example, was founded in 1945 as a showcase for modern music and as part of a concerted effort to keep the town's name on the map.

> Yet it is here that the Wagnerist Dream has been best realised in England. That dream, truly interpreted, did not mean that the English soil should bring forth performances of Wagner's music copied from those at Bayreuth. It meant that the English soil should produce English music and English drama, and that English people should perform them in their own way.[7]

The fact that Boughton's English music and drama *was* in some ways Wagnerian in scope and content was ignored by Shaw, and, somewhat ironically, the rustic nature of *The Immortal Hour* made it well suited to performances in a town with neither lights nor theatre. Most importantly for Boughton—and much later for Britten—people attended and sustained this relatively isolated festival, and its host managed to attract the support of important music critics.

Two hundred years before the first Glastonbury Festival, however, the Three Choirs Festival was formed—its later momentum due partly to the provincial rivalry of its rotating hosts Gloucester, Hereford, and Worcester. It operated on a quite different social level from that of Glastonbury. The popularity of community singing and sol-fa in schools in the late nineteenth century meant that the Joneses were now singing rather than listening ('keeping up' was an irrelevance in this rather sincere activity), and the performance of large-scale choral and orchestral works guaranteed a large, if often filial, audience. As a further precedent to Aldeburgh, works were commissioned or written for the Three Choirs Festival, shaped by the large numbers participating, the unusual acoustic of the particular venue, and the Festival's proto-Christian baggage. If not single-handedly driving the English oratorio tradition, the Festival was at least its kindly caretaker.

Further groundwork was laid as a result of the folk-music revival at the turn of the century and the later, more nationalist manifestations of the 1930s and 1940s. The reinforcement of rural identity through cultural artefact gave music extra-programmatic value; performance became a communion of nationalist ideals. A festival need not take folk music as its centrepiece, nor need it focus on local art and environs (as Aldeburgh *did*) in order to reinforce the idea of community; once a town or village had set itself up as a cultural focus, this sense of identity began to spread outside the immediate locality. Moreover, the revival of interest in assorted folk traditions had brought with it new icons for new congregations; people became used to seeking community outside the Church, and finding it outside the class-based restrictions governing the social hierarchy of most localized societies.

Hovering over all these festivals was the famous example of Bayreuth. A celebration restricted entirely to one composer's music, Bayreuth soon adopted

[7] George Bernard Shaw, 'The Music of the Future', quoted in Stradling and Hughes, *The English Musical Renaissance 1860–1940*, 193.

some of the mythical, quasi-religious postures and terminology of the operas presented there: audience members became pilgrims, their journey to the isolated Festival a pilgrimage; performances became rituals; and the direction of the Festival was dynastic. Elitism was thus reinforced—validating the Festival's restricted repertory and prompting a wholesale invention of traditions.

Perhaps because of these (sometimes successful) precedents for Aldeburgh, the new Arts Council immediately decided to back Britten's proposed festival: £500 was made available—just over 2 per cent of the Council's budget for miscellaneous music grants, but over 20 per cent of the Festival's entire income in 1948.[8] There were, in fact, two principal reasons for the Council's enthusiasm. First, the music panel, which included Eric Walter White as a member, clearly considered Britten an important figure and national figurehead: support for his venture might help placate critics of the new Council. Second, the Aldeburgh Festival's goals appeared to be unsullied (at least on paper) by the elitist associations of 'The Opera'—the Council was already having to defend in some quarters its support of opera at Covent Garden. The Festival, therefore, was the perfect counterbalance—an embodiment of the egalitarian provincial policy of the Council, as outlined by Steuart Wilson, the first music director of the Arts Council, in the first music panel paper, written less than six weeks after VE Day. The Council was to 'inspire and assist the small undertakings rather than be the direct provider of concerts, but to create the larger undertakings such as Summer Festivals (but not to call them "English Salzburgs")'.[9] John Maynard Keynes, the Council's Chairman, expanded this philosophy in a broadcast and subsequent article in *The Listener*. The people, he argued, needed neither bread nor cake, but theatres:

> And let such buildings be widely spread throughout the country. We of the Arts Council are greatly concerned to decentralise and disperse the dramatic and musical and artistic life of the country, to build up provincial centres and to promote corporate life in these matters in every town and county. It is not our intention to act on our own where we can avoid it. We want to collaborate with local authorities and to encourage local institutions and societies and local enterprise to take the lead.[10]

Arguing against the concentration of artistic resources in London, Keynes wished for a diversified country where people developed ideas and cultures different from those of their neighbours. 'Nothing can be more damaging than the excessive prestige of metropolitan standards and fashions. Let every part of Merry England be merry in its own way.'[11] Keynes completed his oration with

[8] ACGB, *Annual Report 1948–49*, 26; BPL, *Aldeburgh Festival 1948 Report*, 5–11.
[9] Music Panel Paper No. 1, 23 June 1945. ACGB, Advisory Panel on Music, Minutes.
[10] John Maynard Keynes, 'The Arts Council: Its Policy and Hopes', *The Listener* (12 July 1945), 31.
[11] Ibid.

the fatwa-esque words 'Death to Hollywood'—a passionate attempt to stem the forward march of American values propagated by films, GIs, and the late Glenn Miller.

Rhetoric aside, the Council and the Aldeburgh Festival were perfect bedfellows. The latter was provincial, producing 'local art', independent, 'merry', and in the hands of extremely talented directors and performers. Moreover, the first Festival made a profit of £300—vindicating the Council's investment, though no vindication was required. The £500 Council grant makes annual appearances in early Festival accounts, increasing in value in 1954 and again in the 1960s. Out of the handful of festivals supported by the Arts Council (a growing figure during the 1950s), Aldeburgh was one of the 'high earners' of Council funding, running behind the Cheltenham Festival of Contemporary British Music (for obvious reasons), the York Festival, and the triennial appearances of the Leeds Festival, but consistently on a par with the prestigious Three Choirs Festival. By 1962 the hierarchy of funding had changed: the Three Choirs Festival was near the bottom of the pile, while Aldeburgh was in second place—beaten only by the unique and therefore incommensurable inauguration of Coventry Cathedral, which attracted £7,500 and the first performance of Britten's *War Requiem*.[12]

The history of the Aldeburgh Festival in Britten's lifetime falls more or less into three distinct periods: one of modesty and struggle (1948–58); one of financial consolidation and rising artistic ambitions (1959–66); and one of expansion (1967–76). The three sections exploring the Festival's history in this chapter, however, do not correspond exactly with the obvious chronological divisions. The first section looks at the artistic and financial climate of Aldeburgh in the period 1948 to 1958. The second does the same for the years 1959 to 1968—thereby taking on board the first two years of the Snape Maltings concert hall. The last section explores the influence of the Festival on Britten's own music.

House of Straw: Artists, Money, and the Floundering Fifties (1948–1958)

It was Aldeburgh's unexpected surplus in 1948—rather than the prospect of further Council funds—that set the agenda for future Festivals. It suggested that music *could* be self-supporting, as long as certain tastes were catered for, precise patterns identified. Once it was decided to make the Festival an annual event, identifying the prospects was a simple operation: audited accounts were included in an annual report. Catering for the tastes suggested by these early attendance

[12] Figures taken from Arts Council Annual Reports. Accounts were for year ended 31 March.

patterns would foster trends, further reinforcing notions of demand and supply. To many composers, the notion of demand and supply is suspect—a denial of artistic individuality. To Britten, however, writing for the public was a 'duty' and a challenge—he frequently disparaged composers who wrote in a 'vacuum'. Yet, despite the constraint, the economic pressures of the Festival would at different times influence Britten in his choice of artists and in the works he composed for Aldeburgh.

Income and expenditure for the 1948 Aldeburgh Festival is outlined in Table 5.1. Almost every event in the nine-day Festival was profitable; the one exception was an exhibition of *Peter Grimes* models and materials which lost £12. The overall deficit of £300—the result of administration and other costs—was turned into a surplus, once private donations and the Arts Council grant were taken into account. A breakdown of these figures for income and expenditure suggests a number of factors that influenced programming of future Festivals. The English Opera Group received a fee of £750 for its three appearances (less than it would get for appearances elsewhere after the Festival), yet the Festival's

Table 5.1 Aldeburgh Festival income and expenditure (£), 1948[a]

Expenditure Common expenditure	*£*	*s.*	*d.*	*Income* Surplus over expenditure	*£*	*s.*	*d.*
Hire of electrical appliances	43	9	2	Opera	14	11	11
Transport of pianos etc.	34	13	6	Serenade and chamber music	37	19	9
Performing rights	2	5	0	Pianoforte recital	46	12	0
Caretakers	3	0	0	Choral and orchestral concert	42	14	6
Donation to parish church	50	0	0	Recital (Pears and Britten)	172	0	0
Festival programme	422	6	0	Recital (Zorian String Quartet)	80	9	9
				Recital (verse and music)	32	17	3
Administration	486	1	8	Children's concert	6	4	0
Publicity	227	10	10	Art exhibition	43	14	0
				Lectures	48	1	11
				Festival Club	57	7	9
				Festival dance	115	15	3
				Programmes and books	278	1	2
				Deduct deficit (*Grimes* exhibition)	12	9	5
				Total deficit	306	6	4
Total	1,269	6	2		1,269	6	2

[a] BPL, *Aldeburgh Festival 1948 Report*.

further expenditure on opera was only £100 or so—£25 for the hire of the hall, £12 for the orchestra's travelling expenses, £9 on miscellaneous expenses, and £65 to construct an orchestra pit and alter the flooring of Aldeburgh's Jubilee Hall. There were no royalties paid (these may have been absorbed into the EOG's production costs) and tickets sales were £120 more than the Group's fee—a result of the lower overheads for the company (no commissions and negligible charges for hire of venue), which consequently could exact a lower fee. And although the week did nothing to offset the EOG's mounting deficit, expenditure was at least covered by income—a sufficiently unusual event in the Group's short history to ensure that it returned for future Festival appearances.

The piano recital demonstrated another neat Festival principle: limited overheads and a 'big name' would almost certainly guarantee a profit. In normal circumstances, it would be difficult to limit these overheads in the case of a starring artist; yet Noel Mewton-Wood, covering for an indisposed and indisputably more famous Clifford Curzon, was the first in a long line of important, often young, soloists to perform at Aldeburgh for far less than he would receive in London or—more significantly—other provincial centres. Mstislav Rostropovich, Galina Vishnevskaya, Sviatoslav Richter, Yehudi Menuhin, Julian Bream, Dennis Brain, and the Amadeus Quartet were among those who performed at the Festival over the years for little or no fee. There was also some bartering and payment-in-kind: Britten exchanged Menuhin's 1957 Festival appearance (expenses £34) for a concert by himself at the violinist's small festival in Gstaad. Likewise, Britten's appearances in Russia were partial repayments for Rostropovich's concerts at Aldeburgh. This exchange of artists was, in effect, a further donation of revenue to the Festival by the composer (and often his partner, Pears); such bartering, however, does not appear in letters or accounts; it was an unacknowledged thread running through the Festival economy in its first forty years. There were those who considered the purchase with musical services of membership of the Festival 'Brotherhood' almost Faustian. Robert Tear, for example, later derided the Festival atmosphere in his autobiography *Tear Here*. And there were those who simply could not afford to trade their time and skills for a place in Aldeburgh's pantheon. Eric Crozier left the EOG and the Festival in the late 1940s because he couldn't earn enough to support his family.[13]

One significant partnership was not fully developed in Crozier's period of association with the Festival, but seeds were sown and the outcome was very important. The BBC was naturally interested in broadcasting concerts from Aldeburgh—especially since the Festival often included a Britten premiere, a spectacular, even unique, combination of artists, or the only appearance of a soloist in the country at that particular time. A 1957 memo from the Head of the

[13] Kildea interview with Crozier, 11 Apr. 1994.

BBC's Transcription Service illustrates further aspects of the Corporation's interest: 'There has been the closest co-operation between Britten and ourselves over the Festival for the past two years. For our part we get very good performances out of Aldeburgh; they do interesting things, and the transcriptions made sell exceedingly well.' And most strikingly, given the festival culture developing in Britain in the 1950s: 'Overall, Aldeburgh is far cheaper for us than Edinburgh.'[14] The first Festival played on the BBC's involvement—whether consciously or not. The Zorian Quartet, for example, was paid only £72 for its recital in 1948, but broadcasting fees of £31. 10*s*. 0*d*. were generated, some of which the quartet received. Such remuneration would later sweeten the (sometimes) bitter pill of low Festival fees. By 1957, for example, the Head of Transcription Service could write that 'Britten has always been quite frank with me in admitting that if the BBC take any appreciable number of programmes from the Aldeburgh [Festival] this represents a big financial gain to the artists and tends to encourage them to accept . . . comparatively small fees'.[15] The broadcasts were also of artistic or promotional value to the musicians. Performers were not always aware of the extent of the BBC's subsidizing role. In 1963 Reiss reported to Britten that the Festival would receive £750 directly from the BBC as a facilities fee; in addition, the Corporation would pay half of Menuhin's £500 fee, and two-thirds of Bruno Hoffmann's fee of £75.[16] In Aldeburgh's twentieth year, bolstered by interest in the Maltings, broadcast fees were £5,708; in the following year, without the novelty of the Maltings' inaugural season, the fees nonetheless remained at a respectable rate—£3,249.[17]

The BBC's influence eventually extended into Festival repertory and the technicalities of staging and performing. The 1959 Festival prospectus, for example, proudly refers to the Corporation in a number of places and with the rather understated phrase 'The B.B.C. Transcription Service presents . . .'—quaintly redolent of the dinner-jacket culture once associated with news broadcasts. This practice became quite common in the 1960s; the use, however, of the BBC to subsidize programmes that the Festival could not afford to mount on its own did limit Britten's autonomy, however slightly.

[14] Memo from M. A. Frost, 13 May 1957. BBCWAC, Outside Broadcasts—Sound, Aldeburgh Festival, file 1, 1955–8.

[15] Ibid. Frost noted that the BBC's relationship with artists appearing at the Aldeburgh Festival was much stronger than with those booked for Edinburgh. He attributed this to received intelligence that the Edinburgh Festival authorities were keeping 75 per cent of the artists' broadcasting fees as a commission.

[16] Reiss to Britten, 1 Aug. 1963. BPL, Aldeburgh Festival Correspondence, 1963. Hoffmann played the glass harmonica in works by Reichardt, Schulz, Naumann, and Mozart.

[17] *Aldeburgh Festival 1967 Report*; *Aldeburgh Festival 1968 Report*. BPL, Aldeburgh Festival Correspondence, 1967 and 1968.

By far the most important performers to appear regularly at the Festival in its early years at less than their market value were Britten and Pears. Their reputation as recitalists, though recent, was by now considerable: recordings of the *Seven Sonnets of Michelangelo*, the *Serenade*, Op. 31 for tenor, horn and strings, and the folk-song settings had assured this. More to the point, their reputations were 'bankable'. Drawing no fee and incurring just £5 in expenses meant that, in effect, the two musicians donated over £170 to the 1948 Festival. The Britten–Pears recital was the most financially successful event of the first Aldeburgh Festival, and it became a treasured refrain of subsequent ones.

Yet for all the optimism generated in 1948, the following ten years of the Aldeburgh Festival saw significant changes in its financial infrastructure (Table 5.2). Between 1948 and 1958, expenditure on individual Festival events more than tripled; administration and general costs increased almost threefold. Box-office receipts doubled, while receipts from programmes and the sales of miscellaneous goods increased from £327 to £2,152. The Arts Council grant—flauntingly impervious to inflation—remained close to its inaugural level of £500.

The most important indication of the changing financial infrastructure, however, is the steady increase in the working deficit—the difference between total expenditure and total box-office and 'other' receipts. Between 1948 and 1958 the working deficit increased by almost 900 per cent—from £306 to £2,670. Although the labour-intensive nature of Western art music defeats most attempts at rationalization, in the space of eleven years the directors of the Aldeburgh Festival were facing a challenge from that most simple of market equations—that demand should pay for supply (as it had come close to doing in 1948). This disregard of market economics poses a number of questions: since box-office income did not increase at the same rate as Festival expenditure, were audiences diminishing? Were artists no longer willing to work at 'Aldeburgh rates', or was it simply that the Festival's programmes were becoming more complex and expensive? How did the directors deal with the problem and how did this affect the artistic output of the Festival and its founder composer?

Table 5.2 highlights a number of 'key years' in the Festival's early history. Although the data suggests a degree of directorial analysis and reaction in these key years, which is not *entirely* accurate, the information assembled is nonetheless rather telling. In 1951 expenditure on individual concerts was £1,000 more than in both the previous and following years. In 1953 box-office income was lower than that of the first Festival; consequently (or incidentally . . .) the working deficit was at its highest to date. In 1956 income from subscriptions and donations increased by around 50 per cent, yet the biggest change in this particular source of revenue had been in 1954, when it increased fourfold over the previous year. Significantly, box-office income in 1954 did not decrease, in spite of

Table 5.2 Aldeburgh Festival income and expenditure (£), 1949–1958[a]

	1949	1950	1951	1952	1953	1954	1955	1956	1957	1958
Expenditure										
Individual events	2,882	2,920	3,897	2,768	3,165	3,335	3,177	4,120	5,546	6,743
General	800	652	691	811	802	622	695	1,127	1,735	1,905
Administration	572	652	971	985	962	1,130	1,085	887	990	1,338
Total	4,254	4,224	5,559	4,564	4,929	5,087	4,957	6,134	8,271	9,986
Income										
Box office	2,740	3,254	3,357	3,001	2,444	2,972	3,157	3,457	4,386	5,185
Other	178	640	633	730	812	672	811	1,289	1,772	2,132
Total	2,918	3,894	3,990	3,731	3,256	3,644	3,968	4,746	6,158	7,317
Working deficit	1,336	330	1,569	833	1,673	1,443	989	1,388	2,114	2,670
Other income										
Arts Council grant	500	500	1,000	500	500	750	659	750	750	750
Subscriptions etc.	196	136	122	52	177	654	710	1,064	1,428	1,914
Total	696	636	1,122	552	677	1,404	1,369	1,814	2,178	2,664
Surplus/Deficit										
Net surplus or deficit	640	306	447	281	997	39	380	426	64	6
Guarantors	339	—	236	324	947	—	—	—	—	—
Reserve fund	12	294	83	127	78	39	420	846	911	906

[a] ACGB, Aldeburgh Festival 1965–70, 1971–2.

the increased subscriptions; either completely new subscribers were found, or old audience members vacated their places in the box-office queue in order to move up into the socially and artistically more elevated position of minor patron.[18]

Each of these 'key years' brings with it a particular theme. Low receipts imply unpopular programmes or performers; high expenditure suggests an increase in artist fees; and an increase in subscriptions and donations suggests either a changing Festival profile or conscious marketing—something previously avoided in Aldeburgh and later denied by Britten: 'we have found that there are enough people who like the kind of things that we like to come and make the Festival worthwhile without a great deal of advertising and of trying to make the Festival known.'[19]

Each theme illustrates a little of the delicate relationship between art and economics at the Festival, which its founders had considered in only the shortest of terms when they had first counted seats in Aldeburgh's Jubilee Hall. It is unlikely that, in 1948, the directors had planned their Festival in terms of cross-subsidization—the conscious balancing of a commercially unpopular concert or work with a sure hit. Instead, they included what they had close to hand: lecturers, art works, poetry, musicians, and the ill-fated *Peter Grimes* exhibition. Risks were minimized: since the first Festival was considered an experiment, balanced books were mandatory if the experiment was to become a tradition. As noted, the directors learnt from the first Festival that well-known soloists offered great box-office returns, as long as it was possible to limit overheads. They also learnt that the *ideal* Festival event involved few artists, was flexible in its repertory, popular, profitable, and budgetable. It was obvious that one or two concerts built on these lines would be needed if the Festival were to survive; if it were to flourish—in both size and repertory—it would need several more.

The urgency of this particular lesson was obvious by the end of August 1948, when the Festival Report was issued. The Report noted that the surplus of £300 was evidence of satisfactory support for the Festival, which could safely be counted on in the future—by no means a foregone conclusion, no matter how accurate it would later prove to be. 'This profit', the report continued, rather contradicting itself, 'is due to certain economies which cannot be repeated.' These included artists working for reduced fees or no fees at all as a gesture to the Festival in its trial year; the Festival manager, secretary, and hon. treasurer managing accounts and running the box office in addition to their own duties (and long before 'multi-skilled' employees slipped into the Civil Service and its

[18] In 1954 ticket prices and venue capacities were comparable with those in 1953.

[19] Benjamin Britten in discussion with the Earl of Harewood, 'People Today', BBC Home Service, 23 June 1960 (pre-recorded in Aldeburgh).

parlance); and a peppercorn rent for the Festival office.[20] The fact that these economies were non-repeatable, and the addition of plans to base the EOG in Aldeburgh from the following autumn, meant that the directors had to temper their expansionist, adventurous mood with careful budgeting and a thorough implementation of cross-subsidy.

The history of the Festival's first years, however, is one of flux: the lessons of one year were not always obvious in the next. As expected *and* predicted, the second Festival was more expensive to mount than the first, but the working deficit was £1,336—which did not include the increased administration costs, and was more than expected. The number of opera performances doubled in 1949: *Albert Herring* returned (it had sold out in 1948), *The Rape of Lucretia* made its first Festival appearance, while Britten's new *Let's Make an Opera*—its commercial value as yet unknown—received its premiere.[21] The EOG's fee was £1,250, but, unlike one year earlier, there were no favours for either party: the Group had been paid the same amount for a week in Cambridge in 1948.[22] Despite this, the EOG's appearance at Aldeburgh in 1949 swallowed up almost half of the Festival's entire expenditure on artistic events, while the increase in the Group's fee—£500 over the 1948 level—accounted for half of the increased artist costs in 1949 (£2,882 compared to £1,862 the year before). So although the directors were keen for visiting artists to receive a decent fee, there was little left to play with. Cross-subsidy, however, was especially apparent in two items in the second Festival: the Cambridge University Madrigal Society (an amateur group) was invited to present an outdoor concert on Thorpeness Meare (few overheads of any sort), while Mr Arthur Ransome was invited to speak, on 'Sailing in East Anglia', thereby contributing to the Festival's middle-class pedigree and continuing a 'trend' of lectures outside the subject of music that remains firmly in place today.[23] Guarantors were called up to the sum of £339, and as a result, the following year's Festival was one of stability and consolidation.

In 1951, the first of the Festival's key years, expenditure on concerts increased by £1,000 over the previous year while the ever-important working deficit rose to £1,569—£1,300 more than in 1950 (Table 5.2). These bread-and-butter figures seem ridiculously small compared to the relative finances of an arts festival today and the growth in inflation, but in the context of Aldeburgh's budget they are considerable. A factor restraining the 1951 expenditure, however, was the Festival of Britain, which was to encourage many artistic enterprises to

[20] BPL, *Aldeburgh Festival 1948 Report.*

[21] Britten's works in the Festival are considered below.

[22] BPL, EOG General Files 3, Annual Accounts 1949–58.

[23] Ransome (1884–1967) is chiefly remembered for his hugely popular children's novels, which reflected his keen interest in sailing, fishing, and the countryside. In the event, illness prevented his attendance

wander outside realistic programming and budgeting—all for the Greater Glory of Britain. The Chairman's letter to Guarantors following the 1951 Aldeburgh Festival began by referring to this: 'Having read in the papers about the fearful losses sustained by various Festivals this year, you may have been feeling anxious about Aldeburgh . . .'.[24] With some justification: Guarantors were called on for 3*s*. 4*d*. in the pound to help cover the £1,000 jump in concert expenditure over the previous year. The events contributing to Aldeburgh's working deficit included the English Opera Group (a surprisingly small £129), concerts of *Jephtha* and *Saint Nicolas* (£269), an orchestral concert (£220), and two concerts by the Grenadier Guards Band (£132). Those generating a surplus included the hardy annual madrigal concerts (£9), a chamber-music concert (£43), a Verdi concert (£83), the Festival dance (£118), and, of course, the Britten–Pears recital, which had expenses of 18*s*. (performing right) and receipts of £138. In 1951 the directors rather cannily tapped into Aldeburgh's environmental vein; with its marshes and woods, the area remains a haven for birds and naturalists, and a lecture and accompanying bird film in the Festival made a profit of £149. Yet a Mozart concert (including the Symphony No. 11, K.84 and the Piano Concerto K.459, performed by the EOG Orchestra with Britten directing from the keyboard) managed a deficit of £49—and this after a broadcasting fee of £190, much of which went to the instrumentalists.

In comparison to 1951 (and reinforcing the ebb and flow of early Aldeburgh fortunes), the 1952 Festival demonstrated considerable control over expenditure. This was another emerging pattern: a year of relative parsimony following a year of excess. And by 1952 the structure of Festival programming had 'standardized'—at least enough to make the compilation of Table 5.3 a relatively simple affair. Although new ideas often made their way into programmes, the events listed in Table 5.3 formed the basis of each Festival. And although a 'core' programme made good sense in terms of financial planning and the speedy invention of popular Festival traditions, Table 5.3 illustrates that such a structure did not guarantee financial stability.

The key years of Table 5.2 are given *some* flesh here, although the data does not give an indication of expenditure, receipts, or ticket prices: a large deficit, for example, does not necessarily indicate poor audiences or expensive artists. Loss-makers from the 'core programme' of the 1953 Festival included one performance only of *Albert Herring*; the two orchestral-choral concerts (a mixed bag to celebrate the coronation, and a performance of Handel's *L'Allegro*); a chamber-music recital of Tchaikovsky's Sonata for Piano, Bartók's Sonata for Two Pianos and Percussion, and Debussy's *Estampes*; the Haydn–Mozart concert (including Haydn's Horn Concerto in D with Dennis Brain, and Mozart's Piano Concerto

[24] Cranbrook to Aldeburgh Festival Guarantors, 1951. BPL, Aldeburgh Festival Accounts, 1951.

Table 5.3 Aldeburgh Festival surplus/deficit figures (£), individual events 1952–1958[a]

	1952	1953	1954	1955	1956	1957	1958
Opera	−126	−185	−644	−478	−1017[c]	−1111	−1602
Orchestra (and chorus) I	66	−233	−31[b]	−15	−173[d]	−169	−246
Orchestra (and chorus) II	−75	−227	−159	−124	—	−108	43
Opera concert	77	35	83	76	104	59	—
Chamber music	67	−39	29	104	107	99	56
Music and poetry	−6	−3	8	—	203	14	—
Mozart–Haydn concert	53	−86	—	—	−154	−187	—
Music on the Meare	−16	−46	2	1	−2	−3	−2
Britten–Pears	239	187	193	133	177	183	176
'Name' concert I	78	67	—	127	120	443	239
Choral concert	—	—	22	4	−5	−160	−242[e]
Lectures	30	55	38	26	−2	21	−5

[a] BPL, Aldeburgh Festival Annual Accounts, 1952–8.
[b] Janáček concert, chamber group and voices.
[c] Two different operas, the double-bill, and *Let's Make an Opera*.
[d] Handel's *Samson*.
[e] A series of five concerts.

K.465 with Britten); madrigals from *The Triumphs of Oriana*; and Jill Balcon and Cecil Day Lewis reciting verse. The two events from this list that *generated* relatively little revenue were *Albert Herring* and the chamber-music concert. The opera was probably a convenient experiment in a busy period (*Gloriana* had claimed some of the EOG's star players): was it more economical to do just one performance of an opera or several? The equation changed each year, depending upon the programme; but the EOG gave better value for money over a number of performances: one appearance, with a fee of £460 (compared to £925 for three performances the year before), gave the Festival *no* opportunity to recover costs (despite a full house), whereas three performances at £925 (or indeed six at £1,250) gave it a *slight* chance of doing so. A single opera performance was not a feature of future Festivals: it was considered that, ideally, a work should remain in the EOG's repertory, and multiple repeats rather than single performances were required.

The chamber-music concert, featuring music by Bartók—even worse, music with percussion instruments, his Sonata for Two Pianos and Percussion—

stewed in its own juices, attracting an audience of just 56 per cent of capacity, perhaps a victim of historical antipathy towards Bartók's music in Britain.[25] This concert, the one performance of *Albert Herring*, and the premiere of Lennox Berkeley's Stabat Mater (audience 34 per cent of capacity), help to explain the low box-office revenue in 1953—specific events rather than a more sinister general decline in interest.[26] These, however, accumulated a high working deficit: the lesson was that, although the Festival could absorb the losses from one unpopular programme in any year, putting on a number of them would result in large claims on Guarantors (£947)—a limited resource.

There were fewer losses on core programmes in 1954 than in the previous year; they were also more predictable.[27] There were two performances of Berkeley's *A Dinner Engagement* and Arthur Oldham's *Love in a Village*, and a further two of *Lucretia*. Although box-office sales were relatively good, costs were high because of the Berkeley premiere, and the working deficit was correspondingly large. Bach's *St John Passion* was also expensive. But the most important feature of 1954 was not the relatively containable losses on ambitious programmes, but rather the creation of a new audience: the increase in the number of subscribers, without a reduction in box-office sales. The Festival's programme most certainly played an important part in this: *St John Passion* by Bach and by Schütz; the first Aldeburgh performance of *Winter Words*; a collaboration between Poulenc and the Amadeus Quartet; the 'Archduke' Trio and the 'Death and the Maiden' Quartet. There was gentle deference to the canon, and any wanderings outside it (Berkeley and the first *musique concrète* performances in England) were nonetheless incorporated into the Festival with great taste and skill.

Programming was probably not the only factor to increase audiences. There is no doubt that the reputation of a festival that could attract such diverse personalities as the composer Francis Poulenc, the contralto Kathleen Ferrier, the viola player William Primrose, and the eccentric Edith Sitwell, was fast spreading. But exactly where was it spreading to? In 1968 Britten was asked whether there was a

[25] See Malcolm Gillies, *Bartók in Britain* (1989).

[26] An Arts Council report on the 1953 Festival listed an overall attendance of 66 per cent of capacity. This figure is partially deceptive: large venues (e.g. the parish church, capacity 500) were frequently used for events that were unlikely to attract capacity audiences (verse and music, Berkeley, etc.). However, according to the Council Report, the principal reason for the figure of 66 per cent, and the correspondingly low income, was that as a condition for using the parish church, 200 free seats had to be available, at any performance, for parishioners and townspeople. The Arts Council also suggested that there was little disposable income among the 1953 visitors, as evident in the 'complete failure, from a sales point of view, of the Festival Book'. Books generated £192 in sales in 1953, compared to £272 the year before. ACGB, Music Department, 1948–55.

[27] It is not clear whether the problem with the parish church had been solved by 1954.

danger that Aldeburgh might become too fashionable, too 'Glyndebourne'. He conceded that this was possible—and that the threat came from the 'county' as much as from London.[28] Of course snob audiences at Aldeburgh were alive and well before 1968, and the 'county' set (both geographical and generic) offered an easy target. But, in the county's defence, by the end of his life Britten and the Festival had come to be fully accepted into local consciousness: a degree of chauvinism was inevitable. Though not every detail of the composer's life was known (in 1971 a student at a local secondary school told her teacher, with no small degree of confidence, that 'Benjamin Britten performed a concert for the Prince of Cothen in 1717 to 1723'[29]), at least the *spirit* of his contribution to national culture was understood. Not everyone welcomed the Festival's intrusion into the Aldeburgh community: Humphrey Carpenter describes a cartoon by Horner from around 1951 in which black-tied concert-goers mingle with a group of fishermen, one remarking, 'Ar, in the old days a man could break into a bit of a shanty any time without someone a'bobbin' up to arrange it for'm'.[30] Although such jokes had been made at the expense of the English folk revival for some time, they were probably apposite here.

It was apparent from the very first Festival that Britten was not interested in cultivating a London audience. Twenty years later he articulated this ('ideally one would like to keep the audience a local one'[31]), but his views were made clear much earlier through his attitude to London music critics. E. M. Forster touched on Britten's isolationist approach in a curious article for *The Listener* immediately after the first Festival; and if the eminent author was not sowing the seeds of discontent, he was at least watering them. 'The Aldeburgh Festival has not been mentioned much in the papers. Its promoters were not able to invite critics and reporters owing to the restricted accommodation, and many people never even heard of it in consequence.'[32] Limited space was indeed a problem; as the Festival grew—increasingly becoming an important forum for Britten premieres—demand for press tickets intensified, and their allocation became the source of contention. The income/expenditure equation left little room for the luxury of complimentary seats, and critics, if adverse, met with little sympathy from the sensitive composer. Britten's views on music criticism were well known: in an article in the March 1952 edition of *Opera* he had described the majority of British music critics as 'unobservant if not actually inane', 'riff-raff', and barely competent. Britten's earliest experiences—when his works were

[28] Harold Rosenthal, 'Aldeburgh and the Future', *Opera*, 18 (Autumn 1967), 8.

[29] BPL, Rosamund Strode's Papers.

[30] Carpenter, 304.

[31] Rosenthal, 'Aldeburgh and the Future', 7.

[32] E. M. Forster, 'Looking Back on the Aldeburgh Festival', *The Listener* (24 June 1948), 1011.

dismissed with platitudes such as 'if it is just a stage to get through, we wish him safely and quickly through it'—had left him scarred.[33]

As a result of the fractious relationship between composer and critic, Aldeburgh Festival staff donned kid-gloves to deal with both. A press release concerning the premiere of Lennox Berkeley's *A Dinner Engagement* listed subsequent performances which critics might attend, since (owing to the small capacity of the Jubilee Hall) the Festival could not afford to increase the usual allocation of press tickets.[34] Ten year later, when the Festival's fortunes were much more secure, the gloves came off, and a feud between Britten and one independent-minded critic made both the national press and good reading. Charles Reid, critic for the *Spectator*, was blackballed from Aldeburgh following his harsh criticisms of extra-musical matters in 1961 and an allegedly biting riposte from Britten himself. Harewood intervened on Reid's behalf in 1964, but to no avail. In 1966 the *Spectator* took up the cause of Britten's *bête noire*. In the subsequent correspondence Stephen Reiss attempted to take over from Britten the responsibility for Reid's exclusion—not entirely successfully. 'Our authority for associating Mr Britten with the decision to blackball Charles Reid from Aldeburgh stems principally from a letter written to Mr Reid by Mr Britten himself some years ago,' wrote Nigel Lawson in the *Spectator*. 'If, however, Mr Britten now wishes to dissociate himself from this foolish vendetta, then let him say so . . .'.[35] A subsequent letter from Reiss to John Cruft, music director of the Arts Council, developed the issue: 'The question is: how far are we obliged to coddle the Press, give them V.I.P. treatment and endure their gratuitous insults?' How could the Festival possibly justify cosseting individuals such as Charles Reid, who had 'over-wined and dined' before his previous onslaught; or Martin Cooper (*Telegraph*), who once wrote a bullying letter because he was not given two free tickets for each event; Peter Heyworth (*Observer*), who left it until the last minute before he announced that he would 'deign to visit' the Festival; and the critic whose ticket found its way onto the black market.[36]

As with so much correspondence, the actual subject is less important than the issue illuminated in the cross-fire. 'Coddling the press' has long been an important

[33] H. C. Colles on *Our Hunting Fathers* in *The Times*, 26 Sept. 1936.

[34] BPL, Aldeburgh Festival Correspondence, 1954. The EOG's Basil Douglas responded to the press release and Sweeting's carve-up of press tickets with little respect for at least one sacred cow: 'On examining your press-list it would appear that the Manchester Guardian and Birmingham Post have prior claim to Punch and The Sunday Times whose musical claims I would say were negligible. It is particularly important that the Guardian should not be omitted.' Douglas to Sweeting, 11 Mar. 1954. BPL, Aldeburgh Festival Correspondence, 1954. Douglas had apparently missed Britten's *Opera* article, in which he said 'my doctor has ordered me to give up the *Manchester Guardian* because of the lowering effect reading its London Dramatic critic has on me; he clearly hates the theatre. And I wouldn't dream of buying *The Listener*: that ear is too withered.'

[35] Nigel Lawson, *Spectator* (1 July 1966).

[36] Reiss to Cruft, 5 July 1966. ACGB, Aldeburgh Festival 1965–70, 1971–2.

part of the music industry. The composition and performance of large-scale music cannot be divorced from criticism and marketability: musicians need to be paid, audiences attracted. The role of the music critic in shaping trends, influencing the canon—no matter how short-term this influence may be—should not be underestimated. Reiss, in his letter to Cruft, makes it clear that critics were suffered rather than cherished in Aldeburgh. The Festival aspired to autonomy—complete with subverted market values—and press criticism was not needed for bolstering either audience numbers or Britten's self-worth.

In his biography of Britten, Carpenter makes much (and at the same time very little) of the change in the composer's personality over the first six years of the Festival. He quotes Norman Lumsden, an early EOG and Festival performer, who remembers Britten as 'one of the boys you might say. But then it gradually changed, just like the Festival changed, until it was very difficult to approach them [Britten and Pears]. We called them the Royal Family.'[37] Although Lumsden's analogy is difficult to reconcile with the state of much of the monarchy today, his meaning is nonetheless clear. Ever eager to identify dysfunctional personality as the cause for Britten's behaviour, Carpenter ignores the strong cases put forward by both the EOG and the Festival. Britten was primarily responsible for the artistic direction of both groups, and he felt the economic pressures strongly. It would have been no source of pride to him that Aldeburgh was *compelled* to pay less than market rates for artists, even if he was rather proud of the fact that many artists happily performed at the Festival regardless of fee. As a result, Britten would have been sensitive to his artists' feelings, and extremely touchy about any suggestion of exploitation. Much easier, altogether, to distance himself from the front line. Furthermore, although Britten was happy to take on any compositional challenge, the constant need for works that were *financially* suitable for both the Festival and the Group would have compounded the pressure he would have felt in dealing with artists.

This pressure surfaced after the 1954 Festival. Britten and Pears wrote to F. V. Hussey, the chartered accountant responsible for auditing the Festival's accounts, dismayed by his remarks at the AGM.

> We were spurred to write this letter, as you may guess, by your remarks at the A.G.M. on the 1954 Festival Balance Sheet, and in particular by your expression of alarm at the growing Expenditure of the Festival. You expressed a strong hope that Expenditure would in future be kept down. This, to be frank, was not at all what we had expected. We had hoped for a certain amount of mutual patting on the back that in 1954 our Income had triumphantly topped our Expenditure, high though the latter may have been, and that our guarantors had not been called on at all. Your remarks took the wind out of our sails and we had nothing to say in answer.

[37] Carpenter, 319.

Income had, indeed, topped expenditure—or at least had come within £39 of doing so (Table 5.2). But this was the result of a dramatic rise in subscriptions rather than of economies in administration or programming, which was not what Hussey was really after.

In fact, however, you are not asking us to raise our Income so much as to cut our Expenses. Our chief expense lies in the cost of Administration, which we were assured at the AGM cannot, under the present régime, be carried on for less. Our other main expense is the Deficit incurred in the programmes of the Festival, chief among which have always been the Opera Performances & the Choral Concert. This year's Festival (1955) is already planned on previous lines & would be difficult radically to alter.[38]

Yet the directors managed to control, if not radically alter, the shape of the 1955 Festival: expenditure was kept under the 1954 rate, while income from nearly all sources increased, creating a surplus of almost £400. Finances were helped by the Festival premiere of *The Turn of the Screw*, which attracted much interest, and by taking care to include only a few other labour-intensive events.

Britten's and Pears's chastened schoolboy response to Hussey also included a reference to the 1956 Festival, which clearly links Festival content with income/expenditure estimates. 'For 1956', they wrote, 'in response to your demand for economy, we propose . . . a programme of quite different scope from previous years.' The Festival was to last only four days; there was to be no opera—an immediate saving of £500; and the simple nature of the programme would allow the management of it to be undertaken by volunteers—cutting management expenses by around £600.[39] The proposed programme was modesty itself: the Amadeus Quartet with Britten; the Festival ball; Bach's *St John Passion* (resurrected from previous years, making it cheaper to put on and bringing with it a popular following); a lecture-reading by Forster; Music on the Meare; a concert given by the Mozart Orchestra with Britten conducting; and a recital by Britten and Pears.[40]

This draft is almost unrecognizable when placed next to a later plan, or indeed the final Festival programme. By 15 July 1955 the Festival was back to nine days in length, and contained most of the programmes eventually featured. Economy was still evident: lectures by both Pears and Forster, while the Zorian Quartet was to appear a few days before the first concert by the Amadeus Quartet, and although the suggested duration was still one day shorter than the Festival would actually last, the proposal was ambitious. The reason for the directors' change of

[38] Pears and Britten to Hussey [draft], undated [early 1955]. BPL, Aldeburgh Festival Correspondence, 1955.

[39] Ibid.

[40] A number of extra events were crossed out on this draft: a concert by the Purcell Singers; Dennis Brain directing an orchestral ensemble; and a lecture and opera concert, both to be given on a proposed fifth and last day of the Festival.

heart is not clear—although following the 1955 Festival, its manager, Elizabeth Sweeting, was replaced by Stephen Reiss, who was more aggressively business-orientated than his predecessor. This change in leadership is apparent in the 1956 accounts: they suggest modern, self-conscious business tactics, far removed from the more amateur practices hitherto associated with British arts management. There was greater revenue from subscriptions and 'other' fees; ticket prices were raised, with correspondingly higher box-office income;[41] administration expenses were at their lowest for six years; and, in contrast to the relative modesty of the directors' initial thoughts, artists of international stature presented recitals.[42] The Festival was far removed from the original four-day plan; here was a turning point in Aldeburgh's fortunes, and this style of management remained a feature of the Festival throughout the 1960s.

If Britten felt uncomfortable in the company of the rank-and-file musicians who made up the Festival, he showed no such hesitation with the international artists he invited to Aldeburgh. Fees were set, negotiated, or waived with the confidence that visiting artists would be spoilt by the hospitality, musicianship, and, often enough, specially composed music of their host. Festival programmes were determined by a particular artist's presence—but often these programmes were suggested by Britten himself. Judging by Menuhin's reply, Britten's invitation for him to play at Aldeburgh was anything but casual:

> Of course, I would like to play the 'new' E Minor movement as part of the third Brandenburg. I must also see the suite with trumpets which you originally had in mind!
>
> The Telemann sounds an excellent idea to begin the program. I am particularly pleased to play the slow movement of the Schumann Concerto. I am so happy you want this. I haven't played it in some years and have been meaning, in any case, to restore it for the Schumann Centennial in, I believe, 1960 [1956]. By the way, it is, I believe, the 200th anniversary of Haendel next year. Would you like to record the six sonatas with harpsichord, as well as the Bach?[43]

And so a Festival was planned, while a second Schumann centenary in a matter of years was narrowly avoided. Similar contact occurred with other composers and performers. Mátyás Seiber was asked for the first English performance of his *Portrait*, which he agreed to conduct with 'great pleasure'.[44] Malcolm Arnold was positively 'delighted' that the first performance of the guitar concerto he was writing for Julian Bream should be given at the 1959 Festival, and was

[41] The maximum price of tickets for non-opera performances was raised from 10*s*. to 15*s*.

[42] Specifically Poulenc, and perhaps Edith Sitwell.

[43] Menuhin to Britten, 29 Jan. 1958. BPL, Aldeburgh Festival Correspondence, 1958. It is interesting to note that here was a performer suggesting recording repertory, rather than a producer or record company. This was partly the result of Menuhin's status as a major performing artist, but it also reflected the expansion of the record industry that followed the invention of the LP.

[44] Seiber to Britten, 15 Dec. 1958. BPL, Aldeburgh Festival Correspondence, 1959.

honoured to be asked to conduct it.[45] Mstislav Rostropovich had the Sonata for Cello written for him, 'on condition he came to Aldeburgh!'[46] Alfred Deller and Owen Brannigan were asked to come to Aldeburgh, to create the roles of Oberon and Bottom in Britten's new opera, *A Midsummer Night's Dream*. In their replies, both artists illustrated the esteem with which they viewed the composer, and the honour attached to an Aldeburgh invitation. 'It has taken me two days to recover from the shock!' began Deller. 'After all, my only stage experience was with the Church Dramatic Society, six performances of "Laburnam Grove" and I was young then and my mind . . . much more alert, do you and Peter think I could do it! if so, I would consider it a privilege to make the attempt.'[47] Pears wrote a reassuring reply. Brannigan, who was to play the part of Bottom, was less nervous, but equally self-deprecating. 'I am delighted and honoured indeed that for the fourth time you are entrusting me with the enviable opportunity to introduce yet another of your, always wonderful, creations.'[48] And, later, when he had seen the score: 'The "falsetto" will annoy Deller!'[49] In fine Festival tradition, the honour of the invitation was more important than negotiating and collecting a set fee.

It is clear, therefore, that the change in the financial infrastructure during the Festival's first eleven years—the move from demand almost covering supply to a working deficit of £2,760—was not the result of any *one* factor. Audiences were not diminishing but increasing. Opportunities for growth in box-office revenue were limited, since ticket prices were kept at the same rate for most of this first period, probably in an attempt to keep the Festival accessible to local people;[50] opera ticket prices increased in 1954, those for some other concerts in 1956, while entry to a Britten–Pears recital remained at the same rate until 1957. Some artists lost the pioneering spirit that had led to their first appearance (and low fee) at the Festival, and their inclusion became more expensive; there were *always* exceptions: the Amadeus Quartet, Forster, and Menuhin (at times), for example. In this first period, programmes became progressively more ambitious, and consequently more expensive. Sudden changes in costs from year to year (Menuhin

[45] Arnold to Britten, 18 Dec. 1958. Ibid.

[46] John Warrack, 'Benjamin Britten: Musician of the Year in Conversation with John Warrack', *Musical America*, 84 (Dec. 1964), 272. This sonata, and other works written for Rostropovich, are examined below.

[47] Deller to Britten, 21 Aug. 1959. BPL, Aldeburgh Festival Correspondence, 1960. The lack of experience showed in production, and Deller did not accompany the cast when the opera moved to Covent Garden; critics had not greeted his involvement positively. Deller had written to Britten after the opera's first season telling him to 'delete me when you think fit'. Carpenter, 396.

[48] Brannigan to Britten, 29 Oct. 1959. BPL, Aldeburgh Festival Correspondence, 1960.

[49] Brannigan to Britten, 15 Mar. 1960. Ibid. The other three roles were Swallow, Collatinus, and Noye.

[50] The ratio of high-priced to low-priced tickets may have changed in this period. This is not clear in the records.

on no fee at one Festival, £500 at another) made planning difficult and the curtailment of expenditure almost impossible. Aldeburgh's directors did attempt to deal with this problem, but did not really succeed until the Festival's 'second period'—1959–68.

House of Brick: Towards Snape Maltings (1959–1968)

The 'second period' of the Aldeburgh Festival differed considerably from the first. The financial stability that had so eluded the directors between 1948 and 1958, and had made adventurous, long-term planning almost impossible, became a feature of Festivals in the 1960s (Table 5.4). A comparison between the information presented in Tables 5.2 and 5.4 illustrates the degree to which the Festival had changed. Expenditure on individual functions increased from nearly £6,000 in 1959 to over £38,000 in 1968; expenditure on events had been £1,862 in 1948 and £6,743 ten years later. In 1968 box-office receipts were £44,000; ten years before they had been £5,000, while at the very first Aldeburgh Festival they had been half this amount. Even allowing for inflation (which was higher in the 1960s than the 1950s), the growth in income was exponential. During this 'second period' the working deficit increased, but so did funds from the Arts Council, subscriptions and revenue from 'other' sources. In each case the *factor* of increase is important. Box-office income increased by a factor of nine in the ten years from 1959: it had merely doubled between 1948 and 1958. In 1968 total expenditure was almost seven times higher than it had been in 1959: it had done no more than treble between 1948 and 1958.

Such dramatic changes in the Festival's income and expenditure suggest striking changes in its operation and organization. Some of these changes are easy to explain. In 1967 the Aldeburgh Festival celebrated its twentieth birthday with a royal opening of its new concert hall at Snape and an extended season: twenty-four days rather than the previous eleven to fourteen. The Snape Maltings permitted bigger events, larger audiences, and higher-priced tickets: despite the artists frequently performing in it and the renovations it underwent, Aldeburgh's Jubilee Hall carried with it a whiff of village life. Joan Cross—among other things the original Ellen Orford and Queen Elizabeth the First—recalled the 1948 Festival on its twentieth anniversary. Aldeburgh 'contained a village hall, rather ugly and quite peculiarly unfitted for performances of opera'.

There was little space and no technical equipment for what would be needed. The 'stage' was, in fact, a room slightly above the level of the main hall, and it had a ceiling which would only impede the movement of scenery. The orchestra pit was tiny. When it was eventually used for the first festivals, the harp and the percussion of the English Opera Group's Chamber Orchestra overflowed each side into the auditorium, and

Table 5.4 Aldeburgh Festival income and expenditure (£), 1959–68[a]

	1959	1960	1961	1962	1963	1964	1965	1966	1967	1968
Expenditure										
Individual events	5,806	9,743	8,777	8,455	6,965	12,859	12,453	14,136	29,504	38,502
General	1,993	3,064	2,611	3,127	3,685	4,882	6,579	7,197	12,466	13,409
Administration	1,486	1,732	3,042	3,296	3,690	4,269	4,642	5,536	7,162	11,746
Total	9,285	14,539	14,430	14,878	14,340	22,010	23,674	26,869	49,132	63,657
Income										
Box office	4,972	8,995	7,058	7,200	8,173	13,702	12,512	14,637	34,650	44,168
Other	2,192	2,461	2,493	2,852	3,740	4,708	6,117	6,080	9,290	8,407
Total	7,164	11,456	9,551	10,052	11,913	18,410	18,629	20,717	43,940	53,575
Working deficit	2,121	3,083	4,879	4,826	2,427	3,600	5,045	6,152	5,192	10,082
Other income										
Arts Council grant	750	1,000	2,500	2,500	2,000	2,500	2,750	3,000	4,500	5,000
Subscriptions etc.	1,683	1,692	2,276	5,201	4,258	5,958	4,043	3,860	3,000	6,032
Total	2,433	2,692	4,776	7,701	6,258	8,458	6,793	6,860	7,500	11,032
Surplus/Deficit										
Net surplus or deficit	312	391	103	2,875	3,831	4,858	1,748	708	2,308	950
Special write-off	—	—	—	2,417	4,474	4,470	1,000	—	—	—
Reserve fund	1,217	826	723	1,182	539	927	1,675	2,383	4,691	5,641

[a] ACGB, Aldeburgh Festival 1965–70, 1971–2.

were tactfully hidden by screens draped with rugs and eider downs. . . . Plainly Britten's vision was far greater than mine. I did not foresee the immense success of the first festival or the amazing developments of the following years.[51]

The new concert hall destroyed any lingering illusions of a haphazard Festival: it was chic and, despite its location and external appearance, metropolitan; admission *could* be priced accordingly. Ticket prices had actually started creeping up in 1964–5—partly because of the high number of international soloists by then performing in Aldeburgh, and partly in an effort to keep the Festival profitable in preparation for the immense changes it would undergo once the new concert hall was completed. In 1967, with the Maltings in use, the price of tickets remained more or less at the same level as in the previous year; the use of the new hall, however, meant a reduction in the number of other Festival venues that had traditionally allowed gradation in ticket prices. The Festival was now concentrated around Snape Maltings, the Jubilee Hall, and Aldeburgh Parish Church—each charging one price for all seats at any event.

Snape was by no means the Festival's first attempt at widening its performance platform and increasing its income: a plot of land at Adair Lodge in Aldeburgh was discussed and bid for in 1956, while in 1959 the Jubilee Hall was expanded following a leaflet campaign that would not have seemed out of place in an American election.[52] But these were unsatisfactory compromises, offering limited return on investment. Nonetheless, recovery of the investment in the Maltings Hall was immediately promising. In its inaugural season, the profit on the Britten–Pears performance of *Die schöne Müllerin* at Snape was £1,113—nearly double that made on their *Winterreise* in the previous Festival.[53] The profit on an Amadeus Quartet concert in 1967, at £863, was almost three times greater than in 1966.[54] Suddenly orchestral concerts and the performance of larger choral works made money. Although the virtual secession from Aldeburgh to Snape would cause resentment among residents and nostalgists, True Believers had long seen the need for a proper concert hall, and were willing to pay, in large numbers, for the privilege.

[51] Joan Cross, 'Twenty Years On', *Opera*, 18 (Autumn 1967), 10–11.

[52] Council of the Aldeburgh Festival Minutes, 20 July 1956. BPL, Aldeburgh Festival Correspondence, 1956. The 1959 leaflet asking for donations for the Jubilee Hall renovations included the following: 'for 12 years composers and designers and producers have been compelled to create and design and produce small operas which can only just squeeze into the Jubilee Hall stage[.] for 12 years the orchestra pit has so cramped the players that they can scarcely draw a bow[.] for 12 years we have discussed all sorts of improvements and even planned a new theatre[.] 12 YEARS IS LONG ENOUGH'. BPL, Aldeburgh Festival Correspondence, 1959.

[53] BPL, Aldeburgh Festival Accounts, 1966 and 1967. Tickets for the Britten–Pears recital in 1966 were actually more expensive than in 1967—40*s*. rather than 30*s*.

[54] BPL, Aldeburgh Festival Accounts, 1966 and 1967. Ticket prices were 30*s*. and 20*s*. for the Quartet's 1966 Jubilee Hall appearance (with Peter Graeme, oboe, and Gervase De Peyer, clarinet), and 30*s*. for its Snape Maltings concert in 1967 (with Britten).

The Festival's extended duration resulted from this new metropolitan thinking: marketing had finally found its way into Aldeburgh's bosom. A queen, a new hall, an inaugural concert, and a twentieth anniversary were perfect ingredients for a heady marketing push. It was a necessary approach: although tickets for many Festival events were traditionally devoured by subscribers, and even though (perhaps in deference to the Cold War and the cult of James Bond) talk of an Aldeburgh black market had some currency in the 1960s, it was by no means certain that there would be the audiences to fill the new hall over the longer period of the Festival, or indeed in the long term. Yet, despite the increase in length, the working deficit—the difference between income and expenditure—in the Festival's twentieth year was less than it had been in the previous year, and was similar to the figure for 1965—a comforting thought for the planners of future Festivals.

Ironically, expanded overheads and the new metropolitan style increased the Festival's claims on the Arts Council, which had always been well disposed towards it since it fulfilled the Council's promises to the provinces, but involved relatively little of its money. Communications between the Arts Council and Aldeburgh were always direct: in 1954, for example, both Kenneth Clark (Council Chairman and regular lecturer at the Festival in the 1950s and 1960s) and Eric Walter White (Music Officer and Britten biographer) wrote to the composer concerning his grant application. 'We considered your cri de coeur yesterday and did what we could. We hope it will be sufficient help,' noted Clark, while White confided: 'We did our best for the Aldeburgh Festival at yesterday's meeting of the Executive & managed to get the guarantee increased to £750: but it wasn't easy, because, as you know, our own Treasury grant remains constant, so any increases on individual items can be made only at the expense of something else.'[55] Such Club-land chumminess was not always so down to earth: in June 1957 the American airbase near Aldeburgh informed Fidelity Cranbrook that all pilots had been informed of the Festival and had been instructed to avoid the Aldeburgh area as much as practicable.[56] The collusion between Authority and Festival knew no earthly bounds.[57]

[55] Clark to Britten, 18 Mar. 1954; White to Britten, 18 Mar. 1954. BPL, Aldeburgh Festival Correspondence, 1954.

[56] Colonel John Robie to Cranbrook, 11 June 1957. BPL, Aldeburgh Festival Correspondence, 1957.

[57] After the Maltings fire in 1969, parliamentary support and sympathy were expressed. 'Mr. Raymond Fletcher asked the Secretary of State for Education and Science if he will give an assurance that public funds will be made available, through the Arts Council or by other means, to facilitate the speedy reconstruction of the Maltings Concert Hall at Aldeburgh, in view of the international importance of the festivals held there.

Miss Jennie Lee: I share the sorrow which every music lover must have felt at the loss of this fine building and I offer my sympathy in particular to Mr. Britten and his colleagues. I am glad to be able to say that the insurance cover, together with the contributions from the public which have been

With the growing stature of the Festival in the 1960s, with a change in government and arts policy, and increasing inflation, a rise in the Aldeburgh grant was inevitable. Harold Wilson's Labour government (1964–70) raised the Council's total grant from £3.2 million to £9.3 million during its term in office; expenditure on festivals, literature, and art increased from 5.6 per cent of the total grant to 11 per cent over the same period.[58] Some changes were already in the air before the arrival of the Labour government: in 1954, the year of Britten's *cri de cœur*, Aldeburgh had received just under 6 per cent of the total Council expenditure on English festivals, whereas this figure was around 18 per cent in 1963, the year before Wilson's premiership began.[59] During Aldeburgh's 'second period' (1959–68) its annual grant increased from £750 to £5,000 (Table 5.4). Snape Maltings consolidated Aldeburgh's position as a leading festival, and the Council's affiliation with this established, successful, *non-metropolitan* affair was good public relations.

There was one other source of revenue that played a considerable role in stabilizing the Festival in the 1960s, but which does not appear in the annual accounts. Britten's indirect contributions to Festival income through his recitals and his heightened bartering skills have been acknowledged above; his direct contributions—either through waiving rights or through personal donations towards the cost of specific works—were equally significant. Although Britten was involved in discussions of the Festival's finances and his possible contributions, his own management's correspondence regarding these is somewhat artful:

> Following on our discussion about the financial problems of this year's Festival [1963], I am now writing to confirm my request for help in connection with the presentation of several of your own compositions. I have estimated that it will cost of [*sic*] £2600 to mount 'The Beggar's Opera' as against takings of only £1100, and that we shall lose a further £300 on the preparation and performance of your new Symphony for Cello and Orchestra, partly on account of the large number of rehearsals required. We shall also lose quite a lot of money on the two Choral Concerts in which your 'St. Nicolas' and 'Rejoice in the Lamb' are being performed. . . . If, therefore, you felt able to make the

flowing in to Aldeburgh, should be sufficient not only to replace the building but to carry out certain refinements in the original design. It is not therefore expected that any call will need to be made on public funds.' *Hansard*, 19 June 1969, 134. The reaction of local children was equally sympathetic: 'Alex' (aged 5½) sent Britten a historically unsynchronized drawing of a Spitfire bombing the Maltings, with the message 'I hope you are a little more cheerful we Do have some fish'. BPL, Maltings Fire Correspondence, 1969.

58 ACGB, *Arts Council Annual Report 1971*. The increased expenditure on art, festivals, and literature was at the expense of opera and ballet, the grant for which fell from 50 per cent of the total Council grant to 28 per cent during Wilson's period in office. This still represented an increase for opera and ballet in real terms, although it indicated a change in the Council's priorities.

59 ACGB, *Arts Council Annual Report 1954*; *Arts Council Annual Report 1963*. A change in the tabulation of Council expenditure makes it difficult to ascertain this figure at the end of Wilson's period in office.

Festival a donation towards the cost of mounting the four works I have mentioned (you generously suggested that £1000 might be possible), it would certainly ease our budget problems very considerably.[60]

In 1966 Britten donated £500 towards the cost of mounting the second of his church parables, *The Burning Fiery Furnace* since, 'despite every ticket being sold we still could not avoid a loss of £987, because of the high cost of production'.[61] Moreover, in 1968 Britten was told that the Festival was expecting a loss of around £2,000 on the performances of *The Prodigal Son* and *Gloriana*, and that if he felt able to make a contribution towards the cost of mounting these works, the management would be extremely grateful.[62] A cheque was immediately dispatched.

In 1969 proposals to institutionalize Britten's contributions to the Festival were formulated. In the wake of the Maltings fire—when ingenuity and economy were needed in equal measure—it was suggested that 'Ben provide with publishers that all his future compositions would be dealt with on the basis that no royalties or performing fees were paid for any performance of his works at the Aldeburgh Festival'.[63] Oxford University Press and Boosey & Hawkes—Britten's previous publishers—would be contacted to see if they would be prepared to make the same concession. Despite Britten's probable involvement in discussions of this idea, it was a throw-back to the turn of the century, when English composers were unlikely to make money on a performance, and a premiere was often the (financial) responsibility of its creator. Certainly Stephen Reiss's language is mildly admonishing—the implication being that the Festival would remain in the black if it weren't for performances of Britten's music, at best an oversimplification, at worst quite wrong. The correspondence and implied discussions demonstrate that Britten was continually reminded of the link between economics and art—as he had been with the English Opera Group, and this was an important influence on the music he composed for the Festival.[64] Moreover, the correspondence demonstrates the dependency culture that the Festival had built around the composer, as the EOG had done some time before.

As in the Festival's first ten years, the financial infrastructure of this second period shaped (and was shaped by) Aldeburgh's artistic output. Contributing artists were no longer limited to those at hand—or, probably more accurately,

[60] Reiss to Britten, 28 Mar. 1963. BPL, Aldeburgh Festival Correspondence, 1963.

[61] Reiss to Britten, 28 Nov. 1966. BPL, Aldeburgh Festival Correspondence, 1966.

[62] Reiss to Britten, 2 Apr. 1968. BPL, Aldeburgh Festival Correspondence, 1968. The actual loss of £1,924 on these two events brought some good news: estimates of income and expenditure were now more accurate than before.

[63] The Benjamin Britten Foundation at Snape, undated. BPL, Maltings Fire Correspondence, 1969.

[64] See below.

those at hand now came from a far wider field, and brought with them international artistic reputations. Menuhin's appearance in the 1957 Festival began this trend; his reappearances over the following two years helped consolidate it. Rostropovich's first Festival performance was in 1961; two years later he was scheduled to give the premiere of Britten's Symphony for Cello and Orchestra and present piano trios with Menuhin and Britten.[65] From 1964 to 1966, however, the number of eminent artists increased, with Richter, Söderström, Janet Baker, and Fischer-Dieskau added to the constellation. This was partly the result of jet travel and the LP, both of which had intensified the cult of the international celebrity performer, but there was another more convincing reason for their presence in this small seaside town. Aldeburgh was an escape from the demands of this perpetual travel, which had grown with each new LP and flight route. Musicians would not come to Aldeburgh for one concert, then disappear; they stayed, often for the duration of the Festival. Moreover, they appeared in more than one capacity: Rostropovich as accompanist or expanding the Amadeus Quartet to a quintet, Richter as duet partner or accompanist. Aldeburgh provided the opportunity for the artists to talk and perform with equally gifted colleagues in a relatively informal environment; outside the Festival, such occasions were limited. The result was truly unique—a contrast to the specialization that had developed in the nineteenth century, and a return to eighteenth-century procedures, before agents articulated an increasingly inflexible market.

The growing financial stability of the Festival in the 1960s allowed Britten to invite a larger number of reputable musicians to Aldeburgh—regardless of any fee reduction that might occur—and to present them in increasingly unconventional programmes. By 1964 it was no longer necessary to detail an important artist's programme in the prospectus: his or her name, or the most cursory reference to the composers likely to be represented in the recital, was enough. With the art of cross-subsidy clearly understood and practised during this second period, the Festival programmes were loosened up; Britten's commitment to the music of his contemporaries, demonstrated in the 1950s, intensified. Poulenc's *opéra bouffe Les Mamelles de Tirésias* was presented alongside Monteverdi's *Ballo delle ingrate* (1958); the 1959 premieres of works by Henze, Seiber, and Arnold stood, if unsteadily, on their own feet, with tickets costing the same as for Menuhin's various Festival appearances that year; the Society for the Promotion of New Music made an appearance in 1960, presenting works by Birtwistle and Maxwell Davies, while in another recital four days later Walton, Frank Martin, and Richard Rodney Bennett stood perhaps more confidently next to Britten and Dowland; Henze was paired with Schumann; Lutosławski conducted his

[65] Postponed owing to Rostropovich's illness.

music long before it became fashionable; the pianist John Ogdon performed Ronald Stevenson—profitably; and Lennox Berkeley's *Castaway* was coupled with Walton's one-act opera *The Bear* (whose choice of plot had been suggested by Pears). In all, apart from the first performances of Britten's works, there were twenty-nine world premieres in the Festival's 'second period', compared with twenty-two in the first.[66] There were also many more second and third performances of works—of greater significance than a premiere for many a composer. Aldeburgh gained a reputation for its support of contemporary music. At times, this reputation was benevolent, if not saintly. Anthony Wright of the publishers Mills Music wrote to Britten in 1959 concerning Elisabeth Lutyens, asking 'if there is anything you can do for her at Aldeburgh next year'.[67] An assistant to Alfred A. Kalmus had written to Britten on a similar mission five years before this. 'Dr. Kalmus . . . wanted to bring to your notice a work by FRANK MARTIN which has only recently been published and which he feels would be particularly suitable for the Aldeburgh festival.'[68] These pieces of contemporary music were often presented by one of Aldeburgh's distinguished soloists; if not, they at least owed their inclusion in the Festival to the presence of such soloists in other programmes, and the resulting subsidy overspill. As Britten retreated more and more into Aldeburgh and the Festival during the 1960s, his ability to attract soloists of such calibre to the Suffolk coast was vitally important; this led to some of his most significant compositions.

Britten as Court Composer

Forster's 1948 article in *The Listener* outlined one vital feature of the Aldeburgh Festival. The author noted how completely the new Festival was integrated into the life of the town: the Festival was shaped by buildings, acoustics, sea fronts, and townsfolk (including one 'hard-bitten' man who, dabbling in critical parlance, found that *Saint Nicolas* was not his 'cup of tea'). The profit-making Festival dance (which never really recovered from its later, Cinderella-like transformation into a Festival ball) was an extension of the directors' community aspirations, while the lectures, art exhibition, verse recitation, and children's concert testified to the underlying philosophical scope of this new venture.

[66] Based on data in Rosamund Strode (comp.), *Music of Forty Festivals*.

[67] Wright to Britten, 9 Oct. 1959. BPL, Aldeburgh Festival Correspondence, 1960. A non-premiere performance of Lutyens's Variations, Op. 38, for flute was presented in 1962.

[68] Harpner to Britten, 2 Apr. 1954. BPL, Aldeburgh Festival Correspondence, 1954. The work in question was Martin's *Sonata da Chiesa*, which had just been premiered at Morley College. Excerpts from Martin's *Everyman* had been performed at Aldeburgh in 1952. A few of his works were given several performances in Festivals over the years.

These environmental factors also had a strong effect on Britten himself—a point he emphasized in an interview with Lord Harewood in 1960:

I think the shape of the Festival—that is, the works you want to perform in the Festival—is very much dictated by the town itself, the buildings, the size . . . and the quality of those buildings. For instance there's this very beautiful church and the churches in the district, that can take a certain number of performers, not too many. Then there is the Jubilee Hall which as you know is a tiny little theatre, holding an audience of not more than 320 or [3]30; [a] very small orchestra, although we've enlarged it this year with a bigger orchestral pit—it will take an orchestra of about forty—but the nature of these buildings dictates the fact that we cannot do big-scale works. Again, the chorus, which is a local amateur chorus, can only perform at weekends, therefore the choral concerts can only be at weekends. What I'm getting at is that the nature of the town and the people working for the Festival dictates very much the shape of the Festival.[69]

Little had changed since Forster's observations some twelve years before. Britten was, however, more specific than Forster about the constricted environment in which he worked. The points he raised—limited space for performers, an amateur chorus available at weekends only (limiting the size and complexity of its contribution), the various acoustics—might be of limited significance to many composers; to Britten, with his antagonism towards 'ivory tower' music, they were of enormous importance.

Six years after his interview with Harewood, Britten expanded his thoughts on music and environment, specifically linking certain works to Aldeburgh and the Festival. 'My life does tend, through the Aldeburgh Festival and other things, to have settled down in the country—in the provincial life rather than in the metropolitan.'

I like at the moment to write pieces which suit the buildings and the occasions down in Suffolk. That is how these small operas have continued, and the church pieces like 'Curlew River' and 'The Burning Fiery Furnace' have developed; although, of course, when occasion has demanded, I have been happy to go back to the bigger forms in 'Budd' and 'Gloriana'.[70]

There were other influences. Since Britten hoped and imagined that much of the audience was local, his compositions often reflected a Suffolk sensibility. Relocating Maupassant's May Queen in Suffolk was not simply good Festival marketing; nor was the move from medieval Japan to medieval England in the church parables. Britten genuinely felt a strong connection with his environment and its constituents. But such sensibility was not always a positive influence on music performed in the Festival. When Holst's *Hymns from the Rig Veda* were

[69] Britten in discussion with the Earl of Harewood, 'People Today', BBC Home Service, 23 June 1960 (pre-recorded in Aldeburgh).

[70] Edmund Tracey, 'Benjamin Britten talks to Edmund Tracey', *Sadler's Wells Magazine* (Autumn 1966), 6.

proposed in 1960, the vicar of Aldeburgh suggested a number of changes 'so as to give them a specifically Christian flavour', thereby rendering them suitable for presentation in the parish church. 'Hymn to the Dawn' was to become 'At Dawn'; 'O Father' was suggested in place of 'O Goddess'; and with a carefree interchange of deities hitherto unsuspected in Hindu worship, 'Saviour' replaced 'Varuna', while Jesus appeared to, and quickly replaced, Indra.[71] The hymn now safely addressed Christian imperialism: more 'Hail Conquering Hero' than anything else.[72] A similar raw nerve was exposed four years later. Britten received a complaint about floodlighting the church exterior ('We feel that being lit up only during festival week, the floodlighting glorifies only man and what he is doing during that special week'), charging admission to concerts ('I expect you know what Jesus said about moneymakers in the temple'), putting up notices that read 'No Admission' on the church doors during rehearsals, and even the use of churches *at all* for Festival concerts.[73] Reiss replied with a deft combination of logic and theology: 'I think you have misunderstood the point about the moneylenders. . . .'[74]

Other, more secular demands were catered for. 'For instance one doesn't write an opera which lasts 8 hours without an interval—that could be socially very inconvenient,'[75] Britten told Lord Harewood—although the composer's thoughts on the social expediency of an eight-hour opera *with* an interval were not touched on. It was more public library than 'ivory tower' composition. Personalities, deities, budgets, acoustics, and musicians all had a stake in Britten's Aldeburgh music. Even works not premiered in a Festival were often composed with the constraints of the Festival in mind: they would soon be performed there. Moreover, the Festival's dependency on the composer—one he enjoyed and encouraged—was most obvious in the constant pressure it placed on him for new works. He spoke of this in 1965: 'If only we had the old, more flexible, even haphazard arrangements for concerts. I've got to decide now exactly how to map out my 1966, what engagements to accept. What I'd like would be to look a month ahead—to be able to say, "Now, I've finished this piece, let's do some concerts." I can't do that.'[76] The financial argument concerning the first performance of a

[71] Memo, undated. BPL, Aldeburgh Festival Correspondence, 1960.

[72] A few years before this there had been a number of conflicts between the vicar and the Festival over use of the church. Concessions were eventually made on both sides. According to Reiss, 'One could hardly say that the vicar was pleasant but he was less disagreeable than hitherto.' Reiss to Britten, 21 Aug. [1955?]. BPL, Aldeburgh Festival Correspondence, 1956.

[73] Colin Smith to Britten, 30 Sept. 1964. BPL, Aldeburgh Festival Correspondence, 1965. Britten was further asked to 'do something towards putting right what we feel amounts to blasphemy towards God', yet whether this concerned specific complaints or was more of a general caveat is unclear.

[74] Reiss to Smith, 5 Oct. 1965. BPL, Aldeburgh Festival Correspondence, 1965.

[75] Britten in discussion with the Earl of Harewood, 'People Today', BBC Home Service, 23 June 1960 (pre-recorded in Aldeburgh).

[76] Warrack, 'Benjamin Britten', 274.

piece by Britten is complicated, but a non-operatic premiere often necessitated a first-class soloist, the composer as accompanist or conductor, a partly ignorant, partly knowledgeable audience, and much media attention. Prestige and good box-office trade resulted—often more of the latter than at other Festival concerts. Over and above this, it was these very features that distinguished Aldeburgh from the many other English festivals—and 'distinction' was an important catchword in Arts Council parlance.

The Aldeburgh Festival premieres of Britten's works are listed in Table 5.5. The table highlights a number of important compositional trends; these include a changing hierarchy of genres, a shift in Britten's compositional priorities, and an intensification in the number of works written for Aldeburgh at the expense of other (metropolitan) locations. In 1960 Lord Harewood asked Britten why, after the first Festival, he programmed so little of his own music. The response was typical Britten:

> Well I feel very strongly about this point. It is not a festival for propagating one's own works. Obviously as—I am a kind of—a composer who likes writing for occasions. It is fun for me to write new operas, new works to fit into the Festival; but essentially I didn't feel—and I hope people are gradually all beginning to feel that with me—that this is not a festival like Bayreuth, which is obviously designed for Wagner's own works. This is *not* the case at Aldeburgh. We are only too happy to do works of all composers of any age or any generation, of any kind, that fits into our plans.[77]

Yet the number of works represented in Table 5.5 is around *half* of those given an opus number between 1948 and 1976, and a handful of others besides. Although this was hardly flooding the market, Aldeburgh was obviously an important forum for presenting, if not 'propagating', Britten's music. Moreover, since Britten traditionally did much of his composing in his 'holiday sabbatical' immediately after each Festival, the table has a further significance: works were sketched and often completed six months before a Festival, yet were squirrelled away for an Aldeburgh premiere. There were still pieces available for other places—commissions or occasional works—but the pattern set during Britten's youth, when the commercial value of a premiere was understood and when prospective 'buyers' were often played off against each other, had changed.

The change in Britten's compositional priorities was quite obviously progressive: as can be deduced from Table 5.5, only four of the seventeen works from the 1950s with an opus number were first presented at Aldeburgh; in the 1960s two-thirds of those pieces with Britten's imprimatur were premiered at a Festival. This shift was partly the result of Britten's move away from opera, a form that had dominated his output in the late 1940s and early 1950s and had necessitated premieres in different theatres around the country. Yet this is a

[77] Britten in discussion with the Earl of Harewood, 'People Today', BBC Home Service, 23 June 1960 (pre-recorded in Aldeburgh).

rather circuitous argument: this diminution in operatic output was due partly to the performance forum offered in Aldeburgh which, as Joan Cross attested, was not naturally conducive to presentations of opera. Regardless of motive, as Britten grew older his compositional activities came to gravitate almost exclusively around Aldeburgh: this intensified the impact and importance of local environmental influences on his compositional style and language in the 1960s—especially before the inauguration of Snape Maltings in 1967, which lessened some of these restrictions.

The works listed in Table 5.5 can be loosely grouped into a number of categories, each constructed around particular constraints or opportunities: works composed for a specific artist; those that owe their existence to a specific acoustic or environment; occasional pieces; and those that were designed for limited financial resources. These categories, granted, are somewhat artificial: although Britten told Harewood that it was fun for him to write new operas, new works to fit into the Festival, the motivation for a piece of music might come from any number of sources, singly or in combination, and jump from one of the above categories to another.[78] Nonetheless, these groupings offer a good perspective on Britten's works, illustrating some of the reasons for the composer's changing hierarchy of genres and his shifting priorities.

The 'occasional works' in Table 5.5 are perhaps the least significant of all the pieces listed. *Variations on an Elizabethan Theme*, a collaboration with a number of other composers on a set of variations on *Sellenger's Round* to celebrate the coronation of Elizabeth II in 1953, is now rarely performed, and is presented more as a curiosity than anything else. Britten's *The Building of the House*, a work composed in the tradition of Beethoven's *Consecration of the House* to mark the opening of Snape Maltings in 1967, has far more compositional integrity than the *Round*, but it is a minor work, and rarely performed.[79] Britten's arrangement of *God Save the Queen* from 1971 is *echt*-occasional music and is performed accordingly; both this and *The Building of the House*, though, are extremely well-crafted works, notwithstanding their near throw-away origins.

The works from Table 5.5 written for specific performers are more important than those written for specific occasions: *Lachrymae* (William Primrose), *Six Metamorphoses after Ovid* (oboist Joy Boughton), *Songs from the Chinese* (Pears and Julian Bream), the Sonata in C and Suites (Rostropovich), *Nocturnal after John Dowland* (Bream), *Gemini Variations* (Jeney twins[80]), the *Songs and Proverbs of*

[78] In his 1966 interview with Edmund Tracey, Britten emphasized this point: 'The singer, the player, the place of the performance—all these give me ideas, and I don't think, if the result is good, that that is necessarily a bad thing.' *Sadler's Wells Magazine* (Autumn 1966), 5.

[79] Britten decided not to tempt fate by performing the piece when the Maltings was rebuilt and reopened after the fire.

[80] See below.

Table 5.5 Britten premieres at the Aldeburgh Festival, 1948–1976[a]

Year	Work	Opus no.	Artists	Venue
1948	*Saint Nicolas*	42	Pears, Ald. Fest. Choir and Orch.	Parish Church
1949	*Let's Make an Opera*	45	EOG, Del Mar	Jubilee Hall
1950	*Lachrymae*	48	William Primrose, Britten	Parish Church
1951	*Six Metamorphoses after Ovid*	49	Joy Boughton	Thorpeness Meare
1953	*Variations on an Elizabethan Theme*	—	Ald. Fest. Orchestra, Britten	Parish Church
1955	'New Prince, New Pomp' (1931)	—	Purcell Singers, Imogen Holst	Parish Church
1955	*Alpine Suite*	—	Aldeburgh Music Club [Recorders]	Thorpeness Meare
1955	Scherzo	—	Aldeburgh Music Club [Recorders]	Thorpeness Meare
1956	Prologue, Song, Epilogue	—	Pears, Dennis Brain, Britten	Parish Church
1957	Courtly Dances from *Gloriana*	—	English Chamber Orchestra, Britten	Jubilee Hall
1958	*Songs from the Chinese*	58	Pears, Julian Bream	Gt. Glemham
1958	*Noye's Fludde*	59	EOG, Charles Mackerras	Orford Church
1960	*A Midsummer Night's Dream*	64	EOG, Britten	Jubilee Hall
1961	Sonata in C	65	Mstislav Rostropovich, Britten	Jubilee Hall
1962	*The Twelve Apostles*	—	Pears, London Boy Singers, Britten	Parish Church
1962	*King Herod and the Cock*	—	London Boy Singers, Britten	Parish Church
1963	Psalm 150	67	Northgate Choir and Orch., Britten	Jubilee Hall
1964	*Nocturnal after John Dowland*	70	Bream	Jubilee Hall
1964	*Curlew River*	71	EOG	Orford Church
1965	*Gemini Variations*	73	Zoltán and Gábor Jeney	Parish Church
1965	*Songs and Proverbs of William Blake*	74	Dietrich Fischer-Dieskau, Britten	Jubilee Hall
1965	*When night her purple veil* (Purcell)	—	Fischer-Dieskau, Alberni String Quartet, Benjamin Britten	Jubilee Hall
1965	First Suite for Cello	72	Rostropovich	Parish Church
1966	*The Burning Fiery Furnace*	77	EOG	Orford Church

1966	*Sweet was the Song* (1931)	—	Purcell Singers, Imogen Holst	Parish Church
1967	*The Building of the House*	79	ECO, East Anglian Choirs, Britten	Snape Maltings
1967	*The Golden Vanity*	78	Vienna Boys' Choir	Snape Maltings
1967	*The Fairy Queen* (Purcell)	—	ECO, Britten	Snape Maltings
1968	*The Prodigal Son*	81	EOG	Orford Church
1968	*In these delightful, pleasant groves* (Purcell)	—	Harper, Baker, Pears, Hemsley, Britten	Snape Maltings
1968	Second Suite for Cello	80	Rostropovich	Snape Maltings
1968	*The Sycamore Tree* (1930)	—	Ambrosian Singers, Philip Ledger	Parish Church
1968	*A Wealden Trio* (1930)	—	Ambrosian Singers, Philip Ledger	Parish Church
1969	*Five Spiritual Songs* (Bach)	—	Pears, Britten	Blythburgh Church
1969	*Tit for Tat* (1931)	—	John Shirley-Quirk, Britten	Jubilee Hall
1969	Suite for Harp	83	Osian Ellis	Jubilee Hall
1971	*God Save the Queen*	—	ECO, Britten	Snape Maltings
1971	Canticle IV	86	Bowman, Pears, Shirley-Quirk, Britten	Snape Maltings
1971	*Dulcibella, whene'er I sue for a kiss* (Purcell)	—	Bowman, Shirley-Quirk, Britten	Snape Maltings
1971	*Let the dreadful engines* (Purcell)	—	Shirley-Quirk, Britten	Snape Maltings
1971	*When Myra sings* (Purcell)	—	Pears, Shirley-Quirk, Britten	Snape Maltings
1973	*Death in Venice*	88	EOG, Steuart Bedford	Snape Maltings
1974	Third Suite for Cello	87	Rostropovich	Snape Maltings
1975	String Quartet in D (1931)	—	Gabrieli Quartet	Snape Maltings
1975	*Suite on English Folk Tunes*	90	ECO, Bedford	Snape Maltings
1976	*Phaedra*	93	Janet Baker, ECO, Bedford	Snape Maltings

[a] Compiled from Aldeburgh Festival programme books; Rosamund Strode's *Music of Forty Festivals*; and *A Britten Source Book*. Works are listed in order of premiere. The table does not list the cadenzas composed for the Haydn Cello Concerto in C (performed by Rostropovich in the 1964 Festival) and for Mozart's Piano Concerto K.482 (Richter, 1966), although both illustrate Britten's flexibility and the Festival's attractiveness from a soloist's perspective. The Courtly Dances from *Gloriana*, performed in 1957, were in a special arrangement for chamber orchestra. The Third Suite for Cello was premiered in Aldeburgh in December 1974, but is included in this table because its first performance was postponed from the 1972 Festival. *Sacred and Profane*, Op. 91, received its first performance at Snape in September 1975, but is not listed in this table as this was after the Festival. A number of other early works (along the lines of 'New Prince, New Pomp' or *The Sycamore Tree*) were first presented at Aldeburgh after Britten's death—a tradition that continues to this day—and have not been included in this table.

William Blake (Dietrich Fischer-Dieskau), *The Golden Vanity* (Vienna Boys' Choir), the Suite for Harp (Osian Ellis), Canticle IV (James Bowman, Pears, John Shirley-Quirk), and *Phaedra* (Janet Baker). Some of these works were blatant bribes: in a letter to Crozier in 1950 Britten stated that *Lachrymae* was written for Primrose 'to reward him for coming to the Festival';[81] as stated above, Rostropovich would be given a cello sonata if he gave the first performance of it in Aldeburgh, while Fischer-Dieskau was invited to Aldeburgh in 1965 with the promise of a new piece (*Songs and Proverbs of William Blake*).[82] Others were written to reward instrumentalists who, by then, were already regular Festival performers (Bream, Ellis, Baker, and Rostropovich again). *All* of the pieces expanded the technical and expressive vocabulary of the particular voice or instrument to a remarkable degree. Britten's works for Pears had been doing this for some time, and his collaboration with Dennis Brain had truly revolutionized the possibilities and expectations of contemporary horn writing. But now his mind (and ear) was being turned to any number of instruments. Mitchell recalls the composition of the *Nocturnal after John Dowland*. 'Ben would sometimes consult Julian, and ask, "Is this possible on the guitar?" And Julian would say, "No it isn't." But then he would take it away and try it and find that it *was* possible, that it worked.'[83] It was the *Serenade* all over again.

Simple things like a soloist's range influenced the shape of Britten's works. Better used to the choir stalls than the opera stage, Deller was quick to detail his vocal geography when asked to sing in *A Midsummer Night's Dream*: 'I'm a bit worried about the compass of the part, what I mean is, if you would tell Ben, when the time arrives, that I like to live here . . .

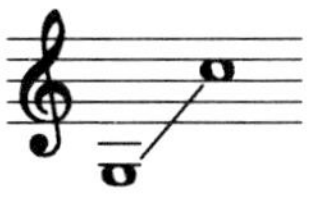

a D is alright [*sic*] if taken in the phrase, but I don't like to sit on it for long!'[84] Deller was duly respected. But the artistic influence of soloists was far greater than the mere range of the parts written for them. Peter Evans reiterates a common critical observation of the time when he says that the *Songs and Proverbs of William Blake*—a sombre, dark cycle, in which Blake's texts are set in music of incredible depth and power—owes its existence to the *sound* of Fischer-Dieskau's voice: 'his unique sound, dark yet unforced even in a high baritone tessitura, is most perfectly adapted to expressions of world-weariness or even of utter fatalism, tempered by a philosophic resignation that never degenerates into

[81] Britten to Crozier, 4 May 1950. Carpenter, 290–1. [82] Ibid. 449. [83] Ibid. 423.
[84] Deller to Pears, 4 Sept. 1959. BPL, Aldeburgh Festival Correspondence, 1960.

emotional detachment.'[85] And of course there were no problems with range, as the high tessitura of Fischer-Dieskau's part in the *War Requiem* had proved.

Britten's relationship with Rostropovich was consummated in the magnificent Sonata in C, for cello and piano, first performed at Aldeburgh in 1961. A semi-serious contract promising six solo cello suites (written on the back of a restaurant menu and offering the works in exchange for an assurance from Rostropovich that he would be restrained when he met a minor British royal[86]) was half-completed when Britten died in 1976. The composer's collaboration with Rostropovich was the second most significant artistic partnership of his life. Britten knew his playing before he knew him personally, and the Sonata was agreed upon only at their second brief meeting. Communication occurred through a translator, and the composition proposed was of a type Britten had barely touched in the previous twenty years: a non-texted, 'absolute' instrumental composition. There was, therefore, an anonymity about the work—one which is rarely to be encountered in Britten before this. The abstract quality was reinforced by another factor: Rostropovich could play almost anything on the cello—yet the personality of his voice came from this strangely impersonal technical facility. Such technical freedom had its greatest resonances in the horn writing for Dennis Brain and the piano writing for the composer himself in the concerto—but not in the vocal writing for Pears which had long been linked to the singer's gradual development of technique.

The cello sonata did not prompt a full-scale return to absolute music; vocal music, in one form or another, still dominated Britten's output, and experiments with non-programmatic ideas were written almost exclusively for Rostropovich. But the use of traditional forms in these works for cello may have been more than a historical nod of homage in the direction of Bach. With no barriers imposed by Rostropovich's technique, these forms acted as an anchor, allowing the most virtuosic of displays within the context of a readily understood musical convention. The technical barriers of the instrument itself—traditionally urging it towards a melodic role—required this; but they were also overcome, never more so than in the three Suites. When writing the Symphony for Cello and Orchestra, Britten informed Rostropovich, 'I must confess I can hear you in every note and every bar, although I fear it may not be worthy of your great art.'[87] Worthy it was; and this grand, formal celebration of emancipated technique and dark, brooding orchestral writing is testimony to the inspiration of one instrumentalist.

Similar influences are to be found in the works written for other artists and for initial performances at Aldeburgh. Britten's letter to Rostropovich could have been written to Bowman, Primrose, Shirley-Quirk, Ellis, and Baker: the 'voice'

[85] Peter Evans, *The Music of Benjamin Britten* (1989), 376.

[86] Carpenter, 417. The royal concerned was Princess Mary; the restaurant was in Lincoln.

[87] Britten to Rostropovich, 15 Nov. 1962. Carpenter, 417.

of each of these is in every note, every bar. The *Gemini Variations* and *The Golden Vanity* are not *quite* in the same league, but they wear their Aldeburgh colours with pride: both brought young boy performers to the Festival—an important compositional motivation and, in the case of the *Variations*, probably the *most* important consideration since it is written for three instruments (piano duet, violin, flute), yet only two performers, Zoltán and Gábor (Gabriel) Jeney—strangely inflexible for all its flexibility. In all, Britten's close relationship with leading artists (the Vienna Boys' Choir and the Jeney twins excepted) resulted in the development of his own compositional technique through the instruments/voices concerned; it also guaranteed the inclusion of at least one 'world-class' performer in every Festival.

Although the *Six Metamorphoses after Ovid* were written with a particular instrumentalist in mind—Joy Boughton—it is a work more shaped by environment than performer. First, the piece is not *technically* difficult: as with *Night Piece*, most of the virtuosity required is in interpretation and, even more so than with the cello suites, in giving a solo 'melodic' instrument a harmonic context. Second, and more convincingly, the work was written for performance outdoors—on the Meare at Thorpeness. Britten was rising to the setting—if not the occasion: Madrigals on the Meare were initiated in the 1949 Festival and *Metamorphoses* was intended to complement the already established conventions of the venue. If sixteenth-century Italy does not immediately suggest a ready compatibility with the pantheism of Ovid's Ancient Greece, that is not because there are not some similarities in theme or imagery—nature in all its allegorical glory being one of these. Although the *Metamorphoses* is now a recital piece and in the standard repertory—of even the most umbratile oboe players—its celebration of the outdoors is obvious in both the subject matter and several acoustical tricks: the quick echoes and sustained notes, for example, which would work very well in a performance in its original setting.

As with the *Metamorphoses*, the three church parables owe their existence to influences from both a particular acoustic or environment and one other category—in this case, limited financial resources. *Noye's Fludde* had been written six years before the first of the parables with an eye firmly on the EOG's troubled accounts. Had it repeated the financial success of *Let's Make an Opera*, it is possible that Britten would have further exploited the children's market rather than moving into the rather austere world of the church parables. Britten stripped the later children's opera of some of the extravagance that had made profits so elusive (elaborate set and costumes), borrowed its principal force (small professional cast and orchestra[88]), and applied it to a combination of Japanese Nō play and medieval English liturgical drama. The financial circumstances of the

[88] *Noye's Fludde*, of course, includes veritable classrooms-full of children in its cast and orchestra.

English Opera Group had long influenced the style and content of Britten's operatic ventures. The 1950s and 1960s saw the EOG move house several times: its first tentative residency at Aldeburgh; the later talk of severing this relationship; and the space made for the Group under Covent Garden's weather-beaten umbrella in the 1960s.[89] But in spite of these changes, Britten preferred both of his charges to remain on speaking terms and he continued to show a strong interest in the direction of the EOG even when most of his energies were consumed by the Aldeburgh Festival.

Britten had recognized the dramatic potential of the Nō play when he first saw *Sumidagawa* in Tokyo in 1956. The gestation was slow but thorough: the twenty-page booklet accompanying the published score details the care taken in the process. 'The style of the first production of *Curlew River*, although suggested by the Japanese Nō theatre, created a convention of movement and presentation of its own.' The production notes, it continued, were intended as a guide to the composer's intentions and the *necessary* style of performance. Gesture, geography, lighting, costumes, masks, and *every* stage direction are listed in the booklet.[90] This lavish book was a goodwill gesture from Faber towards its recent acquisition—Britten; both parties wished to avoid the problems that had so marred the composer's relationship with Boosey & Hawkes during the previous five years. But the booklet's publication was also a recognition that *Curlew River* was a truly original style of contemporary music drama, and deference to the work's symbols was just as important as an explanation of them.

If ever there was a time to write such a work, it was during the immediate period after *A Midsummer Night's Dream*. Never had a work so clearly highlighted the limitations of Aldeburgh's Jubilee Hall. Although the hall had been enlarged and refurbished immediately before *A Midsummer Night's Dream* (the opera was written partly to celebrate the reopening) there were physical limits to what could be done. *A Midsummer Night's Dream* used a larger cast and orchestra than Britten's previous operas, *Noye's Fludde* and *The Turn of the Screw*, and according to Desmond Shawe-Taylor, 'Cranko's production did not wholly avoid the village-hall effect'.[91] But to avoid the village-hall effect was not easy in

[89] The Arts Council had long encouraged collusion between the EOG and Aldeburgh, in the same way that it encouraged the Group's link with Covent Garden in the 1960s. In 1949 Eric Walter White informed the EOG that, with regard to 1951, 'the Aldeburgh Festival Committee might be advised to apply for a grant of up to £2,500, and is likely to get about £2,000. I do not know whether the Council will be able to increase its normal grant to the English Opera Group for that year; so I have suggested that it might be appropriate for the Aldeburgh Festival to commission a new production from the Group on terms to be agreed.' White to Fell, 19 Dec. 1949. ACGB, EOG 2.

[90] 'Production Notes and Remarks on the Style of Performing *Curlew River* by Benjamin Britten and William Plomer', in Britten, *Curlew River*.

[91] Desmond Shawe-Taylor, *Sunday Times*, 12 June 1960.

what was, essentially, a village hall. Extreme stylization and a greater sense of proportion was possible with *The Turn of the Screw*, but even the episodic nature of *A Midsummer Night's Dream* could not totally disguise the large cast (twenty-five) and the resulting cramped effect.

Britten had actually been working on *Curlew River* for some time before he started his adaptation of Shakespeare's masterpiece; the intention was always to mount it in a church. He spoke of his reasons for this in his 1966 interview with Edmund Tracey:

> Perhaps I could say a word here about the church operas, which come really from an inclination I have had, ever since I was a child, for what I might perhaps call the 'Gothic acoustic': where the note reverberates for some time after it is struck or sung, an acoustic which produces a string of notes together, its own form of harmony; and although this is not the only reason I started on these church operas, it was, I think, a very strong one.[92]

This use of a particular acoustic is obvious in the score. Self-generated harmonies are inherent in most of the texture, while Britten's recognition and exploitation of this feature is found in his invention of the 'Curlew sign'—a symbol printed over certain notes or rests indicating that the performer must wait until the other musicians have reached this point in the score before continuing.

There were other factors spurring on the composition of the first parable; 'the development of technique in our instrumentalists, without a comparable development in conducting technique, has been relevant.'

> I am obviously not going to name names, but so often you find a really first-class orchestra suffering under a not very gifted or very intelligent or technically developed conductor; and in these church operas I have given a great deal of responsibility to the players—even the responsibility of following the singers, which after a certain amount of experience they do brilliantly and easily—and this has led to a level of seriousness and creativity in the playing which you don't always get when there is a conductor leading.[93]

Conductors to have worked at Aldeburgh by the time of this interview included Charles Mackerras and Norman Del Mar—hardly amateurs. Yet both have indicated that there was uneasiness in their relationship with Britten—that he never quite let go of the works he asked them to conduct.[94] The new parable circumvented such problems. Moreover, its simple setting could easily be employed again if future parables were composed; indeed, some of the investment in sets and costumes was eventually spread over three different operas.

[92] 'Benjamin Britten talks to Edmund Tracey', *Sadler's Wells Magazine* (Autumn 1966), 6.

[93] Ibid.

[94] Mackerras says that Britten's uneasiness with him resulted from the composer's sexuality. To Mackerras and others, homosexuality in Aldeburgh in the 1950s was simply funny, and any humour was not malicious. This was probably of little comfort to Britten. Kildea interview with Mackerras, 6 Jan. 1996.

The works that do not appear in Table 5.5 of course tell us much about those that do—as well as illustrating something of Britten's priorities for himself and the Festival. Even Britten, canny as he was in wrenching premieres from the commissioning body, could not expect to make a long-term habit of this.[95] Because of this, a firm demarcation between Aldeburgh works and 'other' pieces sometimes developed—but only if the commissioning body was larger and more heavily resourced than Aldeburgh. Works that could be incorporated into the Aldeburgh repertory of course were. But the whole question of the influence of Britten's direct involvement in a performance, his continued association with that work, and its eventual success is important.

Of the twenty-eight works with opus numbers to be premiered outside the Aldeburgh Festival, just over half were commissions (Table 5.6). In many of these cases, sheer scale prevented a performance at the next Festival. Such pieces were more a feature of the first ten years or so of the Festival, before Britten's 'retreat' to Aldeburgh: the *Spring Symphony*, *Billy Budd*, *Gloriana*, *The Prince of the Pagodas*, and *Cantata academica* were all commissioned and performed outside Aldeburgh between 1948 and 1960. The first Aldeburgh performance of the *Spring Symphony* was not until 1967, with the arrival of Snape Maltings. Neither *Billy Budd* nor *The Prince of the Pagodas* was performed at Aldeburgh during Britten's lifetime. And *Cantata academica* received its first Festival performance in 1962, two years after its premiere.[96] During the 1960s no large works were first performed outside Aldeburgh apart from the *War Requiem*, *Owen Wingrave*, and, on a slightly smaller scale, the Symphony for Cello and Orchestra.[97] There were Festival premieres of substantial works—the three church parables, *A Midsummer Night's Dream*—but this period saw a restriction in Britten's composing activities. As far as he was concerned, the Festival provided the musical sustaining power and the emotional security without the dangers of the commercial London concert scene.

Of the non-commissioned works not receiving an Aldeburgh premiere, many were written for regular Festival performers, and some fulfilled the rather loose reciprocity agreed upon when artists such as Menuhin or Rostropovich first performed in Aldeburgh (the Cello Symphony, *The Poet's Echo*, etc.). Moreover, in most cases the premiere outside Aldeburgh was followed by a Festival performance either later that year or the next. In other words, after the formation of the Festival Britten wrote increasingly for Aldeburgh, regardless of where any one piece might first be performed. And the spirit of the Festival is

[95] *Peter Grimes*, *Saint Nicolas*, and the *Spring Symphony*, for example, were first performed by parties other than those who commissioned them.

[96] Strode, *Music of Forty Festivals*, 15.

[97] *Owen Wingrave*'s status is complicated by the fact that it was filmed at Snape, but first seen in a BBC television broadcast. The Symphony for Cello and Orchestra was first performed in Moscow.

Table 5.6 Britten premieres outside the Aldeburgh Festival, 1948–1976[a]

Year	Work	Opus no.	Artists	Venue/event
1949	*Spring Symphony*	44	Concertgebouw Orch., van Beinum	Holland Festival
1949	*A Wedding Anthem*	46	Joan Cross, Pears, St Mark's Choir	St Mark's, London
1951	*Dido and Aeneas* (Purcell)	—	EOG, Britten	Lyric, Hammersmith.
1951	*Five Flower Songs*	47	BBC Midland Chorus, John Lowe	BBC Broadcast
1951	*Billy Budd*	50	Covent Garden, Britten	Covent Garden
1952	Canticle II	51	Kathleen Ferrier, Pears, Britten	Nottingham
1953	*Gloriana*	53	Covent Garden, John Pritchard	Covent Garden
1953	*Winter Words*	52	Pears, Britten	Leeds Festival
1954	*The Turn of the Screw*	54	EOG, Britten	Teatro La Fenice
1955	Canticle III	55	Pears, Dennis Brain, Britten	Wigmore Hall
1955	*Hymn to St Peter*	56*a*	Choir of St Peter Mancroft	Norwich
1956	Antiphon	56*b*	St Michael's Choir	Tenbury Wells
1957	*The Prince of the Pagodas*	57	Covent Garden, Britten	Covent Garden
1958	*Nocturne*	60	Pears, BBC SO, Rudolf Schwarz	Leeds Festival
1958	*Sechs Hölderlin-Fragmente*	61	Pears, Britten	BBC Broadcast
1959	*Fanfare for St Edmundsbury*	—		Bury St Edmunds
1959	*Missa Brevis*	63	Westminster Cathedral Choir	Westminster Cathedral
1960	*Cantata academica*	62	Basler Kammerorchester, Paul Sacher	Basle University
1960	*Fanfare for SS Oriana*	—		Vessel launch
1961	The National Anthem	—	RLPO, Pritchard	Leeds Festival

1961	Jubilate Deo in C	—	Choir of St George's Chapel	Windsor
1962	*War Requiem*	66	CBSO, Meredith Davies, Britten	Coventry Cathedral
1963	*A Hymn of St Columba*	—	The Ulster Singers, Havelock Nelson	Donegal
1963	*Cantata misericordium*	69	Orch. de la Suisse Romande, Ansermet	Geneva
1963	*Night Piece (Notturno)*	—	Various	Leeds Piano Comp.
1964	Symphony for Cello and Orchestra	68	Moscow PO, Rostropovich, Britten	Moscow
1965	*Voices for Today*	75	Various	New York, Paris, Lond.
1965	*The Poet's Echo*	76	Vishnevskaya, Rostropovich	Moscow
1967	*Hankin Booby*	—	ECO, Britten	Queen Elizabeth Hall
1969	*Children's Crusade*	82	Wandsworth School Choir, Burgess	St Paul's Cathedral
1970	A Fanfare for D.W. [D. Webster]	—	ROH, Covent Garden	
1971	*Who are these Children?*	84	Pears, Britten	Edinburgh
1971	*Owen Wingrave*	85	ECO/BBC, Britten	BBC Broadcast
1975	Canticle V	89	Pears, Osian Ellis	Bavaria
1975	*Sacred and Profane*	91	Wilbye Consort, Pears	Snape
1976	*A Birthday Hansel*	92	Pears, Ellis	Cardiff
1976	*Tema 'Sacher'*	—	Rostropovich	Zürich
1976	String Quartet No. 3	94	Amadeus Quartet	Snape

[a] Compiled from Aldeburgh Festival programme books; Rosamund Strode's *Music of Forty Festivals*; and *A Britten Source Book*. Works are listed in order of premiere. *Five Flower Songs* received its premiere in a private performance by amateurs. *Night Piece (Notturno)* was the test piece in the 1963 Leeds Piano Competition, and was thus performed by many pianists. *Voices for Today*, written for the twentieth anniversary of the United Nations in 1965, was given a simultaneous triple premiere in New York, Paris, and London. Britten's incidental music for the plays *Stratton* (1949), *Am Stram Gram* (1954), and *Old Friends are Best* (1955) are not included in this table. Similarly, small works, such as his edition of Purcell's *Job's Curse* (1950) or a timpani piece written for James Blades in 1955, which did not receive an opus number and have seldom been performed since their premiere, are not in this table.

obvious in these works; the restrictions in size, scope, and economy relate less to the premiere than to the first, and subsequent, Aldeburgh performances. Canticles II, III, and V are a case in point. Composed for some of the great musicians of the twentieth century and first performed outside Aldeburgh, these works were consummate musical experiences, but highly flexible since they were not labour intensive and were popular (especially the earlier ones). Similarly, *Winter Words*, *Sechs Hölderlin-Fragmente*, *The Poet's Echo*, and *Who are these Children?* were first performed outside the Festival, but there can be no doubt, from their scale and the personnel involved in their presentation, that Britten had in his mind Aldeburgh performances when he composed the works.[98]

The significance of this shift from the pattern of the 1950s is most obvious when one looks at Britten's music as a cultural product occupying or articulating both genre and the canon. Although referring to film, Steve Neale outlined some of these patterns in a 1990 article. In it he talks of the 'role and importance of specific institutional discourses . . . in the formation of generic expectations, in the production and circulation of generic descriptions and terms, and, therefore, in the constitution of any generic corpus'.[99] Aldeburgh had its own specific institutional discourses—never more obvious than in Britten's relationship with Decca and his publisher, whether Boosey & Hawkes or Faber Music. The audience and financial patterns of the Festival brought certain generic expectations. These were further reinforced by Decca, which, by the 1960s, was recording Britten's works soon after their Aldeburgh premiere and, through sales figures and critical reaction, compounding the Festival's own institutional discourses. The informality of Britten's negotiations with Decca belied their seriousness. A conversation with Decca's John Culshaw over a gin and tonic at the Red House during the Festival charted the next (or next-but-one) recording session; patterns again informed expectations. The process was two-sided: canonical elevation meant that certain artists were long associated with certain works, and other performers were often unwilling to take on the piece—unless their performance aligned itself closely in style and sound to that of the original exponent (something the young Robert Tear was alternately lauded and criticized for, depending on how far he strayed from Pears's formidable artistic interpretations) or was given Britten's approval. This of course created the paradoxical situation of a *canonic* work being performed by a select group of artists in Britain; it did, however, increase the importance and power of the Festival, where artists from this group could often be found performing the very work with which they were associated.

[98] *Winter Words* received its first Aldeburgh performance in 1954; *Sechs Hölderlin-Fragmente* in 1959; *The Poet's Echo* in 1968 (two performances); and *Who are these Children?* in 1971 (September—its first Festival appearance in Aldeburgh was in the following year).

[99] Steve Neale, 'Questions of Genre', *Screen*, 31/1 (Spring 1990).

Many commentators have described Britten's increasing retreat into Aldeburgh as a negative force, which compounded his move from the large stage after *Peter Grimes*. It is certainly true that without the Festival Britten would have undertaken more commissions, writing for different forums with their own (often large-scale) expectations, and responding to different articulations in the market. But Britten's responses to Aldeburgh's own articulations, and his subsequent manipulation of the wider market through his 'authorized' recordings, resulted in a long list of masterpieces, without the composer having abdicated control over his product.

Chapter 6

Recording a Reputation

> Uncle Matthew was no respecter of other people's early morning sleep, and after five o'clock one could not count on any, for he raged round the house, clanking cups of tea, shouting at his dogs, roaring at the housemaids . . . and all to the accompaniment of Galli Curci on his gramophone, an abnormally loud one, with an enormous horn, through which would be shrieked 'Una voce poco fà'—'The Mad Song' from *Lucia*—'Lo, here the gen-tel lar-ha-hark'—and so on, played at top speed, thus rendering them even higher and more screeching than they ought to be.[1]

Nancy Mitford's 'Uncle Matthew' is the patriarchal English squire personified. Above the chimney-piece in the hall of his large country house he proudly displays the entrenching tool with which he bludgeoned to death eight German soldiers in the First World War. Blood and hair has never been removed from it lest the story be doubted, the verismo undermined. To him Oscar Wilde is a 'sewer', clearly not a literary criticism, since the only book he has ever read is *White Fang*—a work he found so impressive that he has never bothered to read another. He sits—and more frequently sleeps—in the House of Lords, protesting once from the floor that Peeresses should be kept out of the chamber since, once in, they would be certain to use the Peers' lavatory. He speaks of 'writing-paper' not 'notepaper' and is firmly against the education of women. But this rich, prejudiced, and deeply uncultured person nonetheless knows parts of the 'Mad Scene' from *Lucia di Lammermoor*—not usually a trophy of the ignorant. Moreover, 'Uncle Matthew' (in reality Mitford's own father) has catholic, seasonal tastes: *Lucia* is eventually replaced by 'Thora' ('I live in a land of roses, but dream of a land of snow'), who lasts a full winter.

In truth, Uncle Matthew is interested in neither Donizetti nor popular music, but this episode from Mitford's life says much about the production and consumption of music in the 1920s and 1930s. That the gramophone—*echt*-modernist

[1] Nancy Mitford, *The Pursuit of Love* (1967), 20.

child of a revolutionized industry—managed to penetrate the deeply hostile and inward-looking walls of a country house is significant in itself. Its place in many homes did not result from the sort of thinking that had put pianos in the front rooms of the working classes in the late nineteenth century—pianos which often remained mute but which nonetheless fulfilled a well-understood criterion of social status and mobility.[2] Rather, the gramophone was at first a toy—successfully re-creating the voice, but little else. Yet unlike many of the pianos bought in the late nineteenth century, this new musical apparatus was actually played—for much of the day in the Mitford household—which suggests a sudden change in leisure patterns. It is true that neither Uncle Matthew nor his family gave the gramophone undivided attention in the way that people were just starting to do with radio; lives carried on, but to the accompaniment of Donizetti, Thora, or whoever else happened to be in fashion at the time. But this is not another sign of ignorance in this particular upper-class family: it was a general pattern in gramophone 'consumption'. Domestic Muzak was born. Rather ironically, this change in the way people listened to music—returning, full circle, to the way opera in Mozart's time was heard, before giving way to a new culture of concentrated attention—was partly the result of the gramophone's limited technology. Each record contained around four minutes of music (eight, once double-sided discs were introduced)—hardly enough to promote sustained entertainment or broad erudition. As such, the gramophone encouraged the short popular song, but it left art music severely truncated or pillaged.

One repercussion of the limited recording space on each record was that, quite unlike radio, each piece of recorded music was repeated over and over again—a wholly new aesthetic in music education. In art music the prima donna became a consumer item—consolidating a trend begun by Jenny Lind and others. Certainly fashions and trends were provoked by, and resulted in, the rather eclectic output of the various recording companies—companies that at first appeared and disappeared in great numbers and with little warning owing to primitive technology and limited overheads.[3]

The gramophone is the last century's most striking symbol of the potent influence of technology on music. After a shaky beginning, the various stages of its evolution made an impact on popular and art music. The three-minute jazz piece or popular song (its legacy still with us today) was a child of the wind-up gramophone. As acoustic recording technology improved, so did the variety of instruments and sounds successfully committed to disc—a lesson that many composers learned and took heed of in the music they put forward for recording.

[2] See Ehrlich, *The Piano*.

[3] Without exclusive technology confined to any one company and with a high threshold of consumer tolerance, many were encouraged to involve themselves in this new industry, in a way similar to the early internet businesses of the 1990s.

When electric recording was introduced in the late 1920s, representation of instruments and voices became that much truer. When the LP appeared in the late 1940s it brought with it composers such as Bruckner and Mahler, whose music had been only superficially explored under the regime of the LP's short-playing ancestor.[4] The reputation of these composers quickly rose, owing to greater dissemination and easy repetition of their previously dismissed or misunderstood works. And accompanying the introduction of magnetic tape in the late 1940s (which allowed editing) and stereo recording in the 1950s was a more sophisticated mixing desk and a more professional record producer, marking the beginning of impossibly high standards and expectations in (doctored) performances.

The gramophone eventually irrevocably changed reception and perception of music. Unlike radio, where the listener choice was limited to tuning into a programme or not, the gramophone allowed consumer selection. The facility of choice turned art music into a serious mass-market proposition. In itself, this represented an incredible change in the perceived role of art music, and in the nature of its audience. A composer might gain critical success in the opera house or the concert hall, and the same composer might be held in high esteem by executants—as measured through sheet-music sales or performing-right royalties—but popular success could be judged only through a popular medium. Radio, for all the naive sophistication of its listener surveys, could not provide an accurate measurement in this regard—something conceded when it began broadcasting 'hit parades' based on sales of records. Yet the gramophone, through its associated sales and marketing mechanisms, provided a measure of a work's popular resonance. Moreover, with the gramophone the music critic—learned, distanced, and unanswerable—had a new performance forum on which to comment, a new audience to educate. And unlike a live performance, a review could be compared with the record concerned: the distance between critic and audience was breaking down, and the relevance of each judgement was easily questioned if it flew in the face of 'public opinion', a powerful, *measurable* force.

The gramophone challenged the autonomy of critical opinion by encouraging mass public opinion. Each force became aware of the other—consumers when deferring to the new record guides, critics when writing about best-selling records. Although the relationship between critic, consumer, and composer has never been easy, it has nonetheless been intriguing to study, ever since early courtship. But to concede that such a relationship often exists gives rise to awkward questions. To what extent was critical opinion shaped by popular opinion, or vice versa? And was this new mass market seductive enough to affect composers and their music—in the way it clearly was with 'popular' music?

[4] Exceptions were recordings of Mahler's *Das Lied von der Erde* and Symphony No. 9, released, to subscribers, on the HMV label.

Benjamin Britten might as well have been talking about Uncle Matthew when in 1964 he said 'Anyone, anywhere, at any time, can listen to the B minor Mass upon one condition only—that they possess a machine. No qualification is required of any sort—faith, virtue, education, experience, age.'[5] This appears at best petulant, at worst prudish (a virtuous listener?). But although Britten undoubtedly demonstrated at various times in his life both petulance and prudery, he showed from the first an enthusiasm for recording—as much for its use of technology (an altar at which he worshipped in the 1930s) as for the opportunity of committing 'authentic' versions of his music to the public and posterity. The relationship between popular and critical opinion of Britten's music over his whole lifetime is a fascinating and varied study, not least because he was involved at the beginning of many of the most rapid changes in the gramophone's later development. His use of the new medium from the 1930s onwards tends to undermine his Aspen Award sentiments, at least in their most simplistic reading. More importantly, it demonstrates yet again a composer quite at home with technical innovation, and not at all reticent about how this innovation could be used to his advantage.

To analyse Britten's critical and popular reputation according to periods of gramophone history is a somewhat artificial exercise. For a start, it elevates the gramophone to a dominant position in Britten's life. Although that is not a true picture, neither is the opposite. Moreover, to treat their histories in parallel highlights the relationship between composer, critic, and consumer. These three forces are sometimes completely independent; there is also frequent overlap and symbiosis.

The chief periods of gramophone history in Britten's lifetime are 1925–49 (the invention and refinement of electrical recording); 1950–7 (the introduction and rapid rise of the long-playing record in Britain); and 1958–76 (the advent of the stereophonic record).[6] It is significant that a subsequent new period of gramophone history, revolving around the introduction and general acceptance of the compact-disc player in the 1980s, did not render the recordings of the preceding period obsolete as had happened at each previous stage of the gramophone's development; heightened technology averted this.[7] In Britten's case, the

[5] Benjamin Britten, *On Receiving the First Aspen Award* (2nd impression 1978), 20. Stravinsky had said something very similar thirty years earlier: 'Today anyone, living no matter where, has only to turn a knob or put on a record to hear what he likes. Indeed, it is in just this incredible facility, this lack of necessity for any effort, that the evil of this so-called progress lies . . . For one can listen without hearing, just as one can look without seeing.' Igor Stravinsky, *An Autobiography* (1958), 248–9.

[6] Pre-recorded stereophonic reel-to-reel tapes first appeared in 1954, four years before the first stereo records.

[7] This was often artistic obsolescence as much as technical obsolescence, fuelled by consumer demand for new recordings. Ironically, the large number of CD reissues of early stereo recordings has been driven by consumers certain that performers today do not reach the standards of those in the 1960s.

combination of this advanced recording technology and the composer's personal involvement in each recording project from the late 1950s onwards has meant that only recently have other conductors and record companies challenged his master's voice, often coming a very poor second in the process. No other composer-executant active in the age of stereophonics—Stravinsky included—can make this claim.

Electric Recording: 1925–1949

Britten's father thought himself prudent rather than prudish when he refused to buy either gramophone or wireless while his children were young: music-making was their personal responsibility. Britten could listen to the radio or the gramophone at the homes of various family friends, but his early introduction to the great symphonic works came about in the same manner as it had for most musicians before the advent of recording: through piano transcriptions and arrangements. Although this gave him little understanding of orchestration, there were certain advantages: he could at least learn the complete piece rather than the truncated versions peddled by the various gramophone companies or pedalled by enthusiasts of the pianola. For as a boy Britten could have heard Schubert's 'Unfinished' Symphony on a record lasting only eight minutes, compounding the sins of its title by being incomplete as well. This was a time when recordings emerged from the most unlikely circumstances. For example, in a typical recording session in Columbia's London studio a few years before Britten's birth, the 'French horns, having to direct the bells of the instruments towards the recording horn, would turn their back on it and were provided with mirrors in which they could watch the conductor. The tuba was positioned right back away from the horn and his bell turned away from it; he also watched in a mirror. The big drum never entered a recording room.'[8] This was a time when Beethoven's Fifth Symphony was recorded with six violins, two violas, and no timpani or double bass. Tubas were often used to double or replace the cellos. The result, according to Compton Mackenzie, who founded the magazine *Gramophone* in 1923, was that a recorded orchestra often sounded like the noise of a merry-go-round 'several streets away', and the piano like a banjo—and this from an advocate and enthusiast for the new technology.[9] *Punch* (described by Mackenzie as a magazine representing the views of the man on the golf course rather than the street) was dismissive of many of these early stages in the gramophone's history; but in the excitement surrounding this new product, it was something of a lone voice.

[8] Gellatt, *The Fabulous Phonograph* (1977), 180.

[9] Compton Mackenzie, 'The Gramophone. Its Past: Its Present: Its Future', *PMA*, 51st session (1924–5), 102.

When electric recording was introduced in 1925, the acoustic process became obsolete almost overnight. The technology that replaced it was developed and refined over the next twenty years (especially so as a result of the Second World War), but the principle remained the same: a pair of microphones could be placed above an orchestra rather than musicians being placed around an acoustic horn; and these microphones turned sound waves into electric signals.

The recording culture that Britten encountered in the 1930s was built around these techniques and principles. Yet the English art-music market had been decimated at the beginning of the decade. The combined effect of the American Depression and consequent slump in international trade, high unemployment in Britain, and the collapse of the gold standard culminated in a merger of HMV and Columbia (forming EMI) after their joint profits of £1.42m. in 1930 fell to £160,000 in the following year.[10] This disaster made the industry even more market-driven than before and dominated by mainstream repertory. Walter Legge, then a junior producer at HMV, initiated one way of circumventing this by devising a subscription system. Projects were advertised, subscriptions collected, and records made—in this order. This scheme was enormously popular (the Wolf Society, for example)—a most successful marriage of demand and supply. The system, of course, did not favour young composers, relying as it did on the interest and support of large numbers of the cultured (and moneyed) classes, whose tastes had not kept abreast of the developments in contemporary British music.[11]

Britten did benefit from the EMI monopoly and specialist subscriber market, but in a roundabout way. In the mid-1930s Decca entered the competition, initiating a series of cut-price recordings with conductors such as Sir Henry Wood and ensembles such as the Boyd Neel String Orchestra.[12] Decca's approach to the market differed from that of its older, more established competitors. When its first recordings were criticized as 'rackety, harsh, and overamplified', it invested in new microphone and master-disc technology, which greatly improved quality and gave the young company a reputation for innovation— although it was some time before Decca threatened EMI's pre-eminent position.[13]

Decca's innovative spirit was not limited to the development of gramophone technology. Its contract with ensembles such as Boyd Neel's was part of an attempt to corner areas of the market neglected or completely ignored by other companies (EMI was able to sign up bigger names). This policy brought about

[10] Michael Chanan, *Repeated Takes* (1995), 80.

[11] In an enthusiast's market, however, any project was theoretically possible—Beecham recording Delius, for example.

[12] The Decca record company was formed in 1929 when an older company of the same name (which manufactured portable phonographs) was bought by a London stockbroker, Edward Lewis. See Chanan, *Repeated Takes*, 81.

[13] Ibid.

Britten's first gramophone recording, although the credit for it must be shared with Boyd Neel. In 1937 Neel's orchestra was invited to perform at the Salzburg Festival in August, on condition that it play a new English work. Having encountered Britten's music in the film *Love from a Stranger*, and aware of the speed with which the composer worked, Boyd Neel commissioned from him a work for Salzburg. The *Variations on a Theme of Frank Bridge* was the result. Its successful premiere in Salzburg was followed by performances at the Proms and the 1938 ISCM Festival, and it was recorded for Decca in July 1938. Britten was pleased with the records, but further offers of commercial recordings did not immediately follow. Indeed, three years later Britten noted that the only works of his on record were the *Variations*, the *Simple Symphony*, and his *Soirées musicales*.[14] Moreover, each of these recordings was produced by Decca; Britten had yet to attract the attention of other labels.

The first recordings of Britten's works from the period of the electric gramophone are listed in Table 6.1. Since there are a number of huge delays, which seem extraordinary to early twenty-first-century eyes, this recording profile must be analysed in terms of Britten's reputation at the time.

The first thing to note about Table 6.1 is that only twelve of the works with opus numbers were recorded by British companies (or subsidiaries) before 1950. Apart from the three already listed, these were *Seven Sonnets of Michelangelo*, *Introduction and Rondo* and *Mazurka Elegiaca*, *Hymn to St Cecilia*, *A Ceremony of Carols*, *Serenade* for tenor, horn and strings, *The Young Person's Guide to the Orchestra*, *The Holy Sonnets of John Donne*, and his String Quartet No. 2. *Matinées musicales* must be added to this list: although according to Parsons's discography it was released in 1951, it was almost certainly recorded before then since it was first issued on 78s. Of these thirteen recordings, eight were made by Decca, three by HMV, and one each by Columbia and MGM/Parlophone.

The timing of these recordings delineates rather well the patterns of critical reception in Britten's first fifteen years as a professional composer. It also highlights two different compositional periods within these fifteen years—periods that Britten himself recognized. This compositional division is a little less complex than the critical divisions, although the two clearly overlap. In early March 1942, less than two weeks before being offered a commission for *Peter Grimes*, and only fifteen days before beginning his journey back to England, Britten told Kit Welford that he had 'reached a definite turning point in my work, & what I most want is to be able to think & think & work & work, completely undistracted for a good period of time'.[15] Hints of a turning point in Britten's music had come two years earlier with the *Sinfonia da Requiem* and the *Michelangelo Sonnets*. In these two pieces, an evenness and certainty of touch is obvious,

[14] Britten to Abe Meyer, 2 July 1941. DMPR 824.

[15] Britten to Welford, 1 Mar. 1942. DMPR 1021.

although this cannot necessarily be said of the work that separates them (*Diversions* for piano (left hand) and orchestra), nor of those that follow (among other things the *Introduction and Rondo alla Burlesca*, *Paul Bunyan*, the posthumously published and titled *American Overture*, and the *Scottish Ballad*). But *St Cecilia* was followed by a string of extraordinary pieces; as Mitchell says, the success of *Grimes* must be looked at in terms of these very works and the sureness of touch they exhibit.[16]

This certainty of technique and dramatic structure was noticed by the more perceptive British critics. Ernest Newman attended the premiere of the *Michelangelo Sonnets* at Wigmore Hall in September 1942, and wrote that they were 'evidently of exceptional quality, but the style is so unexpectedly different from that of Mr Britten's other recent works . . . that one can record only the general impression made by the first performance'.[17] His 'general impression' was favourable. The accuracy and prescience of Newman's review sets it apart from much of the often petulant criticism that had been written about Britten in the 1930s. Even the *Variations on a Theme of Frank Bridge*—a real hint of what was to come—was casually dismissed by the critic of the *Observer* with the patronizing caveat, 'Mr Britten's Variations were worse than we have been told, but better than we had feared'.[18] The lineage of this sort of criticism is easily traced through *Our Hunting Fathers* ('if it is just a stage to get through, we wish him safely and quickly through it') back to the *Sinfonietta* ('Mr Benjamin Britten in a Sinfonietta for ten instruments showed that he can be as provocative as any of the foreign exponents of the catch-as-catch-can style of composition').[19] Moreover, there was something English and cosy in this lineage, caught perfectly in William McNaught's preview of the *Sinfonia da Requiem*: 'For some years past a number of people have been admiring his undergraduate cleverness while wondering when it was going to couple itself with a graduate mind and purpose.'[20]

One of the most influential proponents of this antagonism was the musicologist and critic Jack Westrup. Two months before the premiere of the *Michelangelo Sonnets* Westrup previewed the first English performance of the *Sinfonia da Requiem* in typical style in *The Listener*:

'O for a trace of clumsiness somewhere!' wrote a critic of Benjamin Britten's 'Les Illuminations'. The exclamation might seem at first sight peevish. Critics generally have

16 DMPR 54.

17 Ernest Newman in the *Sunday Times*, 27 Sept. 1942, quoted in DMPR 1078.

18 *Observer*, 10 Oct. 1937, quoted in DMPR 515.

19 H. C. Colles on *Our Hunting Fathers* in *The Times*, 26 Sept. 1936; *Daily Telegraph*, 1 Feb. 1933, quoted in DMPR 300.

20 W. McNaught, *The Listener* (30 July 1942), quoted in DMPR 530. In this preview McNaught is generally positive about the *Sinfonia da Requiem*, but the language and retrospective view are significant.

Table 6.1 Britten's works 1932–1949, first commercial British recording[a]

Opus no.	Title	Completed	First recorded	Label
1	*Sinfonietta*	July 1932	May 1965	Decca
2	*Phantasy*	October 1932	released April 1951	Esoteric/Saga
3	*A Boy was Born*	May 1933	January 1957	Decca
4	*Simple Symphony*	February 1934	March 1939	Decca
5	*Holiday Diary*	October 1934	June 1982	Chandos
6	Suite for Violin and Piano	June 1935	1967	Supraphon
7	*Friday Afternoons*	August 1935	July 1966	Decca
8	*Our Hunting Fathers*	July 1936	June 1961 [released 1981]	BBC Enterprises
9	*Soirées musicales*	August 1936	November 1937	Decca
10	*Variations on a Theme of Frank Bridge*	July 1937	July 1938	Decca
11	*On This Island*	October 1937	June 1969 [released 1981]	BBC Enterprises
12	*Mont Juic*	December 1937	1971	Lyrita
13	Piano Concerto	July 1938	1957	HMV
14	*Ballad of Heroes*	March 1939	July 1990	EMI
15	Violin Concerto	September 1939	July 1970	Decca
16	*Young Apollo*	August 1939	April 1982	EMI/HMV
17	*Paul Bunyan*	April 1941	May 1987	Virgin
18	*Les Illuminations*	October 1939	January 1954	Decca
19	*Canadian Carnival*	December 1939	April 1982	EMI/HMV
20	*Sinfonia da Requiem*	June 1940	September 1953	Decca
21	*Diversions*	October 1940	July 1954	Decca
22	*Michelangelo Sonnets*	October 1940	November 1942	HMV
23/1	*Introduction and Rondo*	November 1940	January 1944	Decca
23/2	*Mazurka Elegiaca*	July 1941	January 1944	Decca

24	*Matinées musicales*	June 1941	1951	MGM/Parlophone
25	String Quartet No. 1	July 1941	1951	Esoteric/Saga
26	*Scottish Ballad*	October 1941	April 1982	EMI/HMV
27	*Hymn to St Cecilia*	April 1942	January 1943	Decca
28	*A Ceremony of Carols*	October 1942	December 1943	Decca
29	Prelude and Fugue	May 1943	September 1961	Westminster
30	*Rejoice in the Lamb*	July 1943	April 1957	Decca
31	*Serenade*	April 1943	May and October 1944	Decca
32	Festival Te Deum	November 1944	1963	Decca
33	*Peter Grimes*	February 1945	December 1958	Decca
34	*The Young Person's Guide to the Orchestra*	December 1945	*c.*October 1946	Columbia
35	*The Holy Sonnets of John Donne*	August 1945	August and December 1947	HMV
36	String Quartet No. 2	October 1945	November 1946	HMV
37	*The Rape of Lucretia*	May 1946	July 1970	Decca
38	*Occasional Overture*	September 1946	May 1984	EMI
39	*Albert Herring*	April 1947	April 1964	Decca
40	Canticle I	September 1947	April 1961	Argo
41	*A Charm of Lullabies*	December 1947	March 1962 [released 1981]	BBC Enterprises
42	*Saint Nicolas*	May 1948	April 1955	Decca
43	*The Beggar's Opera*	May 1948	June 1992	Argo
44	*Spring Symphony*	June 1949	November 1960	Decca
45	*The Little Sweep*	May 1949	October 1955	Decca
46	*A Wedding Anthem*	September 1949	January and February 1984	Hyperion

[a] Compiled from Charles Parsons, *A Benjamin Britten Discography* (1990); Ray Crick's discography in Michael Kennedy, *Benjamin Britten* (1993); Evans, Reed, and Wilson, *A Britten Source Book* (1988); Malcolm Walker, 'Benjamin Britten: Discography of Commercial Recordings as a Performer' (1993); J. F. Weber, *Discography Series XVI: Benjamin Britten* (1975); and DMPR. This table deals with complete recordings only of those works to which Britten allocated an opus number. There was some international mobility in the industry in this period, presaging that of today. Some MGM discs were distributed in the UK (including recordings of the Royal Opera House orchestra). Supraphon and Esoteric (Saga) were both distributed in the UK. Excerpts of *The Rape of Lucretia* and *Peter Grimes* were recorded long before their first complete release. Excerpts from *Friday Afternoons* appeared on disc before the 1966 recording, from which No. 4 was omitted.

plenty of clumsiness to worry them without wishing there were more. But the point of view is quite intelligible. Britten has published work after work displaying a complete technical assurance; and if nothing but technical assurance were looked for, there would be nothing but praise for this music. What disturbed this critic was the feeling that the technique had become an end in itself and that invention, in the fullest sense, had been left to take care of itself. It is a view that not a few people share about Britten's work, and its prevalence will explain why his music has so often aroused hostility. The hostility arises not from a lack of sympathy or a failure to understand his idiom but from exasperation at what seems a prodigal use of a conspicuous talent.[21]

Britten's heartless but magnificent technique was a critical leitmotiv during the 1930s. Although the *Variations on a Theme of Frank Bridge* partly changed this, the change was short-lived, as the critical climate soured considerably with the advent of war. Many writers were openly hostile towards Britten and his music during the war. The *Musical Times*, for example, embarked upon a vitriolic campaign, the resonance of which was felt for some years. As noted above, in June 1941 it published a letter from the respectably mobilized Pilot Officer E. R. Lewis, which denounced the 'favour recently shown to a young English composer', and followed this with an editorial that suggested that 'there are even worse fates than being unable to go on living and "composing in America", and one of them may be the consciousness of having saved one's art and skin at the cost of failure to do one's duty'.[22] Some members of the BBC were implacably opposed to Britten. And the honorary treasurer of the Royal Philharmonic Society suggested that Ernest Newman's enthusiasm for the young composer would be better directed at those involved in a 'programme called the Battle of Britain; a programme in which Mr Britten has no part'.[23] Practicalities and prejudice meant that only three of the works Britten composed after leaving for America were performed in England while he was away: *Les Illuminations*, *Canadian Carnival*, and the Violin Concerto. One side-effect of this was a heightened critical interest in Britten's music after his return to England and performances recommenced.

There was a touch of the 'prodigal son' about Britten's return in 1942. Although many took the role of the Older Brother, resentful that the sibling should regain a position of privilege having once rejected it, many were prepared to play the Forgiving Father, and welcome Britten back into the fold. This latter role was probably slightly easier to assume: Britten was a professional, and much art in England at the time was haphazard, vulgar, amateur, and self-consciously entertaining or uplifting (the theatre critic Philip Hope-Wallace,

[21] Westrup, 'The Virtuosity of Benjamin Britten', *The Listener* (16 July 1942), 93.

[22] DMPR 870–1.

[23] Baker in *The Times*, 15 June 1941, quoted in DMPR 958–9. This episode and the period in general is discussed in more detail in Ch. 2.

caught in a theatre during an air raid, commented: 'How squalid to be killed at this disgusting little farce.'[24]) Britten, particularly as composer of the folk-song settings, uplifted and entertained, but with a professionalism quite unknown to much wartime entertainment.

Hope-Wallace's sentiments were part of an intellectual reaction that longed for serious art and saw defiant survival of high culture as an essential element in the anti-Nazi war effort. The writer John Lehmann describes a poetry reading given by the Sitwells in 1944:

> As Edith got up to read, and began with her poem about the air-raids in 1940, 'Still Falls the Rain', the warning whistle was sounded in the Club. She had, I believe, never experienced a doodle-bug raid before; but she seemed quite unperturbed. . . . the rattle grew to ominous proportions, and it was impossible not to think that the monstrous engine of destruction was poised directly overhead. . . . Edith merely lifted her eyes to the ceiling for a moment, and, giving her voice a little more volume to counter the racket in the sky, read on. . . . Not a soul moved, and at the end, when the doodle-bug had exploded far away, the applause was deafening.[25]

There was similar applause for the *Seven Sonnets of Michelangelo* on its first London outing, and for similar reasons: the work defied the circumstances of its performance (if not its composition), was neither vulgar nor amateur nor too 'highbrow', and was presented by two musicians who had recently returned to wartime England from the safety of America. The songs brought about a new critical approach to the prodigal composer—Jack Westrup notwithstanding. Edward Sackville-West, a friend and admirer of Britten's, called them the 'finest chamber songs England has had to show since the seventeenth century, and the best any country has produced since the death of Wolf'.[26] He also noted their popular appeal, referring to the 'enthusiasm of a numerous audience'. Britten and Pears recognized the cycle's popularity at its first performance. 'Wednesday night was a grand success. Peter sang wonderfully & everyone was quite astounded. We were booked to record it for HMV immediately after the show!!!'[27] And later: 'We have recorded the Michelangelo for HMV and they have sold enormously. It is remarkable (or isn't it remarkable, Elizabeth) how much everyone loves the Sonnets. We do them to very simple audiences & they all say it is what they have been waiting for. They have made a tremendously deep impression.'[28] The songs' near-explicit celebration of the love between Britten and Pears through the cycle's dedication ('To Peter') and the narrative content of the sonnets, disguised admittedly by the Italian in which they were sung ('My will is in

24 Robert Hewison, *Under Siege* (1977), 169.
25 Ibid. 170.
26 Sackville-West in the *New Statesman* (3 Oct. 1942), quoted in DMPR 1077.
27 Britten to Ursula Nettleship, undated. DMPR 1076.
28 Pears to Elizabeth Mayer, 13 Feb. 1943. DMPR 1078.

your will alone, my thoughts are born in your heart, my words are on your breath'), was, perhaps none too remarkably for the period, left untouched.

The positive reaction to the premiere of the *Sonnets* explains HMV's immediate interest, while the commercial success of the consequent records accounts for the commitment of various gramophone companies to the works that followed (Table 6.1). It is clear, though, that HMV was motivated by immediate popular response and not by critical reaction to the *Sonnets* (the offer of a record contract came before any reviews were published). As Ralph Hawkes later wrote, such an approach was unusual. 'It is a well-known fact that, except in a very few isolated instances, the gramophone companies with all their wealth have never taken the initiative in issuing any composer's works before they have been fairly well established through publication and performance.'[29] His house composer was of similar mind. In 1940 Britten told Sophie Wyss to persuade Decca to record *Les Illuminations*: 'as it had such good notices it ought to sell quite well.'[30] HMV's immediate offer on the *Sonnets* was therefore unusual and significant, and formed an obvious demarcation between Britten's pre-war and wartime works. There had been a 'popular response' to certain of his pieces before the war—the Piano Concerto and the *Simple Symphony*—but these were fewer in number and were not recorded until some years after their first performance; even then, they had to wait until the critical tide had started to turn as a result of the *Variations on a Theme of Frank Bridge*.

Britten was well aware of the change in critical and popular reception of his music. He wrote to Elizabeth Mayer in May 1943:

> Do you know I'm going to do some more playing now—I'm doing the Scottish Ballad with Clifford Curzon again at the Albert Hall soon—& we're going to do some records together—my pieces, & probably the Schumann & Mozart . . . I'm also doing some more records with Peter (probably the folk-songs & some Schubert). So I'm busy, you see. I am a bit worried by my excessive local success at the moment—the reviews that the Sonnetts [*sic*], St Cecilia, the Carols, & now the quartet have had, & also the fact that Les Illuminations is now a public draw! It is all a little embarrassing, & I hope it doesn't mean there's too much superficial charm about my pieces. I think too much success is as bad as too little; but I expect it's only a phase which will soon pass.[31]

It is no coincidence that at this time Britten began to take recording slightly more seriously. In doing so he also came to see the relationship between critic and gramophone as important. In December 1942 Britten told the scholar (and friend) Alec Robertson that he 'loved the article you wrote in the Gramophone [about the *Sonnets*], it ought to sell lots of sets. I hear they are going very well—

[29] Ralph Hawkes, 'Composer and Economics', *Tempo*, NS 1 (1946), 11.

[30] Britten to Wyss, 15 Mar. 1940. DMPR 780.

[31] Britten to Elizabeth Mayer, 22 May 1943. DMPR 1152.

certainly every shop I go to has sold out.'[32] Robertson's review of the recording was yet to appear in *Gramophone* (it was published in the January edition), so Britten's emphasis on their popular appeal was probably meant to impress (and possibly influence) the critic for his future writings. Later Britten commented to Robertson on another work: 'I'm sorry I wrote crossly—but I was sick about the Mahler . . . and also that you weren't going to review St. Cecilia, & say how atrocious you thought the performance is . . .'.[33] His enthusiasm for the recordings of his music, and his desire that they be recognized by critics, was probably partly motivated by the process of rehabilitation he was then undergoing, with both critics and self-styled patriots. There was reassurance in the large numbers of 'ordinary citizens' who found pleasure in the records of the *Sonnets*. The writer Frances Partridge, for example, entered in her diary her reaction to the records: 'When [Lawrence Gowing] asked me over to listen to records I went somewhat unwillingly, but I'm very glad I did, for they were Benjamin Britten's *Michelangelo Sonnets*, and I felt I was hearing a work of genius for the first time.'[34] The records were a Sitwellian gesture, with Britten raising his eyes to the German bombs overhead, before continuing his work. They were, moreover, a vindication of the Appellate Tribunal's decision to grant Britten unconditional exemption from military service; his music would be part of the war effort.

The gramophone was also, of course, a valuable source of income, although as Hawkes explained in 1946, this did not come directly from large record sales. English copyright law, framed in 1912 when the potential of the gramophone was not yet recognized, prescribed that the composer and publisher share a royalty of just over 6 per cent of the selling price of each record. Thus, of the 6*s*. paid for a double-sided record, the composer received just over 2*d*. The financial gains of this medium were obviously less direct. As Hawkes noted, 'Gramophone recordings are valuable to a composer in that they spread his reputation quickly and widely, stimulate "live" performances and sales of the printed copy, and can be broadcast from radio stations all over the world with considerable performing fees accruing in consequence.'[35] Some critics agreed. In his review of the *Serenade* William Glock suggested that 'HMV or Columbia or Decca should record this . . . as soon as possible and the BBC should see that the country is made aware of its new masterpiece'.[36]

[32] Britten to Robertson, 17 Dec. 1942. DMPR 1109.

[33] Britten to Robertson, 24 May 1943. DMPR 1156. The letter continued: '—as it is, some other nit-wit in the Gramophone didn't even notice it (& Eric Blom calls it "unbelievably perfect"): Do you really think I should pass that?' The reference to Mahler probably stemmed from the cancellation of a proposed recording.

[34] Frances Partridge, *A Pacifist's War*, quoted in DMPR, 1079.

[35] Hawkes, 'Composer and Economics', 11.

[36] Glock in the *Observer*, 24 Oct. 1943, quoted in DMPR 1176.

The single most important change to the British critical climate surrounding Britten's music came about with *Peter Grimes*. Although not absolute, there was rare unanimity in critical response to the opera, with all the main papers and journals publishing long, considered, and mostly enthusiastic reviews.[37] These were accompanied by various profiles of the composer himself—a ready sign that his music had come to enjoy a popular resonance with the journal-reading middle classes. By 1948 Britten's reputation was enough to sustain a glowing tribute by Edward Sackville-West in *Vogue*. In the same year Britten's international reputation took off—exemplified by his appearance on the front cover of *Time*, with a fishing-net in the background and the composer earnestly gazing into the distance, his mind on Higher Things. The article itself is divided by a number of sub-headings, each compatible with the Metropolitan Opera's production of *Peter Grimes*. 'Punch & Power', 'Crude but Sympathetic', 'The Vicious Society', 'Impacts & Climaxes', and 'Harsh and Helpless' punctuate what can most charitably be described as journalese. But its inclusion in this particular magazine testifies to Britten's new international reputation.

Enthusiasm for *Peter Grimes* and its composer was not confined to the papers and journals. The premiere, according to Joan Cross, was an immediate success with the audience ('There was silence at the end and then shouting broke out. The stage crew were stunned: they thought it was a demonstration. Well, it was but fortunately it was of the right kind'[38]), while the critic of the *New Statesman* told readers of a bus trip in 1945 where the conductor at one point shouted 'Sadler's Wells! Any more for Peter Grimes, the sadistic fisherman!'[39] As a result, the British Council planned a recording of the opera in collaboration with Decca. William Walton, however, advised that 'something less commercially viable should be selected'.[40] Excerpts were made, and today are testament to a remarkably sweet-voiced Pears, but a full recording did not take place until 1958.

As Table 6.1 establishes, the period between the completion of Britten's works and their first recording was at the very least a few years. Decca's intention to record *Grimes* immediately after its premiere was therefore a marked departure from this pattern. It was of course completely understandable: as William Walton suggested, the opera's popular and critical acclaim meant that a recording was likely to be a commercial success (although record sets were expensive). The fact that *Grimes* was not recorded until thirteen years after its first performance is significant, given the enthusiasm for Britten's music after 1945. But as Table 6.1 illustrates, few of Britten's works after *Grimes* were quickly committed to record. This was partly a result of Britten's preoccupation with

[37] The critical response to *Grimes* is well documented, particularly in DMPR 1253–65.

[38] Cross in *The Times*, 1 June 1985, quoted in DMPR 1263.

[39] DMPR 1264.

[40] Susana Walton, *William Walton: Behind the Façade*, 125.

opera in the years following *Grimes*, a genre that bristled with practical difficulties in the days before the LP. But a further unexpected factor proves to have been the competition between Decca and HMV, each of whom ran a stable of 'exclusive' artists. Rudolf Bing, Manager of Glyndebourne, alluded to the problem in a letter to the British Council two months before the premiere of *The Rape of Lucretia*. Having been approached by the two record companies—each interested in recording the new opera—Bing stated that the

> difficulty is that some of our singers are tied to H.M.V. and some to Decca, but I think we would find no difficulty in collecting one complete cast to record for either Company. I think I am right in assuming that Mr. Britten himself would rather favour Decca. At the same time Glyndebourne used to collaborate with H.M.V., who did complete recordings of three of our pre-war productions.[41]

By late June Britten's preferred option was no longer Decca. In negotiations with J. D. Bicknell of HMV, Britten outlined his preconditions: the complete work was to be recorded; Pears, Kathleen Ferrier, and Ernest Ansermet were to be involved despite their contractual obligations with Decca; Walter Legge was to have nothing to do with it.[42] Bicknell was not interested in recording the complete opera, finding the bulk of the first scene ill-suited to the gramophone ('but from the commencement of a tenor solo by the male chorus, describing Tarquinius' ride from the Camp to Rome, until the end of the Act there is some magnificent music').[43] His preferred option was that extracts be recorded, that Nancy Evans sing the title role rather than Ferrier, and that Britten conduct.[44] As an emollient, though, HMV expressed regret at 'the difference of opinion which had taken place in the past', and looked forward to offering Peter Pears a contract in the near future (since 'both he and Mr. Britten are dissatisfied with the records that Decca have made').[45]

Britten's compromises over this recording far outweighed those of HMV and of the British Council, which was partly financing it. Only three-quarters of *Lucretia* was recorded, using four of the nine musicians Britten originally specified—a marked contrast to the relationship and power he would enjoy in

[41] Bing to Donald (British Council), 6 May 1946. GFO, *The Rape of Lucretia*, 1946. This letter was written at Britten's suggestion. There were two complete casts involved in this production, which accounts for Bing's confidence in assembling one for a recording.

[42] Bicknell to Mittell, 27 June 1946. BPL, EMI Correspondence, *The Rape of Lucretia*. Britten and Pears had a poor relationship with Legge, which would have been exacerbated at this time because of their friendship with Nancy Evans, Legge's ex-wife.

[43] Ibid. The review of this recording in Sackville-West's and Shawe-Taylor's *The Record Guide* (1951) lamented the cuts: 'It is a pity that some of the best music in the first scene should have been omitted . . .'.

[44] Ibid.

[45] Ibid. The dissatisfaction was with Decca's recording of the *Hymn to St Cecilia*, which Britten considered 'atrocious'.

the production of his recordings from the 1950s onwards. Pears was one of these, but Britten had to compromise on Ansermet (replaced by Reginald Goodall), Kathleen Ferrier (Nancy Evans), Otakar Kraus (Frederick Sharp), Anna Pollak (Flora Nielsen), and Owen Brannigan (Norman Lumsden). Only two-thirds of the first scene was recorded (less than the average for the rest of the work)—more than Bicknell had originally desired, but less than Britten had wanted. Moreover, Bicknell's opinion of this scene was probably more to do with its slow dramatic pace than with the music and its effective transference to disc—an outlook considerably different from that of the composer. Britten's chamber-scale writing was actually ideal for the recording process employed by HMV at the time. For the previous twenty years composers had been writing music with the requirements of the gramophone and the radio in mind. As Michael Chanan establishes, Kurt Weill used stark textures in his *Berliner Requiem*, commissioned by Frankfurt Radio, so that it would suit the medium for which it was written, while Schoenberg stated that radio and gramophone 'are evolving such clear sonorities that one will be able to write much less heavily instrumented pieces for them'.[46] In the late 1940s heavy string textures did not transfer well to gramophone; nor did the piano, but solo wind instruments, the harp, and the voice did. The decision to excise 'Tarquinius does not dare' from the first scene could possibly be 'justified' because of its low string texture (although the same sonority is used in an earlier section included in the HMV recording), but the rest of the score has a clarity particularly well suited to the electric gramophone.

When Decca discovered that Britten was seeing another record company, it reacted badly.

> It seems a pity that since we did so many of BENJAMIN BRITTEN's early recordings, culminating in the recording of 'SERENADE FOR TENOR HORN AND STRINGS' which the Gramophone Reviewers cited as a 'a triumph and great service to English Music' that at no time did either Mr. Britten or yourself give any indication that these negotiations were in progress with another Company. Indeed, had it not been for my letter to you, I suppose we should have remained completely in the dark until the recording had appeared under another label.[47]

But the contractual problems presented by competition between Decca and HMV were not the only factor limiting the number of Britten recordings in the post-war period. Despite Bicknell's suggestion that Britten should furnish him with a list of his works that he would like to record,[48] the relationship quickly deteriorated, as Roth noted in May 1950:

[46] Chanan, *Repeated Takes*, 116.

[47] Gibbs to Bing, 12 Aug. 1946. GFO, *The Rape of Lucretia*, 1946.

[48] Bicknell to Mittell, 27 June 1946. BPL, EMI, *The Rape of Lucretia*.

Quite frankly, the fact that they have not recorded any of your large works and Mr. Bicknell's view, as expressed in Gishford's letter to him, seem indicative of an attitude which could not encourage you to make a further contract with H.M.V.-Columbia. It seems fairly obvious that there is some opposition to your work inside H.M.V.-Columbia, and even if one would attempt to talk to the people at the top, I cannot imagine that we would get much satisfaction, as the smaller people on the artistic side could always obstruct or sabotage any instructions they may get. My personal opinion, therefore, would be to finish with H.M.V.-Columbia, as you do not seem to get there the atmosphere you want.[49]

Although Roth was rather partial to conspiracy theory, the fact remains that few recordings of complete Britten works were released by HMV in the years following *Grimes* (Table 6.1)—a period when interest in the composer ran high and commercial exploitation would have seemed opportune—notwithstanding the tired economy into which these records would have been released. Roth's closing sentiment was taken on board, and Britten entered the era of the long-playing record with a renewed commitment to Decca.

The Long-Playing Record: 1950–1957

Decca's own commitment to Britten increased in the period 1950–7. The company appeared genuinely hurt by Britten's dalliance with HMV. Before then it had seen itself as the torch-bearer, pompously (and incorrectly) writing to Bing in 1946: 'As you know, we have been making records of all Benjamin Britten's works.'[50] But Britten returned to Decca with a strengthened hand; the company was determined to give the composer no reason to look further afield. Britten's contract with Decca was not at first exclusive: he recorded some folk songs with HMV in 1950, and the same company released his Piano Concerto in 1957—but Decca's recordings invariably involved the composer as performer, giving Decca something of a commercial and artistic advantage. In this period of the LP, Decca filled some of the holes in its catalogue (Table 6.1). *A Boy was Born* and *Rejoice in the Lamb* were recorded in 1957; *Saint Nicolas* and *The Little Sweep* in 1955; *Les Illuminations* in 1954, and the *Sinfonia da Requiem* in 1953. More importantly, in certain instances Decca shortened the interval between premiere and recording (Table 6.2). *Winter Words*, *The Turn of the Screw*, and *The Prince of the Pagodas* were committed to record within a year of their first performance. The increased capacity of the LP and the general climate of accelerated catalogue building were factors in this quick turn-around—especially for the long, dramatic works. But as Table 6.2 establishes, Decca was by no means indiscriminate in the recordings

[49] Roth to Britten, 18 May 1950. BPL, Boosey & Hawkes Correspondence, 1950.

[50] Gibbs to Bing, 12 Aug. 1946. GFO, *The Rape of Lucretia*, 1946.

Table 6.2 Britten's works 1950–1957, first commercial British recording[a]

Opus no.	Title	Completed	First recorded	Label
47	*Five Flower Songs*	Spring 1950	1963	Argo
48	*Lachrymae*	May 1950	1964	Esoteric/Counterpoint
49	*Six Metamorphoses after Ovid*	June 1951	1954	Concert Hall Society
50	*Billy Budd*	November 1951	December 1967	Decca
51	Canticle II	January 1952	January and April 1961	Argo
52	*Winter Words*	September 1953	March 1954	Decca
53	*Gloriana*	March 1953	October and November 1992	Argo
54	*The Turn of the Screw*	September 1954	January 1955	Decca
55	Canticle III	November 1954	January and April 1961	Argo
56*a*	*Hymn to St Peter*	Summer 1955	*c.*1963	Alpha
56*b*	Antiphon	March 1956	1962	Esoteric/Saga
57	*The Prince of the Pagodas*	Autumn 1956	February 1957 [abridged]	Decca
58	*Songs from the Chinese*	Autumn 1957	September 1963 and March 1964	RCA
59	*Noye's Fludde*	March 1958	November 1960 and July 1961	Decca

[a] Compiled from Charles Parsons, *A Benjamin Britten Discography* (1990); Ray Crick's discography in Michael Kennedy, *Benjamin Britten* (1993); Evans, Reed, and Wilson, *A Britten Source Book* (1988); Malcolm Walker, 'Benjamin Britten: Discography of Commercial Recordings as a Performer' (1993); J. F. Weber, *Discography Series XVI: Benjamin Britten* (1975); and DMPR. This table deals with complete recordings only of those works to which Britten allocated an opus number. Argo was part of the Decca label. A recording of Canticle II with Pears and Norma Proctor was made in April 1957, but never released, while one of Canticle III, with Britten, Pears, and Barry Tuckwell, was made in February 1959, only to suffer a similar fate.

it produced. *Billy Budd*, *Gloriana*, and Canticles I and II all had to wait some time for a commercial recording—forty years in the case of the coronation opera. Certainly Britten was not happy with either *Budd* or *Gloriana* as it stood, extensively revising one and temporarily dropping the other. Their tardy entrance to the record market was probably the result of the poor response and puzzlement that each work had aroused at its premiere: they were not considered commercially viable.

The resumption and intensification of Britten's relationship with Decca prompted much resentment among other musicians. Most young British composers encountered the sort of problems outlined by Hawkes in his 1946 article: a new work needed to establish itself through sales and performances before a record company would take it on. But performances and sales of scores were stimulated by familiarity with a piece as much as by curiosity, which is where the gramophone became a decisive factor. There was, therefore, much resentment of Britten's ready access to both publishing house and recording company. But this resentment had actually begun in the late 1940s, as a backlash to the success of *Peter Grimes* and Britten's subsequent international reputation. An article in the September edition of the *Lantern* epitomizes the new style of criticism: complimentary but begrudging. 'Benjamin Britten is probably the cleverest and certainly the luckiest composer of the age. . . . everything he touches turns to gold, everything he writes at once flames into the most incandescent publicity.' And of particular relevance: 'As one disgruntled elderly composer remarked to me, "Benjamin Britten has only to blow his nose and they record it!" '[51] The critic Scott Goddard located the turn in critical favour rather closer to *Grimes*: 'There had been much publicity over this production, valuable for the event itself, though it did no good to the work. Generous enthusiasm was immediately countered by spiteful antagonism, each answering each before the opera had even been seen. It became impossible to mention the work without discussion degenerating into argument.'[52] Another critic supports Goddard: 'Britten is also a cult. He is indisputably the Golden Boy of contemporary music, immensely successful and immensely fashionable. His success is due to two courses: exceptional gifts and *exceptional opportunities* for putting them over.'[53] And this line was reiterated by the composer Denis ApIvor: 'Most fantastic of phenomena is the extraordinary coterie which appears to have gathered around the young composer Benjamin Britten.'[54] But as ApIvor established, dissenting voices were consigned to the wilderness, unable to compete with Britten's pre-eminence

[51] Stephen Williams, 'Britten the Too-Brilliant', *Lantern* (Sept. 1947), 2.
[52] Scott Goddard, *British Music of Our Time*, quoted in DMPR 1264.
[53] *Penguin Music Magazine* (May 1947). My italics.
[54] Denis ApIvor, 'Contemporary Music and the Post-War Scene', *Critic* (Spring 1947), 46.

after *Grimes*: 'it is almost as difficult to find any criticism of Britten's work as it is to find a combination of instruments or voices he hasn't written for.'[55]

Three events in the early 1950s threatened Britten's reputation as music's golden boy. The first was his return to grand opera in 1951 after a six-year absence. To varying degrees, *Billy Budd* antagonized critics and public, with both groups expecting another *Peter Grimes*. The second occurred one year later when Donald Mitchell and Hans Keller released *Benjamin Britten: A Commentary on his Works from a Group of Specialists*, which was considered by many to be at best uncritical, at worst sycophantic. The third was in the following year when Britten's *Gloriana* received its premiere and much of the remaining critical sympathy quickly disappeared.[56] Whereas the mixed reaction to *Billy Budd* was on the whole confined to the relatively narrow world of opera and music criticism, the response to *Gloriana* spilled over into the public domain. As referred to in Chapter 4, the MP and critic Beverly Baxter wrote a pompous review of *Gloriana* in the low-brow *Maclean's Magazine*: 'there is one subject that still divides friends and families. I refer to the gala Coronation production of Benjamin Britten's opera, Gloriana . . . Even the porters in the Covent Garden vegetable market will put down their baskets and argue about it.'[57] Martin Cooper in the *Spectator* perceived 'an almost sadistic relish of glee' in the musical world at the opera's failure.[58] Several hundred letters concerning the opera were sent to *The Times*; in America the *Herald Tribune* chronicled domestic critical reaction,[59] while Tony Mayer in *Opera* confidently referred to 'L'Affaire "Gloriana"'.[60]

'L'Affaire Britten' was an altogether more complex situation. Although the venomous response to *Gloriana* was partly to do with the work itself, there is no doubt that it was fuelled by Mitchell's and Keller's book, and by Britten's own article on music criticism, which had appeared in *Opera* in March 1952, a year before the royal gala performance (as Cooper wrote in his *Spectator* article: 'The fact is the fashion has changed and it is now smart to underrate Britten's music'). The seam running through critical reception of Britten's music in the 1930s was now revisited and mined with some enthusiasm. The timing of Britten's article was almost as unfortunate as its content: it appeared just after Mitchell's and Keller's book and, as noted above, described critics as, among other things, inane riff-raff. Moreover, he called for a dismantling of the profession as he saw it, in its place erecting a system of serious, intellectual debate:

[55] Denis ApIvor, 'Contemporary Music and the Post-War Scene', *Critic* (Spring 1947), 46.

[56] See Ch. 4 and Antonia Malloy, 'Britten's Major Set-Back? Aspects of the 'First Critical Response to *Gloriana*', in Paul Banks (ed.), *Britten's Gloriana*, 49–66.

[57] Beverly Baxter, 'The One Sour Note of the Coronation', *Maclean's Magazine* (1 Sept. 1953), 4.

[58] Martin Cooper, *Spectator* (19 June 1953), quoted in Carpenter, 358.

[59] Joseph Newman, 'Britten Opera Stirs Storm', *New York Herald Tribune*, 14 June 1953.

[60] Tony Mayer, 'L'Affaire "Gloriana"', *Opera* (Aug. 1953), 456–60.

Who are these serious critics to be? At the risk of appearing Irish, I say at once—not critics. There should be no such profession as criticism. Musicologists, of course, are quite different, and this is a sadly neglected profession in this country—but there should definitely be no regular critics. Criticism must be a side line. To go through life living off other people's work clearly has too degrading an effect. Therefore let the composers, the performers, the publishers, the concert promoters, the musical administrators, the intelligent amateurs too perhaps, take time off occasionally to write reasoned judgments on the work of their colleagues. I have no fear that it will lead to undue bias or jealousy; on the whole, the better the artist, the more he understands the problems of his colleagues and so will realise what they are trying to do, and be sympathetic towards it. There is much less risk of bias here than in the sourness of the *failed* artist who has had to turn to criticism to live. Again, in giving judgments the important thing is 'truth,' and that can often fly out of the window if the critic is worrying about his career, about his editor's or seniors' reactions to his writings, about the memorable or witty quality of his phrases. Again, his reactions must remain fresh; he must continue to love the art he is writing about (my doctor has ordered me to give up the *Manchester Guardian* because of the lowering effect reading its London Dramatic critic has on me; he clearly hates the theatre. And I wouldn't dream of buying *The Listener*: that ear is too withered).[61]

Backlash to the Britten article and the Mitchell/Keller publication was considerable. True Believers associated themselves with the book and dissociated themselves from the style of criticism attacked in the article; trenchant critics did the opposite. Either way, music critics came out of it rather badly. Ernest Newman tried to walk the middle ground: 'A book on Benjamin Britten has recently appeared which is likely to exasperate some worthy people; it is frankly of the adoring order, its tone reminding us at times of the slogans of a presidential election—"I boost for Ben," "We're smitten with Britten," and the like.' But a week later, he was slightly more partisan: 'The general opinion, I fancy, even among those of us who think highly of Mr. Britten, is that his incense-bearers are inclined to pitch their song of praise in rather too high a key, and with insufficient modulation from it.'[62] Newman, who had first fought the 'Battle of Britten' in 1941 over the composer's residence in America, was drawn into a new campaign of the same name. Henry Raynor in *Musical Opinion* noted the divided critical reaction to the book before stating that hostility was positive: 'We cannot demand that the critics cease to examine each new work as it appears. The hostile, who are looking at Britten's music for qualities it does not possess . . . will help us in the task of evaluating new works as they appear.'[63] *Scrutiny* published a damning review of both the book and much of Britten's music, under the title 'The Cult of Benjamin Britten'. Noting that a symposium

[61] Britten, 'Variations on a Critical Theme', *Opera* (Mar. 1952). See Britten's collected writings on music in Kildea (ed.), *Britten on Music* (forthcoming).

[62] Ernest Newman, 'The World of Music', *Sunday Times*, 11 Jan. 1953 and 18 Jan. 1953.

[63] Henry Raynor, 'The Battle of Britten', *Musical Opinion* (July 1953), 597.

was usually 'the privilege of the dead or of the venerably established living', Robin Mayhead was surprised to find 'a uniform tone of eulogy prevailing throughout the present volume, eulogy sometimes hysterical and almost always dogmatic'.[64] He added 'superficial', 'slick', and 'pretentious' to this list of charges.

Much of the critical reaction to this book was in the very least agenda-driven, when not actually unfair. F. R. Leavis, the powerful literary scholar-critic and founding editor of *Scrutiny*, had long viewed the 'Auden generation' of poets with antipathy; Britten's politics and his association with the key figures of this group would have ensured that he was similarly viewed and could expect a rough ride in the pages of this particular journal. Yet *Scrutiny* represented only one defined critical school in this period; other antipathies were almost certainly fuelled by the publication of this book. In the preface to the 1981 reprint of *Music Survey*, the journal Mitchell and Keller edited from the late 1940s, some of these critical camps were discussed by the two editors, with almost comic results. Mitchell recalled a remark made to him by Eric Blom of *The Times*: 'the fact of the matter is we just don't want Mahler here.'[65] Similarly, Frank Howes of the same newspaper took Mitchell aside when he was to review a concert that included Schoenberg's First Chamber Symphony: 'Well, you know, we have a policy about him.'[66] Quite apart from such 'policies', Mitchell and Keller broke one of the golden rules of criticism at the time: they used the pages of *Music Survey* to attack the views of other critics. Thus Mitchell remembered a review of the journal written by Frank Howes: 'He wrote that the editors of *Music Survey* may have had interesting ideas, though less than elegantly expressed, but that the important lesson they had not yet learned was that dog does not eat dog.'[67] Their list of foes in this preface is long and all-embracing—from *The Times* to the BBC ('You can't overestimate the degree to which we were regarded as outcasts'). Thus, when their symposium on Britten appeared, which both men viewed as a natural extension in style and intellectual approach of *Music Survey*, other critics were undoubtedly keen to settle some scores.

If this had remained an intellectual cat fight, the effect on Britten's music would have been minimal. But because of the link between criticism and popular reception, many were worried that Mitchell's and Keller's book would provoke growing hostility towards Britten's works. This was undoubtedly the motivation behind a letter from Boosey & Hawkes's Anthony Gishford to Donald Mitchell, no matter how tactful the prose:

On reflection, I think I am not prepared to let you loose on GLORIANA. I have no doubt that you would do an excellent piece with every word of which I should be in

[64] Robin Mayhead, 'The Cult of Benjamin Britten', *Scrutiny* (Spring 1953), 231–9.

[65] Donald Mitchell and Hans Keller (eds.), *Music Survey: New Series 1949–1952* (1981), [preface].

[66] Ibid.

[67] Ibid.

agreement, but rightly or wrongly it seems to me that the Mitchell-Keller combine is in some slight degree at present [in danger] of getting itself regarded as a kind of self-appointed Britten claque. Believing as I do in the integrity and value of your criticism, I am not disposed to give any encouragement to this.[68]

Britten himself considered that such hostility was limiting performances and damaging his reputation. Gishford was dispatched to Edinburgh in 1955 to build bridges:

I said that, rightly or wrongly, you had the impression that some sort of prejudice existed against you in the Edinburgh Festival: your Spring Symphony had been performed at the Tanglewood Festival, the Holland Festival, the Leeds Festival, but that although it was always held out as a kind of bait to get you to Edinburgh, it invariably got postponed. The English Opera Group were invited to perform at the Venice Festival, the Holland Festival, the Florence Festival etc., but never at the Edinburgh Festival. It appeared that the only capacity in which Edinburgh really wanted you was as a recital accompanist.[69]

Although Britten was often accused of persecution mania, his complaint in this instance was valid. He had experienced (and learned to recognize) institutional prejudice towards his music during the Second World War, when the BBC and the Royal Philharmonic Society had blocked performances of his works. Moreover, Rudolf Bing, Britten's sparring partner from Glyndebourne, was director of the Edinburgh Festival from 1947 to 1949, and he may have retained some of his prejudice.

Bayan Northcott was not yet a critic in this period; he was, however, part of the record-buying public. 'I can recall as a schoolboy in the 'Fifties with what excitement we awaited the appearance of each new work or recording; the discs of "The Turn of the Screw" must have been on my record-player daily for months on end.'[70] The fruits of the LP revolution were obvious in the 1950s: as Northcott notes, many people were weaned on gramophone recordings, experiencing the work live much later. This type of consumerism was seemingly independent of mainstream critical commentary on individual works: possession, collection, exchange, and discussion made up the LP discourse, in turn fuelling the record industry. A new form of criticism was developed to deal with this revolution. Although its origins lay in the *Gramophone* magazine, which was founded by Compton Mackenzie in 1923, record criticism greatly increased in intensity and importance during the 1950s. *The Record Guide*, edited by Edward Sackville-West and Desmond Shawe-Taylor, first appeared in 1951, riding the waves of enthusiasm generated by the products it described, which were now

[68] Gishford to Mitchell, [1953]. BPL, Boosey & Hawkes Correspondence, 1953. The article was probably intended for *Tempo*, Boosey & Hawkes's journal. Mitchell was then a young journalist and critic.

[69] Gishford to Britten, 1 Sept. 1955. BPL, Boosey & Hawkes Correspondence, 1955.

[70] Bayan Northcott, 'The Anguish of Benjamin Britten' [obituary], *Sunday Telegraph*, 5 Dec. 1976.

released into a slowly recovering economy, one that did encourage a degree of consumerism. It fast became a bible for art-music consumers. Although slightly pro-Britten because of Sackville-West's connections with the composer, the book is self-consciously impartial, and gives little indication of the storm brewing in the various critical camps outside the world of the gramophone. The twenty-one Britten works listed (including six folk songs) receive intelligent reviews. The music is discussed, as is the effectiveness of the recording. Most pieces elicit firm recommendations (the author shared Britten's reservations about the *Hymn to St Cecilia* records, although it is unlikely that Sackville-West was not fully aware of the composer's reservations about this recording). The foresight of the recording companies is praised: 'Where Benjamin Britten is concerned, the recording companies cannot be accused of stinginess.'[71] But the enthusiasm was muted slightly in the 1955 edition of *The Record Guide*: 'For reasons unconnected with the popularity of his music, the present situation of Britten recordings is not very satisfactory.'[72] The authors lamented the absence of *Sinfonia da Requiem* from the catalogue (it was actually recorded in 1953), and also of the Violin Concerto, the three Canticles, *Rejoice in the Lamb*, and the *Spring Symphony*. As Table 6.1 establishes, these works were slow to appear on record—the concerto had to wait for twenty-five years. What was the rationale guiding the various companies?

It probably took account of two factors: a hostile critical environment (was it indicative of the general public's view of Britten's music?) and the actual number of records sold. For all Northcott's retrospective enthusiasm for Britten recordings, for all the blossoming collector culture of the time, sales in this period were actually rather modest—certainly compared with American figures. In the three months from November 1955, Decca's 1953 recording of *A Ceremony of Carols* achieved sales of 580 in Britain; in America, 4,459 were sold in the same period.[73] Between May and July 1956 only seventy-four copies of the same record were sold in Britain. Although new on the market, *The Turn of the Screw* sold fewer than 400 sets in Britain in the three months from November 1955: double this number were purchased in America and, as will be seen below, new recordings of Britten operas managed much higher sales in Britain in the 1960s. *The Record Guide* might deplore the lack of a recording of the *Sinfonia da Requiem*, yet the British public felt otherwise: once it was issued, only 154 records were sold between November 1955 and January 1956, in the three months from May 1956 only ten. The comparison between the two countries is equally startling in the 1940s: 3,200 records of Britten's *Introduction and Rondo* were sold in America in October and November 1946, whereas only 163 copies

[71] Sackville-West and Shawe-Taylor, *Record Guide*, 1951, 143.

[72] Sackville-West and Shawe-Taylor, *Record Guide*, 1955, 164.

[73] These and all subsequent sales figures are taken from Decca royalty statements, kept at BPL.

were sold in Britain in October of the same year. There was hardly a thriving market for (Britten) recordings in England. Moreover, gramophone companies could not afford to disregard the American market and its enlightened record culture. But the American market was guided by American taste.

Sackville-West and Shawe-Taylor turned their attention to the differing perceptions of British and American taste in their 1951 record guide. In a discussion of the six Britten folk-song arrangements on disc, they noted that there were 'many more in the published volumes that would be well worth recording; and indeed two further Decca records by Pears and Britten (including the heroic *Bonnie Earl o'Moray* and the romantic *Ash Grove*) have actually appeared in America, where they are hugely popular. Why they have not been issued in the country of their origin is an insoluble mystery.'[74] The authors had a point: the songs' absence from British catalogues was almost as curious as their inclusion in American lists. *Echt*-British, the perfect length for the gramophone, and cheap to produce, the records would surely have quickly made their way in the British market. But why their success in America? They were, after all, the sort of thing that one American conductor (Bernstein?) had in mind when he fatuously dismissed English music as 'too much organ voluntary in Lincoln Cathedral, too much Coronation in Westminster Abbey, too much lark ascending, too much clod-hopping on the fucking village green'.[75]

Britten's village green was emblematic of America's marriage of high culture with the mechanisms of mass culture—the former diluted sufficiently to make it part of the latter.[76] The folk-song settings were in English, were accessible and therefore anti-elitist, and were on the American market at the same time that Toscanini was making the 'serious' gramophone record a (mass) cultural icon. Record clubs ensured wide distribution, and the demand was so thoroughly different in America during the 1950s that its market was often looked to—and appeased—before Britain's. Moreover, this period was one of great affluence in America: record collectors were buying everything. This affluence (absent from Britain) and America's huge population guaranteed considerable sales.

The result was scarcely satisfactory for Britten. As Shawe-Taylor said in 1952, 'It is extraordinary that England, possessing in Benjamin Britten a composer of world-wide appeal, should leave America to make the only records of some of his most important music.'[77] Where, he asked, were the British recordings of the *Spring Symphony*, the *Sinfonia da Requiem*, the Violin Concerto, excerpts from *Grimes*, *Albert Herring*, and *Billy Budd*, *Saint Nicolas*, *Les Illuminations*, *Rejoice in the*

[74] Sackville-West and Shawe-Taylor, *Record Guide*, 1951, 148.

[75] Stradling and Hughes, *The English Musical Renaissance*, 174.

[76] Dwight Macdonald, 'Masscult and Midcult', excerpts repr. in Joseph Horowitz, *Understanding Toscanini* (1994), 6–7.

[77] Desmond Shawe-Taylor, 'Discography', Mitchell and Keller (eds.), *Benjamin Britten*, 360.

Lamb, and the two Canticles? 'Whether it is a contractual difficulty or sheer lack of enterprise which is responsible for these omissions, they are a standing reproach to our generally progressive gramophone companies.'[78] They were extraordinary omissions from the gramophone catalogue. But a more telling omission was *The Little Sweep*, which was not recorded until 1955. Despite the opera being a perfect length for an LP, a hugely popular success in Britain in the late 1940s and early 1950s, and an altogether perfect candidate for mass British consumption, it had closed after only five performances on Broadway, dismissed by the New York critics. American success for a recording was therefore placed in doubt, and British companies kept the piece waiting for some years. Similarly, *Billy Budd* was not well received in America in the 1950s. It was given a (condensed) NBC television broadcast in 1952 and one stage performance at Indiana University in the same year. The next American production was not for another thirteen years.[79] Had the response been otherwise, a recording might have been produced; but without an apparent market on either side of the Atlantic, *Billy Budd* remained unrecorded until 1967. It is a little difficult to reconstruct the thinking of record companies in this economically turbulent period, but such genuflection at the American altar surely directed the thinking of recording companies, at least until Britain began to replicate some of the consumption patterns of its transatlantic cousin.

There is one more point to consider. For all their near-exclusivity, Decca's mono LP recordings of Britten's music did not have quite the same degree of authority as did the later stereo recordings. This is partly because Britten took recording more seriously in the age of stereo, and partly because of the technical omniscience developed at Decca under John Culshaw's watchful eye. The combination of these factors was to give Britten's recordings an authority and authenticity far above those of the 1950s. As the sociologist Pierre Bourdieu identifies, such authority tends to increase the value of the product and in turn influence sales:

> For the author, the critic, the art dealer, the publisher or the theatre manager, the only legitimate accumulation consists in making a name for oneself, a known, recognized name, a capital of consecration implying a power to consecrate objects . . . or persons . . . and therefore to give value, and to appropriate the profits from this operation.[80]

Before Culshaw, the record producer with the greatest powers of 'consecration' was Walter Legge. His imprimatur was enough to mould both record sales and the reputation of the individual artist or ensemble. Culshaw had similar authority; his

[78] Desmond Shawe-Taylor, 'Discography', Mitchell and Keller (eds.), *Benjamin Britten*, 360.

[79] Mervyn Cooke, 'Stage History and Critical Reception', Mervyn Cooke and Philip Reed (eds.), *Benjamin Britten: Billy Budd* (1953), 141.

[80] Pierre Bourdieu, *The Field of Cultural Production: Essays on Art and Literature* (1993), 75.

sympathetic collaborations with Britten in the 1960s revolutionized the composer's discography, income, and popular reputation.[81]

The Stereophonic Record: 1958–1976

For all his modernist, multi-media credentials, Britten remained curiously isolated from the developing stereophonic technology. When HMV proposed a stereo tape recording of his Piano Concerto in 1956, Britten sought information about the new technology, and received this reply:

> With regard to your enquiry as to what a Stereosonic Tape Recording is, my Secretary, Miss James, went to hear a demonstration of this the other day at the New Gallery Cinema when a recording of the Dvorak Cello Concerto was played, and she is of opinion that it represents yet another advance in recording technique. It was explained that the recording had been made from a large number of microphones distributed amongst the orchestra, recording simultaneously on separate channels, and it was played back from two separate players, one on each side of the stage, which were connected to twenty five separate speakers. The result was realistic three-dimensional sound which gave the impression that the orchestra and soloist were present on the stage. These recordings will be for sale to the public although the market is at present limited, and H.M.V. say that it is likely that the recording of your PIANO CONCERTO will also be issued on ordinary L-P records at a later date.[82]

Such demonstrations of the new technology were popular at the time, reminiscent of the Lumière brothers' first public cinema screening to a tiny audience lacking any real understanding of the significance of the event, any inkling that the market was about to change beyond recognition. Why Britten remained ignorant of the technology two years after its introduction is a little curious: although many of his colleagues delighted in a carefully cultivated philistinism where musical innovation was concerned, Britten had always shown himself open to new technology. And although, as the above letter concedes, the market for stereosonic tape recordings was limited (owing to the expense and clumsiness of reel-to-reel machinery), it was only a matter of time before the technology would be cheap and the recordings accessible on disc. Decca must have been exploring the technology at this time (it cannot have emerged as a market leader in 1958 without first having invested huge sums and effort into the new technology), and it is perhaps symptomatic of Britten's relationship with the gramophone company, or indeed his outlook on recordings in general, that he was not told of developments. He was possibly caught unawares by the stereo

81 See Culshaw's autobiography, *Putting the Record Straight*, for an account of this remarkable man.

82 Jackson to Britten, 28 Mar. 1956. BPL, Boosey & Hawkes Correspondence, 1956.

Table 6.3 Britten's works 1958–1976, first commercial British recording[a]

Opus no.	Title	Completed	First recorded	Label
60	*Nocturne*	September 1958	September 1959	Decca
61	*Sechs Hölderlin-Fragmente*	Summer 1958	November 1961	Decca
62	*Cantata academica*	September 1959	March 1961	Decca
63	*Missa Brevis in D*	May 1959	1959	Argo
64	*A Midsummer Night's Dream*	May 1960	September and October 1966	Decca
65	Sonata in C, for cello and piano	January 1961	July 1961	Decca
66	*War Requiem*	January 1962	January 1963	Decca
67	Psalm 150	May 1962	July 1966	Decca
68	Symphony for Cello and Orchestra	May 1963	July 1964	Decca
69	*Cantata misericordium*	July 1963	December 1963	Decca
70	*Nocturnal after Dowland*	November 1963	1966	RCA
71	*Curlew River*	March 1964	June 1965	Decca
72	First Suite for Cello	December 1964	July 1968	Decca
73	*Gemini Variations*	March 1965	July 1965	Decca
74	*Songs and Proverbs of William Blake*	April 1965	December 1965	Decca
75	*Voices for Today*	July 1965	May 1966	Decca
76	*The Poet's Echo*	August 1965	July 1968	Decca
77	*The Burning Fiery Furnace*	April 1966	May 1967	Decca

78	*The Golden Vanity*	August 1966	October 1969	Decca
79	*The Building of the House*	March 1967	July 1990	EMI
80	Second Suite for Cello	August 1967	July 1968	Decca
81	*The Prodigal Son*	April 1968	May 1969	Decca
82	*Children's Crusade*	January 1969	October 1969	Decca
83	Suite for Harp	March 1969	February 1976	Decca
84	*Who are these Children?*	Summer 1969	November 1972	Decca
85	*Owen Wingrave*	August 1970	December 1970	Decca
86	Canticle IV	January 1971	November 1972	Decca
87	Third Suite for Cello	March 1971	1980	ASV
88	*Death in Venice*	March 1973	April 1974	Decca
89	Canticle V	July 1974	February 1976	Decca
90	*Suite on English Folk Tunes*	November 1974	April 1977	Columbia
91	*Sacred and Profane*	January 1975	October 1976	Decca
92	*A Birthday Hansel*	March 1975	February 1976	Decca
93	*Phaedra*	August 1975	March 1977	Decca
94	String Quartet No. 3	November 1975	March 1978	Decca
95	*Welcome Ode*	August 1976	January and March 1990	Chandos

[a] Compiled from Charles Parsons, *A Benjamin Britten Discography* (1990); Ray Crick's discography in Michael Kennedy, *Benjamin Britten* (1993); Evans, Reed, and Wilson, *A Britten Source Book* (1988); Malcolm Walker, 'Benjamin Britten: Discography of Commercial Recordings as a Performer' (1993); J. F. Weber, *Discography Series XVI: Benjamin Britten* (1975); and DMPR. This table deals with complete recordings only of those works to which Britten allocated an opus number. Argo was part of the Decca label.

revolution—one as dramatic as that following the Lumières' experiments with film—and consequent transformation of the music market.

Britten's first significant contribution to this revolution was his 1958 recording of *Peter Grimes*. Employing technology Britten had known nothing about only two years earlier, the *Grimes* recording is a masterpiece—a musical and technical feat every bit as significant as the *Ring* cycle, on which Decca was then embarking. Despite developments in technology and musical technique since 1958, this recording remains superior to its later rivals on so many points, a lasting endorsement of the Decca process. It was critically and publicly acclaimed on its release: in the year from 1 February 1959 almost 1,000 stereo sets and 1,600 mono of *Grimes* were sold in Britain. A separate issue of the 'Sea Interludes' in the same period reached sales of 740 stereo and 1,786 mono. These figures suggested that there *was* a sizeable British market for Britten's music, independent of America and Canada (which incidentally bought only 1,600 sets of *Grimes* in 1959), and it cemented Britten's relationship with Decca. The company now wasted little time before committing each new Britten work to disc (Table 6.3).

The disgruntled older composer who had complained in the 1940s about Britten's nose-blowing would have had cause for complaint in the 1960s. The delays of the mono LP period were forgotten and nearly every work was recorded within a year or so of composition. Any delay was usually caused by the non-availability of artists (Cello Suites, *The Poet's Echo*, *A Midsummer Night's Dream*, etc.). The one exception was Britten's overture for the new Snape Maltings, *The Building of the House*, which was not recorded until 1990. Given that it had been well received at its premiere (Andrew Porter predicted that it would have 'lasting value'[83]), critical disapproval was not the reason for tardy commitment to disc; a more likely cause was the problem of finding suitable companion pieces (the overture is fairly short), or perhaps Britten was ambivalent about this minor 'occasional' piece. But consideration of critical disfavour lost all influence in the stereo era, when each piece was recorded regardless of critical opinion. *Owen Wingrave* is a remarkable example of this: it was recorded before its premiere, was available for purchase immediately after the television broadcast, and sold 1,190 sets in the first few months of its release—three times the sales of *The Turn of the Screw* in its first three months on the market, despite, on balance, a more positive critical response to the earlier work. Here was a remarkable strategy in play, appropriated from popular music: if the timing and marketing was just right, negative critical opinion could be crushed by hype. And there was plenty of this: feature articles, previews, interviews with the composer and the cast, and a lengthy explanation of the opera's genesis by John Culshaw. The critical reaction to the opera was not as enthusiastic as the pre-broadcast hype, but that was almost

[83] Andrew Porter in the *Financial Times*, 3 June 1967.

irrelevant as far as sales were concerned. The opera tapped into the *War Requiem* market (outlined below), and benefited from its ready-made BBC audience. Screening on television was symbolic of Britten's status in the 1960s—a composer, writing for a mass market, whose works were hardly affected by critical vicissitudes. Once all publicity surrounding the opera had ceased, sales dropped dramatically; in October to December 1971 only a hundred sets were sold in Britain. But this seemed only to support the idea that it was the amount of publicity—not its message—that was driving the record industry.

Surely here is Toscanini's legacy—a triumph of marketing as much as of music, and a public for the gramophone quite distinct from that for live performances. Many people, for example, got to know of *Grimes* through Decca's recording of the 'Sea Interludes', which found a place in the sparsest of collections. Here was a revolution in consumption, partly because Britten, like Toscanini, invested each recording with his own authority. And if the cult of Toscanini was responsible for his huge gramophone sales in America, a lesser cult of Britten was doing the same thing for his music in England—doubly important, since the market was so much more specialized. Furthermore, Britten, like Toscanini, had a strong rapport with his record company. Mitchell says that Britten 'fell for what Culshaw was selling him, and I was sorry to see him taken in by it. John treated him like a version of Wagner—"Yes, Master, No, Master"—and I didn't care for it. The manipulative side of it was all too transparent.'[84] This paints Culshaw in a rather poor light, for he was clearly a man of vision, and the cooperation between composer and producer nurtured a series of remarkable recordings, regardless of the precise commercial nature of Decca's motivation. The relationship, however, is indicative of Britten's control over the production of his works and his independence from the London musical scene. What had begun in 1947 with the formation of the English Opera Group, and had continued with the Aldeburgh Festival in the 1950s, was completed in the 1960s with Decca. Once the Maltings was built, the mountain had to come to Mohammed; Decca's Britten recordings thereafter took place at Snape. Even *Owen Wingrave* was recorded amid the cluttered, quite hopeless set-up at the Maltings, rather than in the modern (London) television studio wanted by almost everyone but Britten.

There was now a genuine cult of Benjamin Britten—not in the narrow, ritualistic sense long described and dismissed by critics, but rather in the sense of there being recognition and consumption by mass, rather than specialized, markets. Although the roots of this transformation lie in the 1958 *Peter Grimes* recording, it was actually the *War Requiem* LP that finally changed Britten's position among the general music public. The tone of criticism for this work was

[84] Carpenter, 504.

almost reverential: indeed Peter Shaffer considered 'criticism impertinent': 'I believe it to be the most impressive and moving piece of sacred music ever to be composed in this country . . . the most profound and moving thing which this most committed of geniuses has so far achieved.'[85] William Mann wrote of a Festival Hall performance after the recording had been released that the '*War Requiem* has caught the public imagination to an almost unheard-of degree'.[86] Most critics were similarly unstinting in their praise. The recording was released in May 1963 and sold over 200,000 sets in five months.[87] Britten's attitude to the gramophone changed as a result. Although only a year later he dismissed the loudspeaker as 'the principal enemy of music',[88] it was not entirely convincing, as he made clear in a rather pompous letter to Ernst Roth: 'As you know, I value very highly the *authentic* recordings of my works, and wish to keep my contact with the Decca Company (who is most sympathetic to the idea) very close indeed. . . . It does not seem to be understood in the firm [Boosey & Hawkes] that these major recordings are to be encouraged in every way rather than to be regarded as a muisance [*sic*] . . .'.[89]

The commercial success of the *War Requiem* recording was not the only reason for Britten's change in attitude. He was now aware of the gramophone's true potential, and this altered his outlook. Not only could the gramophone popularize a work (the expectation with *Owen Wingrave*), it could also 'canonize' it—without recourse to the traditional path of live performance, public reception, and, most importantly, criticism, which had been trodden by most canonic works. As Joseph Kerman says, 'a single recording of a modern piece can attain canonical status because usually the composer has been involved with it.'[90] Canonic aspiration was no vainglorious desire on Britten's part, but simply fulfilment of his compositional creed: 'I can find nothing wrong . . . with offering to my fellow-men music which may inspire them or comfort them, which may touch them or entertain them, even educate them . . . I want my music to be of use to people, to please them, to "enhance their lives".'[91] A canonic work touched and enhanced with a certainty guaranteed by the composer. Although, in Kerman's term, 'Repertories are determined by performers, canons by critics',[92] the gramophone altered canonic criteria. As a result, the composer-critic-consumer balance shifted considerably in the 1960s: critics had very little sway with a canonizing gramophone and a consecrating producer.

[85] Peter Shaffer, *Time and Tide* (7 June 1962), quoted in Carpenter, 410.
[86] William Mann, *The Times*, 13 Dec. 1963.
[87] Carpenter, 411. This presumably is a worldwide figure given the British sales listed in Table 6.4.
[88] Britten, *On Receiving the First Aspen Award*, 20.
[89] Britten to Roth, 13 Jan. 1963. BPL, Boosey & Hawkes Correspondence, 1963. My italics.
[90] Joseph Kerman, *Write All These Down* (1994), 47.
[91] Britten, *On Receiving the First Aspen Award*, 12, 21–2.
[92] Kerman, *Write All These Down*, 37.

If hype rather than well-informed criticism was driving record sales, there was much to be found in 1963, the year in which Britten turned 50. Concerts, parties, celebrations, feature articles, a festival, and a *Festschrift* played their parts. Britten's 'slighted child' *Gloriana* was given a concert performance, and met with a success so remarkably different from the response to its appearance ten years earlier that few could have doubted Britten's elevated role and status. Britten was not convinced. 'I feel that . . . these concerts are memorial rather than celebratory, & these nice things being written are really obituaries,' he told William Plomer.[93] And to William Walton he said, 'I don't think any composer has ever felt less confident than I—especially somehow when the public praise seems to have got rather out of hand!'[94] There was, of course, a backlash. Stravinsky eloquently led the charge, observing that the 'Battle-of-Britten sentiment' was so thick and the applause so loud for the *War Requiem* that he could not hear the music: 'Kleenex at the ready, then, one goes from the critics to the music, knowing that if one should dare to disagree with "practically everyone", one will be made to feel as if one had failed to stand up for "God Save the Queen". The victim of all this, however, is the composer for, of course, nothing fails like success.'[95] Twenty years earlier the 'Battle of Britten' had been hostile; it was now adulatory. Public perception had changed remarkably—especially given that both 'battles' were fought over Britten's (supposed) reaction to war.

How accurate was Stravinsky's final charge? As Table 6.4 illustrates, Britten's popular success endured throughout the 1960s. Each new recording was bought in huge numbers as soon as it appeared on the market. Interest in the LPs was sustained by the close proximity of premiere and record release: public and reviewers alike expected the one to follow the other rather quickly, and this in turn generated a high degree of expectation—from composer and public alike. It is hard to think of another British composer from the last century whose new works were charted in the popular consciousness and press of the British public with such assiduousness. And there were many new events to anticipate: Britten made around forty different stereo recordings of his own works—as either conductor or pianist. Table 6.4 also illustrates greater initial interest in new Britten recordings from 1963, the year of the *War Requiem* discs. The Symphony for Cello and Orchestra, *Curlew River*, and a new recording of the *Serenade* each achieved sales of several thousands in the first year on the market, whereas in the 1950s *The Turn of the Screw*, *The Little Sweep*, and *The Prince of the Pagodas* had each sold considerably fewer discs in the initial year. This was certainly partly to do with new stereo technology from 1958 onwards, but, as sales figures for *Peter Grimes* establish, there was actually a considerable market for Britten's mono recordings that, for whatever reason, had not really been tapped before 1958.

[93] Carpenter, 420. [94] Ibid.

[95] Igor Stravinsky, *Themes and Conclusions*, 26–7.

Table 6.4 UK sales of Britten's Decca recordings, 1958–69[a]

	1958	1959	1960	1961	1962	1963	1964	1965	1966	1967	1968	1969
A Boy was Born	1213	2[illegible]3	241	254	290	401	379	254	224	173	110	100
Les Illuminations	—	—	—	—	—	—	—	—	—	1997	1231	240
A Ceremony of Carols	993	69	815	787	1164	1093	1177	1313	709	283	—	—
Serenade	—	—	—	—	—	—	7108	3224	1630	1995	1781	6282
Peter Grimes	—	2607	1348	844	488	611	569	547	400	447	460	323
Sea Interludes	—	2526	536	612	687	675	440	355	384	384	144	—
The Holy Sonnets of John Donne	—	—	—	—	—	—	—	—	—	—	1764	—
Albert Herring	—	—	—	—	—	1715	189	139	102	141	41	—
Billy Budd	—	—	—	—	—	—	—	—	—	—	6973	246
The Turn of the Screw	111	173	134	205	254	200	279	209	162	141	663	536
The Prince of the Pagodas	255	140	123	114	90	136	107	107	110	98	1246	309
Nocturne	—	—	720	1105	582	768	288	159	61	81	—	—
A Midsummer Night's Dream	—	—	—	—	—	—	—	—	—	3026	752	230
Sonata in C, for cello and piano	—	—	—	876	1750	2390	813	653	263	283	188	153
National Anthem	—	—	—	—	3420	1142	—	—	—	—	—	—
War Requiem	—	—	—	—	25632	10590	3796	2693	2755	2732	864	—
Symphony for Cello and Orchestra	—	—	—	—	—	—	4772	2630	1276	790	742	207
Cantata misericordium	—	—	—	—	—	—	—	4119	984	432	469	338
Curlew River	—	—	—	—	—	—	—	3080	2808	1078	656	171
The Burning Fiery Furnace	—	—	—	—	—	—	—	—	—	2639	1599	203

[a] Based on Decca Royalty Statements 1958–69, BPL. These statements are not issued according to the calendar year; each column in Table 6.4 runs from 1 February in the year listed to 31 January in the following year. Where individual records of a set achieved varying sales, the average has been listed here.

Table 6.4 illustrates one final point: high initial sales quickly gave way to much lower sales. There were exceptions—the *Serenade*, for example—but the extremes of *Billy Budd* (6,973 in its first year, 246 in the next) were rather more typical. This pattern reinforces the notion of 'hype sales' in the years following the *War Requiem*. This was Britten as 1960s pop star and cultural icon, with each new hit superseding its predecessor—and there were plenty of hits to go round. This was the same Britten who turned up in the pages of a Peter Shaffer play alongside the seducer, Bob, and the seducible Doreen. ('I think Britten's the greatest composer in the world. I mean, he writes tunes, not just plink-plonk. I hate all that twelve-tone stuff, don't you? It's sort of not-human. I know what I'll play you! (*Grabbing an album*) PETER GRIMES! Decca's done the most marvellous recording of it.'[96]) This consumerism suited the sound and message of the *War Requiem*, but it was rather lost on less accessible works. Yet since many pieces began their public life in the relative isolation of the Aldeburgh Festival (BBC transmission notwithstanding), educating or enticing an audience through live performances over a sustained period of time was rather difficult: the gramophone therefore had an important role to play and Britten, who by this stage had settled into a pattern of Aldeburgh premieres, was well aware of it. The paradox of a composer committed to writing for 'the people', yet performing relatively little outside of his specialized Festival, could not have been lost on Britten. The recording industry allowed him to serve his public, circumvent the established base of the British music industry, London, and allow him the rural sanctuary in which he thrived.

Even if Britten had *popular* appeal in the 1960s—as Table 6.4 suggests—is it possible that Stravinsky's comments have any force? There is no doubt that Britten changed his style in the 1960s: most works from this decade are intimate, in both scale and intention. Harewood, who knew Britten well, thinks this new intimacy stemmed from the *War Requiem*'s reception: 'I think he felt the easy success was an outrage and an invasion of privacy.'[97] He discussed it in the context of *Gloriana*, the last 'public' work before the *War Requiem*. 'I have little doubt that the initial public and critical failure of *Gloriana* was a turning point for Ben. It shut him in on himself and he became even more private. He had made a great public gesture and the public had, so to speak, rejected him. He had risked writing for other than "his" audience . . . had given instead a hostage to fortune and had forfeited it.'[98] Where failure had once prompted a retreat into the arms of Aldeburgh, now success did the same. Yet Harewood's assessment is only partially true: *Curlew River* was planned some time before the *War Requiem* was composed, and the intimate style of the new parable was in part influenced by the economic strictures of the

[96] Quoted in Muriel James to Britten, 6 Sept. 1965. BPL, Boosey & Hawkes Correspondence, 1965.

[97] Harewood, *The Tongs*, 148.

[98] Ibid.

Festival and the English Opera Group and was not a deliberate retreat from the large scale and success of the *Requiem*. Moreover, the parable was critically well received, and it sold over 3,000 copies in its first year on the British market—two good reasons to repeat the formula. But Harewood is certainly right on one point: since nearly all Britten's works after the *War Requiem* were composed with an Aldeburgh Festival performance in mind, before the advent of the Snape Maltings Concert Hall, intimacy followed quite naturally.

Stravinsky had some critical allies in the 1970s. Many critics considered Britten's music 'cold' or 'impersonal' in this period. In his obituary of the composer, Bayan Northcott wrote that magical and atmospheric qualities gradually deserted Britten's music in the 1960s. 'It is said that he feared the colossal success of his "War Requiem" in 1962 was more a matter of its sentiment than its invention, and the steady stripping down of texture in subsequent pieces certainly suggested an artist in search of some more basic self.'[99] Others disagreed: Shawe-Taylor considered the church parables to be 'beautifully shaped works of art',[100] although in the obituary he wrote for the *Sunday Times* he noted a 'dryness' in Britten's later works. Shawe-Taylor had expressed similar sentiments ten years earlier: 'Those who may have feared that the two church parables and last year's William Blake cycle heralded an increasingly austere period in Britten's work will take heart from these picturesque and lyrical songs [*The Poet's Echo*].'[101] Following Britten's death Peter Heyworth wrote that after the Symphony for Cello and Orchestra 'his style grew more sparse and in the process a certain narrowness of range became apparent, especially when his later music is measured against the astonishing promise of the works he wrote before "Peter Grimes" . . . Perhaps a greater openness to cross-fertilisation might have served to extend his range.'[102] These were common criticisms of the time—that somehow 'sparse' textures indicated a 'narrowness' or contraction of talent and musical language. And the retrospective critical shift represented by Heyworth regretting that the promise of the 1930s was never fulfilled—a decade in which most of Britten's new works were dismissed or carped about by critics—is a savage irony. Britten himself noted the change in his critical fortunes, commenting to Philip Ledger that perhaps his music was not seen as modern enough: 'Perhaps I'd be a better composer if I were more avant-garde.'[103] The mantle of experimentalism fell on Tippett, whose reputation grew, it seemed, at the expense of Britten's. Robert Tear observes that it must have been painful for Britten to realize that 'Michael seemed to be ascending in public esteem while he, at best, was stationary', while

[99] Northcott, 'The Anguish of Benjamin Britten'.
[100] Shawe-Taylor, 'The Meeting of East and West', *Sunday Times*, 16 June 1968.
[101] Shawe-Taylor, 'Two Aspects of Britten', *Sunday Times*, 24 July 1966.
[102] Peter Heyworth, 'Putting Our Music on the Map', *Observer*, 5 Dec. 1976.
[103] Carpenter, 535.

Mitchell recalls that to university students in the 1970s, Britten was 'absolutely "out" . . . fashion had gone totally against him'.[104]

While it is true that sympathy for Britten's music waned in intellectual circles, a new recording would nevertheless sell in large numbers. In its first six months, *A Prodigal Son* sold over 2,300 copies in Britain alone. Similarly, *Lucretia* managed sales of over 1,100 in its first three months on the British market, while the disc of the Piano Concerto and the Violin Concerto sold nearly 2,000 in a similar period. But the slump in sales came much more quickly than before, and was more severe: *Lucretia* sold only sixty-six copies in its second three-month period, *Wingrave* eighty-eight. New recordings had driven sales in the 1960s, but with ill-health and fewer new works, there was little to record, and royalty statements are consequently somewhat sparser. Works such as the *Serenade* and the *War Requiem* continued to sell well, but others failed to match them. But Britten remained generally popular with a wide audience: a Decca compilation ('The World of Benjamin Britten') sold more than 4,000 copies over six months in 1970, and he was deemed acceptable for another compilation—'Classics for the Motorway' (a disc the composer would have particularly hated, given his Aspen speech)—and even managed an appearance on Decca's 'Big Stereo Test Cassette'.

Although the gap narrowed between public and critical opinion in the 1970s, it never closed: Britten's public reputation remained independent of the critical consensus. A 1964 article in the high-circulation *Daily Mail* listed the riches that followed his popularity: £53,000 in the composer's royalties on the *War Requiem* recording in its first fourteen months; £1,000 royalty on the sale of scores (representing 3,575 copies); £10,000 as part of the Aspen Award; £300 for each of the thirty recitals given by Britten and Pears every year outside Aldeburgh; and a £1,000 standard conducting fee.[105] Such were the fruits of the gramophone. But the gramophone served an even more important role in Britten's life—namely to link all his separate compositional activities. Works for Aldeburgh, the English Opera Group, Glyndebourne, Covent Garden, and the BBC all ended up on disc. Moreover, in the 1960s and 1970s the gramophone allowed Britten to control his output—all from the relative isolation of Aldeburgh. Royalty statements kept his finger on the public pulse: critics abdicated and cultural relativism reigned supreme, something the composer had wanted since the 1930s. This is perhaps closer to Britten's meaning when he spoke of 'authentic' recordings: the gramophone allowed him to tidy up unfinished business, to revisit periods in his sadly short life, and to reinvest works with new life and a new critical and popular reception. Even today this process continues. First recordings of previously unknown or unvalued Britten works trickle out of Aldeburgh at a steady pace. Incidental music for radio dramas—written as bread-and-butter

104 Ibid. 534–5.

105 'Britten: Master, Composer, Man Against War', *Daily Mail*, 3 Aug. 1964.

pieces in the 1930s—are now on disc. Sketched works are completed (with considerable skill and knowledge of Britten's changing harmonic language) and recorded. Pre-LP recordings of *Grimes* and *Lucretia* are available. Pieces forgotten or ignored by the composer are committed to disc. Radio broadcasts have jumped from sound archive to record shop—unthinkable (and illegal) only a few years ago—each disc reminding us of the incredible legacy of Britten the Performer, in his own music and in that of others. Selling Britten is almost as easy now as it was in the 1960s. The triumph is Britten's: having spurned the Luddite excesses of many of his colleagues from the 1930s to the mid-1970s, he went on to record what remains today, at least in part, his own reputation.

BIBLIOGRAPHY

Manuscript Sources

The following archives have been used extensively. Collection titles and shelf-marks are given in the main body of the book.

Arts Council of Great Britain, London.
British Broadcasting Corporation Written Archives Centre, Reading.
British Broadcasting Corporation, Broadcasting House, London.
British Library, Manuscript Room, London.
The Britten–Pears Library, Aldeburgh.
Glyndebourne Festival Opera, Lewes.
Oxford University Press, Oxford.
Royal Opera House Covent Garden, London.
Sadler's Wells Opera Papers, Finsbury Library, London.

Secondary Sources

Important articles used in the book are listed below. A number of newspapers and journals have been quoted in the book, particularly in relation to the critical response to Britten's music, as have several BBC interviews. These are cited in the main body of the book, but not listed here.

ADAMS, RICHARD, *A Book of British Music Festivals* (London: Robert Royce, 1986).

APIVOR, DENIS, 'Contemporary Music and the Post-War Scene', *Critic*, 1/1 (Spring 1947), 45–7.

The Arts Enquiry: Music (London: PEP, 1949).

AUDEN, WYSTAN, *Paul Bunyan: The Libretto of the Operetta by Benjamin Britten with an Essay by Donald Mitchell* (London: Faber & Faber, 1988).

—— and ISHERWOOD, CHRISTOPHER, *The Dog Beneath the Skin or Where is Francis?* (London: Faber & Faber, 1986).

BANFIELD, STEPHEN, *Sensibility and English Song: Critical Studies of the Early 20th Century* (Cambridge: Cambridge University Press, 1988).

BANKS, PAUL (ed.), *Benjamin Britten: A Catalogue of the Published Works* (Aldeburgh: Britten–Pears Library, 1999).

—— (ed.), *Britten's Gloriana: Essays and Sources* (Woodbridge: Boydell Press, 1993).

BOURDIEU, PIERRE, *Distinction: A Social Critique of the Judgement of Taste* (London: Routledge & Kegan Paul, 1986).

—— *The Field of Cultural Production: Essays on Art and Literature* (Cambridge: Polity Press, 1993).

BOYLE, ANDREW, *Only the Wind will Listen: Reith of the BBC* (London: Hutchinson, 1972).
BRETT, PHILIP (ed.), *Benjamin Britten: Peter Grimes*, Cambridge Opera Handbooks (Cambridge: Cambridge University Press, 1989).
——'The Britten Era' (Proms Lecture, 17 Aug. 1997).
——WOOD, ELIZABETH, and THOMAS, GARY (eds.), *Queering the Pitch: The New Gay and Lesbian Musicology* (New York: Routledge, 1994).
BRIGGS, ASA, *The Collected Essays of Asa Briggs*, vol. iii (Hemel Hempstead: Harvester Wheatsheaf, 1991).
——*The History of Broadcasting in the United Kingdom* (London: Oxford University Press), vol. i, *The Birth of Broadcasting* (1961); vol. ii, *The Golden Age of Wireless* (1965).
——'Problems and Possibilities in the Writing of Broadcasting History', *Media, Culture and Society*, 2 (1980), 5–13.
BRITTEN, BENJAMIN, *Curlew River: A Parable for Church Performance* (London: Faber & Faber, 1964).
——*On Receiving the First Aspen Award* (London: Faber & Faber, 1978).
——'Speech on Receiving an Honorary Degree from Hull University', *London Magazine*, 3 (Oct. 1963), 89–91.
——'Variations on a Critical Theme', *Opera* (Mar. 1952).
BRITTEN, BETH, *My Brother Benjamin* (Abbotsbrook: Kensal Press, 1986).
'Broadcasting and the Composer', *B.B.C. Handbook 1928*.
CAREY, JOHN, *The Intellectual and the Masses: Pride and Prejudice among the Literary Intelligentsia, 1880–1939* (London: Faber & Faber, 1992).
CARPENTER, HUMPHREY, *Benjamin Britten: A Biography* (London: Faber & Faber, 1992).
——*The Brideshead Generation: Evelyn Waugh and his Generation* (London: Faber & Faber, 1989).
——*The Envy of the World: Fifty Years of the BBC Third Programme and Radio 3 1946–1996* (London: Weidenfeld & Nicolson, 1996).
——*W. H. Auden: A Biography* (Oxford: Oxford University Press, 1992).
'Chamber Music in Broadcasting', *B.B.C. Handbook 1928*.
CHANAN, MICHAEL, *Repeated Takes: A Short History of Recording and its Effects on Music* (London: Verso, 1995).
'Composing for Wireless', *B.B.C. Handbook 1929*.
COOKE, MERVYN (ed.), *The Cambridge Companion to Benjamin Britten* (Cambridge: Cambridge University Press, 1999).
——and REED, PHILIP, *Benjamin Britten: Billy Budd*, Cambridge Opera Handbooks (Cambridge: Cambridge University Press, 1993).
COX, DAVID, *The Henry Wood Proms* (London: BBC, 1980).
CROSS, JOAN, 'Twenty Years On', *Opera*, 18 (Autumn 1968).
The Crystal Palace and its Contents (1851).
CULSHAW, JOHN, *Putting the Record Straight* (London: Secker & Warburg, 1981).
CUNNINGHAM, VALENTINE, *British Writers of the Thirties* (Oxford: Clarendon Press, 1993).

DENT, EDWARD J., *A Theatre for Everybody: The Story of the Old Vic and Sadler's Wells* (London: Boardman & Co., 1945).

The Disastrous consequences which are likely to arise to the manufacturing trade of this country from the carrying out of the proposed Great Industrial Exhibition of all nations in 1851 (Dalton: privately published, 1850[?])

DOCTOR, JENNIFER, *The BBC and the Ultra-Modern Problem: A Documentary Study of the British Broadcasting Corporation's Dissemination of Second Viennese School Repertory, 1922–1936*, Ph.D. thesis, Northwestern University, 1993 (Ann Arbor: UMI, 1995).

—— *The BBC and Ultra-Modern Music, 1922–1936: Shaping a Nation's Tastes* (Cambridge: Cambridge University Press, 1999).

DONALDSON, FRANCES, *The Royal Opera House in the Twentieth Century* (London: Weidenfeld & Nicolson, 1988).

EHRLICH, CYRIL, *First Philharmonic: A History of the Royal Philharmonic Society* (Oxford: Clarendon Press, 1995).

—— *Harmonious Alliance: A History of the Performing Right Society* (Oxford: Oxford University Press, 1989).

—— *The Music Profession in Britain since the Eighteenth Century: A Social History* (Oxford: Clarendon Press, 1985).

—— *The Piano: A History*, rev. edn. (Oxford: Clarendon Press, 1990).

—— 'Taste, Function and Technology: Some Conjectures', *Proceedings of the Second British–Swedish Conference on Musicology: Ethnomusicology* (Skrifter från Musikvetenskapliga institutionen, Göteborgs universitet, no. 26, 1991).

EVANS, JOHN, REED, PHILIP, and WILSON, PAUL (eds.), *A Britten Source Book* (Aldeburgh: Britten–Pears Library, 1988).

EVANS, PETER, *The Music of Benjamin Britten* (London: J. M. Dent & Sons, 1989).

'Feste', 'Looking Ahead II', *Musical Times*, 75 (Feb. 1934), 116–20.

FOREMAN, LEWIS, *From Parry to Britten: British Music in Letters* (London: Batsford, 1987).

FORSTER, E.M., 'Looking Back on the Aldeburgh Festival', *The Listener* (24 June 1948).

FOSS, HUBERT, *Music in My Time* (London: Rich & Cowan, 1933).

GELATT, ROLAND, *The Fabulous Phonograph 1887–1977*, 2nd rev. edn. (London: Cassell, 1977).

GILLIES, MALCOLM, *Bartók in Britain* (Oxford: Clarendon Press, 1989).

HALSEY, A. H. (ed.), *British Social Trends since 1900: A Guide to the Changing Social Structure of Britain* (Houndmills, Basingstoke: Macmillan, 1988).

HAREWOOD, EARL OF, *The Tongs and the Bones* (London: Weidenfeld & Nicolson, 1981).

HAWKES, RALPH, 'Composer and Economics', *Tempo*, NS 1 (1946), 10–12.

—— 'Letter from London', *Tempo* (American edition), 1/4 (Jan. 1941), 1–2.

HEADINGTON, CHRISTOPHER, *Peter Pears: A Biography* (London: Faber & Faber, 1992).

HERBERT, DAVID (ed.), *The Operas of Benjamin Britten* (London: Hamish Hamilton, 1979).

HEWISON, ROBERT, *Culture and Consensus: England, Art and Politics since 1940* (London: Methuen, 1995).

—— *In Anger: Culture in the Cold War 1945–60* (London: Weidenfeld & Nicolson, 1981).

—— *Under Siege: Literary Life in London 1939–45* (London: Quartet, 1977).

HINNELLS, DUNCAN, *An Extraordinary Performance: Hubert Foss, Music Publishing, and the Oxford University Press* (Oxford: Oxford University Press, 1998).

HOBSBAWM, ERIC, and RANGER, TERENCE (eds.), *The Invention of Tradition* (Cambridge: Cambridge University Press, 1992).

HOLST, IMOGEN, *Britten*, 2nd edn. (London: Faber & Faber, 1970).

HOROWITZ, JOSEPH, *Understanding Toscanini* (California: University of California Press, 1994).

HOWARD, DIANA, *London Theatres and Music Halls 1850–1950* (London: Library Association, 1970).

HUGHES, SPIKE, *Glyndebourne* (London: Methuen, 1965).

HYNES, SAMUEL, *The Auden Generation: Literature and Politics in England in the 1930s* (London: Pimlico, 1976).

KEMP, IAN, *Tippett: The Composer and his Music* (London: Eulenburg Books, 1984).

KENNEDY, MICHAEL, *Britten*, The Master Musicians Series (London: J. M. Dent & Sons, 1993).

KENYON, NICHOLAS (ed.), *Authenticity and Early Music* (Oxford: Oxford University Press, 1988).

—— *The BBC Symphony Orchestra: The First Fifty Years 1920–1980* (London: British Broadcasting Corporation, 1981).

KERMAN, JOSEPH, *Write All These Down: Essays on Music* (Berkeley: University of California Press, 1994).

KEYNES, JOHN MAYNARD, 'The Arts Council: Its Policy and Hopes', *The Listener* (12 July 1945).

KILDEA, PAUL, 'World War I and the British Music Industry', M.Mus. diss., University of Melbourne, 1991.

—— (ed.), *Britten on Music* (Oxford: Oxford University Press, forthcoming).

LANDOWSKA, WANDA, *Landowska on Music* (New York, 1964).

LEMAHIEU, D. L., *A Culture for Democracy: Mass Communication and the Cultivated Mind in Britain Between the Wars* (Oxford: Clarendon Press, 1988).

LEVENTHAL, F. M., 'The Best for the Most: CEMA and State Sponsorship of the Arts in Wartime, 1939–1945', *Twentieth Century British History*, 1 (1990), 289–317.

MACKENZIE, COMPTON, 'The Gramophone. Its Past: Its Present: Its Future', *PMA*, 51st session (1924–5).

MCKIBBIN, ROSS, *The Ideologies of Class: Social Relations in Britain 1880–1950* (Oxford: Clarendon Press, 1994).

MAYER, TONY, 'L'Affaire "Gloriana"', *Opera*, 4/8 (Aug. 1953), 456–60.

MAYHEAD, ROBIN, 'The Cult of Benjamin Britten', *Scrutiny*, 19/3 (Spring 1953), 231–9.

MENDELSON, EDWARD (ed.), *The English Auden* (London: Faber & Faber, 1986).

MITCHELL, DONALD, *Britten and Auden in the Thirties: The Year 1936* (London: Faber & Faber, 1979; repr.: The Boydell Press, 2000).

—— *Cradles of the New: Writings on Music 1951–1991* (London: Faber & Faber, 1995).

—— and EVANS, JOHN (comps.), *Pictures from a Life: Benjamin Britten 1913–1976* (London: Faber & Faber, 1978).

—— and KELLER, HANS (eds.), *Benjamin Britten: A Commentary on his Works from a Group of Specialists* (London: Rockliff, 1952).

——and KELLER, HANS (eds.), *Music Survey: New Series 1949–1952* (London: Faber Music, 1981).

——and REED, PHILIP (eds.), *Letters from a Life: The Selected Letters and Diaries of Benjamin Britten 1913–1976*, 2 vols. (London: Faber & Faber, 1991).

MITFORD, NANCY, *The Pursuit of Love* (Harmondsworth: Penguin, 1967).

MORIS, JOHN (ed.), *From the Third Programme* (London: Nonesuch Press, 1956).

[Music Critic of *The Times*], *Musical Britain 1951* (London: Oxford University Press, 1951).

NEALE, STEVE, 'Questions of Genre', *Screen*, 31/1 (Spring 1990).

NORRIS, CHRISTOPHER (ed.), *Music and the Politics of Culture* (London: Lawrence & Wishart, 1989).

Opera in English, Sadler's Wells Opera Book No. 1 (London: John Lane at the Bodley Head, 1945).

Oxford Music: The First Fifty Years '23–'73 (Oxford: Oxford University Press, 1973).

PARSONS, CHARLES, *A Benjamin Britten Discography* (Lewiston: Edwin Mellen Press, 1990).

PEACOCK, ALAN, *Paying the Piper: Culture, Music and Money* (Edinburgh: Edinburgh University Press, 1993).

——'Public Patronage and Music: An Economist's View', *Three Banks Review* (Mar. 1968), 18–36.

——and WEIR, RONALD, *The Composer in the Market Place* (London: Faber Music, 1975).

PRENDERGAST, ROY, *Film Music*, 2nd edn. (New York: W. W. Norton & Co., 1992).

Radio and the Composer (London: Ivor Nicholson & Watson, 1935).

RAYNOR, HENRY, 'The Battle of Britten', *Musical Opinion* (July 1953), 593–4.

Report of the Committee on Broadcasting, 1960 (London: Her Majesty's Stationery Office, 1962).

A Report on Musical Life in England sponsored by the Dartington Hall Trustees (London: PEP, 1949).

ROSCOW, GREGORY (ed.), *Bliss on Music: Selected Writings of Arthur Bliss 1920–1975* (Oxford: Oxford University Press, 1991).

ROSENTHAL, HAROLD, 'Aldeburgh and the Future', *Opera*, 18 (Autumn 1968).

ROSSELLI, JOHN, *The Opera Industry in Italy from Cimarosa to Verdi: The Role of the Impresario* (Cambridge: Cambridge University Press, 1984).

ROTH, ERNST, *The Business of Music* (London: Cassell, 1969).

SABANEEV, LEONID, 'Music and the Economic Crisis', *The Musical Times*, 75 (1934), 1075–7.

——'Music and the Sound Film', *Music and Letters*, 15 (1934), 147–52.

SACKVILLE-WEST, EDWARD, and SHAWE-TAYLOR, DESMOND (comps.), *The Record Guide* (London: Collins, 1951).

——(comps.), *The Record Guide* (Butter Market: W. S. Cowell, 1955).

SAID, EDWARD, *Representations of the Intellectual* (London: Vintage, 1994).

SCANNELL, PADDY, 'Music for the Multitude? The Dilemmas of the BBC's Music Policy, 1923–1946', *Media, Culture and Society*, 3 (1981), 243–60.

——and CARDIFF, DAVID, *A Social History of British Broadcasting*, vol. i: *1922–1939: Serving the Nation* (Oxford: Basil Blackwell, 1991).

SCHOLES, PERCY, 'Broadcasting and the Future of Music', *PMA*, 53rd session (1926–7).
—— *The Mirror of Music 1844–1944*, 2 vols. (London: Novello and Oxford University Press, 1947).
SIDNELL, MICHAEL, *Dances of Death: The Group Theatre of London in the Thirties* (London: Faber & Faber, 1984).
SILVEY, ROBERT, *Who's Listening* (London: George Allen & Unwin, 1974).
STIMPSON, MANSEL, 'Drama and Meaning in *The Turn of the Screw*', *Opera Quarterly*, 4 (Autumn 1986), 75–82.
STRADLING, ROBERT, and HUGHES, MEIRION, *The English Musical Renaissance 1860–1940: Construction and Deconstruction* (London: Routledge, 1993).
STRAVINSKY, IGOR, *An Autobiography* (New York: Steuer, 1958).
—— *Themes and Conclusions* (London: Faber & Faber, 1972).
STRODE, ROSAMUND (comp.), *Music of Forty Festivals: A List of Works Performed at Aldeburgh Festivals from 1948 to 1987* (Aldeburgh: Aldeburgh Foundation, 1987).
TRACEY, EDMUND, 'Benjamin Britten talks to Edmund Tracey', *Sadler's Wells Magazine* (Autumn 1966).
VAUGHAN WILLIAMS, RALPH, *National Music and Other Essays* (Oxford: Oxford University Press, 1972).
WALKER, MALCOLM, 'Benjamin Britten: Discography of Commercial Recordings as a Performer' (1993).
WALTON, SUSANA, *William Walton: Behind the Façade* (Oxford: Oxford University Press, 1988).
WARRACK, JOHN, 'Benjamin Britten: Musician of the Year in Conversation with John Warrack', *Musical America*, 84 (Dec. 1964).
WAUGH, EVELYN, *Vile Bodies* (London: Eyre Methuen, 1978).
WEBER, J. F., *Discography Series XVI: Benjamin Britten* (New York: private publication, 1975).
WELSH, HENRY, 'A British Ministry of Fine Arts', *Musical Times*, 75 (1934), 448.
WHITE, ERIC WALTER, *The Arts Council of Great Britain* (London: Davis-Poynter, 1975).
—— *Benjamin Britten: His Life and Operas*, 2nd edn. (London: Faber & Faber, 1983).
—— *A History of English Opera* (London: Faber & Faber, 1983).
—— *The Little Chimney Sweep* (Bristol: White & White, 1936).
—— *The Rise of English Opera* (London: John Lehmann, 1951).
WHITTALL, ARNOLD, *The Music of Britten and Tippett: Studies in Themes and Techniques*, 2nd edn. (Cambridge: Cambridge University Press, 1990).
WIENER, MARTIN, *English Culture and the Decline of the Industrial Spirit 1850–1980* (London: Penguin, 1981).
WILLIAMS, STEPHEN, 'Britten the Too-Brilliant', *Lantern* (Sept. 1947), 2–5.

INDEX OF BRITTEN'S WORKS

GENERAL INDEX